THE COMPLETE BOOK OF
PATIO AND
CONTAINER
GARDENING

THE COMPLETE BOOK OF
PATIO AND CONTAINER GARDENING

ROBIN WILLIAMS
ROBIN TEMPLAR WILLIAMS
MARY-JANE HOPES

Edited by ROBIN WILLIAMS

WARD LOCK

Acknowledgements

The publishers are grateful to the following for granting permission to reproduce the following photographs: Harry Smith Horticultural Photographic Collection (pp. i, ii, (lower, v (both), xi (both), xii, xiii, xvi, xvii, xix (lower), xx, xxi, xxiv, xxv (lower), xxx (both), xxxii); Outdoor Lighting Supplies (p. xv); Photos Horticultural (pp. ix, xxii, xxiii, xvii, xviii, xxviii). The remaining photographs were taken by Bob Challinor.

With the exception of Figures A1–A10, all the line drawings were drawn by Nils Solberg.

Further information on outdoor lighting may be obtained from Outdoor Lighting Supplies, 325 Old York Road, London SW18 1SS.

First published in Great Britain in 1992
by Ward Lock Limited, Villiers House, 41/47 Strand,
London WC2N 5JE, England
A Cassell Imprint

Copyright © Robin Williams, Robin Templar Williams & Mary-Jane Hopes 1992

British Library Cataloguing in Publication Data
is available upon application to the British Library

Text filmset by Chapterhouse, Formby, L37 3PX

Printed and bound in Hong Kong

ISBN 0-7063-7007-4

CONTENTS

PART VII: *Care and Cultivation of the Patio and Container Garden*

APPENDIX: *Successful Patio Garden Plans*

Introduction

The object in writing *The Complete Book of Patio and Container Gardening* is to guide and assist the reader through the appropriate processes of design and construction towards a patio garden that is aesthetically pleasing, practical, functional, maintainable and last, but by no means least, affordable.

Without skill and knowledge the amateur can find the route to success overly complicated, time wasting and very costly. While no book can guarantee to eliminate these possibilities, it is hoped that the way can be smoothed as much as possible. To this end, *The Complete Book of Patio and Container Gardening* has been structured logically and sequentially. This will help you to decide from the outset which of the processes you could carry out by yourself, and which require the help of professionals.

Consequently, the main part of the book has been divided into four parts:

1. Planning and construction.
2. Decoration and planting design.
3. Plants, planting design, husbandry and welfare.
4. Examples of patio gardens for particular purposes. Plant and construction material sources.

Each main heading has then been subdivided, with each topic dealt with as a separate entity, so avoiding as far as possible the need for cross reference to other subjects which may not be immediately relevant to the project in hand.

The word 'patio' appears to have taken on Chameleonic characteristics in recent years, since it now assumes different and varying meanings. Originally the meaning was quite uncomplicated, 'a small paved area open to the sky and enclosed by house or other walls'. More often than not plants were grown within this area, but most probably the original purpose of a patio was either functional or simply to create cool shade. In Mediterranean countries especially, the most beautiful examples can be tantalizingly glimpsed through gateways and grilles.

Today, the name 'patio' can simply mean an area of paving upon which it is intended to sit – without any reference to its environment. A modern 'patio garden', on the other hand, could mean anything from the tiniest urban yard to any smallish plot attached to a house, and for the purposes of this book this is the chosen interpretation.

The recent patio garden phenomenon has mainly resulted from ever increasing land costs, coupled with the pressures on less and less available building land. Consequently, the modern house plot tends to be modestly proportioned when compared with times past. There are other reasons too, for example high maintenance costs have meant some large houses being divided into smaller units, together with their gardens. In towns and cities gardens have always tended to be smaller than their country cousins.

The best patio gardens do not happen by accident; they result from the very careful consideration of all relevant factors. So what does make a patio garden successful? Clearly it must meet with certain criteria, decided and agreed upon by everyone concerned. If possible, desires and expectations must be fulfilled according to lifestyle. The design should be both aesthetically pleasing and functional and should accord with its immediate environment. Maintenance should be appropriate to the time available and so on. This list is by no means exhaustive but any patio garden, however good it may look on paper, must be considered poorly designed should it not meet the owners' needs.

In view of this, the very first step in the design process is to sit down and compile a comprehensive list of needs and expectations. Only when this is done can the next stage be contemplated, which will be making a plan: The plan is vitally important! To make an analogy, to commence work without a garden plan is rather like starting out on a long journey in an unknown country without a route map. Without any proper means of direction time will be wasted, extremely expensive mistakes can be made and disappointment will inevitably follow. Another piece of sound advice is, having made a plan, stick to it! That is, unless there is some really good and overriding reason for not doing so. The old adage, 'Never change horses in mid stream' is particularly pertinent here. A plan which is to be useful, illustrative and from which we may quantify and lay out the various elements, must be both to scale and in correct proportion. The best way to ensure this is firstly to take accurate measurements of the plot, both horizontal and vertical. An accurate measurement will serve as the basis for the final plan and may then be developed through distinct stages, initially as a 'site analysis', then a functional plan, design outline, then finally a detail plan. These processes are described and reasoned in Chapter 1 'Basic Planning'.

A successful patio garden will result from following good principles of design. These are Simplicity, Balance, Scale and Proportion, Harmony, Interest and Functionality. No modern garden should be designed simply as a geometric exercise on paper, or for that matter on the ground. It should earn its keep by working at all levels.

Simplicity

A garden should never be fussy or appear contrived for its own sake. Simplicity should run through the whole design. This is particularly important in confined areas where the simpler the scheme the greater the illusion of space, bringing with it a sense of calm.

Balance

Every effort should be made to achieve balance not only between one element or structure and another, but between colours also. Any artist will know this to be fundamental when painting a picture and a garden is, after all, a three-dimensional picture! One side of a garden should not dominate the other. In gardens which slope sideways, for example, there is always the risk that features and elements on the higher side will be predominant.

Such a situation can be redressed by including construction or planting to give greater mass and height on the lower side. Colour balance is more difficult to achieve and when, say, it is desirable to make a garden appear larger than it is by this means, an imbalance in colour and texture might well have the reverse effect.

Scale and Proportion

Vertical and horizontal elements must not only be in proportion with each other but also with the overall size of the garden. Very large structures and heavy plantings will only serve to make a small garden appear even smaller. Individual elements and structures should be proportionate to their purpose. Good scale and proportion also extends to planting where trees, beds and borders should neither appear to be understated nor overstated. The popular weeping willow is a good example of the latter, frequently seen growing in areas far too small for it.

Harmony

Harmony is a subjective but important principle of design, yet is often difficult to achieve. The visual unification of the various garden elements brought about by harmony is a constant theme in the book. A patio garden should work as a whole, an entity. Elements, textures and colours should relate one to another and never be a series of bold individual statements. This can be disruptive and unsettling. Of course, there is nothing wrong with the stimulation of contrast, but even this is governed by the laws of harmony. A contrast, therefore, should never become a visual shock.

Interest

A garden might work at all levels yet lack interest. Interest adds 'spice'. Unfortunately not all gardens are interesting, perhaps lacking theme or obvious purpose. Some of the most boring gardens are those which lack mystery, the sort that can be seen in entirety with one sweep of the eyes, leaving nothing to be explored. Even the smallest garden can incorporate illusions, or at least a focal or talking point. Theme gardens can be very interesting, if only to the owner. A patio garden might, for example, be devoted to a collection of sculptures, a particular group of plants, or for fish-keeping. Remember, though, interest is only one principle and its particular manifestations should never be allowed to take over the garden completely.

Functionality

The function of a garden is the motivation for its design. Although listed here as a principle, it is rather more than that and its presence at the end of the list should not be misinterpreted. As already stated, any garden plan that does not meet the needs and expectations of its owner can only be considered to be poorly designed. Function cannot of course exist in isolation if the garden is to be beautiful. The other design principles must constantly be gauged against it during the making of a plan.

General Design Points for Patio Gardens

A patio garden needs to be just as carefully designed as any other type. Indeed, most designers agree that they are more difficult to plan, as each and every square inch of space has to earn its keep. Since space will be at a premium, there will be little or no room for 'dead' or unused areas. Also, any mistakes will be more noticeable by their closer proximity to the house. In many instances, again because of a lack of space, some of the garden features may have to assume dual roles, for example a particular type of paving might be laid not only to permit dry and safe access but also for its light-reflecting properties. Planting may be chosen not only for its beauty, but also for screening or partitioning capability at the same time.

Listed below are the general advantages and disadvantages of owning a small patio garden.

Advantages

1. Less costly to install.
2. Less difficult and time consuming to maintain.
3. More intimate, even cosy, resulting in a sense of greater security.
4. At a more human scale.
5. Can act as an extension to the house, in the manner of an outside room.

Disadvantages

1. Access may be difficult or inconvenient especially when the garden is at the rear of a back-to-back terraced house.
2. Costs of garden installation will be higher if access is difficult.
3. A lack of space might seem claustrophobic.
4. Possibility of lost privacy when overlooked by nearby tall buildings, especially in urban situations.
5. Greater areas of shade relative to proportionally high surrounding walls and fences.

In temperate climates gardens tend to be used far less in winter than in summer. This means that over a year a patio garden may well be viewed more from within the house than actually is visited. A well-designed garden should be attractive when viewed from any angle. In reality, however, because of the circumstances described above, there is usually a 'main' view from the house. The smaller the garden, the more the view tends to be in the nature of an outdoors stage set.

There are two main design approaches when planning a patio garden:

Formal Approach

Here, existing architectural features such as house and boundary walls are incorporated into the garden scheme. In effect this approach continues the architectural concept and the result is a garden with mainly clean and formal lines expressed in either symmetrical or asymmetrical terms. Bold, textural planting of similar 'mass' is sometimes used to offset any suggestion of harshness. Alternatively, limited planting is carried out to echo but not compete with the architectural lines, assuming a supporting role. Each is differently effective and remains a matter of choice.

Advantages of a formal architectural garden

1. Can make a garden appear bigger and more open.
2. Provides more recreational and play space due to uncomplicated horizontal surfaces.
3. More light reflection from uninterrupted surfaces.

In addition, paving used in a formal garden:
4. Has greater unity with the house architecture.
5. Is easier to maintain.

Disadvantages of formal schemes

1. Hard construction materials and installation are expensive.
2. Risk of garden looking austere and unsympathetic.
3. May be too static – less awareness of the changes of season, for example.
4. Inhibiting to the plantsman.

Informal Approach

To be truly effective, informality requires the formal boundaries often associated with patio gardens to be blotted out from view. Unless this is done there will be a conflict of ideas. In effect the patio garden must be 'junglefied'. By planting up the majority of the available space in very small gardens this approach can be extremely effective.

Advantages of an informal garden

1. The view from house windows can be exciting and mysterious (especially when illuminated at night).
2. Boundaries are 'lost' – without any indication of where the garden ends, it can look endless.
3. Maintenance is comparatively low, but only when the plants become mature.
4. Because of the cost of covering an area with plants rather than paving, for example, installation costs are lower.
5. Provides more privacy.
6. Encourages wildlife.

Disadvantages of the informal garden

1. An unbalanced planting, with a predominance of evergreen, will make the garden appear static, even cemetarial if too many tall conifers are included.
2. Tall plants increase the amount of shade.
3. Might seriously reduce the space available for recreational or sitting areas.

There is the possibility of creating a 'hybrid' garden, with a style somewhere between formal and informal, but this would run the risk of taking on the worst features of both as much as the best. That is not to say it should not be attempted but, having taken up the challenge, good imagination will be needed to make it work well.

In conclusion the authors and editor have endeavoured to explain the various topics and operations as clearly and precisely as possible, offering advice not only on 'how' but, equally important, 'why'. An understanding of 'why' makes the whole concept of designing and building a patio garden far more interesting and enjoyable. Where construction detail is described, for example, and in particular the sections dealing with walls and other vertical elements, it is recommended that such construction should not be undertaken without the help of a professional or, alternatively, after having received some training perhaps at evening classes. The book is not intended to be a building manual, rather a source of inspiration and ideas.

PART I

MAKING THE PATIO GARDEN PLAN

CHAPTER 1

Basic Planning

To produce a plan from which we can construct or modify a patio garden, we need firstly to collect and record accurately, information that will enable us to determine the inclusion, position, size and shape of required features.

This will take the form of five progressive stages. The first stage is the preparation of a *site survey plan* indicating the boundaries, levels, house walls, windows, existing trees, etc., in fact all the tangible and measurable elements. The second stage, the *site analysis*, will record details which are less tangible, such as direction of prevailing winds, orientation, beautiful or ugly views, soil type, etc. The third stage, the *functional plan*, will indicate the patio garden's main working components, for example seating areas, lawn, pool and screening. The fourth stage, the *outline plan*, shows in detail the most appropriate position and shape of each element on the patio. The outline plan will result from an assessment of the site analysis in conjunction with the garden's intended function and purpose – for example, first thoughts about set positions for sun lovers might have to be revised when the garden's orientation means an area earmarked for the purpose is discovered to be in the shade. Utilities or services close to the ground surface may also determine the positions or even prohibit the inclusion of some desired features, such as a pool or sand pit.

Bearing just these few factors in mind, it becomes apparent that we need, by some means, to work out, set down and test our ideas before forging ahead. This is the purpose of an outline plan. The outline plan can also indicate the intended construction materials. It is important to know these in advance, since purchasing materials or plants on impulse to create a patio can more often than not lead to disappointing results and prove to be an expensive mistake. Ideas implemented straight from one's head often do not work for any number of reasons. The choice of material may

be incompatible or inappropriate both architecturally and in colour, size and texture to surrounding structures and to each other. It may be that you acquire too few materials, in which case more will have to be sought, and hopefully from the same batch as colour and textural variations often occur. Too many materials means a waste of money and possibly the added inconvenience of having to dispose of them.

Measuring and Recording Accurately

To be truly useful the patio garden site, including those existing elements you intend to keep, must be measured and plotted accurately and to scale. This will allow us to see in advance what may or may not be achieved within a given space. Before starting out, it may be worth checking to see whether a site plan already exists. Measurements might be part of the property deeds, or shown on architect's plans if modifications or additions have been carried out. If the property is a new one, details such as these will almost certainly be found on the planning applications. With older properties such research may be more trouble than it is worth, and similarly if the area concerned is small and therefore easily measured. When survey plans are available, it is still advisable however to take at least one physical measurement in the garden and compare it with the plan. Even when carried out by 'professionals', survey drawings are sometimes inaccurate.

You may find it necessary to increase the scale of the plan to such a size as to allow sufficient detailing. For example, increasing in scale from 1:100 (10 mm = 1 m) to 1:50 (20 mm = 1 m). This is achieved either by redrawing using a scale rule, or using the services of a good reprographic shop. If you choose to enlarge the plan reprographically (which is the easiest option) draw a line on the plan to scale with the drawing, representing

1 m ($3\frac{1}{4}$ ft), and measure the line on the enlarged copy to check the accuracy of it.

Assuming that no plan exists or it is easier to measure the area yourself, some basic equipment will be needed before starting. A tape measure is essential, calibrated in metres or feet (some incorporate both metric and imperial calibrations, each occupying one side or other of the tape). A 3 m (10 ft) retractable steel tape should be sufficient for small patio sites; for larger sites a longer tape of 30 m (100 ft), for example, will be more useful, and these can be hired if you do not already have one. You will need a sheet of paper large enough to contain the drawing at the chosen scale – graph paper is better than plain and can be purchased in pads or rolls. Be careful to ensure that the graph paper's squares are compatible with either the metric or imperial scale rule you choose. A good scale rule will usually have eight different unit scales on it. An ordinary 300 mm (1 ft) rule can be used if you do not possess a scale rule, provided the scale for the measurements and recording the patio in sufficient detail is not likely to be less than 1:100 ($\frac{1}{8}$ in to 1 ft), and no more than 1:50 ($\frac{1}{4}$ in to 1 ft). A sharpened pencil and an eraser will also be needed, together with a pair of compasses with which to fix the boundaries, check the angles of adjoining walls/buildings and the positions of existing features. A directional compass to indicate exactly the orientation of the site, for example, north facing or south-east facing, etc. Finally, a solid surface is essential upon which to place the paper, perhaps a good-sized clipboard or small collapsible picnic table for larger sites. This will serve as a mobile centre of operations, so saving a lot of to-ing and fro-ing when measuring and recording.

CHAPTER 2

The Five Progressive Stages

Stage 1 – Site Plan

Having assembled all the necessary equipment, work can commence. First, determine which scale to use. This will obviously depend on the overall size of the site and the amount of detail required. The dimensions of the site can be roughly assessed by pacing out the maximum distances of both width and length. A good pace is approximately equal to 1 m ($3\frac{1}{4}$ ft). The area which the scaled patio garden will occupy on the graph paper can be approximated: if the patio site measures 10 m × 5 m (32 ft × $16\frac{1}{2}$ ft), for example, the plan could be drawn onto a piece of A4 (210 × 300 mm or $8\frac{1}{2}$ × 12 in) graph paper at the scale of 1:50 (20 mm = 1 m). If the site dimensions were half this size, the scale could be increased to 1:20 (50 mm = 1 m).

Start by measuring and plotting accurately to scale, the outside of the house walls. At the same time, plot the position of doors, including the way they open (that is, in or out), the windows, heating vents, pipes, drains – in fact any items which may affect the position or inclusion of future features or elements. The house wall will serve as a 'base' line and further measurements to establish boundaries and existing elements can be taken from it. Should a self-contained patio be sited at some distance from the house, it will still be necessary to establish a base line from which to work. In this instance it might be an adjacent fence, an existing summerhouse or a garage wall. If no such feature exists, a base line can be created using a piece of string or wire stretched taut between two canes or pegs. Ensure that the canes are as wide apart as possible, pushed into the ground. By measuring and plotting to scale from the base line formed by the canes or pegs and the line, the surrounding area and elements can be measured and recorded.

Simple patio garden shapes, squares, rectangles and so on, can be plotted by taking measurements off the base line at 90° (right angle). Should the site be complicated, how-ever, it may be necessary to use more canes or pegs, forming a triangle with the other two. The third cane is plotted by using a pair of compasses and this system is known as 'triangulation', producing three base lines from which to work. From each of these base lines more measurements can be taken at 90° to establish various points and features; these secondary measurements are called 'offsets'. The process is shown in Fig. 2.1.

Measuring changes in level

Establishing and recording different ground levels within a relatively small area can often be achieved quite simply without having to resort to the use of expensive optical or daunting electronic instruments.

The presence of any existing steps is an obvious indication of changes in level and by adding together the rise of each step, the difference between the two levels can be calculated. Of course, this will only give the immediate change in level at that point. To obtain the changes in level over greater distances, the following three methods can be considered:

Measuring methods

1. A spirit level placed onto a straight piece of timber of known length will, when accurately brought to level, show the rise or fall over that length by physically measuring the gap between the underneath of the end of the timber and the ground (Fig. 2.2). This process can be repeated to give a more detailed assessment of the overall changes in site levels. Find and establish by visual means the highest point of the area concerned. From this point repeat the procedure described, taking measurements at, for example, 2-metre intervals. Go from one side of the garden to the other, then repeat the process at right angles. Plot each point with its measurement onto the plan, eventually to form a grid. Make sure that the point at which the

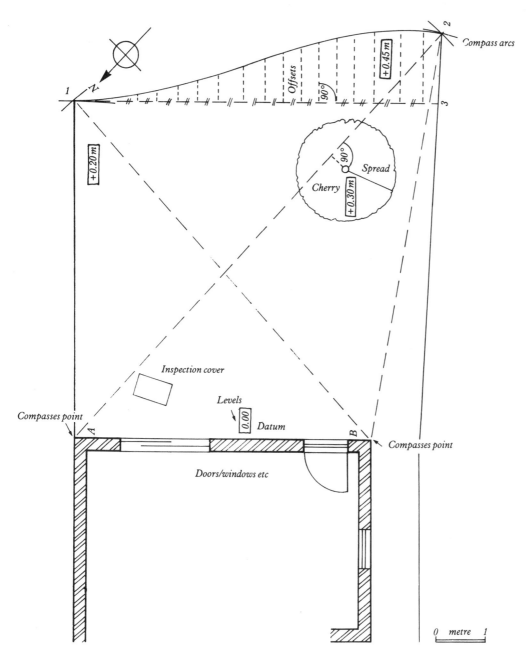

Fig. 2.1 Stage 1. Site plan, showing triangulation and offsets. Triangulation. The arcs are drawn by opening the compasses to correspond to the scaled measurements. For example, place the point of the compass on point 'A' and draw an arc representing the measurement to corner one. Then repeat from point 'B' to corner one. Where the arcs bisect must be the actual position of corner one. A connecting line can then be drawn to represent the boundary from point 'A' to point one. This process is repeated until all corners are established.

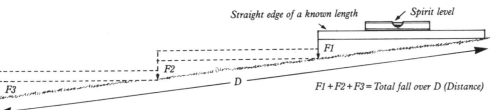

$F1 + F2 + F3 = Total\ fall\ over\ D\ (Distance)$

Fig. 2.2 Using a spirit level placed onto a straight piece of timber of known length.

15

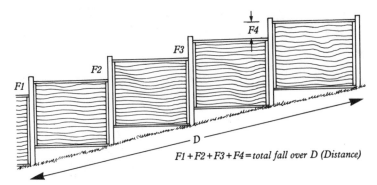

Fig. 2.3 Using level fencing panels fixed between posts.

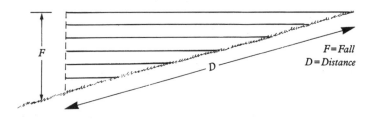

Fig. 2.4 Using a brick wall or block 'reading' the brick courses.

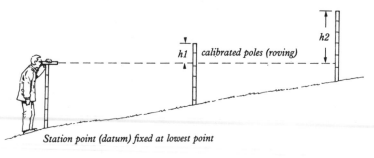

Fig. 2.5 Using a 'hand-held' level to establish spot levels.

previous measurement was taken is the starting point for the next level and so on, until the opposite boundary is reached. By adding together the measured differences in levels at each point, the overall fall can be calculated.

2. Level fencing panels (use a spirit level to check) fixed between posts can be used to indicate the rise and fall in ground levels (Fig. 2.3). As the panels step up or down with the change in level, simply add together the measurement of each step.

Similarly, a level brick or block wall may, by comparison, indicate a change in adjacent ground level (Fig. 2.4). By visually following a particular mortar joint along, starting at highest ground level, the fall can be approximated by physically measuring from the joint to the ground at the point at which the information is required.

3. A hand level is an easily used instrument for quickly assessing and measuring changes in ground level (Fig. 2.5). Although not as

accurate as other more sophisticated optical instruments, it can be used without the assistance of a second person, by the following means.

Fix upright into the ground a 1.5 m (5 ft) long calibrated pole or marked cane at the lowest point of the site, and plot this point accurately on the plan. Try to ensure that from this base position, you can see all the points it is necessary to know the levels of. This is the datum point and should be indicated on the plan as 'datum 0.00'. Now fix into the ground a second calibrated range pole of the same size, at the position where a measurement needs to be taken. Return to the first range pole and hold the level on the top of it. Looking through the viewing aperture of the hand level towards the second pole, fix visually the point at which the 'true' level indicator contained within the hand-held level appears to strike the second pole. The distance from this point on the second range pole to its top represents the rise in the ground. Plot this measurement and the position of the second range pole onto the plan. The process is repeated, with the first (datum) pole remaining in a fixed position, while the second pole is shifted from one point to another, where it is necessary to establish measurements. This means that all measurements will be relative to the datum pole, and since the datum pole is at the lowest point, all measurements will be on the plus side.

Stage 2 – Site Analysis (Fig. 2.6)

Having established and plotted the boundaries and main elements, and assessed any changes in level, take a further close look at the site and indicate on the drawing the less tangible elements. These will include: sunny areas; shady areas; orientation; exposure to prevailing winds; pH and soil type; good and bad views; over-looking neighbours (privacy); services; inspection covers; areas of poor drainage; dry areas; underground routes of various utilities and services; and any overhead cables.

Soil types

Where it is necessary to import soil into a patio garden, the type, quality and pH can be controlled. Where indigenous soil is to be utilized, a check will need to be made of its type, quality, pH and depth.

pH

The pH, in basic terms, means the degree of alkalinity or acidity of a soil, and this is measured on a logarithmic scale from 1 to 14, 7 being neutral. A reading above 7 denotes an increase in soil alkalinity, a reading below 7, an increase in acidity. The majority of soils will be between pH 5.0 and 7.5.

Testing the pH is easily done with the aid of pH soil-test kits which are widely available from outlets such as garden centres. The type of plants growing in the local area may also give a clue to the acidity/alkalinity of the soil. If, for example, rhododendrons, azaleas and other acid-loving plants are thriving, you can probably safely assume that the soil is acid. However, this is not so obvious in the opposite case, as plants that thrive in alkaline soils will usually tolerate moderate acidity. The presence of acid-loving plants showing signs of chlorosis and/or poor growth when others appear healthy, may indicate a neutral or alkaline soil.

Soil type and quality

Find out which type of soil it is; is it a sand, silt clay or loam soil? Although subject to many influencing factors, identifying the soil type will allow you to assess roughly the performance it will give during different climatic conditions. This in turn will influence your choice of plants, and allow you to see what action might be taken to cultivate certain species successfully.

You can assess fairly accurately the soil type and texture of a site by using touch. Moisten a small amount of soil in the hand, making it sufficiently damp to be pliable, but not wet. Now mould it into a ball, ensuring that its original structure is destroyed. The proportions of sand, silt and clay in the soil can be estimated by their following characteristics:

Sand feels gritty when rubbed between finger and thumb. Individual particles can often be seen by the naked eye, and there is little cohesion or binding of particles. General characteristics: good drainage; poor moisture and nutrient retention.

Silt feels smooth, silky or soapy when rubbed between finger and thumb. It is also slightly sticky, although it tends to adhere to and stain the fingers. Grains cannot be distinguished by

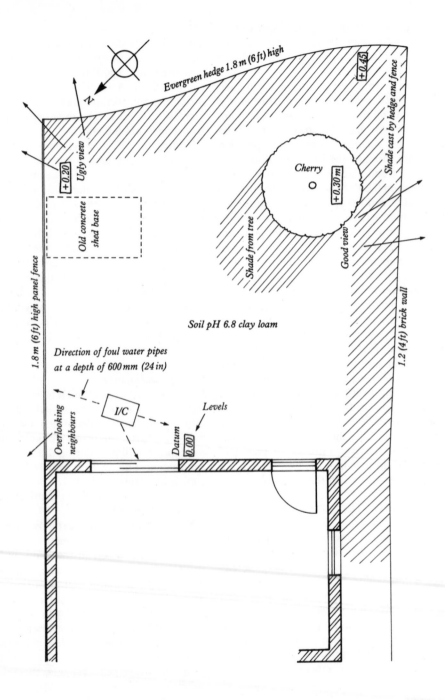

Fig. 2.6 Stage 2. Site analysis.

touch or sight. General characteristics: good drainage, average moisture and nutrient retention; and is susceptible to 'capping', which is surface hardening or crusting when hot weather follows rain.

Clay feels sticky and plastic, and shines when rubbed between finger and thumb. Can be easily shaped into threads and subsequently bent into rings without breaking. Is fairly easy to remove from the fingers and does not stain. General characteristics: poor drainage, good nutrient retention, very slow to warm up following cold weather, cracks following shrinkage in dry hot weather, difficult to cultivate.

Loam is composed of varying proportions and grades of sand, silt and clay. The ball of soil being tested will bind together but feels neither gritty, soapy or sticky when rubbed between finger and thumb. Having identified the soil as a loam, you can also now determine whether it is sandy (light), medium (relatively even proportions of all components) or heavy (clay). Compress the soil ball between finger and thumb. A light loam breaks apart easily, as it has a high proportion of sand, a medium loam breaks apart under pressure and a heavy loam will not break apart at all.

Soil depth

If the soil is to be used for direct planting, its depth will also need to be known. This can be estimated by digging a hole and physically measuring the depth of topsoil in the exposed profile (hole interior).

Service routes

Services will include water, gas, electricity, telephone, oil pipes, waste pipes and storm water pipes, etc. Should any of these services exist within the patio garden their positions, where possible, should be plotted.

It is important to know where the services are, particularly if they are invisible at ground level. This is necessary firstly in order to protect pipes from any damage and, secondly, because they must be allowed for when making your plan.

The depth and direction of sewage and waste water pipes (both storm and domestic) can in some instances be found by lifting inspection covers and drain grilles. Where this is not possible, as will probably be the case with services such as gas, water and electricity, it may be advisable to contact the respective authorities to see if any plans exist that would give this information. If the property is new or has recently been renovated, plans showing details of services will almost certainly be with the builder, developer or architect. Metal detectors can also be used to find and follow the path of cables and metal pipes.

Orientation

Orientation is the position of the site relative to magnetic north. Recording the orientation of the site onto the plan is essential, for it allows us to establish the path of the sun and the resultant areas of light and shade as it travels from east to west. Areas of shade will, of course, be increased by the presence of buildings, trees, fences, walls and other vertical elements. This information will then influence your decisions as to the positioning of various features.

Finding north is achieved either by using a directional compass or by observing the position of the sun at midday. If you are reading a compass, ensure it is not used within close proximity to strong electrical or magnetic fields, or indeed objects containing ferrous metals. This could result in an inaccurate reading.

Wind

If strong winds prevail, the direction from which they blow should be indicated on the site plan. Adequate screening can then be appropriately positioned in the design, thereby reducing its adverse effects.

Views

Indicate the direction of both good and bad views. A particularly good view may be incorporated into the design, either as a backdrop or focal point (see page 125), whereas a bad view may need to be screened or obscured. Screening for privacy is also essential, whether or not you have nice neighbours.

Land drainage

Any areas of poor drainage should be recorded. These may be localized or cover the whole of the site, but in either case a decision either to

19

drain and/or utilize the water can be made at the design stage. The higher the water table, the greater the necessity for a land-drainage system.

The fact that a site, or areas within the site, are poorly drained is not always obvious. This is especially true during dry periods. At such times you may have to search for clues. On hard surfaces such as paving, the presence of dried algae or dirty water marks may be an indication of poor drainage. However these signs may be the result of badly laid paving as well, and so not directly the result of a poorly drained site. In both cases, water that lies on paving can be dangerous as it encourages algal growths and, during freezing conditions, ice; both slippery underfoot. Poor, patchy, yellowing grass may also be a sign of poor soil drainage, especially when a species such as *Ranunculus repens* (creeping buttercup) is seen thriving in lawn areas and borders. In extreme cases sedges may also be present.

During wet weather poor drainage is much easier to detect. Puddles of water often quickly appear within grassed and other areas, retreating slowly and leaving the ground spongy long after the rain has ceased.

These conditions are commonly found on new housing developments where the subsoil, particularly if it's clayey, has become compacted by machinery. Token layers of topsoil spread by the builders soon takes on the characteristics of a sponge, as the subsoil underneath prevents the free passage of water downwards through the soil profile. In summer the reverse is true. This potentially serious situation needs careful consideration at the design stage – it is well worth remembering that prevention is better than a cure.

Stage 3 – Functional Plan (Fig. 2.7)

Before developing the plan further, write down a list (in order of preference) of elements to be included in the patio garden. If a place to sit and read is a priority, a comfortable spot to do just that may be at the top of your list. Taking this a step further, at what time of day is your special place most likely to be used? Should it be in the sun or shade? If, for example, shade is preferred, but the patio site due to its orientation offers none, perhaps the

clever positioning of a pergola or arbor could be used to achieve it.

Taking this list of requirements, together with the information gathered in Stage 1 – the site plan, and Stage 2 – the site analysis, the functional plan can now be worked through.

By this process each item on the list can be carefully looked at and only then given its appropriate position on the plan in basic terms. In some instances more than one feature is likely to benefit from the same position and so a certain amount of juggling must be expected, often meaning the exclusion or relocation of some functional items. This is more likely on smaller sites.

Having earmarked various areas for different functions, these will need to be physically or visually linked by some means or another – for example, by paths, lawns, etc. These linked functional areas are the heart of the plan.

Stage 4 – Outline Plan (Fig. 2.8)

With the functions and location of areas and features now resolved the outline plan can be started.

Each element within the patio garden must now be drawn onto the plan, but this time to scale, showing exactly its eventual size, shape and the position it will occupy. The basic type and size of materials to be used must also be indicated, remembering that whatever their combinations, the materials used should always be in harmony with one another and suit the particular situation/function for which they are intended. Take into account also the need for good access, and leave sufficient or as much space as possible to move around easily and unrestrictedly. If a table and chairs are to be used on the paved patio for example, even these should be drawn to scale on the plan. This will show the actual space the chairs will occupy when pulled out, as opposed to being tucked neatly away beneath the table. As a rule of thumb, a table that measures 1 m ($3\frac{1}{4}$ ft) wide will need perhaps a surprisingly large width of 4 m (13 ft) to accommodate people sitting at each side of the table with space all around (Fig. 2.9). It is important not to cheat when drawing up the outline plan; take care to find out the dimensions of the various elements, and the space they will occupy. That way no-one will be disappointed and the patio garden

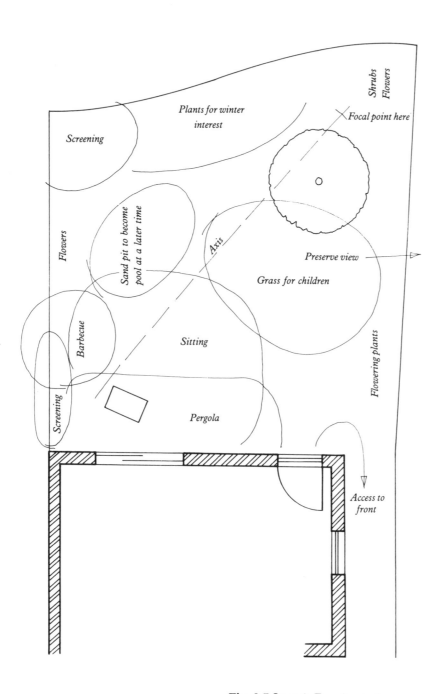

Fig. 2.7 Stage 3. Functional plan.

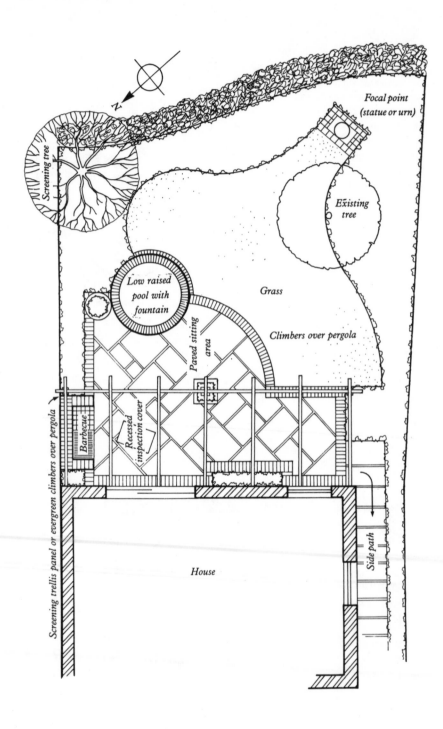

Fig. 2.8 Stage 4. Outline plan.

will not become cluttered as a result. When in doubt, elements like table and chairs, summerhouse, pool etc. can be cut out in plan form from card. These can then be moved about on the developing outline plan, so that their effect and space occupancy can be fully appreciated before being drawn.

On completion of the outline plan, when it can be seen to be entirely satisfactory, then the final detail can be added.

Stage 5 – The Detailed Plan

The detailed plan will include information such as exactly what type of brick or which particular paving is required. Planting will also be included with species, spacings and numbers indicated. It will be necessary to

develop the plan to this degree of finish to ensure that what we planned to achieve or have is exactly what we get. Plans that are not sufficiently detailed means that too much is left too much to interpretation, which can result in problems, particularly if outside agencies are involved.

On completion of the detailed plan it is recommended that it is either inked in or better still traced off using drawing ink. This becomes the 'master copy'. As many copies as you need can then be reproduced by photocopying, taking care to preserve the original. For outside use it is possible to have copies covered with a waterproof film. These can then be wiped clean of mud or dust during construction operations.

Fig. 2.9 Sketch showing how space is calculated to accommodate a 1 m table and chairs.

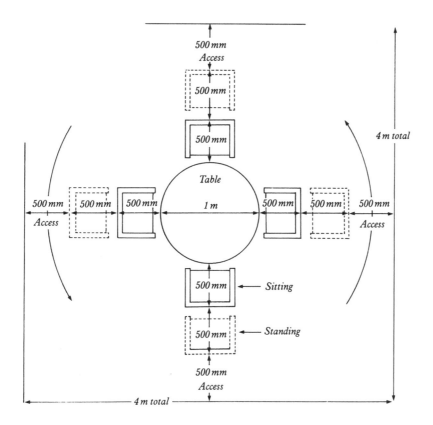

PART II

THE FIRST STEPS

CHAPTER 3

Where to Start

Well, we have a plan but who is going to implement it? Are the services of a landscape contractor to be sought or are you going to carry out the work yourself? It may be, as is often the case, a bit of both. For example, the landscape contractor could construct and lay the hard elements, such as the walls and paving, etc., while you do the planting. Someone else who is skilled at building, on the other hand, may need the assistance and advice of a planting contractor.

If a contractor is to carry out all or part of the work, it is advisable to approach at least three, giving each identical information and making quite clear the scope of works. Inform each one that it is a competitive quote and request that all items be separately and clearly costed.

Never get a contractor to estimate 'blindly', that is without inviting him or her to visit the site first; that way costly extras will be avoided. Poor access; existing features or materials excess to requirements; having to reduce levels; all these will have a profound effect on costs. If such items are not noted, a contractor can hardly be expected to include them in the price. In addition, unless a contractor comes directly recommended, ask for references and if possible to see examples of finished work. To reputable contractors this is standard practice and most will be happy to oblige.

Having received the quotes, the choice of contractor can only be made by you, based on a particular set of circumstances. Remember the old adage, 'You get what you pay for'.

Site Clearance

If you have recently inherited a patio garden from a previous owner, it is advisable not to rush into a programme of complete clearance. It is preferable to play a waiting game, especially if the garden is taken over in summer or mid-winter. In winter, for example, any existing plants will either be dormant or invisible beneath the ground, as is the case with most herbaceous plants and bulbs. In late

summer, the majority of plants will be past their best and mostly without flower. What a pity it would be – indeed, what a waste – if plants such as these were to be removed at least before a proper judgement could be made as to their suitability for a position within the new regime. It is appreciated that almost everyone taking on a new garden will want to impose their own style and personality upon it as soon as possible. There is, of course, nothing wrong with this. In the life of a garden, however, a year is practically nothing and it is eminently sensible to wait at least this time to witness what plants are there, how they look and how they perform. At the end of this period you can then decide which ones will be suitable to keep and which are to go. Those retained will not only save on costs but will be more mature than those purchased new from a garden centre. Most younger shrubs and plants can be moved, with care, to more appropriate places.

Where existing constructions or paving are concerned, these too need to be identified and considered in terms of their suitability for inclusion into the new plan, although this is best done at the planning stage. The route for an existing path may, for example, have been established on a trial and error basis by the former owner. In time, the new owner may discover precisely the same practical reasons for keeping the path where it is, so here again hesitate before indiscriminately clearing things away. This is assuming of course that the existing features are acceptable for reasons of personal taste or preference. If such features are unacceptable under these terms, then they should be removed since their presence will thereafter become an irritation.

The materials arising from clearing unwanted constructions and paving should be carefully examined to see if some or all might be reclaimable, even if only as hardcore. Saving materials such as these will effectively cut costs as any material imported will have to be paid for. Should the patio garden be entirely new, the ground may nevertheless contain builders' rubbish, both organic and inorganic. This is especially so where unconscientious developers have been at work and where a token inch or two of topsoil camouflages all manner of indescribable matter, which will need to be removed.

Removal of rubbish

It is advisable to clear the site of rubbish completely. A site cleared of any moveable obstructions or clutter will make for a better work place. However, take care when removing rubbish from the patio garden site. Local Authorities have strict rules on the collection and dumping of all rubbish, but particularly of garden refuse. In some cases the quantity of refuse will necessitate the use of a skip. If this is the situation check with the Local Authority as there are often guidelines to placement and safety. In many areas, particularly where it is busy or built up, a licence or permit may have to be sought if a skip is required. If in doubt, check.

Setting Out

'Setting out', or 'marking out' as it is also known, means to mark out on the ground, the positions and the dimensions of all the elements in plan form. This includes walls (and the extent of their foundations) paths, sitting areas, lawn, pools, and so on. In basic terms it is the transference of information from the paper plan to the ground. Accuracy is therefore of paramount importance if the patio garden is to replicate the design faithfully.

In essence, the process of marking the ground is like carrying out a survey in reverse, and the same basic techniques can be employed. Straight 'marking out' lines are generally easier to do than curvilinear. For straight lines, pegs can be driven into the ground and lines then attached to them. These are stretched as taut as possible and then fixed by tying. Where a rectangular area of paving is intended, the pegs would represent the corners and the line the peripheral edges. This will not only give a good indication of shape and space but also the area within which excavation or whatever is to take place. Where curvilinear lines must be represented, this obviously cannot be achieved by making the builder's

line straight. In this instance, pegs or canes will mark out the previously plotted curve or circle, spaced at appropriate distances. A line is then passed appropriately in front or behind them to represent the curve, and pulled as tightly as possible. The closer the pegs are placed, the more the line will represent the true curve as opposed to a polygon. Only trial and error will determine the appropriate spacing under a given set of circumstances.

The use of pegs and lines is the traditional way of marking out although it can be rather fiddly and time consuming. They have the advantage, though, of being able to be adjusted and give a strong visual indication. Tall pegs or stakes can indicate the positions of individual specimen trees. On completion of marking out it should be possible to walk through the proposed garden and with the help of a little imagination, anticipate its final appearance.

Professionals sometimes use alternatives to pegs and line, such as dry sand or builder's lime. This is used in a similar way to childrens' *Join the Dots* picture books. Principle points are transferred by measurement from the drawn plan on to the ground as a series of either sand or lime dots. The dots are then joined together by trickling sand or lime to form lines. To assist in the marking out of curves more accurately, a garden hose can be utilized. This is placed on the ground to conform to the sand or lime indicator dots. The sand or lime can then be trickled closely alongside the hose. When the hose is removed, it leaves a true curve or circumference on the ground.

For the very latest in marking out techniques, aerosol sprays are commonly used, but again mostly by professionals. The aerosol sprays have the distinct advantage of being available in many colours. This gives the opportunity of using a particular colour to represent a particular feature or material, so the emerging patio garden can be 'read' more easily without the need to distinguish mentally one representative line of pegs from another. It must be said that these aerosol sprays are expensive. However, since they save a great deal of time and are extremely easy and effective in use, you might well consider the investment to be worth while.

Lastly, chalk is occasionally used to mark

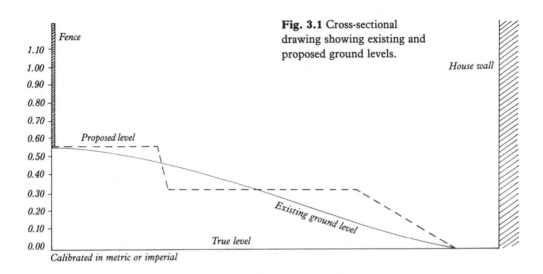

Fence

House wall

Proposed level

Existing ground level

True level

Calibrated in metric or imperial

Fig. 3.1 Cross-sectional drawing showing existing and proposed ground levels.

out, but only where the surface being marked out is hard and where the marking out is only temporary. The first shower of rain will wash most of the chalk lines away, whereas the other methods that have been mentioned will be longer lasting.

Whichever of the methods described above are employed, they will all be more effective if the ground or surface upon which they are used is reasonably flat. Indeed, if the ground is very lumpy or the grass long, the appropriate steps should be taken to flatten it.

On completion of marking out always make a final check. It is much easier and less expensive for adjustments to be made at this point, rather than when construction, cultivation or levelling has taken place. It is at this stage that the care taken during the initial surveying and planning operations will pay dividends.

Setting Levels

Marking out serves to indicate, like the drawn plan, what and where things happen but only in a one-dimensional form. There may well be differences in the surface levels of the patio garden, either existing or proposed, and these will need to be taken into consideration at a very early stage. The original survey or measurement of the patio garden will hopefully show the amount of fall or rise in the ground. To make these more appreciable, it is a good idea to reproduce them as one or a series

of cross-sectional drawings, depending on the complexity of the level changes. This process is not as difficult a task as it sounds. In theory it is simply a vertical plan of the garden (following a specific or axial line) as opposed to the horizontal.

To achieve maximum benefit from cross-sectional drawings they need to be drawn to a scale which should preferably be the same as the main survey drawing. The particular line or lines chosen, upon which to indicate the changes in level, will need a companion line which is drawn horizontally and against which the difference in level may be visually gauged (Fig. 3.1). The cross-sectional drawing might well show existing changes in level compared with proposed changes in level. The full implications in terms of differences, including the associated excavations or making up, can then be more fully appreciated and calculated.

The calculations will be necessary to establish such things as numbers of steps, gradients of ramps and grass slopes, etc. Also, how much soil might need to be excavated and removed or, alternatively, imported or transferred to make up levels. Where ground levels exist or are proposed against a house wall, the finished level (or datum) must be 150 mm (6 in) below the damp proof course. This is particularly important to bear in mind when dealing with paving, and other surfaces (see page 62). When setting levels for any purpose, to

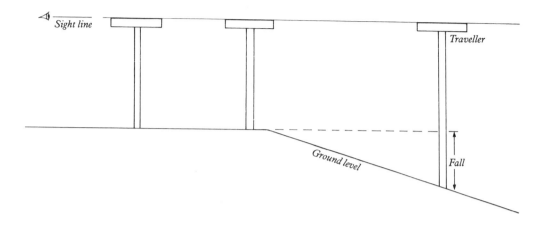

Fig. 3.2 Level setting using T-rods.

establish the bottom-most point of a paving structure for example, all calculations are made downwards from the 150 mm (6 in) below dpc level. Where a patio garden is more or less level and this state of affairs is preferred, then the only level setting that will be necessary will be to establish paving bases, wall foundations, excavations and pool depths, etc. In gardens which mainly slope, however, levels may have to be set to achieve flat horizontal surfaces for a children's play area or for seating perhaps. This means initially setting levels which will be generally different from those existing. Whereas the setting of levels on paper is comparatively easy, on the ground it is more complicated and cannot be carried out independently of the excavation or making up. On the contrary, following establishment of a datum, the level setting is done as operations continue, with continuous referrals back to the datum.

The most efficient means is by using optical instruments or by the use of 'boning T-rods' (see Fig. 3.2). These will need to be used in threes: one at datum; another at distance, which is at the same level as datum; and a third which is a 'traveller'. The first two are fixed,

whereas the traveller moves about. It is from the top of the traveller that measurements are taken, when the tops of all three are in horizontal conjunction. The difference in ground level is read vertically by calibrating the boning T-rods, or by using a steel rule and taking a physical measurement. This operation is illustrated to make the idea clear. If circumstances allow when setting levels, it is always best if datum serves all the different levels in the garden, as opposed to one level being calculated from another, down or up a slope (when any mistakes made will be compounded). Where it is intended to raise the ground upwards from a datum, as opposed to downwards, level setting can be even more difficult to achieve since the process is put into reverse and 'back-sighting' towards the datum will be necessary.

Should a patio garden be very steep, either upwards or downwards, to the extent that it would be exceeding the height, and therefore the range, of a 1.8 m (6 ft) boning T-rod for example, it is suggested that professional help be sought. Under these circumstances, the area being measured would almost, by definition, cease to be a patio garden.

CHAPTER 4

Ground Work

Before excavating to accommodate specific garden features, it will be necessary firstly to achieve general ground levels and contours. When flat areas need to be provided on a sloping site, this might mean carrying out one of three operations (see Fig. 4.1). The first will mean incorporating soil to place over the slope or part of it. The second, to excavate making an area level, removing from site the excess material. Both operations will be costly: on the one hand expensive material needs to be brought in; on the other, materials have to be taken away. If access is restricted, labour costs or DIY work-time will also be greatly increased.

For these reasons the third option, namely 'cut and fill' is usually the best, at least where it is appropriate. 'Cut and fill' consists of firstly removing the topsoil; digging into the ground at the high point of the proposed flat area; and then simply transferring it to the low point. This is done with each successive 150 mm (6 in) layer being thoroughly consolidated until a flat surface is achieved. If necessary, the initial topsoil is now replaced over the new level area or used elsewhere.

With 'cut and fill', the embankment formed where the new level surfaces reaches the original slope will be steeper than before, but equally shared at each side which makes them easier to deal with. However, methods one and two above, will create an embankment of greater steepness on the low or high side respectively. This is a more difficult situation to deal with, perhaps even requiring some physical means of retention.

Before any ground works are commenced and this includes either of the options noted above, all good topsoil should be removed from the immediate area of operations and stacked elsewhere for use at a later date. Good topsoil is such a valuable and costly commodity that it should not be wasted and neither should it be allowed to become mixed with subsoil.

Following the major ground levelling or contouring, specific ground works can commence. These will include excavations of trenches for utility services, drainage, foundations, reduced levels for paving, and so on. Trenches and excavations are best done tidily and precisely, keeping all arisings to the sides of the trenches

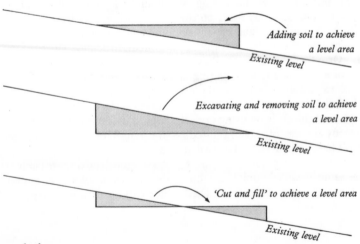

Fig. 4.1 Three methods to achieve a level area.

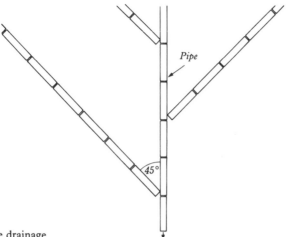

Pipe

45°

Fig. 4.2 Herringbone drainage
system.

Direction of fall and outflow

– near enough to be conveniently deposited but far away enough to prevent it tumbling back into the excavation. Also there should be room between excavations and arisings to allow foot and wheelbarrow passage. All trenches which are to be refilled following the installation of the various services, must be done thoroughly by replacing subsoil in layers not exceeding 150 mm (6 in). Each layer must be thoroughly compacted so that, ideally, there is no soil left over at the end. If trenches or excavations are not properly consolidated, they will inevitably become so later by natural forces, with perhaps serious consequences.

In times of wet weather during ground works, the soil surface should be protected as much as possible. Boards are normally used for this purpose, for not only do they protect the underlying soil structure, they also provide a drier and safer surface from which to conduct operations. The soil is often an early casualty when ground works are badly managed.

Land Drainage

Water retentive and heavy soils are a major problem in any patio garden, especially where areas are to be used for lawn or general planting. The indicators of poorly drained soil are mentioned earlier in the book (see page 20), but moss is the most recognizable symptom.

The main causes of poor drainage are: overly compacted soils due to heavy use by pedestrians and wheeled site traffic; and/or the nature of the topsoil itself, for example, clay or some other impervious layer lying beneath the topsoil. Whatever the reason, the effect is the same: water hangs about on the surface and will not readily disappear.

Poor drainage can often be improved by double digging and incorporating coarse organic material, or sometimes by the addition of garden lime and organic material. The latter treatment is the best for clay. The problem may be more serious than can be cured by either treatment alone and a proper drainage system will then have to be installed. There are four principle methods.

Pipe method (Fig. 4.2)
This utilizes earthenware or plastic pipes (some are ribbed or perforated) of sizes ranging from 75–100 mm (3–4 in) diameter for the main drain and 50–75 mm (2–3 in) diameter for the branch drains. These are arranged in a herringbone pattern and their line frequency appropriate to the poorness of the drainage. The system is set into the bottom of v-shaped trenches (Fig. 4.3a). Over the pipes is placed a 25 mm (1 in) layer of larger gravel with 10 mm ($\frac{3}{8}$ in) of smaller gravel above that. Over the gravel is laid a strip of geo-textile material or, if

31

Fig. 4.3 Four methods of land drainage.
(a) Pipe method
(b) Rubble drain
(c) Brushwood drain
(d) Sand slits.

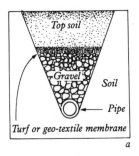

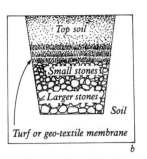

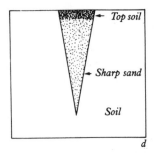

this is not available, inverted turf. This is followed by topsoil backfill. The purpose of the geo-textile material or the turf is to help keep soil particles from filling the voids in the gravel beneath, so making the system less efficient.

In heavy clay it is usual to lay the pipes nearer the ground surface. Any drainage system must slope to an outfall and this will either be into a ditch or, more likely in a patio garden, to a soakaway or the rainwater system.

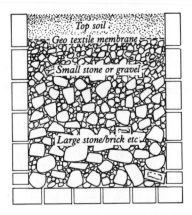

Fig. 4.4 Soakaway

If the latter, permission may have to be sought from the Local Authority, who will probably insist on the inclusion of a silt trap in the system.

Rubble drain (Figure 4.3b)
This is simply a wedge shape excavation, into the bottom of which fairly large stones are placed. Layers of smaller stones are then placed in succession, with an uppermost level comprised of gravel. A layer of geo-textile material or a double layer of inverted turf is placed over this. Finally a backfill of topsoil.

Brushwood drain (Fig. 4.3c)
A traditional method not so often used today. The system is in principle the same as the rubble drain except that brushwood (such as willow or hazel twigs) replace the stone.

Sand slits (Fig. 4.3d)
This method is based on a series of deep but narrow (approximately 50 mm/2 in) slits laid in herringbone fashion. These are filled with sharp sand almost to the surface, and top soil used as a backfill.

Fig. 4.5 Disguising a soakaway within a paved area.

Soakaways (Fig. 4.4)

Sometimes called 'sump drains', soakaways are very large pits approximately 1 m sq (3 ft sq) by a depth that varies according to soil type and the complexity or size of the associated land drain system. This might be anything from 1 m (3¼ ft) to 2 m (6½ ft) deep. In areas of clay soils, the sides ideally should not be left mechanically polished by spade or mechanical plant, as this could make them impervious, so holding in the water. The bottom too should be roughly forked and have brushwood incorporated. On completion of the excavation, the soakaway is filled to within 150 mm (6 in) of the surface and then backfilled with soil or turfed over. Alternatively, the pit may be lined with perforated blocks as shown (Fig. 4.4)

During hot summer weather the position of a soakaway may become obvious due to the drying grass square above it. Thus it is preferable, if it is practicable, to position the soakaway beneath an area of paving (Fig. 4.5).

Water Supply

Alkathene or polythene domestic water pipes should be used for the supply of water to external taps and irrigation systems, etc. To protect against freezing weather a pipe should be laid at least 45 mm (18 in) into the ground. Pipes entering the ground should do so as sharply as possible and be lagged to a minimum depth of 225 mm (9 in) from the surface. Avoid letting the pipe gradually rise to the surface as this will greatly increase the chance of freezing. Any connections below ground level should, where possible, be tested for leaks before backfilling. If the water is not to be connected immediately following the installation of the pipe, ensure that a sufficient length of pipe is spare at each end, to connect when the time comes. Plugging the ends with a piece of rag or newspaper is good practice, as it prevents any materials that may cause blockage from entering the pipe.

Electricity Supply

It is essential to consult a qualified electrician to design and install any electrical systems, particularly those outdoors. Having said that, at this stage the electricity cable or cables are only being placed and not connected.

The cables must be either PVC clad, mineral-insulated or armoured, the latter being preferable but more expensive, and laid at least 60 cm (2 ft) into the ground. Ideally the cable should run beneath paths or paving where there is virtually no chance of them being damaged. Cables laid beneath areas likely to be cultivated should be covered with a single row of bricks to give added protection from penetrating garden tools. As with water pipes, allow for a sufficient amount of cable to connect both the power source and the appliances.

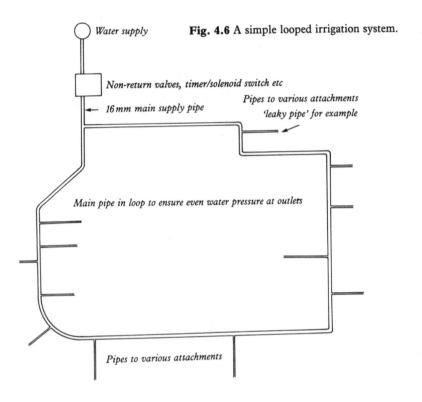

○ *Water supply*   **Fig. 4.6** A simple looped irrigation system.

Non-return valves, timer/solenoid switch etc

Pipes to various attachments
'leaky pipe' for example

← *16 mm main supply pipe*

Main pipe in loop to ensure even water pressure at outlets

Pipes to various attachments

Irrigation of General Areas

All plants will need watering at some time or another and those growing in a patio garden are no exception. Recent summers have been hot and dry. Under these conditions the imperative need to water regularly can soon become a very time-consuming chore. Add to this that watering is most safely and effectively done in late evening or at night, makes the prospect of watering by hand even less appealing, especially on the heels of a long and hard day's work. Another problem during summer is that many patio gardens have to be left unattended while owners are away on holiday, and this is usually at just a time when they need extra attention. The solution lies in the installation of an efficient irrigation system. These range from simple DIY kits to tailor-made electronically controlled systems. The latter will have to be installed by professionals and following their advice.

All irrigation systems work on basically the same principle but have different appliances at varying levels of sophistication, meeting different needs. The majority of systems will be based on a looped single series of mains pipes – 16 mm ($\frac{5}{8}$ in) diameter for example (Fig. 4.6). The fact that the mains pipe is looped ensures an even pressure to all outlets. Smaller branch pipes will be attached with various attachments carrying out specific tasks, for example:

In-line drippers (Fig. 4.7a)
This comprises a 'leaky pipe' with water escaping through small holes of specific sizes at pre-determined spacings. The water percolates via the soil to the roots of nearby plants. This is particularly effective on sloping borders. The pipes can easily be hidden beneath a mulch, which in itself will reduce water loss from evaporation by as much as 50–70%. 'Leaky

pipes' require very little maintenance as there are no moving parts and work on low pressures, effecting a saving on energy costs if being automatically pumped. The pipes are designed to be left permanently in place even in winter, with no risk of them bursting. Additionally, fertilizers can be introduced to the plants at controlled rates provided the necessary technology is to hand.

The 'leaky pipe' system is, where appropriate, the most cost effective. In some instances, it can be connected direct to mains water for small-area irrigation, rather than via a looped mains. The true 'in-line dripper' system uses rigid pipes, whereas those available through garden centres and other outlets are flat pipe systems, but these will mostly fulfill the needs of the DIY patio gardener.

Other systems based on similar principles have adjustable caps positioned at intervals over holes at the top of the pipes. This permits fine tuning of the water flow and at the same time keeps the outlets free from clogging up.

Pot drips (Fig. 4.7b)
These in conjunction with fine-bore leads allow the accurate and controlled watering of pots and containers. These might be independent systems or linked to the looped mains (see page 34).

Mini sprinklers (Fig. 4.7c)
Mini sprinklers are useful for irrigating areas of open but fairly low planting such as rockeries, small herbaceous borders and rose beds. In effect they are small-bore pipes attached and held erect by metal spikes. At the top is either a rotating or fixed sprinkler head. Mini sprinklers, depending on output, will cover a diameter ranging from approximately 3 m to 5.5 m (9 ft–16 ft). To some extent mini sprinklers can be moved about.

Pop-up sprinklers (Fig. 4.7d)
These are used for watering lawn areas, shrubberies and large herbaceous borders. By necessity pop-up sprinklers occupy a fixed position and are linked to a grid or pattern so that no area is left unwatered or, for that matter, overwatered. In areas of lawn it is, of

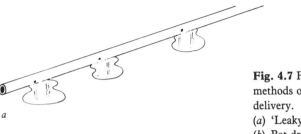

Fig. 4.7 Four methods of water delivery.
(a) 'Leaky pipe'
(b) Pot drip
(c) Mini sprinkler
(d) 'Pop-up' sprinkler.

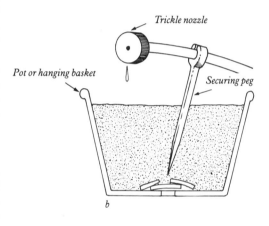

Trickle nozzle

Pot or hanging basket

Securing peg

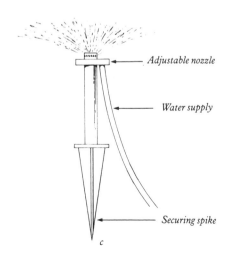

Adjustable nozzle

Water supply

Securing spike

course, essential to have a system where the sprinkler heads are below ground level during mowing operations. However, when turned on, water pressure forces the sprinkler heads to 'pop up' automatically (hence the name) to perform their function. This needs to be carefully programmed, in terms of timing, application and duration, etc. Pop-up sprinklers are therefore part of a fully automated and electronically controlled system that also requires reservoirs, header tanks, and so on. It is unusual for such a system to be connected directly to the mains water. Indeed it would not be permitted.

Pop-up sprinklers at just above ground level will cover an area of up to 9 m (30 ft) diameter; and up to 30 m (100 ft) diameter if the sprinklers are mounted on risers for shrubbery water-

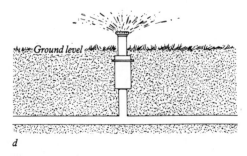

d

Fig. 4.7 *continued*

ing, etc. In the final analysis the diameter of watering will depend to a great extent on the water pressure, ranging from 1 cu m per hour at 30 lbs per sq in, to 5 cu m per hour at 60 lbs per sq in. The latter would be far too powerful for an average patio garden dimension.

PART III

PAVING THE PATIO

CHAPTER 5

Choosing the Surface

There are many ways in which a patio can be surfaced. The choice of material or combination of materials is vast, and will be selected for their function, desired appearance and situation.

In many people's minds, appearance is often the first consideration when choosing material for a patio surface but equally important, and in some instances more so, is the texture. The texture in turn will be determined by the function the particular area has to perform, for example, as a place to accommodate garden furniture, children's play, a barbecue, access to other areas, container gardening, as a utility area. To take the first example, an even surface will be necessary to prevent garden furniture from rocking, which can be irritating and unsettling. On the other hand, for children's play a sufficiently textured surface is essential to prevent slipping, and it should also be easy to clean (likewise for utility areas). The proposed surface to surround the base of a barbecue must also be easy to clean and as grease resistant as possible for obvious reasons. Where a patio also serves as access to another area, especially if not well lit at night, the surface must be even, non-slip, and preferably of a light colour to reflect any light there might be. Surfaces upon which to stand containers may benefit from loose or granular materials since they would retain moisture to be released gradually in the heat of the day. This is beneficial to the plants, whilst providing an attractive foil. An even and firm surface, on the other hand, will facilitate maintenance and make soil spillage easier to deal with.

Having identified a function or functions, the patio surfacing can then be chosen to achieve the desired effect, selected probably from the following materials and products.

Forms of Natural Stone

Gravel

Self-binding gravel is a mixture of graduated sizes from coarse to fine. When dampened and well compacted by means of rolling or vibrating, it forms an even-textured surface. Particle sizes range from approximately 15 mm down to sand.

Crushed stone

This is obtainable in different sizes. Various textures can be achieved depending on the grades and type used. Since this material is multi-faceted, it tends to be more stable. Particle sizes range from 50 mm (2 in) to 5 mm.

Pea shingle

This is naturally water-worn, the grade of which determines textural quality. Pea shingle can unfortunately migrate on slopes since the pieces are round. Particle sizes range from 15 mm to 10 mm.

Cobbles (large pebbles)

Cobbles are normally used exclusively for their textural effect. Sometimes also used for discouraging people from walking over a particular area since they can be extremely uncomfortable under foot, especially if large and widely spaced.

Setts

These are usually in the form of blocks or cubes cut from granite or similar hard stone. New setts have often been 'rough hewn' but eventually become smooth with wear. Second-hand setts can be obtained in this state if preferred.

Cut stone (sometimes called Flags)

Textures will result from the way in which the stones were quarried, then subsequently sawn, cut, split or chiselled. The type of the stone and desired effect will determine which.

Bricks

Clay bricks

These are available in a wide range of textures to suit most needs, from the very rough to the very smooth.

Sand lime bricks
Different from clay in that they are usually only available with a very smooth surface. Only the best quality are frost proof!

Concrete bricks
These often imitate clay bricks with varying degrees of success and have a similar range of textures and forms.

Concrete

Concrete formed either *in situ* or in mould can be finished to achieve practically any texture using the following: trowelling, brushing, tamping, impressing, stippling, exposing the aggregates, and hammering.

Trowelling with a steel trowel will produce a glass-like surface, whilst a wooden trowel provides a soft-dragged texture. *Brushing* using a soft brush will leave shallow smooth-edged lines, whereas a stiff brush will impart fairly deep grooves. *Tamping* is a method mostly used to create a strong texture of pronounced ridges. *Impressing* is a method of marking the surface of wet concrete by mechanical means *in situ*, usually to imitate other materials (setts, for example). This method is more often undertaken by professionals, as it involves the use of specialized equipment. *Stippling* results from a roller being pushed over the wet concrete. *Exposing the aggregate* (the small pebbles or stones within a cement matrix) is achieved by carefully washing away the surface cement, to give the impression of gravel. *Hammering* is usually a finish given to paving slabs at the factory to lightly break up the surface in order to reveal their crystalline structure.

Timber

Timber, while not extensively used as an exterior surfacing in the UK, can – depending on the way it is laid – produce the most interesting textures: for example, *planking* (decking), spaced or butted; *on end*, as sawn-to blocks with the end grain exposed, or as *log rounds* (slices).

The reason for the lack of popularity of timber in a temperate climate is that a planed or smooth surface quickly becomes slippery and therefore unsafe. This alone is a good reason for texturing, and can be achieved by

the following methods: rough sawn or rebated to give different textural patterns. Granulated *tree bark* is obtainable in different grades, from fine through to coarse, and various textures can be achieved depending on the grade.

Paving Patterns
Bricks

Bricks for paving will produce, according to their type, surfaces which range from the rustic to the very precise and formal. Catalogues and visits to builders' merchants will help determine those which are most suitable to produce a particular 'feel', according to the requirements of the design. Used on their own, bricks create an overall surface texturing when viewed from a distance. At close quarters the patterns ('bonds') in which they are laid will range from the dynamic – suggesting movement – to the static. The bonds illustrated are mostly traditional, since all the possible permutations have been more or less exhausted over the years. Bricks may either be laid flat with their largest surface areas uppermost (providing they have no indentations or perforations) or 'on edge'. This will not only have an effect on the overall appearance of the paving, but laying on edge will necessitate half as many bricks again – an important point to remember if low cost is a consideration.

Popular brick patterns

Stretcher bond pattern (Fig. 5.1a). The bricks are laid either flat or on edge in rows, with the joints equally staggered between successive rows. When choosing 'stretcher bond' a decision will need to be taken as to the direction of the brick rows related to the direction of, or main viewing position, of the area being paved. This applies both to a patio and path. When laid running across the patio or path, stretcher bond has a widening effect. Laid so that it runs away from the main view or, in the case of a path, following its route, stretcher bond then becomes strongly directional. It can also make it appear narrower. Stretcher bond has the advantage of negotiating curves, as the brick joints 'flow' with them. For this reason, it is often the best choice of bond since there will be practically no cutting needed.

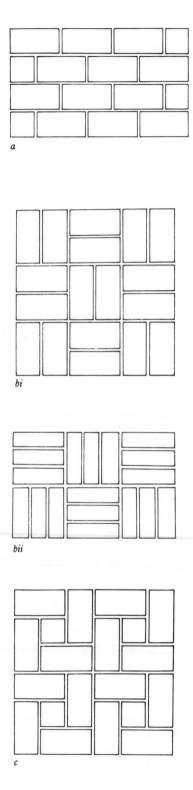

a

bi

bii

c

Basket-weave pattern (Fig. 5.1*b*). Traditionally laid on edge in threes but in most of today's patios, laid flat two by two. This is not only on grounds of economy but for reasons of proportion, as 'basket weave' of flat bricks is less fussy and therefore ideal for larger areas. Basket weave is a static pattern with no apparent directional movement. As such, it suggests calm and is therefore also eminently suitable for sitting areas. The pattern is achieved by laying two (or three) bricks side by side, then alternating their direction by 90° over and over again throughout the entire area. The finished surface resembles woven basketwork.

Flemish pattern (Fig. 5.1*c*). Another static pattern and just as effective as basket weave. 'Flemish bond' is achieved by arranging in series, four flat brick lengths to form a square by overlapping, in such a way as to leave a small square at its centre, equivalent in area to the half-brick which is cut to fill it. Because of the need to cut bricks, Flemish bond is a little more labour intensive, but extremely attractive.

Straight herringbone pattern (Fig. 5.1*d*). 'Straight herringbone' produces a most interesting pattern with each brick laid overlapping in a different direction by 90° to its immediate neighbours. The general direction of the joints will be parallel to the length and width of the area being paved. At the periphery, half-bricks are required to make the edges straight. When a straight herringbone path is laid, there is a degree of movement suggested, but this is not pronounced.

Diagonal herringbone pattern (Fig. 5.1*e*). This is achieved in exactly the same way as the 'straight' version, except it is laid at 45° to the length and breadth of the area being paved. Depending on the way the bricks are viewed, and relative to the area as a whole, there can be a distinct sense of diagonal movement, its visual strength lying between stretcher bond and basket weave. For this reason it is a suitable pattern to suggest a meander. This very traditional pattern has a drawback in that small triangular pieces of brick have to be cut to make up the differences at the edges.

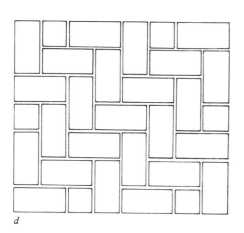

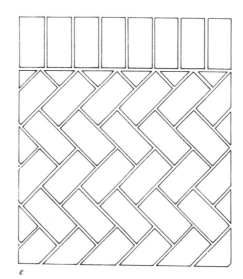

d

e

Fig. 5.1 Popular brick patterns.
(*a*) Stretcher bond pattern
(*bi*) Basket-weave pattern
(*bii*) Basket-weave on edge

(*c*) Flemish pattern
(*d*) Straight (90°) herringbone
(*e*) Diagonal (45°) herringbone pattern
(*f*) Stack or straight pattern.

Stack or straight pattern (Fig. 5.1*f*). This pattern sets up strong directional lines in both directions as the brick joints run uninterrupted from one side of a paved area to the other (the pattern does not include staggered joints). The bricks are simply laid side by side and end to end. For some reason this pattern has a modern look about it and is often associated with contemporary architectural gardens. 'Stack' or 'straight pattern' is occasionally laid to run diagonally across a patio or path with interesting and stimulating effect.

In addition to the above brick-paving patterns, further interesting variations can be introduced by using bricks of different colours and textures. These can range from the subtly harmonious to striking contrasts. Besides occupying the whole of a paved area, bricks are commonly used in conjunction with other materials for edging and design detail.

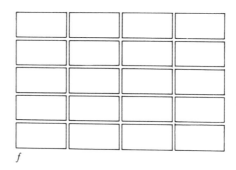

f

Paviors

Some manufacturers produce paviors which do not conform to the familiar brick format and are intended for special purposes. However, for patio use they can be treated as bricks as far as laying is concerned. Regarding the patterns they make, this will depend on the patterning information supplied by the manufacturer and on the format of the pavior itself. The herringbone pattern principle is most often suggested.

Fig. 5.2 Granite setts laid to a traditional 'fish scale' pattern.

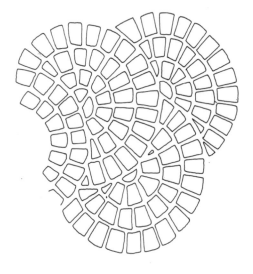

Setts (Fig. 5.2)

Setts can be laid in more or less the same patterns as bricks, especially where their lengths are equal to twice their width. When their proportions are closer to a square they can be laid either with staggered or straight joints, which can run either following the direction of a path or paved area, across it or diagonally to it. The smaller the sett, the greater its versatility in producing interesting patterns – it is the smaller square setts that are used to create the famous 'fish scale' or 'fan' patterns.

Patterns can be heightened or embellished by introducing setts of a slightly different colour. As with bricks, setts are also used in conjunction with other paving materials to form edging and design detail.

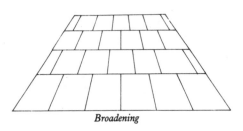

a

Broadening

Lengthening

Fig. 5.3 Concrete slabs.
(*a*) Dynamic effects of paving joints
(*bi*) Hexagonal paving
(*bii*) Static/lengthening
(*c*) Circular paving slabs. Circular slabs associate well with pebbles laid loose or in mortar.

bi   *Hexagonal paving*

bii   *Static/lengthening*

Concrete slabs

Concrete slabs are manufactured in square, rectangular, hexagonal and round shapes. These shapes dictate the patterns. Square paving slabs can only be used in two ways: either with the joints staggered, or straight and uninterrupted. If you lay slabs with staggered joints, have regard to the direction from which the resultant paved area will be viewed (Fig. 5.3a). Uninterrupted joints running away from the eye are seen as being strongly directional, whereas the same pattern turned 90° will have a broadening effect. Concrete paving slabs laid with all the joints straight and in line look the same when viewed from any direction. This presents a non-directional, even static pattern, ideally suited to areas for seating and relaxation.

Rectangular slabs, depending on their individual proportions, can be laid in a very wide range of design permutations, including a false 'random' pattern.

Hexagonal slabs are, even today, fairly unusual for patio and path work but are undeniably attractive in a modern way. Depending on the direction in which they are laid, hexagonal pavings will be mildly directional if the points are in line with the viewing axis (Fig. 5.3b(i)). Conversely, the effect will be

static if the flat sides are in line with the viewing axis (Fig. 5.3b(ii)).

Circular paving slabs are excellent for stepping stones but for 'all over' patio or path surfacing they can be more trouble than they are worth (Fig. 5.3c). Whether they are laid touching each other or spaced, oddly shaped gaps will be left in between which will need to be filled with some other material such as mortar or gravel. This is rarely a satisfactory proposition.

The colours of concrete slabs will vary according to the manufacturer but many colours are available, including buffs, browns, greens, blues, black, grey and white. Mixing too many colours will look garish and will be both visually disruptive and distracting. Although a single colour is often best, there is no doubt that the introduction of a second brings interest. Limiting the choice to perhaps two colours lessens the risk of the paving competing with other patio features, in particular the plants and flowers. In the patio garden, think of the hard elements like paving as a frame, with the plants making the picture.

Fortunately most coloured concrete products fade with age, so after a few years any over use of bright colour will be moderated by nature.

Reconstituted stone

Reconstituted stone has similar sizes and proportions to concrete slabs, most likely based on multiples of 150 mm (6 in) and 210 mm (9 in). Therefore all the concrete slab patterns can be achieved likewise with reconstituted stone slabs.

Natural stone

Natural stone for paving will be most readily available as sawn or cut flags of varying rectangular sizes or as flat polygonal shapes (crazy paving) (Fig. 5.4a). Sawn stone flags are mostly laid in random patterns to take account of their individual random rectangular sizes (Fig. 5.4b). Unlike concrete or reconstituted stone, they will be truly random, as no one flag will be exactly the same as another. It is possible to obtain natural stone flags to form rectangular patterns, using uniform sizes and proportions such as squares. This degree of precision

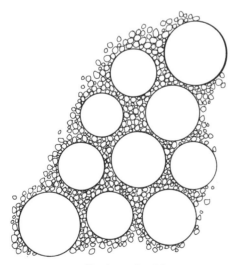

c   *Circular paving slabs*

involves great skill and inevitably more waste at the quarry, which is consequently reflected in the very high unit cost.

Polygonal random flat stones (crazy paving) will, up to a point, bring their own patterns. The more angular the stone pieces, the more 'crazy' the general appearance. Random stones which have rounder corners produce a far softer effect. In patio gardens, crazy paving is nowadays very likely to be used with other materials, such as brick (Fig. 5.4c). The bricks might be used to make a series of 'frames' or 'lattices', which are then filled with random stone. The overall effect of this is one of controlled informality and harmony, which is lacking when crazy paving is used alone.

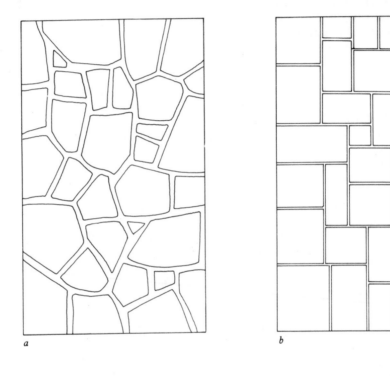

a

b

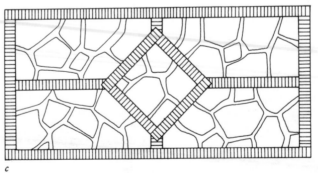

c

Fig. 5.4 Natural stone.
(a) Crazy paving
(b) Random rectangular
(c) Crazy paving with brick detail.

CHAPTER 6

Laying the Paving Surface and Edgings

The main purpose of paving in the patio garden is to provide a safe dry surface to facilitate walking and the use of wheeled vehicles such as cycles, pushchairs, wheelchairs and wheelbarrows. Very occasionally paving is laid just for its appearance, and for its ground pattern. There is sometimes another purpose too, and this is to cover the ground, replacing grass and plants in an attempt either to reduce or remove completely the need for maintenance. Before discussing the various types of paving, it is best to gain an understanding of how it works. This will help you to choose the correct and most suitable specification for a particular set of circumstances.

In Roman times, large slabs of thick stone were laid on compacted soil. These were in reality stone 'rafts'. The loading imposed on each slab was in turn being imposed on the area of soil underneath. A 19th-century engineer called Robert McAdam arrived at a better solution whereby the traffic-imposed weights were dissipated downwards at 45° through several layers of different-sized stone, with the largest at the bottom. This was a flexible pavement, far more efficient than earlier techniques and not having to rely on obtaining, transporting then placing extremely large flat stones. The diagram of a typical macadam pavement (Fig. 6.1) shows how the idea works in principle, and the various layers of material making it up.

Paving terminology	
Formation	The base and sides of the excavation which will accommodate the paving.
Sub grade	The soil (or other indigenous material) beneath the formation.
Sub base	The first and bottom-most layer, comprising the largest stones.
Base	The middle layer of smaller stones that helps to dissipate the load imposed from above.
Wearing course	This course being the uppermost, protects the base from wear and tear.

The material, size and depth of the various courses will depend entirely on the loads

Fig. 6.1 Typical cross section of a macadam pavement.

45

which are to be imposed upon them and the nature of the sub grade. Vehicular traffic obviously requires greater support than pedestrian traffic. Since patio gardens fall into the latter category, only the minimum support will be necessary. Even so it should be emphasized that it is important to get the specification right to carry out the job well. Under-specifying is far worse than over-specifying but either one is a waste of money! For domestic work, sub bases can be made up of almost any hard *inorganic* material – crushed rock, hardcore, brick batts, and so on. Any *organic* materials, such as timber or old wall plaster, should be avoided at all costs. These will degrade or decompose, in time causing settlement. All sub grades should be very well compacted by mechanical means if necessary, before the imposition of the base layers. Base layers should be of evenly graded material, compacted in layers of not more than 150 mm (6 in) at a time. This may mean, for example, that several compacted layers are required to make up an appropriate sub base depth. Where paving flags, bricks or some other hard surfacing is used in a domestic situation, one base course will probably be all that is necessary. Under such circumstances, yet appropriate to the quality of sub grade, the depth could vary from 30 cm (12 in) to 75 mm (3 in). Clay and sandy soils will require the greatest depths, while hard or stony soils the least. In really difficult situations neat cement can be thoroughly mixed with the upper surface 150 mm (6 in) of the sub grade and then thoroughly compacted. After several days, provided the sub grade is damp, the resultant 'soil concrete' will help stabilization.

Laying Wearing Courses – Paving Surfaces

There is an extensive range of paving surfaces. The choice will depend on their suitability in terms of function and appearance. In turn these choices will have a bearing on how the paving is laid. The following descriptive notes all assume that a base is already in place.

Gravel – self binding

Self-binding gravel is a naturally occurring material and must be spread evenly over the base using a shovel and/or a rake. This gravel type (comprising particle sizes varying from 15 mm ($\frac{5}{8}$ in) down to sand) is as a rule supplied damp, straight from the gravel pit or in pre-packed bags. As the material is spread in layers it must be compacted. Obviously the surface must be even and the use of a heavy hand roller, mechanical vibrating roller, or a mechanical compactor (whacker plate) will accomplish this. The final compacted depth will be approximately 20–50 mm ($1\frac{1}{2}$ in). Self-binding gravel, on finishing, should be of even surface, but when used to surface a path it is traditionally laid to camber – that is, higher at the centre than at the sides to form a very gentle hump. This 'profile' helps to direct the surface rainwater away.

All gravel paths look better if they have an edging of some kind (edging materials and types are discussed separately – see page 47) and the edging of the self-binding gravel is used in conjunction with a shaped board, concavely cut to form the camber. The shaped board uses the edging as 'rails', along which it runs horizontally at 90°.

Self-binding gravel paths need to be checked at least once every year (preferably after the hard frosts have passed), and re-raked and re-rolled as necessary. Continuous use and the well-known effects of frost will disrupt the surface and cause holes or irregularities. However, self-binding gravel, if well laid, provides a firm surface for wheels or pedestrian use. Finished levels usually coincide with the top of the edging.

Crushed stone

Crushed stone is taken from the quarry and inland gravel pits, or produced by crushing larger rocks. It is then graded to size and is multi-faceted. Crushed stone is laid using a shovel and rake. Due to the fact that the stone pieces are graded from coarse to fine, there is less 'locking' together than with self-binding gravels. For this reason rolling can only achieve a surface that is temporarily flat. Pedestrian and wheel traffic will dislodge the individual stone pieces. However, since it is multi-faceted, it is still reasonably stable if laid to fairly shallow depths over the base. Depths of wearing courses vary according to stone size, which should not exceed one third of the total wearing course depth. 25–75 mm (2–3 in) depths are considered normal for wearing courses. Stone sizes range from 5–50 mm ($\frac{1}{4}$–2 in).

Disadvantages are that sharp stones can damage high-heeled and soft-leather shoes and if they become lodged in Wellington boot soles, will be taken indoors. Crushed stone is also extremely difficult to cycle over or push a wheelbarrow on.

Crushed stone paths should be slightly lower than adjacent edgings to prevent stone particle migration, especially onto grass where the larger sizes of stone can cause damage to mower blades.

Pea shingle

Pea shingle is laid in exactly the same way as crushed stone and is similar in most other respects too; for instance, the particle sizes are approximately 10–15 mm ($\frac{1}{2}$–$\frac{3}{4}$ in), as taken from the seashore or inland gravel pits. The particles are smooth and roundish, having been water-worn for thousands, perhaps millions of years.

The drawback with pea shingle, compared with either of the previous two types, is that owing to its round shapes it very easily migrates. For this reason it is not the best surfacing for sloping paths. Even if used sparingly, a heap of stones will inevitably soon appear at the bottom of any dip.

Advantages are that both crushed-stone gravel and pea shingle are to some extent self draining, and therefore do not generally need levels incorporated as 'run offs'. Either surface is useful for security reasons since it would be extremely difficult for an intruder to walk over them without making a noise; footsteps on gravel or shingle can be surprisingly audible.

Geo-textile matting

This greyish white blanket-like material based on polymer fibres is sold in rolls under brand names such as Biddim and Terram. It is placed over the formation and under the sub base or base of a path, and lapped partly up the sides to contain the various strata. Its usefulness is as a stabilizer, helping also to distribute loads evenly over the underlying soil. Moreover, it acts as a filter, allowing only water to drain while retaining the fine aggregate particles. Its value is well known in road and path making.

Where paths within a patio garden are concerned, and particularly where the wearing course is open (such as in any gravel path), it really comes into its own! What it also does in this situation is to prevent an exchange of fine soil particles working up from the sub grade through the path matrix to the surface, thereby preventing the path from becoming muddy. While it adds to the cost, the inclusion of geo-textile matting is worth while in the long term.

Edgings

Edges have been included at this point since they naturally follow on from gravels. The purposes of edgings are various. Firstly, they will stop the lateral spread of unfixed or loose materials, which includes the bases as well as the wearing courses. Secondly, they define the edges or limits of paths or other areas. On a practical level, this helps to identify a path route or paved area where the light may be poor, or if there is snow (provided the edging is high enough). On an aesthetic level, edgings have important visual qualities on the ground in linking, directing and generally providing design continuity. Lastly, where grass abuts a path, (provided the level is correct) edgings make excellent mowing strips (Fig. 6.2a) and, where soil abuts, they are a means of keeping it off the paved surface (Fig. 6.2b).

Edging materials

Where any of the 'hard' materials are used as edging, such as brick, stone, setts, concrete or terracotta, they are best built into or laid on a concrete foundation, and haunched at the rear for additional stability (this means to bring the concrete up at the rear to just below the upper surface) (Fig. 6.3).

Brick

Almost any durable frost-proof brick makes a good edging. They may be laid in a variety of ways according to the desired effect. Stretchers will impart a neat narrow edge of 65 mm ($2\frac{1}{2}$ in) in width if laid singly. If laid on flat then the edging will be 100 mm (4 in) in width, but of course any 'frogs' (see page 77) would have to be laid downwards. Perforated bricks would not be suitable if laid flat since the holes would be clearly visible. Laid flat, bricks may be in a more pleasing proportion to an overall path

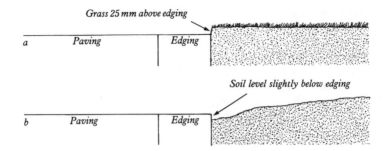

Fig. 6.2 Edgings.
(*a*) Edging as a mowing strip
(*b*) Edging for soil retention.

Grass 25 mm above edging

| a | Paving | Edging |

Soil level slightly below edging

| b | Paving | Edging |

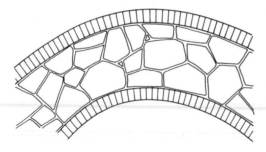

Fig. 6.3 Typical cross section showing foundation and haunching for 'hard' edging.

15 mm gap between top of edging and haunching

| Edging | Paving |
| Base |
Soil
Concrete haunching
| Sub base |
Geo-textile membrane

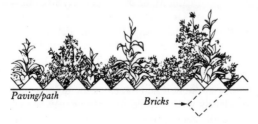

Fig. 6.4 Brick edging laid as header.

Fig. 6.5 Bricks on slant (45°) as edging.

Paving/path   *Bricks* →

width, however this will depend on individual taste. Bricks laid as header (Fig. 6.4) will form a very pronounced edging of approximately 215 mm (9 in) in width; for normal straight runs and very gentle curves laid with the flat (100 mm/4 in) side uppermost. To negotiate tight curves, the 65 mm (2½ in) stretcher face upwards (on edge) is best. When bricks are used as edgings, they double up as good flat mowing edges too.

Bricks on slant make a most attractive if not entirely practical edging (Fig. 6.5). The bricks are laid either in mortar or simply set into the soil at 45°. The largest face of the brick may be facing forward, with stretcher at the top, or alternatively laid so that the largest face is uppermost with the stretchers at the side. In either instance no 'frogs' should be visible.

Pre-cast concrete edging

Pre-cast concrete edgings, because of their comparative low cost and the fact that they are readily available, are most commonly used.

They are supplied in two lengths: 300 mm (1 ft) and 900 mm (3 ft). The 300 mm (1 ft) length is most suitable for negotiating curves. Depths vary but are normally either 150 mm (6 in) or 215 mm (9 in). Thicknesses are either 35 mm ($1\frac{1}{2}$ in) or 50 mm (2 in) for heavier duty. Beyond these sizes they are known as 'kerbings' and are not generally appropriate to patio gardens. The tops of pre-cast concrete edgings are given shapes – square, chamfered, bull-nosed or half-round. A number of manufacturers, recalling Victorian times, have also recently been decorating the tops of their edgings with rope and scalloped patterns. The textures of pre-cast edgings tend to be smooth as they have usually been cast with wet concrete. Colours are varying shades of grey (according to the particular cement and aggregate mix), although some manufacturers produce them in pastel shades of red, buff and green.

Following a building line, concrete edgings are laid over a shallow foundation 75–100 mm (3–4 in) deep by approximately 150 mm (6 in) wide of concrete, which is also brought up against the back of the edging (haunched) to within 25 mm (1 in) or so of the top. This is eventually hidden by backfilling with soil or whatever. In the event of a gravel path as opposed to something more stable, the haunching is carried out at both sides, but to a lower point on the path side if the edging is intended to project above the path level.

Concrete edgings are normally butt-jointed rather than mortared. This is done on the grounds of convenience, while at the same time making a thermal-movement joint. Concrete for bedding and haunching will most likely be 1:3:6 (cement: sand:15 mm aggregate).

Setts

Setts are cut from very hard stone, like granite, and are cuboid in shape. Their use as an edging material is very well known indeed, not only for patio gardens but also for roadways. They are extremely tough, attractive and adapt themselves to straight paths or curved. They can be fixed perpendicularly at the side of the path, flush to the path's surface or at a batter (sloped), in which case the abutting soil is taken right up to the uppermost edge of the setts. Sett sizes vary but for the patio, smaller ones of 100 mm sq (4 in sq) or 150 mm sq (6 in sq) are the best proportion. They are available new or secondhand – the latter being smoother and lending a more mature appearance to the path.

As a rule setts are laid with a strong mortar, e.g. 1:3, and the joints are always pointed – usually 'bird beak' or 'snail trail' (see page 86).

Stone edging

Stone edging is used traditionally in formal or rustic settings. Where there are random stone pieces, these are pressed either straight into the ground or into a concrete base. As previously mentioned (see page 47) this offers up to the elements the most vulnerable facets of the stone and splitting may follow. Therefore, where a really permanent edge is required, only the strongest stone of an homogenous nature should be used.

Random stone makes an attractive edging but may present mowing problems if grass grows too closely beside it.

If stone edgings have been especially cut, their purpose would have been known, therefore it is to be expected that a suitable, durable stone was selected by the mason.

Terracotta/burnt clay edging

There has recently been a revival in the use of terracotta as a path-edging material. Victorian styles are being reproduced in many forms, including the well-known 'rope' pattern. Expensive but very effective, terracotta creates a mature or 'olde worlde' atmosphere in a patio garden. Optional colours are in red, blue/black and buff. Lengths are approximately 215 mm to 300 mm (9 to 12 in); heights are in two sizes, approximately 150 mm and 215 mm (6 in and 9 in). When choosing the height it is worth considering how much of the edging is intended to be seen above ground level.

Traditionally these edgings were placed end to end in a narrow trench, with soil compacted around the base. The use of concrete at the base of the trench will make a more stable fixing but this method has its drawbacks in that it prohibits them from being moved for possible re-use at a later date. Terracotta edgings are designed to be seen above ground so that their decorative merits can be appreciated. Apart from the aesthetic value of

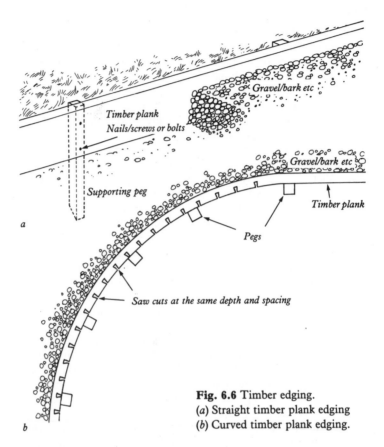

Fig. 6.6 Timber edging.
(a) Straight timber plank edging
(b) Curved timber plank edging.

terracotta edging, its practical use is in retaining adjacent soil, and in keeping low-growing plants at bay.

It must be remembered that these edging units tend to be brittle and if grass is growing close to them, great care must be taken not to cause damage when using the mower.

Timber edging

There are two ways in which timber can be used as edging. Firstly, upright with the end grain uppermost, and for this poles varying in diameter from 50–100 mm (2–4 in) (appropriate for the depth and width of the path) are driven into the ground and concreted in. Depending on the desired effect, the poles can then be trimmed either to path level or left upstanding rather like a low wall. Another method is to saw the poles off at slightly different heights, giving an interesting and rather novel finish. Timbers, of course, are not necessarily round and it is possible to purchase

ready-made edging systems which utilize square-sectioned hardwoods in a choice of sizes.

Timber used on end as edging will be stable provided the pressures from path material on the one side and soil on the other are more or less equal. However, these pressures are not always equal, for example when the path surface is lower than the surrounding soil level. This situation would need to be compensated for by sinking the poles well into the soil, perhaps by as much as two or three times the length showing above ground. All poles used for edging purposes (except the hardest of woods) will need to be pre-treated with preservative.

Timber in the form of horizontal planks supported by stakes is commonly used as edging (Fig. 6.6a). Again, depending on the depth and width of the path, the correct choice must be made in terms of timber thickness and to some extent depth, although it is possible, if unusual, to make up the total edging height by the use of several planks. Sideways pressures could be considerable so the timbers need to be of adequate proportion to carry out the task well without bulging. Planks of 25 mm (1 in) thickness are the norm, but 200 mm to 500 mm ($\frac{3}{4}$ in to 2 in) may be required in some circumstances.

When paths are curved it will be necessary to curve the edging too (Fig. 6.6b). If the planks are stout this will not be possible unless vertical cuts are made into them, to approximately two thirds to three quarters of their thickness. The distance between the cuts will be determined by the amount the plank needs to curve – the closer together the cuts, the greater the capacity to curve (you could have as little as 25 mm/1 in between cuts). To achieve a specific curve will be a matter of trial and error.

Without exception all timber edgings must be fixed to a stake, ensuring stability. The stakes must therefore be strong enough in themselves to do the job. Another consideration is that the stakes must be driven into the ground to an adequate depth and be firm enough to prevent them leaning under pressure. A minimal cross sectional size would be 50 mm sq (2×2 in) rising to 75 mm sq (3×3 in) if the edging timbers are heavy or the path deep and wide. The length of the stake supporting the edging will not only depend on the height of the edging itself but also on the soil type into which it is driven. Soils like stiff clay are more supportive than others. To take an example, if a path's structure amounts to 150 mm (6 in) in depth and assuming that there will be 25 mm (1 in) to be left above the path level to the top of the edging boards, in clay the overall stake length would need to be approximately 500 mm (19 in). In a loamy soil the length may need to be extended to 750 mm (30 in).

Fixing
The edging boards are usually fixed when the stakes have been driven into the ground. The nails are driven into the boards so that the nail heads are flush with the board on the inside (path material side). Nail sizes will correspond to the thickness of the board but will be at the very least 50 mm (2 in) long and, depending on the board widths, a minimum of three nails for

each stake. Care must be taken to support the back of the stakes when hammering the nails, otherwise the stakes may become dislodged and out of line. Alternative methods are screwing or bolting – both are more than adequate and ensure a firm fixing. Screws and bolts should always be well greased before use. An added advantage is that the boards can be easily disassembled at any time.

The distance between stakes will vary but they must be close enough to prevent the lengths of board between them from bulging outwards under pressure from the path materials. The closer they are, the less pressure there will be on individual stakes. A typical spacing between supporting stakes would be 1 m ($3\frac{1}{4}$ ft). (Stakes are always cut to a point in order that they may be driven into the ground more easily and accurately.) This spacing may need to be reduced to negotiate curves. For really tight curves the stakes will need to be very close, indeed 300 mm (1 ft) apart, for example. Another factor in the equation is the available lengths of the boards. These must be butt jointed, the joint coinciding with the centre of a stake, to which the butted boards are to be fixed. Path edgings are laid following a builder's line to ensure accurate longitudinal and crossfalls.

On completion of the edging installation the stakes should be trimmed at the top with a saw to either finish flush with the edging, or just below it if the stakes are not intended to be seen. Occasionally the trimming is carried out at an angle (weathered) to ensure that rain water is shed quickly and does not penetrate the end grain and so shorten the life of the stake. An extra application of preservative is recommended for the top of the stakes following trimming.

Thick metal pins or angle iron can be used instead of timber stakes, but for small projects these are expensive and certainly not as aesthetically pleasing.

Laying Cobbles (Large Pebbles)
Cobbles are smooth water-worn pebbles supplied in graded sizes from 25 mm to 100 mm (1 in to 4 in) diameter and more. A pebble smaller than 25 mm (1in) diameter could not be laid satisfactorily in the way described below.

Cobbles need to be laid in a bed of mortar to make them stable. The mortar mix must be strong yet comparatively 'flexible' on setting, to cope with any thermal movements. A mix of 1:4 (cement:sharp sand) with a plasticizer added would be ideal. There is, however, a strict sequence to follow:

1. Over a properly laid base, strong temporary timber form work must be set up. Its purpose will be to contain the concrete and mortar, since a precise edge will be required. If, however, a permanent edging, such as brick, is planned, this will need to be positioned first and would then replace the temporary timber edge. Permanent edging may become stained with cement; this can be avoided by covering it tightly with strips of polythene which must also be wrapped down the edges and fixed with blobs of mortar.

2. Concrete is then mixed and placed within the area formed by the edging so that on completion approximately 50 mm (2 in) of concrete remains under the cobbles. Prior to laying, the cobbles need to be just damp (not wet) and the mix fairly workable (but not so wet that the cobbles sink without trace!) It must be remembered that when it comes to the point of pressing the cobbles in, the mortar will be displaced and its level will rise. It is extremely difficult to calculate by how much, so a couple of 'dummy runs' using a seedtray, for example, is highly recommended. The mortar is placed to cover an area which can be safely cobbled before it starts to set. The time must also allow for mortar of sufficient depth to be trowelled off smoothly. This is essential. On reaching the periphery the mortar is lapped up to the top of the edgings on the inside by a trowel. This is necessary because on being displaced by the cobbles, mortar will cling and not rise up against the edging inside surface to the same extent as the main body of the mortar rises. This results in a peripheral 'valley' which would hold rainwater if left.

3. Having put in the correct depth of mortar and dealt with the edges, the cobbles are very carefully and evenly placed over the entire area. A large flat piece of wood or ply is then placed across the cobbles and pushes them in, so achieving consistent pressure over the entire area. The pressure is kept up until the cobbles are well keyed and the mortar matrix reaches the desired level. The entire area must be left for at least a week before being walked over. Should minor 'patching up' be necessary it must be done immediately. For this purpose raised and supported planks should be used from which to work (i.e. not pressing on the cobbles). Thermal movement joints will be necessary, over 5 m in every direction. The closeness of the cobbles is a matter of personal choice, though 60 kg ($1\frac{1}{4}$ cwt) of cobbles will generally cover approximately $1\frac{1}{2}$ sq m. On completion the polythene used to cover and protect any permanent edges can be cut away. It does not matter if a portion of polythene below mortar level is left.

Laying Setts

Over a constructed base, a fairly dry bed of 1:1:6 (cement:lime:sand) mortar is laid to a depth of 25–50 mm (1–2 in). The depth may need to vary according to the depth of the setts. For this reason it is better to use setts of consistent size, and this can only be guaranteed if they are new; old or secondhand setts may well differ in depth! The bedding mortar is not trowelled flat, but rather raked to create a series of minor peaks and troughs. This is best because being semi-dry, the mortar does not displace so easily. The peaks and troughs will allow displacement in various directions over the very small distances between them, resulting in almost a full bed on the placement of the setts. Final level adjustment is achieved best with semi-dry mortar for comparatively small units like setts. If a full wet mortar bedding were used, on placing one sett the displaced mortar would travel sideways and cause the immediate neighbouring setts to rise. The setts are bedded in by hammering via a piece of stout timber in the nature of a buffer. To hammer the setts directly could result in breakage and uneven surfaces. Normally several setts are hammered in together to achieve continuity. The setts would of course need to be laid either to overall levels or cross falls and this is, as usual, achieved by following builder's lines, leaving open joints of approximately 15 mm ($\frac{5}{8}$ in) wide. Sett joints are then pointed as a separate operation with a 1:3 mixture of cement and sharp/gritty sand. This can either be brushed in as dry mix, well tamped and 'watered' (with a watering can complete with can rose), or by using a wet mix. This would need to be trowelled in and finally brushed (using a soft brush) to impart a texture. When pointing setts, this is best done via planks or ply sheets so that individual setts are not disturbed or dislodged in the process. Setts gain support and stability from the mortar which surrounds them as well as that underneath. In their unsupported state they are vulnerable.

Setts are not the best surface for walking or for tables and chairs, since the surface can never be truly even. They do however have an exciting textural quality and many patterns can be achieved, including 'fish scale'.

Laying Cut Stone (Flags)

Depending on the desired ground pattern, flags may be laid as random rectangular, regular rectangular, square and so on. Since they are cut natural stone, by definition they will be expensive; however, if all six sides are cut as opposed to the normal four or perhaps five, then this will make it a very expensive proposition indeed. On the other hand, what it will mean, is that all the stone will be of a uniform thickness, making their laying considerably easier. To take the usual situation, though, cut stone flags will probably not only be of varying proportion but thickness too. Natural stone flags vary from 25 mm (1 in) to as much as 150 mm (6 in) – for example Old York flags. The thinner a stone is, (relative to its overall size), the weaker it will be. For this reason, thin-section stone (perhaps chosen on account of cost) will need to be laid on a solid bed of mortar. Here, 'spot bedding' (when mortar only partially covers the area underneath the slabs) would be inappropriate, as a heavy weight, imposed on the flag and between the underlying supporting mortar spots, could result in the stone cracking. This then points to three choices when it comes to laying stone flags.

The full mortar bed system

This is virtually the same as previously described for setts, both in practice and for the same reasons. Over a prepared base a semi-dry mortar mix is spread to an appropriate depth and raked to achieve peaks and troughs. The mix on this occasion would be something like 1:1:6 (cement:builder's lime:sand). Each piece will then be individually bedded following lines and using a straight edge. The depth of mortar must accommodate any individual variation in stone thicknesses, therefore the extremes of thickness, up and down, must be taken into account before work commences. Stone must be damp (not wet) to allow better cohesion with the mortar and to prevent premature drying of mortar by the suction of the stone. Joints will be left open to be pointed later. The widths of joint will be in proportion with the size of the stone flags being used but will vary from 10 mm ($\frac{3}{8}$ in) to 40 mm ($1\frac{1}{2}$ in) for the very large flags. Pointing is carried out with wet mortar rather than dry, trowelled in using a 1:4 mix (sand:cement). The mortar should penetrate right down the joint and bond with the bedding mortar. Various joint finishes can be achieved, from smooth to brushed. Where there is even the slightest risk of delamination, as might be experienced with some sedimentary stones, it is recommended the mortar be brought up to the stone's upper surface in order to keep moisture out. Making a shallow 'channel' of a joint will only encourage water to linger and provide a greater opportunity for penetration into the stones' strata.

The advantage of the semi-dry method of full bedding is that it allows the paving to be used a little earlier than mortar spot method which takes longer to give support.

The mortar spot method

With this method of laying stone the mortar must be really flexible. It is then placed in generous applications or spots over the base but within the area of a particular stone to be laid. In other words, each stone is laid separately and every time the area it will occupy, judged. Mortar spots number, four, five or six accordingly to the stone size. What is important is that on tapping the stone into place and to level (using lump hammer via timber), the mortar is in sufficient quantity and adequately flexible to displace and cover almost 100% of the stone area. Should it exude slightly beyond, that is not a bad thing since it will then link strongly with the neighbouring stone's mortar. Using the mortar spot method permits a degree of accuracy in individual stone levelling that the semi-dry method does not. Pointing is carried out separately but because the bedding mortar is wetter to start with than with the semi-dry solid bed method, this operation must be delayed for several days at least, to permit the bedding mortar to set. The pointing mix is as before, 1:4 (cement:sand), and the already mentioned note regarding joint sizes, etc., applies. Butt jointing of cut stone is not recommended as any small gaps may harbour weeds, and frost may cause damage to edges by differential movements.

Laying on sand
Unless cut natural stones are laid as stepping stones through grass or soil (where in any case gravel is preferred underneath) sand is not recommended as a bedding medium. It is unstable, in that water running beneath the slab and over the base will unevenly displace it, perhaps causing undulations at the surface. Secondly, it is far less efficient to lay the stone flags on sand. This is because the sand base must be perfectly prepared to receive each individual stone. Should a stone be found to be too high or low it would then need to be completely lifted out for the necessary adjustments to be made, there being little displacement or flexibility with sand when 'bedding in' flags. Weeds also gain a foothold far more quickly in sand joints than those which have been filled with mortar. Sand as a bedding material is more time consuming and therefore less cost effective, and is less supportive.

Laying Crazy Paving (Random Flat Stone Pieces)
Crazy paving is laid using the same dry full bedding method as previously described and is similarly pointed. Since crazy paving stone is normally derived from stratified rock, pointing right to the top of the stone level is recommended. This helps to prevent lateral water penetration during wet weather, so reducing the risk of delamination by frost. Joint sizes will conform to the gaps left by adjacent stone shapes, but widths between 15 mm ($\frac{5}{8}$ in) and 25 mm (1 in) are best. The mortar joints can be lightly brushed while still wet, or trowelled smooth. Individual stones should never actually touch each other, or have very narrow

joints that cannot be pointed. 'Twice weathered', known also as 'bird beak' (see page 86), is not a recommended joint finish as it tends to form a series of water barriers between individual stones, so preventing efficient run-off. Crazy paving is laid using line and straight edge to achieve even levels and run off. A pre-laid edging to the area of crazy paving will also help to establish levels and falls and will prevent the stones at the periphery from cracking away. This edge could be of timber, brick or setts, etc. Stone surfaces vary according to the stone used – some types are quite uneven and are best used where rustic paths and areas are intended. Uneven stone types are not good for accommodating tables and chairs – these will rock irritatingly – and the flattest stones should be used instead for this situation. Being a natural material, individual stones will vary in thickness but for crazy paving, the best range is from 25–50 mm (1–2 in).

Laying Broken Concrete Slabs
As a substitute for natural stone, some patio garden makers 'recycle' old broken concrete paving slabs as 'crazy paving'. Some concrete slab manufacturers sell their 'failures' for the purpose, and it has been known for retailers to smash up perfect slabs to sell! Too many colours are not recommended for aesthetic reasons, as they can distract from surrounding plantings and flowers. The advantage of using broken slabs is that they will most probably be all of the same thickness. Also there will be plenty of pieces with a perfectly straight side with which to form an edge. Re-using existing materials in this way when renovating or reforming a patio garden, can save a great deal of money and in several ways. The paving itself costs nothing; you will not have to pay to have materials taken away. New materials are costly, as are labour and transport charges to get them on site; also, many people prefer the instantly mature look that recycled materials give. This principle does not only apply of course to paving slabs, but to many other materials as well.

Laying Brick Paving
There are no apologies for repeating the warning about bricks used as paving. It is so impor-

tant that they should be hard wearing, durable and frost-proof – by no means are they all. It must be borne in mind that on the ground, bricks will be subjected to individual as opposed to shared pressure, as when built into a wall. They will also be subject to individual wear by pedestrian and wheeled traffic. Bricks for paving, if made from burnt clay, will need to be one of the following types: engineering, semi-engineering, class one hard stocks, or hard wire cuts. Despite the apparently short list there are many varieties of each so there should be one which is just right for a particular purpose, situation or appearance. It just needs a little research. Secondhand bricks may be used for paving but only after having established exactly what type they are. This can sometimes be difficult. Mixed secondhand bricks are always a doubtful proposition. In the main, new house bricks, e.g. sand faced, flettons will not be suitable. It is essential to check with the manufacturer a brick's suitability for paving before ordering.

Concrete bricks will mostly have been made as being suitable for paving but only the very hardest sand/lime bricks are suitable. Again, check with the manufacturer.

The method of laying bricks will, to a great extent, depend on the type of brick being used (see Chapter 5 'Choosing the Surface'). Basically, there are three methods: mortar bedded and mortar jointed; mortar bedded and butt jointed; and dry laid with butted joints. To a lesser extent the brick patterns or bonds will dictate the method of laying.

Bricks mortar bedded and mortar jointed
This is the most common way, using bricks which have 90° profiles all round (i.e. no chamfers), and probably having a 'frog' (see page 77). Over a properly prepared base, damp (not wet) bricks are laid along a line and with a straight edge, following the previously described semi-dry full mortar bed method. Using 1:1:6 (cement:lime:sand), the bricks are individually pressed or tapped into place, 'frog' down, conforming to the chosen pattern or bond, and leaving open joints of approximately 10 mm ($\frac{3}{8}$ in). After three or four days the bricks can be pointed using a 1:4 (cement:sharp sand) mortar, making sure that the mortar is in contact with the bedding mortar. The mortar

can be applied wet or dry, as previously described, but the wet method is preferred to a dry mix since, in this instance, it is more controllable. Also, the cement dust might quickly stain the entire brick surface, which can be extremely difficult to remove. Coloured ready-mixed mortar can be used, to which cement and water must be added. As described in the previous section 'Laying Setts' (see page 52), and for the same reasons, planks or ply boards are recommended from which to carry out the pointing. Joint finishes will be a matter of choice but brushed or bucket handle are the most popular, and suitable. Diagonally laid patterns, of which herringbone is the best example, must have a positive edging to stabilize the small odd triangular brick pieces resulting at the edges. This edging could be brick 'stretcher' or 'header'. The bricks may also be laid on edge or flat (frog down), depending on the required effect. However, when using bricks of common proportion on edge, one third more of the quantity will be required than if used flat in order to cover the same area. Additionally, the distance from any adjacent damp-proof courses and the upper surface of the base needs to be calculated to allow for the extra depth of the 'on edge' brick wearing course.

Mortar bedded and butt jointed
Here the bedding mortar and method is exactly the same as before but the bricks are butt jointed (i.e. actually touching with no open joints). Even so, it is strongly advised to brush sharp sand into the cracks as this helps to 'lock' the bricks together and thereby give extra support. Secondly, this helps to keep dust and detritus out, which may support the growth of weeds at some time in the future.

Unless specifically made to be butt jointed (and the majority of clay bricks are not), problems will be experienced in achieving certain patterns or bonds – basket weave for example. Bricks are very carefully shaped and proportioned to allow for mortar joints. For example a common brick stretcher is equal in length to two headers and a 10 mm ($\frac{3}{8}$ in) centre joint. Take the joint away (and in effect this is what happens with butt jointing) and the stretcher is longer by 10 mm ($\frac{3}{8}$ in) than two headers placed side by side. You can see, therefore, that in even a small area some bonds are unachievable.

Paving bricks that are meant to be butt jointed are readily obtainable and some have chamfered profiles (arises) around the upper surfaces. On laying, these form 'valleys' when butted together, resembling v-shaped joints. As pointing bricks is a time-consuming exercise, whichever method is employed, you will find that butt jointing is much quicker and less expensive.

Dry laid with butted joints

This is a comparatively recent method of laying bricks for paving, based on the principle that the loads imposed by pedestrian or wheeled traffic from above are transferred and dissipated evenly, both sideways as well as downwards. To achieve this balance the bricks are either especially shaped, or laid to a particular pattern and in conjunction with a uniquely designed base, interestingly not requiring cement and water as constituents – but all 'dry' materials (apart from the edging). What is important is that the brick pattern or joint lines should be diagonal to the direction of the main traffic flow. Diagonal herringbone is therefore eminently suitable for the purpose (see page 41).

Note: at a 100 mm (4 in) depth or more bricks cease to be known as bricks and are instead called 'blocks'.

With any paving, success mainly depends on the quality and depth of the base and sub base. With dry-laid bricks and blocks this method is particularly true. A typical cross-section (Fig. 6.7) for heavy domestic light traffic use (where perhaps the occasional parking of cars is expected), would reveal the following:

A. Sub grade well consolidated.
B. If required, a geo-textile membrane.
C. 100–150 mm (4–6 in) consolidated hardcore (depending on expected loads and subsoil type).
D. A maximum 50 mm (2 in) special grit sand bed. The run-off or falls are built in at this point.
E. The bricks or blocks 65 mm or 100 mm ($2\frac{1}{2}$ in or 4 in) depending on traffic.
F. Dry grit sand brushed into joints.

The special grit sand bed must be perfectly even and uniformly consolidated before laying any bricks. When this operation is complete, the bricks are placed in accordance with the chosen pattern, via planks or boards (so as not to disrupt the sand surface). On completion, the same grit sand is brushed in to fill any small spaces or cracks between the bricks completely. The whole area is then well compacted by a mechanical vibrating plate. These can be hired by the day. This might mean four or five separate passes in different directions to ensure maximum compaction. Not only does this bed the bricks into the sand base, but it also shakes the surface sand downwards between the butted bricks, locking one against the other. This operation is an essential and important part of the method. If an area cannot be entirely completed in one session, then vibrating should cease approximately 1 m ($3\frac{1}{4}$ ft) short of the 'placed' bricks limit. To vibrate to the very edge of the

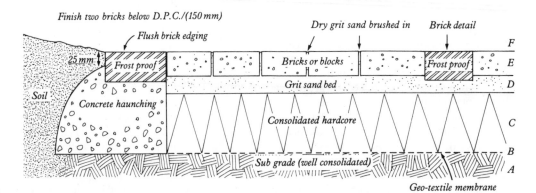

Fig. 6.7 Typical cross section for dry-laid paviors (bricks or blocks).

Finish two bricks below D.P.C./(150 mm)
Flush brick edging
Dry grit sand brushed in   Brick detail
25 mm   Frost proof   Bricks or blocks   Frost proof   F / E
Soil   Grit sand bed   D
Concrete haunching   Consolidated hardcore   C
    B
Sub grade (well consolidated)   A
Geo-textile membrane

bricks might ultimately result in slight differences in surface level, should there be any change in circumstances, for instance overnight rain, or more or less passes with the vibrating plate during the next session. For maximum penetration the sand used for brushing in to the joint before compaction should be bone dry, as should the paved brick surface itself. It is not unusual for a second sand dressing to become necessary after a few months. Rain will sometimes achieve what the vibrating plate will not, that is, an immediate 100% sand-joint fill.

Although referred to as the 'dry laid' method, it does almost without exception call for a restraining edge. This is best achieved by the use of bricks laid on a concrete foundation, complete with 'haunching', in the traditional way (see page 67). The majority of manufacturers producing bricks and blocks to be 'dry laid', issue precise laying instructions/specifications. They consider this to be important if their product is to succeed. The 'dry laid' method is, comparatively speaking, simple, inexpensive and very effective, provided the specification is followed correctly.

Laying Concrete Paving

Concrete is used in two distinctly different ways for making paving: firstly, in wet form for casting and moulding *in situ*; and, secondly, as ready-made products, such as paving slabs, bricks and blocks. Either of these is suitable for patio paving purposes. Paving slabs can be sub-divided as follows:

Plain concrete

Plain concrete can be grey or coloured, and with different textures, depending on the mixture of cement and aggregates. These have been wet-cast or hydraulically pressed.

Reconstituted stone

Reconstituted stone can also be coloured and textured. It results from a combination of crushed stone and cement which has been mechanically compressed, the characteristics of the natural stone remaining more or less intact.

Laying concrete paving slabs

These are laid in exactly the same way as natural cut stone, using either the semi-mortar or spot mortar methods, as already described (see pages 52–53). The advantage of using pre-cast paving slabs is that, provided they are all from the same manufacturer and are of the same type and thickness, less mortar and less effort will be required to lay them.

As with bricks, paving slabs are made in sizes to allow for mortar joints, while others are designed to be butt jointed. If there is an

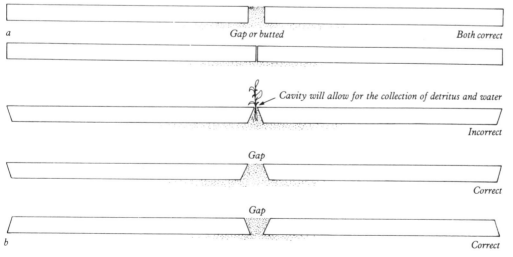

Fig. 6.8 Open and butted paving joints.
(*a*) Paving slabs with square sides
(*b*) Paving slabs with angled sides.

a   *Gap or butted*   *Both correct*

Cavity will allow for the collection of detritus and water

Incorrect

Gap

Correct

Gap

b   *Correct*

allowance for joints in the slab's proportion but you want them to be butt jointed, as with some bricks, you will find certain patterns cannot be achieved, so check first! However, a few patterns are unaffected in this way, for example using units all of the same size with unbroken joints running in both directions; or perfectly square units laid as stretcher bond. It should be noted that the manufacturing method of a slab sometimes also has a bearing on whether the joints used are mortared or butted.

A paving slab produced by hydraulic pressure on a semi-dry mix in an open 'frame' former, will have sides which are square and at 90° to the flat faces. Alternatively, pouring a fairly wet mix into a metal tray mould will produce a slab with sides which are slightly angled. The mould sides have to be angled (wider at the top than at the base) to allow the slab to be tipped out when set. This would not be possible if the sides were at 90°. On the ground the slab with the 90° sides can be butt or mortar jointed (Fig. 6.8a). The angle-sided slab cannot be butt jointed for the following reasons: if the upper surface of the concrete, exposed in the mould is ultimately to be the wearing surface, the sides of the slab, when laid next to its neighbour, are angled in such a way that the joint is narrower at the top than at the bottom (Fig. 6.8b). This means that two comparatively sharp edges are brought into contact, making them vulnerable to frost-caused differential movement and then subsequent chipping. Detritus will quickly fill the void beneath the joints, encouraging the growth of weeds. If, on the other hand, you intend to use the opposite surface of the slab (formed against the bottom of the mould) as the wearing surface, the resulting joint will obviously be narrow at the bottom and wider at the top. In this case it would seem possible to fill the v-shaped channel (created by the butted slabs) with mortar. However, this is not satisfactory either, as the joint mortar is then independent of the bedding mortar and will crack when subjected to frost, to lift out when the area is swept. Moving the slabs apart slightly will ensure that the joint mortar keys with the bedding mortar.

On a safety note, if the intended wearing surface is formed at the bottom of a steel tray mould when cast, it should be textured. Concrete cast wet against smooth steel will produce an almost glass-like surface. This is potentially very dangerous, especially in wet or icy conditions. As a general principle, when one side of a paving slab is smooth and the other side textured, it is the *textured* side that is meant to be laid uppermost to provide a good and safe foothold.

Paving slabs are manufactured in multiples of either 215 mm (9 in) or 300 mm (1 ft). Permutations result in different slab sizes which can be used to create many attractive set patterns. Random patterns are also popular. The rule of thumb with random paving is not to let a joint run uninterrupted for more than three slabs in any direction. More than three is unattractive and the eye soon picks this up. It is usual to brush butt joints over, with a fine yet sharp sand, to fill any tiny gaps and to assist the slabs in locking together. When mortar joints are called for, these are normally finished with 'bucket handle' (see page 83). The most suitable jointing mix for grey slabs will be 1:3 or 1:4 (cement:sharp sand). If the slabs are coloured, a contrasting or harmonizing colourant can be added to the mortar; alternatively, use one of the ready-mixed coloured mortars.

Concrete paving cast *in situ*

Casting wet concrete *in situ* is an alternative to laying ready-made individual units. Generally it is a less costly way of making a paved surface, and under some circumstances easier, although possibly not as convenient. Indeed, in the wrong hands it can be positively messy! *In situ* concrete surfaces are rarely left untextured or untreated in a patio garden, since in its raw state its lack of appeal is almost universal. As patio gardens tend to be small and the paved surfaces readily seen, there is little point in introducing an unsympathetic element.

Yet with quite simple treatment, concrete can make an attractive and practical contribution. *In situ* concrete needs a good base – vitally important since any subsequent settlement would manifest itself as disfiguring cracks, especially if the concrete surface is plain. There are no joints for the cracks to follow, as with bricks or paving slabs for example. Over a sound base, 'form work' of some kind is erected to surround the area to be

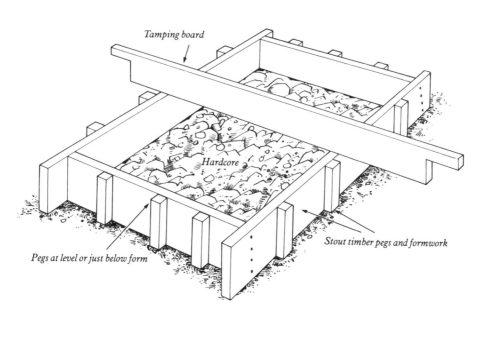

Fig. 6.9 'Form work' for *in situ* concrete paving.

Tamping board

Hardcore

Pegs at level or just below form

Stout timber pegs and formwork

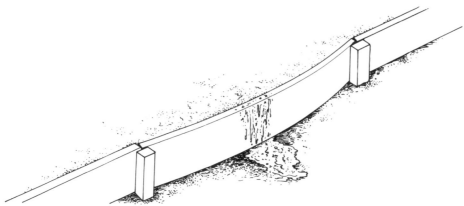

Fig. 6.10 Bulging due to insufficient support; the result of form work being too thin and stout pegs being positioned insufficiently close together to give adequate support!

concreted (Fig. 6.9). This could be stout timbers (see page 50) or, if the concrete is being used in conjunction with some other material, like brick, the edging and detail could be built in first. This will then double as form work. Whatever is used must be extremely strong since the pressures of wet concrete on edgings and frame work, especially when being tamped or compacted, are enormous (Fig. 6.10). For these to give way or bulge at the wrong time could spell disaster. As concrete begins to set fairly quickly and there will be little time to carry out running repairs to the form work, then continue with placing the concrete.

Forward planning is essential, as is the sequence of laying if more than one area is being cast at a time. This is especially true if areas of concrete are large and adjacent to each other. A very obvious but often unasked question on such occasions is, 'Where shall I stand to do the work?' Certainly not on the area just about to be laid! In this context the

59

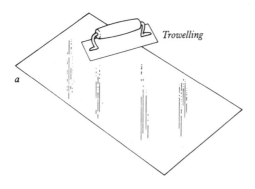

Trowelling

a

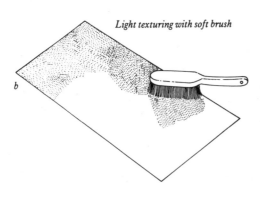

Light texturing with soft brush

b

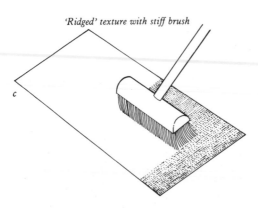

'Ridged' texture with stiff brush

c

Fig. 6.11 Surface texturing to *in situ* concreting.
(*a*) Trowelling   (*b*) Brushing
(*c*) 'Ridged' texture with stiff brush
(*d*) Exposed aggregate.

logistics of laying concrete, or for that matter any paved area, must be worked out in advance. Don't wait until the work actually starts. There will already be quite enough to think about.

Concrete will either be mixed by shovel, mechanical means or delivered as ready-mixed (see page 95). The size of the project and access to the area concerned will determine which. For paving work, where a good finish is required, a 1:2½:5 (cement:sand:aggregate) mix is recommended. 'Batching' should be done by volume; and if the concrete is to be mixed by shovel or mechanical means, a bucket can be used for this purpose, as described earlier (see page 58). Materials should be scrupulously clean, including the water. When concrete is placed, care should be taken not to tip it from too great a height as there is a risk of partial separation, an 'un-mixing' of the sand and aggregate. When a very special surfacing is required using white cement or particular aggregates, for example, then only the upper 50 mm (2 in) need be of that mix. (50 mm/2 in is the minimum depth, otherwise a hard frost might penetrate and lift it). The lower level can be of common concrete, it's the upper surface that needs to be roughened sufficiently to key with the upper decorative surface mix.

As mentioned previously, concrete need not be drab or uninteresting. Listed below are examples of texturing methods:

Tamping
This is carried out with a plank which is progressively lifted a little then dropped onto the still wet concrete surface to produce a series of ridges. This particular technique is useful in creating a fairly non-slip surface, more often than not for service paths, etc. If used for an area that will accommodate tables and chairs, then for the sake of their stability, care must be taken to ensure that the ridges are not too pronounced.

Trowelling (Fig. 6.11*a*)
After the concrete has been compacted and levelled (usually by tamping) the surface can be smoothed, using a flat trowel or float – the latter being a rectangular steel thin blade with the handle at the top. Either can produce a very

smooth surface, which could be a potential danger in wet or icy conditions. To overcome this, a wooden float is used to impart a swirled lightly textured finish that will create a safer surface.

Brushing (Figs. 6.11b and c)

A pronounced texture is produced by drawing a brush across a flat, wet, unset concrete surface. This results in a series of lines which can be straight, alternating in direction, or swirled, according to taste. The strength of line will depend on how much pressure is applied with the brush and the stiffness of the brush bristles. A dummy run treating wet concrete placed in a seed tray will show exactly how the surface will look after using a particular brush.

Stippled

Stippling is achieved by pushing a roller of some kind (e.g. steel/plastic piping, or a pole) across a trowelled, yet still unset concrete surface. This has the effect of 'plucking' the surface slightly, to produce an interesting yet safe texture.

Exposed aggregate (Fig. 6.11d)

This technique commences after completely smoothing the surface of the concrete by trowelling. The top 50 mm (2 in) might be of a specific mix to produce a preferred colour contrast between the cement and a special aggregate for example, or you could use the aggregate in the main body of the concrete, which is more likely. The method is at the critical moment when the cement is set just enough to 'hold' the aggregates, the surface cement is washed away using a soft brush and water (via a hose with arose attached). This is a skilled operation as too little washing will be ineffective, while too much may dislodge the aggregates and once this has happened, it is practically irreparable. Dummy runs are recommended for this in order to get the timing and the washing process just right. Above all the exposure must be consistent across the whole area.

Note: Throwing aggregate onto a wet concrete surface will not produce a satisfactory 'exposed aggregate' finish and should be avoided.

Marked concrete

This is a very popular finish. Following trowelling and then texturing with a soft brush for example, false joints can be marked into the surface with a bucket-handle tool. These 'joints' can be made either with straight lines (using a straight edge as a guide), to give an impression of rectangular paving slabs, or using random lines to look like crazy paving.

Hammered

Not a job for the amateur, this process is carried out by mechanical means after the concrete has completely set. In effect the concrete surface is chipped away by hammering to produce an attractive texture not unlike exposed aggregate, except that the interior (often chrystalline) of the surface aggregates are seen as opposed to the washed surfaces. The hammering results in a fine overall texture.

Impressed concrete

A technique developed in the USA and carried out only by professionals who work under licence. In principle, a special-mix wet concrete has a pattern stamped into it mechanically. Almost any finish, colour or pattern is available – random (crazy) paving, rectangular paving, setts, tiles, cobbles, etc.

Coloured concrete

Pigments for concrete can be obtained from most builders' merchants, together with instructions for use. Colour charts are available giving comparative examples of how, using white cement will slightly alter the colour when compared with Ordinary

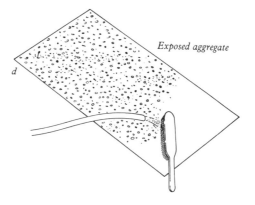

Exposed aggregate

d

Fig. 6.12 Where water running towards the house is unavoidable, it must be channelled away.

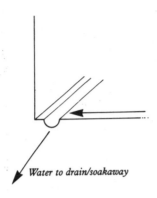

Water to drain/soakaway

Portland cement. Manufacturers advice on adding pigments must be heeded, since it may well mean modifying the amount of cement in a mix, since the addition of colour might otherwise weaken it. The cost of concrete pigment will depend on its source and chemical structure. Qualities of pigment vary considerably, and the more colour fast are the most expensive. For the sake of economy, the general rule is to use pigmented concrete on only the upper surfaces. Regarding colour fastness, buffs and browns tend to be the most suitable for resisting the effects of strong sunlight.

In situ concrete and thermal movement joints

Should an area of *in situ* concrete exceed more than 4.5 m (15 ft) in any direction (including paths) a thermal movement joint should be incorporated to allow for expansion and contraction. Cement naturally tends to shrink a little on setting but thereafter is subject to the normal thermal movements brought about by changes in the ambient temperature. Without thermal joints the concrete will expand and contract regardless, causing unsightly cracking. Thermal movement joints, at their simplest, can be narrow open gaps of 2.5–5 mm ($\frac{1}{8}$–$\frac{1}{4}$ in) or bitumen-impregnated felt, or strips of fibre board, which are two examples of products manufactured for this purpose. A skilled designer will arrange for paving edgings and detail at the surface to coincide with thermal movement joints, so

making them less obvious. Where timber is used as form work to mark out various and adjacent concrete areas, it is sometimes left in the ground to contribute towards the paving pattern. Where this is possible, the timber will also serve as excellent thermal movement joints. Any timbers so used should of course have been treated with preservative, or at least be of a durable type such as oak or cedar.

Surface Water Drainage

The importance of effective surface water drainage cannot be over emphasized. The main purpose of laying paving is to provide a dry and safe surface on which to walk. The presence of water or ice will jeopardize this basic requirement. Sloping paving surfaces are designed as drainage facilities and are commonly known as 'run offs'. The angle will vary according to local circumstances. Falls such as 1/100 or 1/120 are effective yet virtually undetectable and are interpreted as, respectively, 1 cm fall for every 1 m travelled, or 1 in fall for every 10 ft travelled.

It is always better if the 'run off' can be directed away from the house. This is not always possible, in which case special arrangements may have to be made (Fig. 6.12). Care must be taken never to 'box' water into an area, especially if it has walls or some other upstanding feature on all sides. This unfortunate situation can be averted at the planning stage. The series of diagrams illustrated in Fig. 6.13 are the most common 'run off' problems, with solutions. Surface rainwater should under no circumstances be directed to the foul water drainage system (against the law in most Local Authorities) nor, in some cases, straight into the storm water system – a point worth checking at the local council office. A number of authorities will permit the latter but only via a silt trap! Soakaways can be the answer in other circumstances but the difficulty in many patio gardens is that there simply will not be the available space. Surface water can either be directed into gullies, and from there into underground pipes, or collected into channels at the surface and then directed to an outlet. Sometimes both. Since water is a valuable commodity, it should wherever possible, be utilized: this might mean filling a small reservoir (perhaps underground if space will

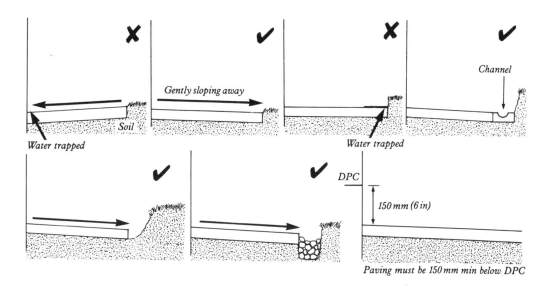

Fig. 6.13 Diagrams showing surface water
drainage problems for paving and their solutions.

not allow otherwise), water butts, or directing the water straight into shrub or plant beds. Obviously this flow would need to be controlled so that plants were not washed out in times of heavy storm. The gardener, appreciating the importance of conservation, will incorporate such ideas into his or her plan at the design stage.

CHAPTER 7

Steps and Ramps

Steps contribute greatly to the appearance of a patio garden, giving both interest and a sense of width or space. Their practical function is of course to enable the visitor to get from one level to another. To be able to do this comfortably and safely will depend largely on the height of each step and the size of the area of foothold. In practice these are called respectively, 'riser' and 'tread'. There is a relationship of good proportion between the two. The golden rule is always that this proportion is consistently maintained throughout the entire flight. In other words the risers should all be exactly the same, as should the treads. The angle at which a flight of steps goes up or down is called 'the pitch slope'. This should never be more than 40° in a garden and preferably less. If more than 40°, the ascent, but more importantly the descent, will appear dangerous. Steps should enable a comfortable gait to be established and maintained. Indoors, and when associated with a hand rail, the 'pitch' sometimes does exceed the 40° limit. The table below shows a selection of well proportioned riser/tread relationships.

Riser		Tread	
180 mm	(7 in)	200 mm	(11 in)
165 mm	(6½ in)	330 mm	(13 in)
150 mm	(6 in)	380 mm	(15 in)
140 mm	(5½ in)	410 mm	(16 in)
130 mm	(5 in)	430 mm	(17 in)
115 mm	(4½ in)	460 mm	(18 in)
100 mm	(4 in)	480 mm	(19 in)

It will be noted that the shallower the riser the deeper the (front to back) tread. It is generally considered that the minimum height for the riser should be 100 mm (4 in) – below this it ceases to be a step and becomes more a means of tripping up! At the other end of the scale, 180 mm (7 in) is given as the maximum – any higher and the step becomes uncomfortable to ascend and alarming to descend, especially if there is no hand rail or side walls. What may decide a particular relationship of riser to tread may not be for visual effect alone, or for reasons of comfort. The decision may have to be made on purely practical grounds, in terms of how much space is available to accommodate the steps! If an area is already small and the rise from one level to the next is comparatively high, how will the steps be accommodated? Both factors must be borne in mind, and this is where the Riser/Treads table will be useful.

There are many ways to accommodate a flight of steps, and these are listed below:

1. Projecting outwards into the lower area entirely.
2. Half (or some other proportion) within the upper level and half in the lower (or on a slope).
3. Entirely within the upper level (or within a slope).
4. A proportion within the upper or lower level – but then turning in one direction or the other.
5. Zig-zagging or curving within or mostly within the upper level or on a slope.

These five options can be achieved in various ways or styles, according to tastes and needs. As with the risers, the width of a flight of steps will not always be decided upon by a desired visual effect, rather by space which may be a limiting factor. It is best, if like the paths with which they are often associated, that steps can accommodate at least two people walking side by side. Of course this is not always possible. Bearing in mind that steps should always be safe to ascend and descend, the inclusion of a hand rail or side walls, is advantageous, especially if steps project beyond the actual place where there is the change of level. In poor light there could also be a danger of stepping off the sides. For example, if only three steps of 150 mm (6 in), risers equal to 450 mm (18 in) in total, are left unguarded, there exists a potentially dangerous situation, particularly for the elderly and small children.

For the sake of safety, the presence of steps should be made as obvious as possible. This may entail changing the material from which the treads are made to that of associated paths or paving. (Incidentally, a change of material textures underfoot is most helpful to people with impaired vision.) A second technique is to ensure a strong horizontal shadow line on the riser; this is probably of more value on the ascent and is achieved by allowing the tread material to project (oversail) beyond the riser. Effective even in poor light. The third technique is to illuminate the steps if possible.

Materials for Steps

Steps are normally constructed from the same or harmonizing materials as the associated architecture and paving.

Brick

Bricks make excellent steps and can be used for both risers and treads. An attractive alternative is the use of bricks for risers, with some other material for the treads. However, as with any bricks used outside on the ground, they must be frost-proof.

Stone

Stone has long since been a popular material for making steps, from the very rustic rockery steps to the very sophisticated, where stone has been dressed and honed to a perfect finish, and the 'nosings' (front tread edge) sometimes carved to be decorative.

Concrete

Concrete poured into shuttering is one method of step making. According to the surface treatment, the appearance will range from the utilitarian to the decorative. Concrete is also used to make 'dummy' steps, reinforced and over which is applied a decorative finish with some other facing material.

Reconstituted stone

Reconstituted stone can in most respects be used as natural stone. There is one drawback, however, when using reconstituted stone paving slabs as treads: if they are of only 25 mm or 30 mm (1 in or 1½ in) thick, as many are, they tend to look mean and out of proportion with the overall height of the riser.

Another down point is when the same paving slabs have been cast in a mould, the sides of which are not 90°. These give a rather sharp and therefore easily damaged nosing to a tread.

Timber

Timber is extensively used for making steps, either entirely or in conjunction with some other material. Particular attention should be paid to the quality of the timber, which should be selected with discretion when intended for use outdoors. Soft woods will definitely need to be treated with a preservative. If left untreated or untextured, they quickly become slippery with wear or when wet. To correct this, either the treated wood is saw grooved, or textured mechanically. Alternatively, a surface treatment is given by applying a sand-based paint or preservative for example, or a strip of stapled chicken wire. Soft wood steps have a tendency to degrade rather more quickly than the hard woods. Generally speaking soft wood is more affordable and may be a factor when making a choice. As steps, timber/planks are either laid horizontally with supporting posts, or inserted vertically into the ground. Situation will determine the actual form of the timber and the range is quite large: sawn planks, cladding (outer slices of tree either with the bark on or off), logs, poles, ex railway sleepers, etc. Timber may be used to form step risers only, with the tread composed of gravel or brushed surface concrete perhaps. This is an eminently suitable style for an informal patio garden.

Ramp Gradients

Ramps are used as an alternative to or in conjunction with steps. However, they can only be employed where there is plenty of room, since ramps take up far more space than steps to overcome the same change in level. On a practical note, provided the slopes are gentle, ramps are to be preferred to steps, as they are far more able to facilitate pushing prams, wheelchairs, bicycles, shopping trolleys, wheelbarrows, and so on. For this reason a ramp gradient should not exceed 14% (one in seven) but preferably be below 10% (one in ten). The particular situation and the main use to which the ramp is to be put will also be determining factors.

The surface of a ramp needs to be very carefully chosen. This is true of any paving of course, but ramps in particular. Rain or ice will quickly turn even a gentle gradient from a safe surface into a potentially dangerous one, especially for the frail or elderly.

The majority of ramps are paved with the same material as that of adjacent or associated paving and on many occasions inadvisably so. Close texturing across the direction of the ramp will maximize its effectiveness as a safe surface. This may be achieved by using tamped concrete, or brick laid in stretcher bond for example. Ridged tiles too are very suitable and are even better if they have a matt surface. Where ramps are curved, their design must be carefully worked out, since the angle at bends is often unavoidably increased. To this end the appropriate maximum gradient should be calculated at and from these points and not from a straight section.

Like steps, hand rails are often associated with ramps, and indeed under some circumstances they would be essential.

PART IV

WALLS IN AND AROUND THE PATIO

CHAPTER 8

Patio Walls

There are three basic wall types: load-bearing; free-standing; and retaining. Each is differently designed according to their function.

Load-Bearing

The load-bearing wall, as the name suggests, will be supporting or carrying something. The best example of load-bearing walls are house walls, which of course carry the roof, floors, stairs, furniture, etc. Apart from glasshouse or conservatory bases, and items like built-in barbecues, load-bearing walls do not figure greatly in patio garden construction. Load-bearing walls need to be designed by an architect working in conjunction with a construction engineer.

Free-Standing

Free-standing walls are exemplified by boundary walls. These can demark an area or boundary, provide security and privacy, protect and screen. Often they perform all these tasks, sometimes just one. Any impression that a free-standing wall only has itself to support is not entirely true. It must withstand the sideways pressures of wind, or other physical elements, as well as general gardening activities. It should be of a thickness relative to its height to make it a stable and sound structure.

A free-standing wall will need to be kept as dry as possible and built of the best materials you can afford in order to ensure its long life.

Retaining Walls

Whereas the load-bearing wall's loads are imposed from above, the retaining wall's load is imposed from the side. The material retained is usually soil, but could be some other substance, including water. Retaining walls, again like load-bearing walls, are usually built to a very strict specification and the higher the wall the more necessary this becomes. Such wall design is usually under-taken by architects and engineers, even for quite low retaining walls. The weight or pressure behind some walls can be calculated in many tonnes – this factor may be grossly underestimated by the amateur. Retaining walls have extended foundations which must be tied into the wall above. Retaining walls are thicker relative to their height than other types – the 'rule of thumb' is that their thickness should be at least equivalent to one third of the height – and may also slope back on the front face or both faces to lower the centre of gravity and therefore gain additional stability. The wall will be thicker at the base than at the top. Retaining walls have a drainage system at the rear to cope with water which may otherwise be trapped and gather there. Retaining walls also need to be kept as dry as possible and only first-class materials should be used in their construction.

Foundations

Before a wall of any kind can be built, it will be necessary to provide it with a firm foundation. To a great extent the future success of a wall in terms of its stability will depend on this. The job of the foundation is to create the situation whereby any local settlement or movement in the soil will not affect the wall in any way. Modern foundations are made almost exclusively of concrete. For general patio garden purposes there are two foundation types (there are many more but these lie within the province of civil engineers fulfilling very particular needs).

Raft or platform foundation (Fig. 8.1)

As the name suggests, this is a slab of concrete laid on and partly in the ground, occupying the entire area of the construction or building it is supporting. A raft foundation can double as floors for a garage or shed, for example. The fact that it is virtually floating on the ground over a larger area tends to make this type of foundation stable, along with the walls above.

Fig. 8.1 (*a*) Raft or platform foundation (*b*) Typical cross section through raft foundation with 'downstand'.

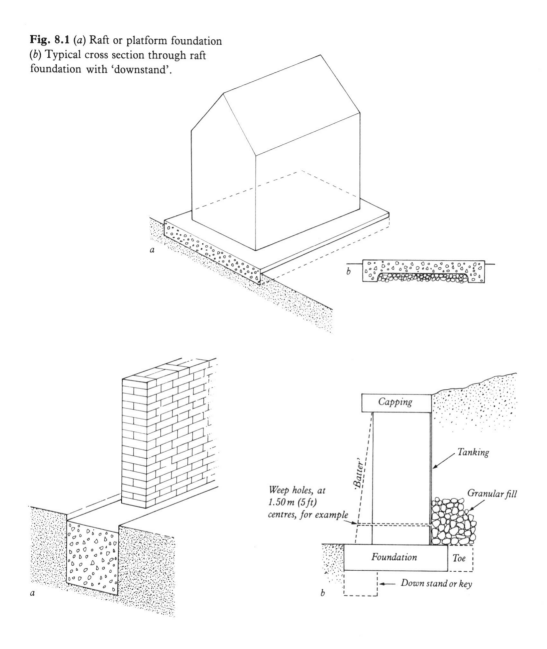

Fig. 8.2 (*a*) Strip foundation (*b*) Retaining walls.

Check points before and after building a retaining wall:

1. Soil good if no heel print. Organic soil has no load bearing properties.
2. Keep front of wall unexcavated i.e. no trenches. Drain the rear of the wall if possible and keep excess weight from the top of the wall. Shrubs are good planted behind the wall top – they bind the soil and de-water it.
3. Must be undisturbed soil at wall front (nothing soft). If so, drop foundation down and/or put 'key' or downstand on foundation. Downstand must be at least as deep as foundation thickness.

Even so, the depth of concrete must be such that it does not crack under pressure due to either a lack of support from the soil underneath or through weight differentials above. To help prevent this happening, raft foundations are often reinforced with steel mesh and have their periphery edges cast downwards into the soil rather like an open inverted box. This formation provides the greatest stability as it decreases the risk of soil displacement from beneath.

Strip foundations (Fig. 8.2a)

A strip foundation is the most familiar type. It is comprised of a strip of concrete extending out beyond the thickness of the proposed wall, and following the route of the wall. (Unlike a raft foundation which covers a whole building area). Strip foundations are used for freestanding and retaining walls. Width is calculated using 'rule of thumb', multiplying the wall thickness by two. In other words if the wall is 225 mm (9 in) thick, the strip foundation will be 450 mm (18 in) wide. The wall normally sits centrally over the foundation, so in this instance approximately 100 mm (4 in) of foundation would extend outwards on each side of the wall. Retaining walls normally need even wider foundations but the additional width is put entirely on the side of the material being retained, that is, at the rear. This founda-

tion extension is called a 'toe' (Fig. 8.2b). This makes for greater stability since the materials being retained behind the walls are bearing down on the 'toe', making it less likely for the foundation and the attached wall to tip over. The toe is usually equivalent to half of the normal foundation width.

Because a foundation's function is to support a wall safely, this may mean going into the soil sometimes to considerable depths, depending on the local soil types. In extreme cases the foundation could mean being as deep as the wall is high. The wall's size and proportion will also help determine the size of the foundation as well as its function. Again, these calculations are definitely not a job for the amateur and apart from the very smallest walls it is important to seek professional advice. Each situation calls for a different specification. It would therefore be unwise and possibly dangerous to give detailed advice here. Speaking generally however, flexible clays and very sandy soils are the least stable, requiring the deepest foundations; stiff clays and organic soils are better, tending to be more stable, while previously undisturbed hard chalk and compacted gravel soils are best, requiring the shallowest foundation (Fig. 8.3). A foundation's depth is calculated downwards, starting from the lower limit of adjacent cultivated top soil, where and if it exists.

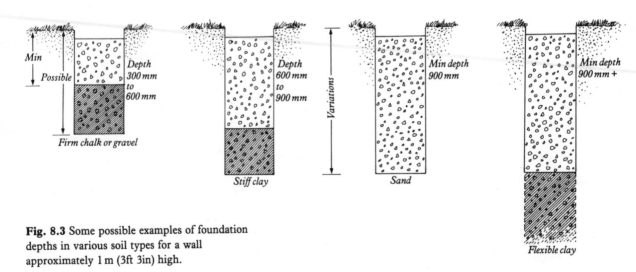

Fig. 8.3 Some possible examples of foundation depths in various soil types for a wall approximately 1 m (3ft 3in) high.

Where patio/boundary walls are abutting a public place or footpath and are over 900 mm (3 ft) high, your Local Authority Building Regulations Department will need to be consulted (although precise rulings may vary between Local Authorities). A badly built or under-specified wall – and this includes the foundation – could present a physical danger to both passers-by and you.

If you are not employing an architect or professional garden designer, at least seek advice from the local Building Regulations Officer; they are extremely helpful in these matters. Where garden areas are designated 'open plan' – and many are – a patio wall may not be acceptable anyway, so always check before building commences. Where the proposed wall is to run between properties, either at the side or at the rear, again consult the local Building Regulations Officer. As a general rule, for reasons of safety and amenity, walls are only permitted up to a height of 1.8 m (6 ft).

Walling Materials

From the design point of view it is essential that the styles and materials of walls be in keeping with local or adjacent architecture. This will ensure continuity and avoid an 'added on later' look. Elements in a garden always benefit from at least appearing to be part of an overall scheme or having been designed as an entity, even if this is not the reality. Walls make strong visual statements and form very much the structure of a patio garden. Walling materials bring with them their own textures, colours and characteristics, so contributing enormously to the whole. Materials for walling include bricks, natural stone, concrete blocks, terracotta, timber and peat blocks.

Bricks

Bricks are made from either one of three materials: baked clay, concrete or sand/lime.

Baked clay bricks

Baked clay is the traditional method of brick making, dating back thousands of years. Colours vary to include oranges, reds, buffs, yellows and blues. Textures vary from the hand-made rustic to the very smooth and very strong mechanically made engineering bricks.

Sizes can vary too, although there is a common brick size which is the one mostly used. Clay bricks can be completely even on all faces, whilst some have perforations and others have indentations known as 'frogs'. The perforations or 'frogs' are provided to ensure that the building mortar keys into them, giving added strength to the wall from which they are made. Clay bricks are variously made for a purpose or to perform a particular function. This means that many bricks are made for interior use only and would break up in wet or frosty conditions. Some are made for outdoor use but only in circumstances where they may be protected from the effects of adverse weather conditions, while others will stand up to practically anything Nature cares to inflict upon them.

To ensure the right brick is chosen for the job it is imperative to anticipate exactly the conditions the bricks in the form of a wall will experience. Armed with this information, only then can the particular brick be chosen. It will also need to meet with other criteria such as colour, texture and size. Fortunately most brick manufacturers, either directly or through builders' merchants, willingly provide as much detail as requested regarding their products, including individual brick properties and their suitability for special purposes.

High cost may prohibit the use of a preferred brick which is totally impervious and with which it was intended to build an entire wall. If this is the case, provided the cheaper substitute brick is still of an exterior, albeit lesser quality, it could be incorporated into the main body of a wall, making sure it was kept as dry as possible. This will necessitate sealing off the wall top with a coping, which could be either an especially manufactured unit, or using at the top extremely tough frost-proof brick. The phrase used in the trade is that such a brick is of 'coping quality'. At the base, for reasons of stability, it may not be safe to use a flexible damp proof course, in which case several courses of the same impervious brick previously suggested for coping, with strong damp-resisting, mortar would make an excellent substitute.

Concrete bricks

Concrete bricks usually conform in size to that

of a common clay brick. They tend to be dense and hard, with the colour having been introduced by various pigments during manufacture. Concrete bricks are rarely as aesthetically pleasing in a wall as clay bricks and their colours are not as permanent.

Sand/lime bricks

Sand/lime bricks are meant mainly for interior use. They can be utilized outside occasionally but it must be stressed that only the best quality should be used, and their suitability approved. These need to be sealed top and bottom, to keep the wall dry. Pigments are used to introduce pastel shades but the natural colouring of this brick type varies from white to cream.

Natural stone

This is stone taken from the quarry and sawn, then cut or split into building blocks or pieces rather than being crushed and mixed with cement. The latter method, alas, is the fate of most stone these days, since it is far more economical in terms of labour and convenience. Nevertheless, there are times when only the real thing will do.

There are as many stone types not being suitable for wall building as there are suitable. Stone for walling needs to be stable, durable, resistant to splitting, and of an appropriate texture and colour. Stone characteristics will be determined by how and from what the rocks were originally formed. As there are numerous rock types it is only possible to give a limited list of examples as follows:

Stone	Type
Granite	Igneous
Sandstones } Limestones }	Sedimentary
Slates } Marbles } Quartzites }	Metamorphic

Granite

Granite is one of the hardest known rocks and has a chrystalline structure. It is prohibitively expensive, especially when cut and polished. It is not often used in patio wall building, unless used in a 'rubble' form and is locally available in sizes which can be conveniently handled. In civil building works it is often used as cladding, when large flat and comparatively thin sheets are fixed vertically to supporting walls, giving the impression of huge blocks. Pink, red and grey/green are some of the rarer granite colours and are difficult to obtain. Light to dark grey is more readily available.

Sandstone

Most sandstones are useful for walling. A good building sandstone is homogeneous in structure, comprising small pieces of sand (of varying sizes according to the particular stone source) which have over millions of years become compacted by immense pressure into a singularity. York stone, perhaps the best known of all, is a sandstone of fine particles in colours from light buff to dark brown and grey. Pennant is another of the sandstone family but tends to consist of larger particles with a colour range from blue/grey to green/grey, with occasional rustic veining. Sandstones can be cut, sawn and 'dressed' (i.e. tooled to a particular shape or face texture) with comparative ease. It is also attractive when used in random shapes and sizes for wall building.

Limestone

Sedimentary rocks like limestone can differ in appearance and performance according to their formation. Some limestones result from the very finest clay particles being laid down and then subjected to immense pressure. Such stones are called carboniferous limestones, indicating the era of their formation. Examples are Cheddar (Somerset) and Westmoreland stone.

Other limestones, whilst being sedimentary, are comprised of the fine calcereous remains of marine animals laminated into distinct bands by the pressures of subsequent overlying deposits. Examples of this type of rock (suitable for wall building) are Portland stone, a dense, fine type which cuts well and is durable, also Doulton stone, which is not quite as fine. These stones have colours ranging respectively from white to creamy buff.

Oolitic limestones are characterized by the very small shell remains of ancient marine creatures – namely oolites. Colours vary from cream to yellow ochre. Typical examples are Cotswold and Bath stones.

Incidentally, a word of caution when building with stones like these and for that matter any which are not truly homogeneous: they must be built into the wall 'on bed'. In other words, so their striations are horizontal in the wall, as they were laid down millions of years ago. To build such stone perpendicularly (in the manner of vertical crazy paving for example) leaves the natural laminations of the stone exposed and vulnerable to water penetration. Subsequently frost damage followed by rapid deterioration could take place.

Flints

Flints, while not being strictly sedimentary stone in themselves, are nevertheless nodules composed largely of silica, found in sedimentary chalk deposits. Flints are traditionally used as 'snapped', that is whole flints broken in half to reveal a glassy grey/brown to black interior. Rarely are they now 'knapped', a further stage whereby snapped flints are further cut to present the random-shaped glassy facets as squares or rectangles.

Slate

Slate is an example of a metamorphic rock. It has an easily recognized individuality of form, and its colours are dark grey and dark blue. More often used for paving and roofing, slate is only occasionally used as a walling material. Its appearance can be very pleasing, either in cut blocks or thin section. Because of its colour though, it can be difficult to combine visually with other walling materials. In areas where it has been quarried, it relates well to existing architecture, which most likely is built of slate also. The weathering properties of slate are excellent and it is sometimes used as a damp-proofing layer in a wall at the top or bottom. It is almost impervious to water.

Marble

When used outside, marble does not resist the effects of the weather at all well. In industrial or urban areas polluted atmospheres can quickly etch the marble's surfaces. Frost can also be destructive. Therefore, a marble wall

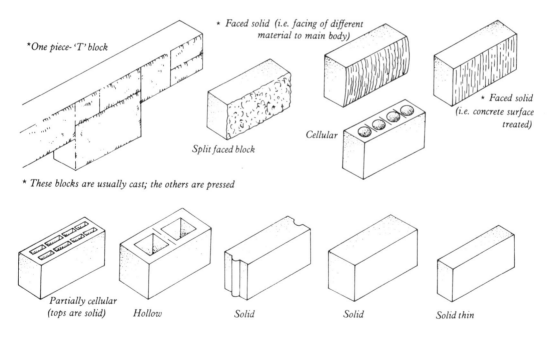

Fig. 8.4 Some concrete block types.
Most of the blocks having no special facing are available in lightweights as well as normal weight and are usually meant for internal partitioning work. Half blocks and other standard specials are also available. Sizes vary but usually 'course' with bricks.

should be well protected and built in as sheltered a position as possible.

Concrete

Occasionally one may see walls made from wet concrete which has been poured into vertical shuttering. Unless the interior of the shuttering has been specially lined or treated to give a texture or pattern to the resultant wall surface, it will be ugly. However, poured concrete walls are used regularly as the rear and unseen portion of a retaining wall, into which has been introduced some reinforcing steel. Inevitably a facing of brick or stone will have been added to make it visually acceptable. Composite walls such as these are not uncommon.

Concrete walls are also built from plain concrete blocks, or reconstructed stone blocks emulating the real thing. Basically the principle of manufacture of both types is the same. It is the ingredients and moulds which make the difference. Reconstructed stone with the right ingredients and moulds can imitate practically any building stone in the world. Popular imitations are of York, Cotswold, Devon and Portland. Even the various

'tooling' marks can be faked. 'Tooling' marks result from the various cutting or chiselling activities associated with real stone. Historically, these were deliberately left on many natural stone facings to impart individual textures and patterns. Reconstructed stone blocks are available in convenient sizes to facilitate just about any natural stone bond.

The common concrete block too has its place in the patio garden, provided it is of a good quality and 'fair faced'. The resulting wall has an uncomplicated and fine-textured surface. Common concrete blocks (known in the trade as 'con blocks') are available in many sizes and forms (Fig. 8.4). It will be remembered that con blocks are all made in sizes to 'course' with common bricks. Additionally the ends can be flat or vertically grooved. Colours are naturally in shades of grey according to the cement and aggregate used in manufacture. Pigmented concrete is occasionally used. Surfaces range from 'open' to fine close textures.

Piers for concrete block walls (Fig. 8.5) need to be carefully spaced.

Bonds for block work are based on the stretcher bond principle but this will depend entirely on the block thickness relative to its

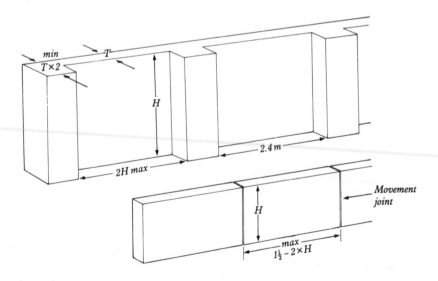

Fig. 8.5 Piers for block walls.
1. Piers *at least* twice as thick as wall
2. Piers spaced *not more* than twice wall height
3. For 100 mm thick walls pier spacings not more than 2.4 m

4. All walls above 2.0 m, consult architect or building inspectors department; if abutting a public place then 1.0 m
5. Expansion control joints at distances not exceeding $1\frac{1}{2}$–2 × wall height.

length; therefore one-quarter bonds and one-third bonds are not uncommon. Because of concrete's well-known high thermal movement rates, true bonding at junctions and piers is not always advised; instead butt joints are made, so allowing movement to take place while strength is achieved by the introduction of expanded metal wall ties at each course, thereby linking the walls or piers together (Fig. 8.6). Perforated and hollow con blocks can be filled with tamped concrete during construction to add strength. Where re-inforcing metal rods are called for, these are bedded in the foundation; hollow blocks are then 'threaded' on to the rod, then mortared in the usual way; and the hollows are filled with concrete to make a very strong wall structure.

Depending entirely on quality, concrete blocks can be left in a natural state but are often painted. Some walls made of concrete blocks have their surfaces rendered (coated) with mortar. This finish can be smooth or textured. Occasionally rendered surfaces are very roughly textured indeed, resulting in a very dramatic play of surface light and shade. Different textures can be applied by pebble-dashing also, a well known but now less

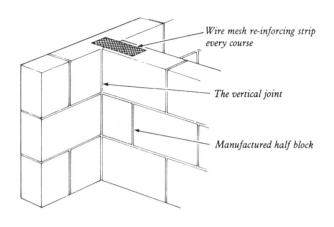

Fig. 8.6 A simple 'T' junction in blockwork.

Fig. 8.7 Concrete screen unit walls (methods of support).

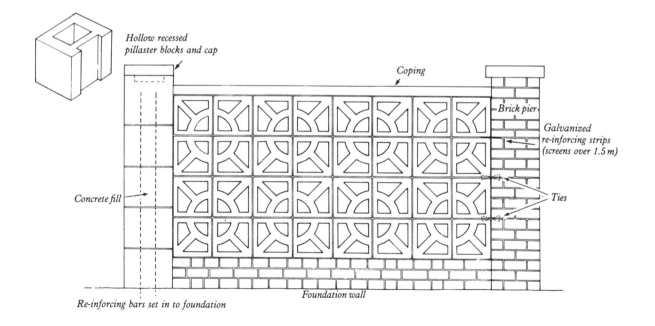

popular technique. This involves throwing pebbles of a selected grade and colour evenly onto a still-wet concrete mortar coating.

Concrete screen blocks made with a series of patterned holes in them are used where absolute privacy is not required (Fig. 8.7). The patterns are available in what seems endless permutations. They make excellent hosts for climbing plants. Another attractive aspect of screen blocks is the interesting light and shade patterns they make when light shines through them. Because the screen units have normally square faces 300 mm sq (12 in sq) and 100 mm (4 in) thick, it is not possible to bond them. Unless specific techniques are used this will result in a weak wall structure. For this reason some reinforcement or other support is necessary. This is provided at the sides, beneath and over the block units.

Terracotta

Terracotta can be used as a wall-building material in the form of tiles or as units for screen walls. These are not used very much on their own to build walls but in conjunction with other materials, hence their modern role is mostly confined to detail and decoration. The terracotta used even for these purposes must be durable and frost resistant. Where tiles are concerned, these may be seen as part of a capping or embellishment. Where detail calls for small radii arches and openings, tiles are particularly useful, as a brick is too thick to negotiate tight curves. When used to build open screen walls, terracotta can be supplied as separate pieces intended to be put together to make up one unit, unlike concrete blocks where the units are whole. This is mainly due to manufacturing processes, bearing in mind that terracotta is the result of firing clay which is far less controllable in terms of the product's uniformity than pouring concrete into a mould.

For the tile or screen units, colours tend to be within the darker range of reds or blues – which can be taken as an indication of their durability resulting from special clay type and high temperature firing.

Composite walls

There are several reasons why some walls are built with more than one basic material type. It may be too expensive to use a particular material exclusively throughout a wall. For example, it might be positioned in the visible faces only, with less expensive materials making up the rear. Alternatively, it might be a question of strength. This is exemplified by flints which tend to be small and certainly do not make successful quions or piers. These are traditionally supported and framed by brick or stone blocks. Most walling materials and units can be used in combination, provided they are in harmony. Permutations popularly include: stone/brick; flint/brick; flint/stone; concrete/brick, and so on. Sometimes the materials are physically bonded, while others are simply held together by specially made ties. Combinations must be visually compatible and in harmony with each other. Introducing a material into the new work which is already incorporated into associated or existing architecture will achieve this.

Timber

Timber is gaining in popularity as a wall-building material, although it does beg the question, when does vertical timber begin to be a wall and cease to be a fence? There is no doubt at all when a row of very straight timbers are set into the ground to hold back the soil, this is a retaining wall. When used in this way the rule of thumb concerning retaining walls will still apply – that thickness of the wall should be approximately one third of its height.

Where a high wall is called for, this may mean a series or rows of timbers, one positioned in front of the other. Since it would be unusual to incorporate a conventional concrete foundation beneath timbers used for soil retention, they will need to be set well into the ground, in some cases up to half their length. Even then the soil in which they are placed should be very well consolidated around them. This is assuming the wall is largely made up of vertical timbers. Where the majority of timbers are horizontal, they would need to be supported by very stout timbers indeed, set at pre-determined distances which would definitely then have to be placed in concrete to prevent their being pushed over – not only by the retained soil but by the weight of the timbers themselves!

When timbers are used vertically to create the equivalent of free-standing walls, for the sake of stability they must be concreted in at the base, as here again a conventional concrete foundation would be inappropriate and impractical. Timbers for walls are by definition larger in cross-section, either as square-round or half-round, than those used for fencing purposes.

To keep water out, it is advisable to complete the wall with a timber coping. Not only will this prevent moisture from penetrating any 'end grain' but it will make the overall appearance far more attractive. It goes without saying that the thickness of the coping should be in keeping with the proportions of the timber wall. Proprietary brands of timber walling are available; usually these are low – perhaps up to 1 m (3¼ ft) in height – and are manufactured in roll form, where perpendicular poles are fastened together with a series of horizontal wires.

The life of a timber wall can be extended if all the components have been treated at source with a preservative. Some water-proofing material such as a heavy-duty polythene placed vertically against the back (soil side) will also extend the life of a retaining wall.

Styles of Walling

Having decided upon a particular material with which to build a wall, the next decision will concern style. Each material needs to be put together differently, according to the shape, size, strength and other characteristics. Add to this the wall's purpose, its proposed proportion and environment.

There are endless permutations of wall styles according to the materials from which they are made. To begin with, it is important to understand certain principles which will above all make a wall stable and strong. Assuming that a foundation of sufficient depth and width is in place, the next step is to organize the building materials so that the vertical joints are bridged as efficiently as possible by the successive overlying layer up through the wall. This is known as 'bonding'. If bonding is not achieved, the result will be uninterrupted vertical joints running from the bottom to the top of the wall. Such a construction will be inherently weak, and a serious risk of cracking, even collapse

will follow. A sound foundation and good bonding should prevent this occurring.

The strength and required purpose of the wall, its location and the materials from which it is erected, will determine whether or not mortar is used in the construction. In the majority of cases, walls are mortar bound, with the exception of peat and timber.

Brick bonds

As mentioned already, some bonds take their name from the type or style of material needed to achieve them and this is certainly true of bricks. Fig. 8.8 shows the anatomy of a common brick. Fig. 8.9 shows several others for reasons of comparison. The 'stretcher face' or 'stretcher', as it is simply known, is the long narrow side that is apparent in most wall faces, the 'header face' or 'header' is the end. There is an 'upper face' and a 'bed face', the latter being the one that is placed into the mortar bed. The common brick has one, sometimes two indentations on the upper and lower faces, which are known interestingly as 'frogs'. These key into the mortar. The edgings of the bricks are called 'profiles' or 'arrises'. The dimensions of a common brick are: approximate length $215 \times 65 \times 100$ mm ($9 \times 2\frac{1}{2} \times 4$ in). These sizes are worked out on the basis of joints being 10 mm ($\frac{3}{8}-\frac{1}{2}$ in wide). For calculations of height, remember that four courses equal 300 mm (1 ft) – 65 mm $\times 4 + 10$ mm joints $\times 4$. Bricks other than common can vary in size however and this will not then apply.

Before describing the bonds themselves, it is useful to know that the thickness of brick walls are referred to or described in terms of a brick's length. A 'single-brick' wall therefore indicates that it is 215 mm (9 in) thick; A 'brick and a

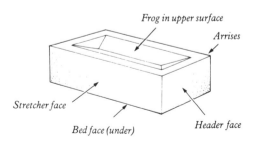

Frog in upper surface

Arrises

Stretcher face

Bed face (under)

Header face

Fig. 8.8 The standard brick.

Useful terminology

Batter

When a wall's sides are not perpendicular, that is, when the wall is thicker at the base than at the top.

Bond

This has in a sense two meanings. Firstly, it describes (when prefixed, for example, English bond) the accepted or traditional arrangements and patterns the building materials make in a wall. The second meaning describes the arrangements of vertical and horizontal joints to bring strength to the wall i.e. 'bonding' as opposed to a particular 'bond'. There are bonds which take their name from the materials or style of materials used to achieve them.

Coping or capping

The top layer of the wall. The term 'coping' is used if it extends beyond the main body of the wall or is of a different material to the main wall.

Course

A course is a single horizontal row of bricks, building materials or building units. In stone-work it can refer to stone pieces making up a distinct band (the bands in this case being the courses). There are brick bonds which need two courses to achieve them, others as many as five or more!

Damp-proof course (dpc)

A means or materials used in preventing water from penetrating the wall at the top or bottom or side.

Jointing/pointing

The method in which the mortar is dealt with or finished between building materials. 'Jointing' describes the treatment to the mortar of which the wall is built. 'Pointing' is carried out as a separate operation. For reasons of cost and or appearance, different mortars can be used at the joint surface.

Lift

The amount of wall built in a day or in a single session. This varies with material weights and season.

Pier (piers/intermediate piers)

An increased dimension of a wall at specific places to add strength and stability.

Pillar/column

An independent structure of brick or stone.

Quoin

The actual corner of a wall. If more or less than 90°, this is called a 'squint' quoin.

Return

Not the corner itself, but reference to the fact that a wall changes direction.

Stopped end

Where a wall ends abruptly and perpendicularly.

Wall face

The face which is most visible (i.e. the outward face).

half' wall is approximately 322.5 mm (13 in); while a 'half-brick' wall is actually 100 mm (4 in) thick, since it is achieved by laying bricks lengthways.

Stretcher bond (Fig. 8.10)

This bond is best known to the layman. Only the stretcher faces of the brick are seen, giving the bond its name. Stretcher bond walls can be either half-brick or single-brick thickness. With the latter, there would be no cross bonding, since the bricks are laid side by side lengthways, with a joint running through the

wall middle. To overcome this potential weakness, either capping or coping at the top will tie the two wall faces together, possibly in conjunction with a cross (header) course at the base of the wall.

An alternative method of strengthening the wall would be the use of specially made metal ties physically linking the two faces. Stretcher bond is an example of the most effective bonding, where the perpendicular joints (known as 'perpends' in the trade) are efficiently bridged by the brick above (as the diagram shows). A 'half bat' (half brick) is

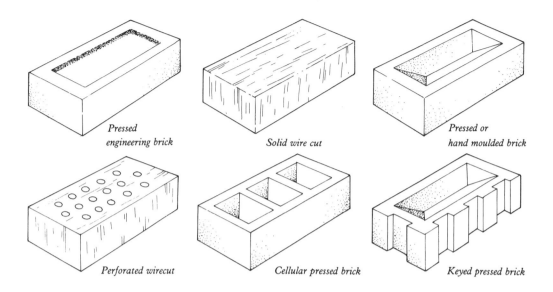

Pressed engineering brick

Solid wire cut

Pressed or hand moulded brick

Perforated wirecut

Cellular pressed brick

Keyed pressed brick

Fig. 8.9 Some special brick types.

required at alternate courses and at each end to make this happen.

Stretcher bond is often used as a cosmetic facing to a less attractive wall.

English bond (Fig. 8.11)

This bond is structurally the strongest, for the reason that it has the least number of uninterrupted joints running vertically through it. English bond is ideal where strength is of primary importance, as opposed to appearance. This is not to say it is not visually pleasing. English bond is achieved by laying header courses alternating with stretcher courses. The header course brick travels as it were from one face of the wall through to the other, whilst the stretcher course travels along the direction of the wall's length, lying side by side. A half of a brick cut vertically down the centre and known as a 'queen closer' is positioned between the first and the second brick and the ultimate and penultimate brick in each header course. This is necessary to push the header course along, relative to the stretcher course lying above and below it, in order to achieve good bonding. This alternating of headers and stretcher courses continues throughout the entire wall, bottom to top. The minimum thickness that a true English bond wall can be is 215 mm (9 in) singly, to accommodate the header course. They can of course be thicker, in multiples of half bricks plus a joint.

Flemish bond (Fig. 8.12)

Considered by many to be the most attractive visually. In Flemish bond the headers and stretchers alternate in individual courses. What we have therefore is one header running crossways through the wall, alternating with two stretchers lying side by side in the direction of the wall's length. The courses above and below do the same thing, except that they are positioned to achieve good bonding so that the header in one course is exactly in the centre of the stretcher above and below. This also produces a characteristic series of what appears to be 'crosses' on the wall face. Queen closer appears in her normal position next to the first and last header at each end of the wall, again necessary to push the bricks along to achieve an efficient bonding. Traditionally bricks with overly burnt header faces – tending to be darker in colour than the stretcher face – were picked out and built in to make interesting patterns in walls. Mainly these took on the

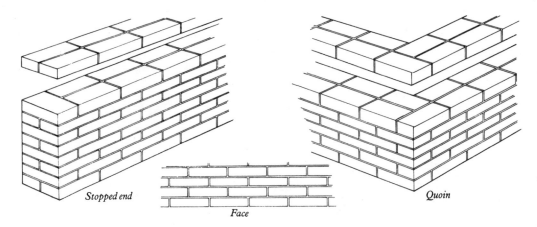

Fig. 8.10 Brick wall in stretcher bond.

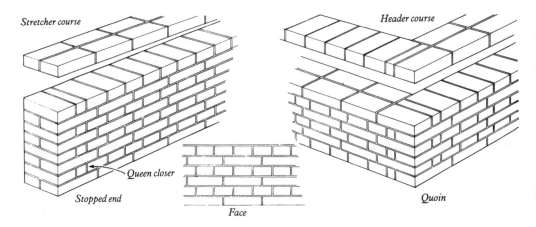

Fig. 8.11 Brick wall in English bond.

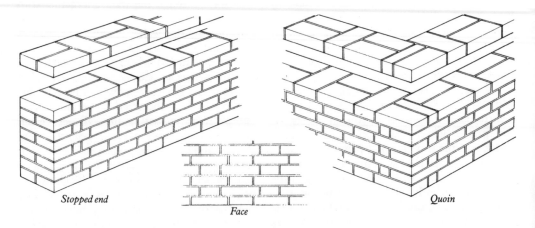

Fig. 8.12 Brick wall in Flemish bond.

appearance of diagonal lines. There is no reason why modern patio garden walls should not benefit from this technique. However, here again walls do need to be a minimum of 215 mm (9 in) thick to permit Flemish bond. They can of course be thicker, in multiples of half bricks, plus a joint.

Header bond

Header is another important bond, although not normally used for a straight section of wall. Its main use is to negotiate curves. Because of this header bond is often used in conjunction with either English or Flemish bond, where the latter makes up the straight sections and on arrival at a bend or curve transforms into header bond, and back again if necessary, with very little trouble.

Superficially, header bond is based on the same principle as stretcher bond, where perpendicular points are bridged by the header positioned centrally above and below. The main difference is the thickness – the half-brick thickness of stretcher as opposed to the full-brick thickness of header bond. The reason it negotiates curved walls better than others is that when a radius becomes small, all stretchers being straight and obviously unbending will produce a many-faceted wall face – with each course having the brick ends projecting slightly beyond the common wall face and by necessity having really wide joints at the front, angling back to very narrow joints at the rear. Using headers results in a smoother curve without the obvious projections, and at the same time reduces the joint widths by doubling their frequency.

Garden bonds

Many years ago when bricks were hand made, they varied in length. When used to construct garden walls which could be seen from both sides, differing brick lengths posed a problem. Most walls are built to a line making one side or the other fair faced and even – in other words, all the bricks having been accurately laid to line. As the bricks were not all exactly of the same length this meant one side or the other of the wall was rough by comparison. Partly because of this, and partly (but more likely) to reduce building labour costs, garden bonds were introduced, all requiring less bricks of exactly the same length. Garden bond walls do not have the strength of their 'parents', but neither do they need it for the role they play.

English garden bond (Fig. 8.13a). Unlike proper English bond, which basically has alternating header and stretcher courses, the garden edition has one course of header followed by an odd number of successive stretcher courses – most likely three, five and seven before the next header course occurs. The number of stretcher courses will rather depend on the wall's height. The header course's main function is to help bind the stretcher courses together.

Flemish garden bond (Fig. 8.13b). Again a variation on a theme. Whereas the 'parent' bonds have headers alternating with stretchers in the courses, here the header alternates with an odd number of stretchers, depending this time on the wall's length. The header is placed directly over the centre of the stretcher group above and below. The number in both English

Queen closer

a

Queen closer

b

Fig. 8.13 The garden bonds in brick.
(a) English garden wall bond
(b) Flemish garden wall bond.

Fig. 8.14
Brickwork bonds
for piers and
columns
(*a*) Bonding of
columns on
isolated pier
(N.B. No column
should exceed 18
times its width)
(*b*) Bonding of
junctions and
piers.

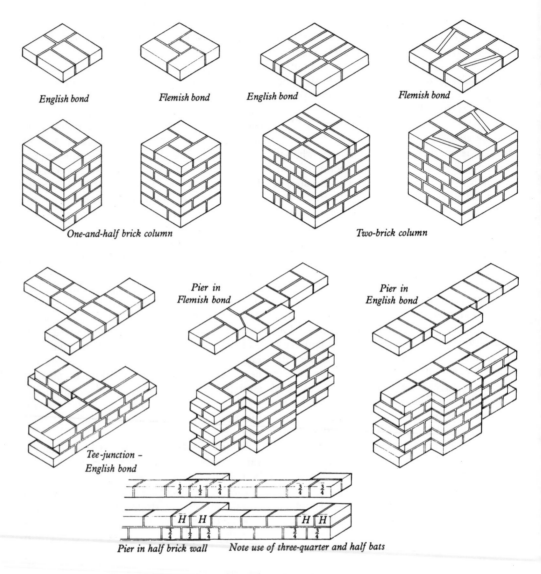

English bond   *Flemish bond*   *English bond*   *Flemish bond*

One-and-half brick column   *Two-brick column*

*Pier in
Flemish bond*   *Pier in
English bond*

*Tee-junction –
English bond*

Pier in half brick wall   *Note use of three-quarter and half bats*

garden and Flemish garden has to be odd for the arrangement to work and to make as efficient a bonding as possible.

False bonds. These are sometimes used where the appearance of English or Flemish bonds are desired but it is neither appropriate nor cost effective to build a wall of 215 mm (9 in) in solid brick. To emulate either bond the false-bonded wall comprises stretchers and snapped headers (half-bats) suggesting the full header. The finished wall or facing could then be 100 mm (4 in) only, or have a secondary reinforcing wall at the rear.

Piers and columns (Fig. 8.14)
Brick-wall bonds are repeated in associated piers and columns.

Piers are normally and properly built as an integral part of the wall and things get very complicated where they meet, requiring specially shaped cut bricks with interesting names – 'king closers' and 'mitred bats' for example. At this level it may be best to contact an experienced bricklayer.

Type of brick
The choice of bricks will be a matter of

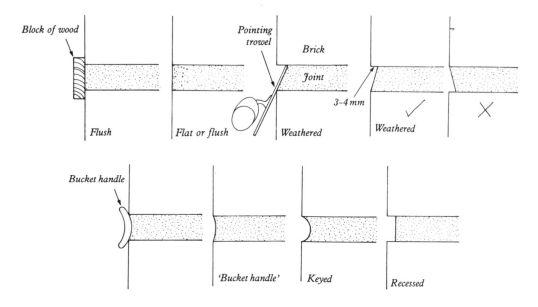

Fig. 8.15 Methods of jointing and pointing brickwork.

individual taste in combination with any associated architecture. The same wall can appear completely different depending on type, from the very rustic to the very modern. Red bricks absorb and hold heat, while light colours reflect it. This is an important point to consider if plants are to be grown against the wall.

Brick jointing and pointing (Fig. 8.15)
The way the joints are dealt with in brickwork will have a profound effect upon the wall's overall appearance – far more than would be imagined. Consequently, careful consideration must be given to the choice.

Adequate weatherproofing is another important factor and the joint finish will determine how much protection will be afforded to the joints in particular, and the wall in general. The most common finishes are named and described as follows:

Flush (sometimes known as 'struck Flush')
Here the joint mortar finishes flush with the face of the wall. Excellent for exposed patio walls, there being no ledges for water to dwell.

Weather struck
Here the mortar is impressed with a trowel so that an angle is formed which runs downwards and outwards. Starts approximately 3–5 mm ($\frac{1}{8}-\frac{1}{4}$ in) in at the top of the joint, and slopes to be flush with the wall face at the bottom. This is good for assisting rainwater downwards from the wall's face.

Bucket handle
A gentle concave depression imparted into the mortar (achieved originally by the use of a bent section of a galvanized bucket handle). Now there is a special tool bearing the name, following the demise of the galvanized steel bucket.

Penny round
Similar to the bucket-handle finish. Historically achieved by using an old penny.

Keyed
Here the impression is a more dramatic concave. In times past a large key barrel would have been used but today a piece of piping does the same job, provided the diameter of it is

only just larger than the width of the joint, to achieve maximum yet controlled penetration.

Recessed

This method is used to push the wet mortar well back into the joint yet to finish squarely, thereby obtaining the most dramatic effect. Unfortunately, it is entirely unsuitable for open or exposed sites, as water would collect on the ledges and might be driven into the wall structure. Recessed wall jointing is also necessary if pointing is to take place later, to provide an adequate purchase to the pointing mortar.

Stone bonds

As with bricks there are stone bonds too, in fact there are many more. Bricks generally conform to precise proportions, whereas stone appears in many shapes, sizes and forms. The bonds are dictated by these factors and the general character of one stone wall can be vastly different from another. The style of stone walls too, varies from extreme formality and sophistication to rustic. Since there are so many bonds, some indigenous to a particular area or adhering to a local or traditional style, only the most popular or the most frequently used are listed below. Good bonding must be achieved as always, and the more randomly shaped the stone, the more difficult this will be.

In mason's terms, 'rubble' is the name given to natural stone pieces (usually as dug from the quarry). In this context, it does not therefore mean left-over builders' hard rubbish. The most common bonds are named and described as follows:

Random rubble uncoursed (Fig. 8.16a)

Here, randomly sized stone (rubble) is put together and bonded with mortar in apparently no particular arrangement, but nevertheless achieving as good a bond as possible. There are no continuous horizontal joint lines either – in other words the stones are 'uncoursed'.

Random rubble brought to courses (Fig. 8.16b)

In effect this is the same as random rubble uncoursed, except that working up through the wall, distinct bands are created. Finishing at a common horizontal level, over this is built another band of uncoursed rubble and then

another, and so on. In high walls there may be as many as five or six bands, the bands representing the courses.

Polygonal rubble (Fig. 8.16c)

Some stones are derived from massive rock faces which have been blasted. In these circumstances the stones are almost in the form of multi-faceted boulders of varying manageable sizes. This bond arises from the use of such stones.

The remaining bonds use stone of more formal shapes, arrived at, either by cutting, sawing or chiselling.

Uncoursed squared rubble (Fig. 8.16d)

This is the more sophisticated edition of random rubble uncoursed. Individual stones have been cut to have rectangular faces. They are still uncoursed, and each of a different size and proportion.

Squared rubble, brought to courses (Fig. 8.16e)

Another sophisticated edition but with the same principle as random rubble brought to courses. The stones, however, have cut rectangular faces.

Regular coursed rubble (Fig. 8.16f)

Here the individual stones are arranged in distinct courses. Each course may be comprised of stones having different lengths but a common height. However, individual courses can sometimes differ in height in the same wall depending on common thickness of the stones from which the courses are made up.

Regular rectangular rubble

This in effect is similar to brick stretcher bond, where stone faces are cut to a proportion where the height is approximately half the length. This produces perhaps the most formal of the stone bonds.

Stone thicknesses

In all instances the thickness, relative to the length of the stones used will dramatically affect the overall appearance of a wall.

No separate bonds have been shown for reconstituted stone blocks. Where these imitate the real thing they automatically share the bonds too.

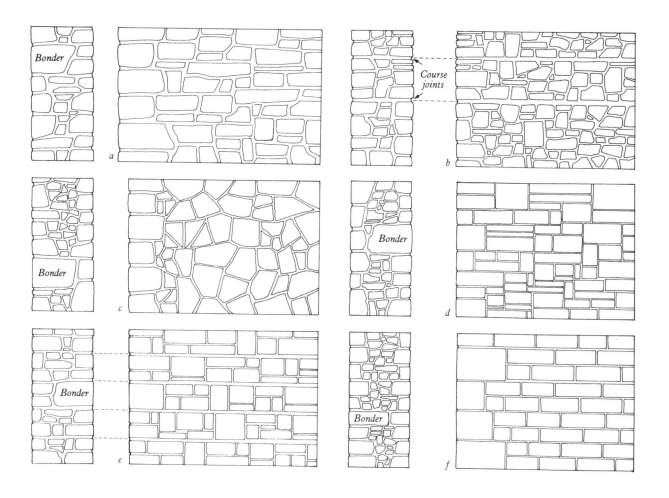

Stone jointing and pointing (Fig. 8.17)

Rubble walls tend to have their own specific and traditional joint finishes. Joint widths depend upon the stone being used and the desired effect, but in general they vary from 10 mm ($\frac{3}{8}$ in) to 25 mm (1 in).

Flush struck

As with bricks the mortar is simply cut off with the trowel and finished flush with the stone's surface. This is a good method to use, especially as certain stones may have a tendency to flake. Flush joints help to seal off and stabilize vulnerable stone profiles, keeping rain out.

Over pointed

In rustic situations the wet mortar is deliberately allowed to project slightly outwards from the wall face, where it is spread a little over the stone's edges. Again this helps to keep moisture out and helps to seal the stone. To look its best the mortar colour should closely resemble the colour of the stone, otherwise it will look like bad pointing. On weathering, over pointing becomes quite acceptable — indeed traditional.

Recessed

The mortar is impressed well back into the joints using perhaps a smooth pebble, a piece

Fig. 8.16 Stone bonds.
(a) Random rubble – uncoursed
(b) Random rubble brought to courses
(c) Polygonal rubble
(d) Uncoursed squared rubble
(e) Squared rubble brought to courses
(f) Regular coursed rubble.

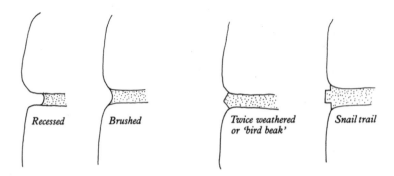

Fig 8.17 Types of stone jointing and pointing.

of rubber hose or bent copper piping depending on the joint width.

Recessed joints will throw each individual stone into relief.

Brushed
This is a further treatment to flush struck where a semi-stiff brush is rubbed over the joint to produce a strongly textured finish.

Rubbed
Another flush joint variation where a ball of hessian imparts its individual texture whilst spreading the mortar slightly over the stone edges. Very occasionally this treatment is given to brickwork.

Bird beak/twice weathered
Using a trowel, the wet mortar is coaxed into a peak (rather like a mountain ridge) following the centre of the joints. This operation must be carried out with the utmost skill since it looks either very good or very bad – there is no in between.

Snail trail
So named because the finished joints look like snail trail. This jointing is useful for bonds such as polygonal rubble, where joint widths are invariably inconsistent due to the nature of the stone.

Coping

A coping is in essence a hat and performs all the functions of a hat. It should afford protection to the top of the wall, firstly to keep the rain out and ideally direct it away from the wall's sides; secondly as a means of decoratively finishing the wall. Like a hat, which seems not only to affect a person's appearance but suggest their character, the same is true of the coping on a wall. Walls constructed in exactly the same style can look quite different, depending on the coping used to complete them.

Good coping should be impervious, frost resistant and designed to shed water not only from its own upper surface but wall faces too, and as efficiently as possible.

The style of coping should be of a proportion and size to be in keeping with the wall below.

Materials for coping

There are many coping materials, including stone, concrete, terracotta (including tiles), bricks and metal.

Stone (Fig. 8.18)
Depending on the required style, stone copings will range from the highly decorative to being simply larger pieces of the wall material extending beyond the wall faces. Preferably copings will incorporate a drip channel

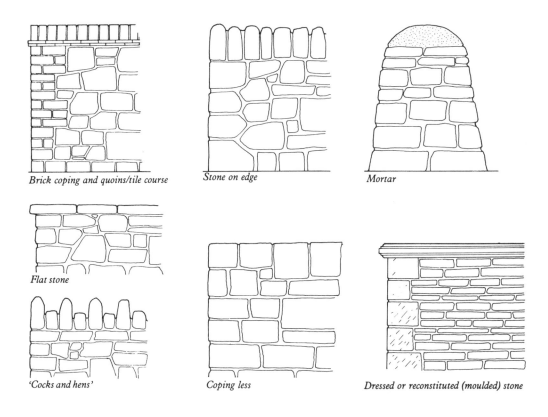

Brick coping and quoins/tile course

Stone on edge

Mortar

Flat stone

'Cocks and hens'

Coping less

Dressed or reconstituted (moulded) stone

Fig. 8.18 Stone copings.

underneath to prevent rain from being transferred to the wall's face.

The best formal stone coping units will be fixed consecutively with bronze dowels, as well as being bedded on mortar. The porosity of the stone coping will determine whether or not a damp-proof course will be necessary beneath it.

Concrete

Concrete either in its 'natural' state or in the form of reconstituted stone has unfortunately a tendency to shrink, especially when new. Consequently, the joint between the coping units can open, possibly allowing water to penetrate the wall below. Damp-proof courses are therefore recommended when using concrete in its various forms for coping. There are circumstances when a continuous or flexible dpc beneath a coping would be unsafe, there being

no direct contact or cohesion between coping and wall. Under such circumstances, should the coping be disturbed there would be a danger of it becoming dislodged and falling off. A waterproof bedding mortar or a tile course underneath will solve this problem.

The versatility of concrete means that copings come in just about any shape, form or colour.

Terracotta

Both the Victorians and Edwardians used terracotta units extensively for wall coping. They are now hardly ever used for reasons of cost and lack of availability. Nevertheless, they are extremely attractive and occasionally may be found in architectural reclamation shops. The units are cellular rather than solid, and sometimes glazed. Colours vary from biscuit to dark red, blue/black and green.

Tiles

These can either be of the flat, ridged or Roman variety and laid in the traditional way on to battens. This means forming the top of the wall into a pitched roof shape, including also a row of ridge tiles at the top. Flat tiles are often used in conjunction with other coping materials in the manner of a dpc while shedding water away from the wall face.

Brick (Fig. 8.19)

These are either ordinary, or bricks of specific shapes, but frost resistant and durable. Available in many textures and colours. Special brick copings are efficiently water resistant in themselves but are small in length compared with other units; therefore, more joints exist per length of wall, necessitating either a dpc, or waterproof mortar for bedding.

Specials

Most natural stone and reconstituted stone copings are available as specials. These are necessary to overcome particular building situations. Examples are for internal and external wall corners, angled and at 90°

stopped ends – curved walls, pier caps, etc. 'Specials' may not be stock items, indeed some have to be cut or moulded to suit a specific situation and will need to be ordered individually. Compared with standard units, specials are very expensive.

Metals (Fig. 8.20)

Usually restricted to copper, zinc or aluminium. In all cases these will be basically sheets of metal, bent and sealed around a concrete or some other core.

Damp Proof Courses (dpc)

If the coping is a rain hat then the dpc used at the base of the wall are the Wellington boots. Dpc's are used to keep water from rising into or penetrating a wall or any construction for that matter. In a retaining or free-standing wall its presence is important to keep walls as dry as possible to avert both frost damage and staining from efflorescence (the manifestation of white salts on the wall's surface); and in the case of retaining walls, to keep algae or moss from gaining a foothold. In a house wall the

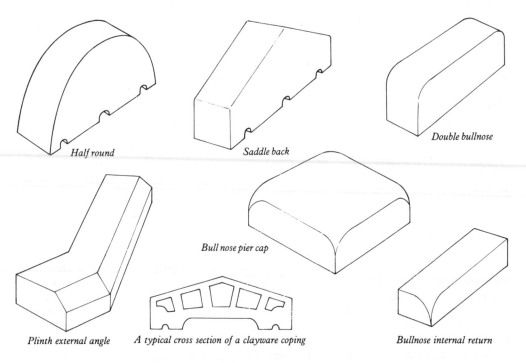

Half round

Saddle back

Double bullnose

Bull nose pier cap

Plinth external angle

A typical cross section of a clayware coping

Bullnose internal return

Fig. 8.19 A few examples of special brick coping shapes available.

Aluminium or zinc

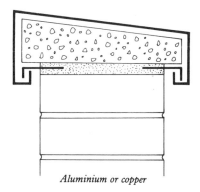

Aluminium or copper

Fig. 8.20 Metal copings. There are various metal copings fixings; here are two of the most common.

dpc's job is not only to keep the walls themselves dry but also the floorboards and plaster, etc. Without a dpc, or where one has been breached, wet rot and other forms of moisture-loving fungi will thrive, causing untold and often unseen damage. Dpc's can be introduced as horizontal or vertical barriers according to the situation. Horizontal dpc's are used, as already mentioned, at the base of walls where capillary action (the attraction of one water molecule to another) takes place and also at the top where gravity pulls the water downwards. Vertical dpc's are employed where it is necessary to keep water from penetrating the side of a wall, where a new wall is built against an existing one and when soil or other materials are raised against walls.

Horizontal dpc materials

Bitumen-coated fibre
This material is normally available in roll form, in various widths (being multiples of 100 mm (4 in) and grades. It is rolled out along the wall's length and bedded in mortar. Construction then continues over it.

Reinforced plastic PVC (polyvinylchloride)
Available in the same form and used in the same way as bitumen-coated fibre.

Slate
A time-honoured and proven material utilized as a dpc. Placed into a wall, top or bottom, in thin pieces and preferably overlapping. Not only is it almost entirely impervious but it adheres to mortar (which flexible bitumastic or PVC's do not) and advantageously does not physically separate the wall above and below.

Clay tiles
Hard and impervious, clay tiles are sometimes used as dpc's. When extended beyond the wall face they can make an attractive, decorative (creasing) course.

Lead
An excellent dpc material used in times past but now only on rare occasions due to its extreme weight and high cost.

Liquid dpc's
These are proprietary brands of bitumen or tar products applied, as the name suggests, in liquid form. When damp-proof coursing a raft foundation or concrete shed floor, for example, liquid dpc's are far more convenient. As a rule it is brushed on in several applications, building up to the required thickness. Manufacturers advise on thicknesses for different situations. Liquid dpc's are always protected at the surface with an overlying sand/cement screed.

Impervious bricks
Engineering bricks make good dpc's. Several courses can be built into the base of the wall in conjunction with a water-proof mortar. For aesthetic reasons they are often included at the top as coping as well. Engineering bricks are

useful for overcoming the physical separation caused by flexible dpc's and are used as an alternative.

Vertical dpc's

Where soils or other materials are placed against walls (especially house walls) to a level above the horizontal dpc, or where constructions have to be kept dry or otherwise protected, as with retaining walls for example, a vertical dpc will be necessary. This can be achieved in several ways by using:

Polythene

Used extensively for the purpose, it must be at least 500 gauge and preferably fixed with battens or some other means rather than being held in place by the pressure of the material it is protecting the wall from. In extreme cases butyl or PVC may be used.

Bitumastic paints

These proprietary-branded products are painted onto vertical surfaces, in a process known as 'tanking'. The surfaces should be flat and clean to make the bitumastic cover as complete and as easy to apply as possible. Where a surface is not flat and clean it may need to be sand/cement-rendered. Building with smooth materials in the first place will obviate the need to render.

Sand/cement render

Sometimes used but only effective if the mix includes a waterproofing agent. The problem with sand/cement renders, as with any mortars, is that it is subject to shrinking and subsequent cracking, leaving the wall vulnerable to moisture penetration.

Air bricks

Air bricks need to be mentioned at this juncture. They allow air to circulate beneath floorboards in the house, preventing condensation and dry rot. It is important to note that air bricks are normally positioned immediately below the dpc and that great care must be taken never to build over or cover them in any way.

Movement Joints

Walls are like everything else subject to the forces of nature, and changes in ambient temperature will cause a wall to expand or contract. When cold, the majority of materials contract; when hot they expand. This simple yet fundamental fact must be borne in mind when building a wall. The longer the wall, the greater will be the effects of thermal movement.

To reduce the risk of damage from this phenomenon, vertical 'open' joints are built into walls to accommodate the movement. Their width and regularity will depend upon the materials used in the wall's construction. For example a wall made of hard bricks could reach 30 m (100 ft) in length before a thermal joint is necessary. Since concrete has greater movement differentials, wall sections built of this material may only be 5 m (16 ft) in length before the introduction of such a joint.

Stone walls, again depending on the type of stone, might reach a length somewhere between, approximately 12 m (39 ft) for example.

Random rubble walls have a greater flexibility than those which are made of rectangular stones and the softer the mortar, the greater the flexibility. Thermal joint widths can vary from 5 mm ($\frac{1}{4}$ in) to as much as 12.5 mm ($\frac{1}{2}$ in), depending on the stability of the building material. The joints may be butted, that is the wall sections positioned exactly end on end; lapped, when the wall is constructed in staggered sections, or integrally lapped. If left as open joints, the latter two provide complete privacy whilst the first may not.

For the sake of appearances the joint gaps are normally filled with flexible materials. This is done by using, in the narrowest joints, a bitumastic dpc (held in by the butted wall ends) alternatively, and more likely with fibre board strips, especially made for the purpose, or possibly mastic which will be pumped in under compression. Mastic sealing compounds are obtainable in many colours which blend with the masonry, so making their presence less conspicuous.

Wall Construction

It must be emphasized that the construction of walls, except very small ones, should be carried out by someone who has the skill and experience to appreciate the importance of a sound and stable structure. The collapse of even a comparatively low wall could result in the death of a child or animal.

It is not possible here to enter into every detail of various wall constructions. There are, however, some sound and basic rules enumerated below to ensure success:

1. Accurately mark the route of the wall and its foundations (Fig. 8.21). This may be achieved by the use of timber profiles at each end in conjunction with building lines. Saw marks on the profiles (more permanent than pencil) will mark the extent of the foundation as well as the wall.
2. Remove any topsoil and put aside for use elsewhere.
3. Excavate the foundation to the required depth using a spade or by mechanical means (Fig. 8.22). The 'spoil' (subsoil) should be moved elsewhere, either to a tip, or for making up levels. The foundation excavation should be perpendicular, not sloping to become narrower at the bottom. If the soil is unstable, shoring may be necessary in the interest of safety.
4. The base of the excavation should be fully consolidated.
5. Concrete of an appropriate mix (see tables at the back of the book) is placed very carefully within the excavation, in layers not exceeding 150 mm (6 in). Each layer must be fully compacted before proceeding with the next. Concrete should not be dropped in from a height, since this can cause segregation of cement and aggregate particles. The side and upper edges of the excavation should be protected so that soil does not inadvertently become mixed with the concrete and reduce its strength. This process continues until the final and top surface level is achieved. This is then tamped or trowelled off fairly smoothly, but not so smoothly that a 'key' will not be provided for the subsequent mortar bed. Check that the foundation surface is level in each direction.
6. Where ground slopes, it will be necessary to provide steps in the foundation appropriate to the building units or material. These need to be as strong as any level foundations.
7. Should they be necessary, reinforcing rods of an appropriate diameter, size and distance will be inserted into the wet mix as the final levels are reached.

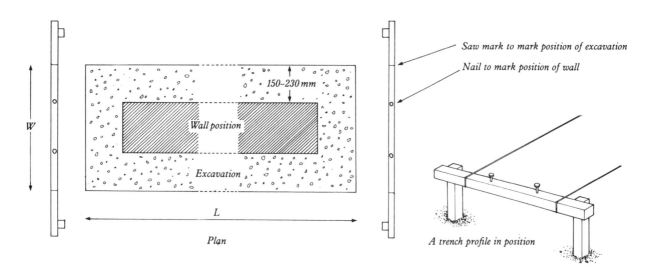

Fig. 8.21 Profile for foundation excavation and wall position.

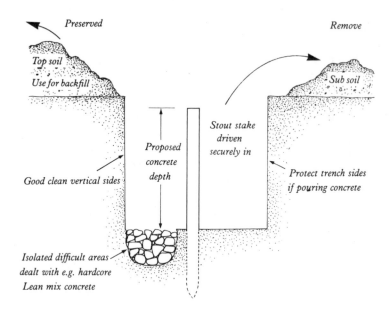

Preserved

Remove

Top soil
Use for backfill

Sub soil

Proposed
concrete
depth

Stout stake
driven
securely in

Good clean vertical sides

Protect trench sides
if pouring concrete

Isolated difficult areas
dealt with e.g. hardcore
Lean mix concrete

Fig. 8.22 A typical foundation trench.

8. Before any building work takes place an appropriate period of time should elapse to allow the concrete initially to set – setting time may vary according to the time of year (longer in winter). Bearing in mind concrete does not achieve maximum strength until 28 days have passed, the initial waiting time could be anything from five days to the full period.

9. Immediately following the installation of the foundation, it should be protected in winter against the frost (which will destroy its surface), or rain which will wash away the surface cement particles; in summer, to prevent it drying out, as opposed to setting. Drying out will destroy the concrete surface. Hessian or straw may be used to cover the concrete although not if the surface is meant to be seen as it can indent and stain the concrete. Polythene is another option but has its drawbacks in winter since it does not protect too well from very low ambient temperatures and has been known to freeze to the foundation surface via the condensed water on the underside. However, provided the hessian or polythene can be supported just above but not touching the concrete surface, either are ideal.

10. When building commences, using the building lines via the profiles, the first wall-end course-corners are built. These need to be accurately perpendicular. The middle section is then built in using lines and a spirit level to achieve straight and perpendicular lines. The dpc will be laid, if required, over the first three courses if these are of brick, blocks or approximately equivalent to 150 mm (6 in) to 250 mm (10 in) in height, if stone or other material. To control pressures on unset mortars, the wall building continues, but only until the first 'lift' is achieved – 'lift' being the section or height of wall built in a single session or day. This ranges from eight to

16 courses of brickwork, or the equivalent in height if stone, depending on the time of year (less in winter). This process continues until the wall reaches its ultimate height. Checks must be made constantly for accuracy, both vertically and horizontally. Mortar (see tables at back) should be of a consistency which is 'workable', in other words, easily used and of a fluidity or flexibility that allows the building material or module to bed into it and then exude between the joints for striking off and finishing. Too dry a mix will make successful bedding difficult and slow, with little exuding from between the joints. Too wet a mix will make weak mortar, which may run out of the joints, possibly causing unsightly staining to the wall surface and, in extreme cases, will increase the risk of effloressence.

11. To achieve the desired joint finish, mortar will either have to be treated as the wall grows or will have to be raked back to be pointed later as a separate operation.

12. The final touch will be the capping (using the same material and flush with the wall's face) or coping (possibly of a different material and extending beyond the wall's face). These will be bedded on with mortar or they may be mechanically fixed (dowels, cramps, etc.). If a dpc is required beneath the coping or capping, it would need to be installed at this point in time. The placing of coping and capping must be accurate if of a 'formal' type, since any deviations will be very obvious.

13. Although, hopefully, every effort will have been made to make a cleaning operation unnecessary, there may be a degree of cement staining which will need to be removed from the wall faces. Also a general tidying up around the new wall will be needed including backfilling the space left at each side between the foundation surfaces and the ground surface.

14. In winter it is advisable to cover the entire wall with a protective material (as described for the foundation) to allow the mortar to set properly before being subjected to rain, frost or low temperatures. In summer a protective material will prevent drying out before the mortar

is adequately set. In extremely hot weather, fine spraying with clean water to dampen the wall (after the initial set has taken place) is recommended. Again, in summer, building materials should not be allowed to become bone dry. If they do, on contact with mortar, they greedily absorb the moisture from it to the extent that the mortar itself becomes dry, making it impossible to set.

15. Before a wall can be 'put to work' the full 28 days' setting time for concrete and mortar must be observed.

Mortar and Concrete Mixes for Walls and Foundations

Mortar

When used for walling, it is nearly always better if the mortar with which the wall is built, is softer than the building material or unit. This may sound illogical, but it's good advice! When movement takes place in a foundation it will manifest itself as a crack or series of cracks in the wall above which will follow the line of least resistance. Therefore, if the mortar is the strongest part of the wall the crack will travel through the weakest – which in this case would be the building material or units – and this would mean physically having to remove the cracked building materials and then completely replace them, which is a difficult operation. If, on the other hand, the mortar joints are softer and weaker than the building material or units, then it will be easier to repair any cracks running through them by simply re-pointing. There is a further reason why softer mortars are used, particularly in stone-wall construction. Hard mortars will attach themselves to stone, and even partially penetrate it if the stones are porous. Subsequently, when frosts occur and the comparatively brittle mortar breaks away, it can take with it some of the stone to which it was adhering. If the same hardness of mortar is used to repoint, damage to the soft stone will be ongoing. Mortars which are softer than the walling also impart a degree of flexibility to a wall as it helps a wall to absorb lateral expansion and contraction differentials brought about by temperature fluctuations (thermal movement).

The constituents of mortar are basically mixtures of cement and either sand or stone dust. Lime is sometimes added, as are other admixes such as plasticizers, accelerators for setting, retarders for setting, water-repellants, colourants and so on. White cement is used occasionally but is approximately twice the cost of Ordinary Portland cement. Below is a table of mortar mixes for wall building. These may have to be adjusted according to variations in the ingredients themselves.

In all mortar mixes, the first number given is

Mortar mixes for general use (using dry materials, not damp).
The cement normally will be Ordinary Portland (OP)

			MIX (RATIO)	
Bricks	Burnt clay – sand/lime – concrete Sheltered sites or work carried out in summer	1:2:9.	{	1 part cement 2 parts lime 9 parts sand
	Burnt Clay – sand/lime – concrete Normal/Open sites or work carried out in Winter	1:1:6.	{	1 part cement 1 part lime 6 parts sand
	All Bricks (except engineering) below dpc or for copings	1:0:4.	{	1 part cement 4 parts sand
	Engineering bricks	1:0:3.	{	1 part cement 3 parts sand

Stone	1:2:10. hard stone	{ 1 part cement 2 parts lime 10 parts sand	to	1:4:16. soft stone	{ 1 part cement 4 parts lime 16 parts sand
	*1:3:10.	{ 1 part cement 3 parts lime 10 parts stonedust	to	*1:0:15.	{ 1 part cement 15 parts limestone dust

NB.

These latter mixes *incorporating lime stone dust or lime stone dust/grit (replacing sand)

Concrete blocks and reconsituted stone   1:1:6.

Cement will be Ordinary Portland (OP)

Concrete mixes for general use: (Using dry materials, not damp)
The cement will be Ordinary Portland (OP)

Rough 'mass' concrete		
Strip foundations	1:3:6	{ 1 part cement (OP) 3 parts sand 6 parts coarse aggregate
Mass concrete (better quality) Raft foundation	1:2½:5	{ 1 part cement (OP) 2½ parts sand 5 parts coarse aggregate
High class work Reinforced work Watertight *	1:1½:3	{ 1 part cement (OP) 1½ parts sand 3 parts coarse aggregate

*Concrete will only be watertight if fully consolidated, dense, and a minimum of 150 mm (6 in) thick.

always the proportion of the amount of cement. The second is building lime and the third, building sand or, where indicated, lime stone dust or lime stone dust/grit. Materials for mortar should be of the best quality and entirely free from soil or other contaminants. The water used for mixing should be clean – preferably of a drinking quality. Mortar materials should always be thoroughly mixed dry before the introduction of water. When added, this too should be fully mixed and in a quantity to achieve a mortar of even consistency which is workable. Always gauge the mortar's dry ingredients by volume, never by 'shovel loads' or guesswork. A bucket is useful for this purpose, filled to the top and levelled off. This way ensures that each mix is the same as the one before. On arriving by trial and error at the correct amount of water to produce the perfect consistency, make a note of it so that all future mixes are the same in this respect. Sand should preferably be stored and used dry, as should cement and lime! When damp sands are used – perhaps after standing in rain – it is very difficult to assess the moisture content day by day, making consistent mixes almost impossible.

Mortars should always be mixed in quantities that can be used up within half an hour and should be protected from drying winds, hot sun and in winter, very low temperatures (less than 30°F/1°C). Once mixed, never try to rejuvenate mortar by adding more water, as this will make it weak – the chemical setting process will already have commenced. It would make sense to mix less at a time if it is found that the batches are not being used up before setting commences. The higher the cement content, the more rapid the initial setting. For these reasons, in some instances with mixes such as 1:4., Plasticizers are used (strictly following the manufacturer's instructions). These entrain air into the mix, which in effect is like millions of minute 'ball bearings' making the mix more workable and delaying very slightly, the tendency of the mortar to dry out. High cement ratio mixes tend to be very stiff and sluggish.

Concrete

The same rules of cleanliness, mixing, storing and using of mortar ingredients apply equally to concrete, since it is virtually the same material as mortar. The difference is that concrete will not contain building lime and the aggregates are much larger. Many people use the name cement when what they really mean is concrete – cement being just one of the ingredients of concrete. Good concrete comprises cement and well mixed and evenly graded aggregates, ranging in size from the largest to the smallest, in predetermined proportion. The largest aggregate size will, to some extent, depend firstly upon the job the concrete has to do and, secondly, the finished concrete depth (thickness). Sizes will vary but for general purposes aggregates range from 25 mm (1 in) down to sand. 'Sharp' sand is used for concrete, as opposed to builder's (pit) sand which is much finer. The reason that the ultimate depth of the concrete has been mentioned in relation to the largest aggregate size is that the latter should not be in size, equivalent to more than a third of the concrete's depth, so as to ensure high ultimate strength. The aggregates, if not pre-mixed, must be mixed thoroughly in a dry state. Sometimes, when tipped on site, a degree of segregation of the particle sizes takes place. This must be corrected by further mixing. Having thoroughly mixed the aggregates, the cement is added dry to the appropriate proportion, then well and evenly mixed before adding the pre-determined amount of water.

Mixing

This routine is to be followed when mixing with a shovel and should be carried out on a very clean and flat surface (a steel sheet for example). Contaminants such as soil will adversely affect the quality of the concrete. All materials should be batched by volume as described in the section dealing with mortar (see page 93). Where a mechanical concrete mixer is employed in which to mix the concrete or mortar, the 'dry' first mixing routine is not always followed, in that the water is placed into the concrete mixer first, followed by the cement and lastly the aggregates. Whichever means is used, either by shovel or mixer, the idea is to coat each and every particle of sand or aggregate evenly with cement. When made wet, each cement particle will, by a chemical process, grow long crystals (resembling microscopic sea urchins); these crystals interlock and bind every particle of aggregate together, which is why it is so important that premature drying out or freezing of new concrete should not take place. This will not only interrupt the chemical process but may actually prevent it from happening at all.

Special cements are available for particular situations but professional advice would need to be taken on their use. One type that is probably used more than others is acid-resistant cement for use in soils with a low pH. Ordinary Portland cement might well be chemically attacked under such circumstances.

Where it is more convenient to use ready-mixed concrete, various mixes can be delivered to site to meet specific requirements. Provided they are given all the relevant information, ready-mix concrete firms will recommend the best mix for the job. If the project is very large, the opinion of a building engineer should be sought as to the most appropriate concrete specification.

Water content will vary according to mix and materials but to take the mix 1:3:6 as an example: if a 50 kg (approximately 1 cwt) bag of cement is mixed with 0.14 cu m. of sand and 0.21 cu m. of coarse aggregate – all perfectly dry – it would be necessary to mix approximately 2 litres of water to make it 'workable' and subsequently reach maximum strength. When purchasing materials from the builders' merchants, aggregates are, unless otherwise specified, supplied as 'all in'. In other words, the first mix in the above table would be then described as 1:9 all in. The term 'all in' describes a balanced mixture of sand and aggregate particles. The use of an all-in aggregate mixture is common practice and although there is not the same control as would result from a precise specification, it is for the majority of garden projects entirely satisfactory.

Compacting concrete on placing, which is essential, can be carried out in several ways, either tamping by board, mechanically or using the back of a shovel. If the mortar is comparatively fluid, a vibrating poker to remove air from the mix can be used (these can be hired). Overly wet mixes, although easier to place, will unfortunately result in weak concrete.

Screens

Screening will be necessary in many patio gardens for a variety of reasons:

1. To provide privacy (this could be from high or low levels) – overlooking windows for example.
2. For reasons of security.
3. To create a micro-climate (to keep strong or cold winds at bay)
4. To render less visible an unattractive view.

All of these practical features could be incorporated into a single screen type or just one feature depending on the relevant requirements.

There is an important point to remember if a solid screen, perhaps in the form of a fence or a wall is placed around an exposed patio garden: any solid vertical object facing a strong wind, will be the cause of considerable turbulence on its so-called lee side. This phenomenon will be detrimental to plants and cause discomfort to people. In other words, the screen might create even greater problems, albeit different ones, than those it was intended to overcome. Certainly, solid vertical constructions are not always the answer. Screens which filter the wind and thereby dissipate its force are best. For example, hedges with their ability to yield and bend, whilst at the same time filtering the strongest of winds, are invaluable. Screens can of course be designed to filter the wind and many do, but rarely can they be made to yield by bending in the way a hedge does. In urban situations however, high winds do not generally present such problems to the gardener, as often the patio will be surrounded by other buildings, all providing a degree of mutual shelter.

If a screen is to be really effective it needs to be at least as tall as an adult person. This might appear to be an obvious statement but where is the privacy that screening is meant to provide if your garden can still be overlooked by someone standing the other side?

Screens as barriers

Walls

These have already been covered in an earlier chapter; however, walls can make excellent screens as well as 'solid' walls. These

Previous page:
Water rendered safe
yet forming a most
eye catching feature
against a backdrop of
rustic brickwork and
patterned pebble
paving.

Right:
Pebbles, whilst not
the most comfortable
surface upon which
to walk, nevertheless
make an excellent foil
for adjacent planting.

Below:
Timber decking,
water and
architectural plants
imply a
Mediterranean
climate in this town
garden.

A simple oriental treatment creates within this town
basement area an illusion of space, light and elegance
(Robin Williams' design).

iv

Opposite page: Pairs of identical containers are often used for flanking steps. These fine terracotta pots contain standard conifers underplanted with trailing plants.

Left:
Reclaimed railway sleepers form the risers and shredded bark the treads in this extremely effective flight of steps – best in an informal setting though.

Below:
Rusticated concrete slabs combine well here with natural setts and the stone of the wall.

Left:
Round wooden stepping 'stones' make a pleasant
informal path.

Opposite page:
A planted terracotta vase makes an effective
intermediate focal point where axes cross.

Logs used as a walling material empathise well with
the plants growing behind.

constructions are known as screen walls or pierced walls (the latter being rather an old-fashioned term). Listed below are materials and descriptions of screen walls:

Screen brick wall. A brick wall with piers at regular intervals for support and several courses of conventional brickwork at the base. Above this level the courses are built in the manner of Flemish bond (see page 80), with spaces left where the headers would have been. Finally, coping is used to cover and reinforce the top and keep out the rain. Variations on this theme can include the use of reconstructed or natural stone.

Concrete screen units. A wall made entirely of specially manufactured units supported at the ends and intermediately by hollow pillaster blocks, which are filled with reinforced concrete. Stack bonded open-patterned concrete units are completed with matching coping pieces.

Terracotta units. Brick piers and base walls supporting terracotta or burnt clay screen units mortared together as panels. The bricks can also be used as a pleasing and effective coping. Of all the screening units, terracotta and burnt clay units are possibly the most attractive and although not so readily available, are well worth seeking out.

Fences

A fence can make an excellent low-cost alternative to a screen wall and there are circumstances where fencing may also be more appropriate. It is usually possible to find the right type of fence to fulfill most requirements.

Close boarded (Fig. 8.23)

Of the solid fences the close boarded is the best and if assembled correctly will prove to be the strongest and longest lasting. It is erected *in situ*, the supporting posts set into the ground in concrete. Attached to the posts are a series of

Fig. 8.23 Close boarded fencing.

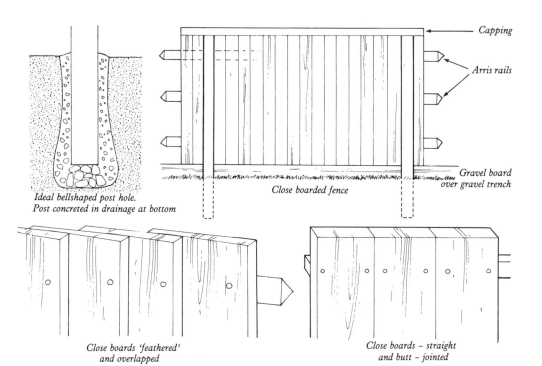

Capping

Arris rails

Gravel board over gravel trench

Ideal bellshaped post hole. Post concreted in drainage at bottom

Close boarded fence

Close boards 'feathered' and overlapped

Close boards – straight and butt – jointed

97

horizontal arris rails, the number of which will be determined by the height of the fence, but usually three or four. Arris rails may be triangular or rectangular, in cross section. At ground level a flat horizontal board (gravel board) is fixed – the reason for its name is that underneath it there should be a shallow drainage trench of gravel. The presence of the trench will prevent the gravel board from becoming permanently damp, so extending its life. Over the gravel board and attached to the horizontal arris rails are the stout vertical close boards themselves. These boards are either butted together, or more traditionally over-lapped. To achieve the latter the boards need to be 'feathered', that is thicker at one side than the other, but this will not be necessary for the butt-jointed boards. At the top of the vertical boards, a flat strip of timber is fixed to form a coping. This must extend outward beyond the face of the vertical boards and will prevent the end grain (the most vulnerable part of any timber) from becoming wet. The whole point of having a timber coping and gravel board is that being probably the first parts to deterio-rate, they may be replaced comparatively easily, while leaving the main fencing timbers intact. Close-boarded fences and their supports are usually made of hard wood, like oak.

The screws or nails used to fix these timbers need to be of a type and quality unaffected by the residual and corrosive saps exuded by oak. Fence posts will be at the very minimum 75 sq mm (3 × 3 in) or more likely 100 sq mm (4 × 4 in).

Close-boarded fences can follow the contours of the ground since they are erected *in situ*. Unlike hard wood close-board fences, which can often be left untreated, soft woods must be treated with a preservative, preferably before erection.

Picket fence

Picket fences always seem to have romantic connotations, reminiscent of times past and conjuring up a vision of roses and clematis scrambling through. Pickets are vertical boards which can have an elaborate and decorative finish to the top but are most often seen with the more simple, pointed or half-round finish. Picket widths vary from fence to fence but are usually from 50 mm (2 in) to

100 mm (4 in), and of 15 mm ($\frac{1}{2}$ in) thickness or thereabouts. The spaces between the pickets are usually equivalent to about half the picket width but can be more or less according to taste or function.

The pickets are individually attached to horizontal arris rails by screws or nails, which in turn are supported by stout posts set in concrete into the ground. It is traditional to shape the top of the supporting post in the same or a complimentary way as the picket tops. Alternatively, the post can be sawn off level and a 'cap' attached to it. This serves to keep water from entering the end grain. The height of a picket fence will of course, depend on individual requirements. As a guide the most likely heights are between 1 m (3 ft) and 1.35 m (4 ft).

A picket fence may be of hard wood, in which case the decision may be to leave it untreated. If made of soft wood, it must be either treated with a pigmented preservative or painted. Painted timber must of course be regularly maintained – an important consideration when making a choice. It must be said however that a white-painted picket fence makes a pretty feature.

Panel fence

Panel fences are a more economical alternative to close-boarded fences. Unlike close-boarded fences which are erected *in situ*, panel fences are supplied ready made. Panels are almost all 1.8 m (6 ft) in length, with various heights ranging in multiples of 150 mm (6 in), from 1 m (3 ft) to 1.8 m (6 ft).

Fence panels are supported between posts which for general purposes will be 75 sq mm (3 × 3 in). Post lengths will vary according to the height of the panel but there must be an allowance in the calculation for approximately 450 mm (18 in) in the ground and approx-imately 100 mm (4 in) extension beyond the top of the panel. Caps of various designs are fitted to the post tops; and whilst giving an attractive finish, they also prevent water from entering.

If the ground is rising, then 'steps' will unavoidably be formed by the level panels. This aspect of erection will have to be brought carefully into the equation as the supporting posts will need to be longer.

Posts are not necessarily made of timber; the alternative concrete is far more permanent but unfortunately has little visual appeal.

It is well known that in temperate climates, hard woods will outlast soft woods but cost may determine which of the two will be used. To extend the life of timber posts used as fence supports, metal 'shoes' can be fitted. These are driven into the ground and the posts are then slotted into the cavity provided. Accurate spacing is essential. You need also to make sure that the 'shoes' are square in the ground and precisely upright. There is an adjustment facility to account for any slight variations in post sizes.

Erection of panel-type fences
As fence panels can vary slightly in length, it is inadvisable to erect the posts in advance. Ideally only the first and last post should be permanently positioned to start with. A line is then strung across from the tops of the first post to the last as a guide to straightness, and against which to gauge subsequent post heights (the line must therefore always be taut!) The panels can then be fixed and the posts erected in sequence, i.e. panel post, panel, post and so on (using a spirit level, check continuously for level and correct vertical line). There is always a possibility that the last space will not amount to a full panel length. This is not an unusual situation. When this problem does arise the panel will have to be reduced by sawing down, but only following the repositioning and nailing on of the end frame piece to the appropriate width. The post caps can then be nailed in place to all the post tops, making sure that they are level.

If it is your intention to concrete the posts in, this will be the last operation, the posts having been temporarily supported by bricks, stones or post cut-offs. If windy weather is forecast to coincide with the concreting operation, it is recommended that angled bracing struts are diagonally positioned and fixed behind each post. These can be removed when the concrete has fully set.

When panel fencing is to be erected on a slope, the first and last post is positioned and a tensioned line fixed as before. This will indicate where the tops of the posts must be. On this occasion though, the work commences at the bottom of the slope, with posts and panels erected in an upwards direction, in the sequence described earlier. Panels must remain level (check with a spirit level) but each panel will step up in accordance with the ground slope. In this case, much longer posts will be needed to take account of the level differentials and it will be necessary to penetrate further into the ground since there will be less soil and therefore less support on the lower side of the post than the upper.

There are many other fence types but these are not immediately connected with patio gardens. Nevertheless, they are still worth mentioning, especially when one considers that not all patio gardens exist in an urban environment.

Wattle and osier hurdles (Fig. 8.24)
These are made from split or entire hazel branchlets (wattle), or the flexible shoots of willow (osier), woven together in exactly the same way as basket work.

Chestnut paling fencing (Fig. 8.25)
The palings are split chestnut branches of approximately 30 mm ($1\frac{1}{4}$ in) dimension, cut into lengths and bound together with horizontal wires.

Bamboo or rush fences
Bamboo or rush fences are used extensively in Japan and China. In the right setting they might well contribute to a patio garden.

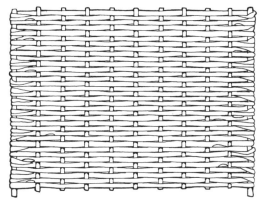

Fig. 8.24 Split hazel wattle or osier hurdle.

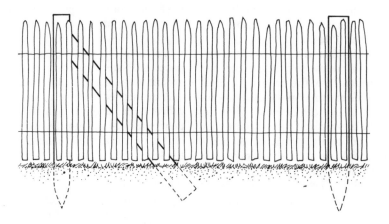

Fig. 8.25 Wire bound chestnut paling.

Trellis

The art of treillage goes back over many centuries and it is as popular a feature in gardens of today as it ever was. The style and function ranges from a basic need to grow a favourite plant against a wall, as a screen, or as a highly decorated panel of *trompe l'oeil*. Starting at a practical level, it must be remembered that the majority of plants have no aerial roots. In a natural situation they would probably be growing through or over host plants and trees. Many of the climbing plants are very beautiful if not spectacular, but it might be inconvenient or impractical to have them growing through other types of plants. Indeed the situation in the majority of patio gardens is that there would probably not be enough space to grow enough host plants and it is here that the trellis really comes into its own.

The style and strength of both the trellis and the manner of securing it must be considered together with the type of plant it is intended to support. An airy entwining plant, such as a member of the clematis family would not need a trellis of the same strength as a fully mature wisteria, which could weigh very heavily. This illustrates the point that for the heavier plants, 'off the peg' concertina-type trellis would not have adequate strength. Strong materials should therefore be used if the trellis is expected to last and give support. This might mean cross-sectional strut sizes of 25 mm (1 in) or more.

The perennial choice must be made between hard and soft woods. Soft wood trellis is less expensive but needs to be treated with preservative or painted, not forgetting that this must be maintained at regular intervals. Unfortunately when the time comes to repaint or repair the trellis, the plants climbing through it may have reached the desired degree of maturity. This presents a dilemma: should the plants be cut back, in their prime, to enable treatment and repairs to be carried out to the trellis, or risk its rapid deterioration? Obviously long-lasting timbers such as oak or cedar are best, since even when untreated they have a longer life span.

Trellis panels can either be secured to a wall with plugs and screws or be 'free standing' and supported by posts. The latter would have to be properly framed to ensure rigidity. Occasionally trellis is fixed as an extension to the top of a fence panel. Units are available specifically for this purpose, in fence panel lengths of 1.8 m (6 ft) and heights of between 300 mm (1 ft) and 900 mm (3 ft), in multiples of 150 mm (6 in). This is a particularly effective way of using trellis. Firstly, it 'softens' any hard-line appearance that the top edge of the fence may have. Secondly, it makes an ideal foil for the climbing plants which are attached to it. Some say that trellis-topped fences are more neighbourly.

When used as a screen, trellis is particularly appealing since it does not totally cut off the area and view beyond, unlike a solid fence or wall. In other words, a sense of space is maintained and with clever planting, a degree of mystery.

By utilizing trellis in this way, what starts out as a simple screen can become an object of interest and delight. As much as providing support for plants and for screening, trellis can be used purely for its architecture. This aspect is particularly relevant to patio gardens. Plain and ugly walls can be transformed and made beautiful; space can be suggested by the use of *trompe l'oeil*, and continuity maintained by allowing the trellis to mirror the architecture of the associated house, although this may mean incorporating arches and curves into the trellis (not an easy process). Decorated panels such as these are best made by experts. For the DIY enthusiast the familiar 'square' or 'diamond' is attainable without too much difficulty.

Vertical poles

Spaced vertical poles set into the ground make excellent screens. The top of each individual pole can be finished in all manner of ways: cut straight, rounded, obliquely or pitched like a roof (twice weathered). The poles might vary in length for interest, resemble organ pipes or be cut off so that collectively the poles resemble waves or a series of apexes. Horizontal wires can be fixed at regular intervals to encourage suitable plants to climb where required. Other materials besides timber might be considered from which to make the poles, e.g. concrete-filled plastic drain pipes, or even concrete pipes.

Timber boards

These must be supported by posts and rails at the rear and can be arranged in many permutations to the extent that they might make textural and abstract pictures or sculptured forms. The boards may be butted or spaced and fixed vertically, diagonally or horizontally or in combination. The boards surface may be planed or left rough-sawn, bringing its own individual texture. Colours can be introduced to give added dimension, using different preservatives of different shades. The thickness and overall dimension of the boards would depend entirely on the effect you wanted to achieve.

PART V

OTHER STRUCTURES AND FEATURES

CHAPTER 9

Decorative Structures

Pergolas

Of all the features in a garden the pergola is probably the most romantic. Not only does it make an excellent host for climbing plants, it provides a cool and interesting walkway in summer. It also creates and changes the play of light and shade and makes a strong architectural statement.

In principle, a pergola is a series of overhead beams held up by two or more rows of opposite and parallel supports. The different forms of pergola are very numerous indeed depending on the materials and how they are used. There are a few basic principles to be considered when embarking on the construction of a pergola. Firstly, the height from the ground to the underpart of the overhead beams: this must be of sufficient height to allow an adult person to walk underneath with at least 300 mm (1 ft) to spare overhead. If you intend to grow plants over the pergola, then you need to take account of this. Take as an example a wisteria, the flower racemes of which will be hanging down sometimes as much as 300–450 mm (1–$1\frac{1}{2}$ft). You can image the consequences of not making an allowance for this! The width of a pergola should be sufficient to allow at least two people to walk through it side by side. The length of a pergola will depend upon the desired effect and the size of the garden. Most pergolas are straight, but there is no reason why they should not be curved. Gentle curves however are preferred to tight curves for two reasons: looked at from the end, the pergola ceases to look like one if the supports appear to cut across the view and; remove any sense of direction. Secondly tight curves call for very complicated arrangements of the overhead beams. In consideration of the width this does not generally exceed 5 m ($16\frac{1}{4}$ ft). Even such a span as this would require very thick timbers just to support their own weight, without the additional weights imposed by plants! Some designers work on specific ratios of pergola height to width to achieve good proportion.

However, other factors come into play such as the nature and size of the supports, the size of beams and the environment in which the pergola is to be placed. Having said that, good proportions must always, of course, be striven for.

Pergola beams

Pre-treated soft woods are more often than not chosen, because of cost. As these have to be regularly re-treated with preservative (depending on the preservative used), this will probably involve disentangling the climbing plants each time. This will not be the case with a good quality hard wood such as oak, which lasts a very long time indeed. But as we know, it is far more expensive.

Pergola beams are divided into two in respect of their functions: the first are called 'bearers' and these rest on the supports and carry the joists (sometimes called 'cross beams' or 'cross members'). Occasionally the bearers will be heavier and larger than the joists because they have not only to carry their own weight but the weight of the joists and any plants there might be as well. Usually though, both bearer and joists are of the same cross-sectioned dimensions, but the way that the one rests upon, or is linked to the other, can vary. Firstly, the bearers can be underneath (and most frequently be running in the direction of the pergola itself) with the joists resting on top, and at 90° (Fig. 9.1). Secondly, the bearers are as before underneath, but the joists have slots cut in the bottom edge of a width corresponding to the bearers themselves, to coincide when positioned at 90° to the top edge of the bearers. On lowering the joist, the bearer penetrates the slots. To what degree will depend on the depth of the slots – usually one third to a half of the joist's depth. This technique is known as partial cross-jointing (Fig. 9.2) and is stronger as a structure than the one simply resting on the other. Lastly, the

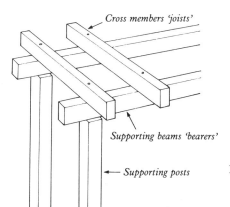

Cross members 'joists'

Supporting beams 'bearers'

Supporting posts

Fig. 9.1 Bearers fully supporting joists.

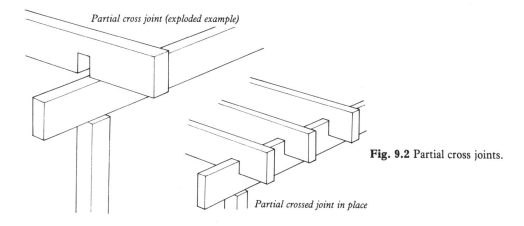

Partial cross joint (exploded example)

Fig. 9.2 Partial cross joints.

Partial crossed joint in place

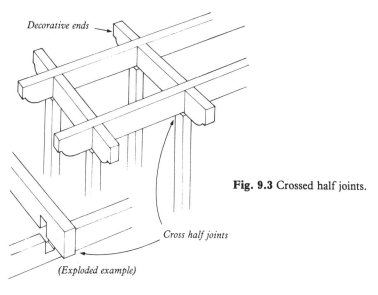

Decorative ends

Fig. 9.3 Crossed half joints.

Cross half joints

(Exploded example)

procedure is exactly as described above but this time the bearer is slotted too. When bearer and joists are coincidentally slotted and to half their depths, this is known as cross-half jointing and when pushed together fully, to lock into each other, results in the top of the bearer being exactly at the same level as that of the joist (Fig. 9.3).

This latter technique allows both bearer and joists to gain a great deal of support from each other. The appearance resulting from each of these three techniques is quite different. The fixing of joists to bearer must be very strong and structurally sound, like the fixing of bearer to supports. This is usually done by penetrating stainless steel pins of, say, 10 mm ($\frac{3}{8}$ in) diameter – coach bolts (these are very long) or hardwood dowels, which pass into holes drilled for the purpose, of the same diameter and glued with an exterior quality product. Screwed on blocks are sometimes also used. Where reinforcing is used in stone or brick supporting columns, this is often projecting beyond the top of the bearers and the bearers then fixed by this means.

Sideways movement is the potential danger as far as the timbers are concerned. Dimensions of the timbers in cross section will, as mentioned, vary with the degree of lightness or heaviness preferred. Some early pergolas have very heavy timbers, perhaps 150×100 mm (6×4 in) in cross section, but two good standard cross sections are 50×200 mm (2×8 in) or 50×250 mm (2×10 in). To some extent the height from the ground will determine which, bearing in mind that when viewed from beneath, the depth of a joist or bearer appears to be less because of perspective.

Pergola columns and posts

Any support arrangement given to the joists and bearers must be structurally sound. The risk is not so much that the weight from above will push the supports into the ground (although this is possible), rather that lateral movement may take place (in conditions of high winds, for example). So whatever mode of support is used, it should be not only stout or strong enough in itself, but be either well supported by or founded well into the ground. The two most often used will be either columns or posts.

Pergola columns

Columns may be constructed from a variety of materials such as brick, stone, concrete (either moulded or as reconstituted stone) or fibre glass. If brick, stone or reconstituted stone are used, they will need to be built in the normal way following the principles of wall construction appropriate to a particular material.

Columns might be straight-sided or, as many are wider at the bottom – becoming narrower in the main and middle section and then becoming wider again just before reaching the top. This gives a more solid and purposeful look to the column and at the same time provides a degree of decoration. Decoration might be applied in other ways too, for example, the introduction of 'creasing' tiles at spaced intervals in a brick column, or small flint panels in one of stone. Whichever of these materials are chosen, not only should the finished column be strong, it should look strong.

If using brick or any other similarly proportioned building unit, the smallest cross section to produce will be 215 sq mm (9 in × 9 in), but such a proportion may only be used for the lightest form of pergola and even then in a sheltered position. For general purposes, a minimum column size would be 300 sq mm (12 in × 12 in), and for some of the larger pergolas 450 sq mm (18 in × 18 in). At these sizes, reinforcing rods of, say, 10 mm ($\frac{3}{8}$ in) diameter can be placed at the centre to be anchored into the foundation, then right up through to project through the top. As previously described this makes an excellent fixing for the timbers. These latter column sizes will apply to random natural stone columns also. Natural stone and poured concrete can also be used to make sound columns. These too need to be strong, of course, and will ideally be of 300 sq mm (12 in × 12 in) diameter. Quite possibly the rounded columns so formed will be simply decorated at the top and bottom, either as an extended and rounded plinth or as a square. Reconstituted stone and poured concrete columns may be purchased from certain manufacturers either whole or in sections. Decorated fibre glass columns are hollow and outwardly resemble marble, for example, but they need to be filled with concrete.

Any column must have a strong foundation. The sizes must, as with walls, be twice the base size of the column, e.g. 450 sq mm (18 in × 18 in), therefore the concrete foundation would be 900 sq mm (36 in × 36 in). If round, say, 300 mm (12 in) diameter the concrete foundation would be 600 mm (24 in) diameter. The depth, as with any construction, varies with soil type and imposed load. This could vary from 300 mm (12 in) to 900 mm (36 in) deep.

Pergola posts

A brick or stone column to support a pergola is by no means always appropriate. To work and look well they need space or associated architecture of the same visual strength. In confined spaces they easily become overbearing. This is where timber posts might be a better option since they have a much lighter appearance, being of less mass. As with a column, a post must be strong enough and look strong enough to do the job of supporting heavy bearers and joists. A post of a cross-sectional size, sufficient to be used for panel fencing, will probably not be strong enough for a pergola. It is therefore, recommended that for the lightest pergola 100 sq mm (4 in × 4 in) be used, increasing in size through 125 sq mm (5 in × 5 in) to 150 sq mm (6 in × 6 in); very occasionally 200 sq mm (8 in × 8 in) might be used for the heaviest of structures. Timber posts may be rounded, even octagonal, but more often than not, square. For more rustic patio gardens, the timber may be left 'sawn', in other words with the saw blade marks deliberately left on the surfaces as a texture. For more sophisticated situations, the posts will have been planed smooth.

Square posts look really attractive if the corners are chamfered. This means the 90° corners are cut or planed off to make a flat surface. The width will vary with the size of the post, but will probably be 5–10 mm ($\frac{1}{4}$–$\frac{1}{2}$ in). It is unusual to take the chamfer from one end of a post to the other, rather it commences at approximately 450 mm (18 in) from the ground to finish approximately 300 mm (1 ft) from the top. A degree of elegance can be introduced by curving the chamfer back to corner, whereas a 45° angle at this point is more positive and matter of fact.

Timbers, depending on the required appearance and cost, can be either treated soft or hard woods – the latter always being considered the best.

Composite and other supports (Fig. 9.4)

A single solid post could be substituted with an arranged group of four, five or six smaller sized posts, provided they amount in cross-sectional

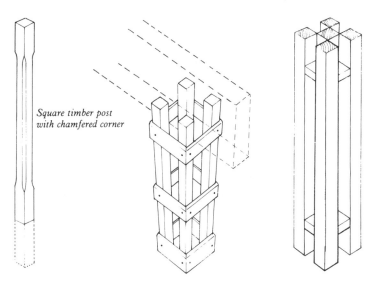

Square timber post with chamfered corner

Fig. 9.4
Composite timber supports.

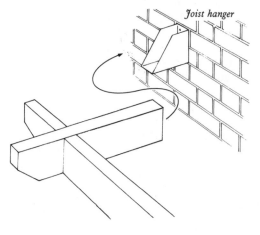

Fig. 9.5 Pergola beam fixed using joist hanger.

Joist hanger

area to a solid post. This way some extremely interesting and attractive structures can be achieved. Metal is used too as a support in the form of large tubes. In Victorian times these were made of cast iron and highly decorated.

Square steel box sections or scaffolding poles could be utilized but would be more in keeping with a pergola of a modern design. Whilst decorative wrought-iron supports (or more commonly and correctly these days, 'spot' welded supports) would place the pergola back in time.

Pergola posts must be well set into the ground to prevent them from leaning during high winds. If not, under the worst conditions this could mean the sideways collapse of the entire pergola. Besides being deeply set into the ground (600–900 mm/2–3 ft), a backfilling of concrete helps enormously. If the hole can be larger at the bottom than the top, rather like a bell in shape, so much the better. Concrete backfills shaped like flowerpots are inherently weak. At the very least, any holes accommodating posts should have vertical sides. If possible, metal 'shoes' (e.g. metapost) ought also to be concreted into the ground, since the effect of a pergola collapsing could be as dangerous as a falling fence.

Not all pergolas are free standing, some are adjacent to, and fixed to walls and have only one side supported by posts. In this state, many

pergolas double up as carports! Where a fixing has to be made to a wall this can be done in several ways, but first make sure that the wall is either strong enough or sound enough to be supportive. Unless you have the necessary skill, it might well be worth employing the services of an architect. On finding that the wall is sound, either a wall beam or wall plate (timber or angle iron respectively) can be attached horizontally, preferably using proper expanding wall bolts (these will be better than screws). When fixing the wall beam or plate, it might be worthwhile running some mastic caulking between the joint formed by the beam/plate top and the wall.

It is not a good idea to create a situation where rainwater might be trapped, thereby risking a permanently damp wall. A timber wall beam in cross section should resemble the bearer proportion of the other side, except it might be necessary to make it a little thicker and so give slightly more purchase for the joists. Any joints necessary in the wall beam itself should be vertical or diagonal. Horizontal, staggered joints may provide joint surfaces upon which rainwater might remain, and also be extremely difficult to reach later when painting with preservative. Wall plates, however, are nearly always made from very heavy-grade angle iron. This would be bolted against the host wall in the same way as a beam. For very long, wall-side pergolas it is advisable to make any metal wall plates in several sections, especially if on a south-facing wall. Expansion and contraction could otherwise present a problem

The alternative fixing device is known as a joist hanger, which may be used with or without a wall beam (Fig. 9.5). In essence it is a steel four-sided shelf which, having been attached to a wall or beam by screws or bolts, will accommodate the end of a joist exactly and thereby give support. Joist hangers are made in several grades and sizes so that most timbers used for pergola work can be accommodated.

Arbours

This was originally a shady retreat or a bower formed by closely planted overhanging plants and trees, supported or trained over lattice work or trellis. This idea has now been extended to include constructions of timber or metal, still used to support plants, but also often beautiful in themselves.

On occasions the plants even take second place! Metal (usually drawn steel wire) is particularly useful in the construction of arbours since it can be bent into many attractive configurations.

Arched Walks

Arched walks make a delightful alternative to pergolas, and especially so if space is limited. While the principles underlying both might be the same, in appearance they are not. There is an intimacy and a sense of enclosure that is particularly relevant to an arched walk. Some walks are simply a series of arches placed at set intervals one after another and following a particular route. On other occasions the arches are actually linked to enclose the route at the sides as well, perhaps leaving an occasional 'window' or 'door'. Climbing plants are normally used to adorn and enclose the arched walks and when the plants have scented flowers, the experience of walking through is wonderful. Careful planning with plants will ensure this experience is extended over a longer period. Even when there is no scent, colour and mottled light makes an arched walk a worthwhile addition.

Arched walks may be made entirely of timber, timber and ropes (these need to be rot-proof as far as possible), timber and wires (either threaded through holes in the timbers or stapled), and lastly, of metal.

Rope Swags

Rope swags are a simple, yet potentially effective and beautiful way of screening at a high level, gently separating one area of a patio garden from another, or flanking a path. Square posts or round poles (usually the latter are decoratively 'turned' on a lathe) are set into the ground at specific distances. The poles are then drilled at the top to take a rope, which is likely to be of 20–25 mm ($\frac{3}{4}$–1 in) diameter, rot-proof and of an appropriate colour – natural, white or green for example – or a chain perhaps made of bronze.

Barbecues

Barbecuing is great fun and the focus of many parties. There is somehow an affinity between a barbecue and a patio garden. Barbecues are either portable or permanent and, if the latter, should make a positive contribution to the overall appearance of the patio. Some barbecues are planned to be focal points as well, so extending their use beyond pure practicability. To do this they must be very well designed and constructed. One important, but often overlooked point about barbecues is that whoever is doing the cooking should surely be able to join in the fun too. This is mostly prevented by virtue of the barbecue being sited so as to face the wrong way! The cook is then obliged to stand with his or her back to guests, so making conversation extremely difficult. If possible, a permanent barbecue should be positioned to allow standing (or sitting) room behind, thus enabling a view over the barbecue toward the main area of patio and general activity: on many occasions space will not allow this facility and the inconvenience will then have to be borne.

All barbecues work on the principle of a base on which rests a burning fuel and a griddle, and over which the food is placed to be cooked. There are degrees of sophistication at all these levels. The fuel will be charcoal (which is said to enhance the flavour of the food in its own particular way), or gas which is piped in but burns through ceramic coals (of which it is said by some that it does not give the same flavour quality as charcoal). It is not advisable to have gas pipes permanently resting in burning charcoal for two reasons. Firstly, the intense heat may cause an early deterioration of the pipes and, secondly, fine dust or ash particles could block the small holes in the pipe. Gas-fired pokers can be used to start a charcoal fire but must be removed as soon as possible for the reasons given above. The most convenient source of gas will be bottled propane.

When a new patio wall is under construction a barbecue can be built to form part of it: otherwise it will have to be built as a separate entity, as most are. The materials from which a permanent barbecue is built should link with other materials of the immediate vicinity so as not to appear as 'yet another feature'. Bricks are often the first choice for construction but reconstituted stone and natural stone closely follow. Styles range from the really basic, comprising two mortarless side walls, supporting a griddle, to an elaborate construction with electric rotisserie, fridge – even a tiled roof with a chimney! Some barbecues are sold in kit form for the DIY enthusiast; others are the result of detailed design drawings, with input from a construction engineer if necessary.

Whichever building material is chosen, one important principle must be borne in mind: where any material gets hot it expands, and the heat generated by burning charcoal is greater than many other solid fuels. If the outer walls of a barbecue are built with mortar and therefore fixed, there should be an allowance within the barbecue for base plates, griddles, racks, etc., to expand and contract without putting any pressure whatsoever on the outer walls. This in turn means leaving space all around the interior, with base plates, griddles, etc., supported by and resting unfixed on 'shelves'. The base upon which the charcoals (or ceramic coals, if gas fired) are placed should always be protected with loose, butted fire bricks. Not to do this can result in a dangerous and literally explosive situation if the base is of concete. Concrete is a very poor conductor of heat and any heating up will be concentrated and not dissipated. Local areas can then become so hot that it expands upwards with tremendous force, perhaps taking hot coals and food with it! On the other hand, if a heavy metal plate is used without a fire brick cover, it may expand and buckle or, if tightly fit, push the barbecue walls out.

With any permanent barbecue, any mortar used must be comparatively flexible to account for general warming and expansion, followed by contraction on cooling. A lime-based mortar is therefore recommended, such as 1:1:6 (cement:lime:sand). Tiles at the top can be bedded in with the same mixture but pointed or grouted with either a 1:4 (cement:sand) mix or flexible exterior grouting mix.

The size of the cooking surface will be determined by a family's needs, but it is better to err on the larger side. It is possible of course to concentrate the fire to one end or the other of the barbecue if the party is a small one. Griddles and other appliances are better if made of stainless steel, not only for reasons of hygiene but if left permanently outside, they would otherwise very quickly become rusty. Should they not be of stainles steel a wipe over

with vegetable oil will afford some protection.

The area around the barbecue at ground level must be protected from unsightly oil or grease staining, although it is almost inevitable. The absorbent surfaces of some bricks and natural stones makes their cleaning extremely difficult. For this reason non-absorbent surfaces in the immediate area are recommended, such as engineering bricks, ceramic or high-fired terracotta tiles.

Permanent barbecues should also have some means of keeping the heat away from adjacent timbers – in the form of fencing, for example – especially if the timber is dry or has recently been treated with an inflammable preservative (creosote and allied compounds, for instance). A small backing wall is usually sufficient to deflect any intense heat, spark or flames.

The working height of a barbecue, permanent or otherwise, is better if the cook does not have to stoop. Over a couple of hours this can become extremely inconvenient and uncomfortable. A good working height will be similar to that in the kitchen, about 900 mm (3 ft), but this can be adjusted to suit 'head chef'!

Portable barbecues

Portable barbecues probably outnumber permanent ones and are useful where space is limited or where a permanent feature is felt not to be appropriate. Some can be left on the patio permanently since they are made to be weatherproof; others must definitely be stored in the dry when not in use. It is as well to check this point at the time of purchase as deterioration can be extremely rapid for non-weatherproof units especially as burning might remove protective surface applications.

Portable barbecues are manufactured to suit most requirements and pockets. The simplest is nothing more than a deep metal tray with a griddle. The most sophisticated will include wheels for transportation, cool box, gas-fired working system, hinged covers, canopy, the lot! Between the two extremes there are many variations.

Patio Pools

As a source of interest and beauty, water is unsurpassed. The addition of even a small area of water can alter the entire character of a patio garden and will almost certainly become the main focus of attention, such is its power of attraction. Water has many moods according to the form it takes. A still surface will be reflective and restful, while a fountain is stimulating and makes a delightful light display. Cascades or falls, on the other hand, are more dramatic and musical as water tumbles from level to level. Water can be included formally or informally. Since patio gardens by definition tend to be formal, water in the same style is usually the most acceptable. Some people, however, resist straight lines in any garden, even patios, and may opt for an informal area of water. This means that there must be very careful planning if it is to integrate well.

The presence of water may be required for one of many reasons: for its reflective properties and its ability to make an area appear more spacious; for its sound when cascading or simply trickling; for its cooling properties in summer, even if the effect is in the mind rather than in reality. As a habitat in which to grow aquatic or marginal plants, or to accommodate fish.

When it comes to positioning a patio pool, there arises a dilemma. Preferably it should be positioned in a well-lit place rather than in the shade, and away from falling leaves and debris. But having put it in a light place, it should not then be left unprotected from the sun's rays, and neither should it be too shallow. The former will cause algae to grow very rapidly and the latter, due to the small volume, will allow the water to heat up excessively. In both cases life-giving oxygen will be lost and, in combination with a high water temperature, will cause both plant and animal life to die. Pools then should be as deep as conveniently possible and the surface given a canopy of at least 25% leaf cover by the inclusion of water lilies, for example, together with oxygenating plants.

Patio pools can be constructed in a variety of ways and by using different materials. When a pool is required above ground level it will be necessary to enclose and contain the water by some means in the nature of retaining wall or other structure. This might be of brick, stone, concrete or timber. However, in themselves these materials might not be waterproof or impervious and so must be treated or lined with

something to make them so. When a pool is set into the ground the same situation exists. The excavated hole, unless in a very particular clay type, will need to be waterproofed and will therefore need to be lined in some way. The soil sides may also have to be supported to prevent them from caving in. An examination of the various materials and combination of materials will be helpful in deciding the best for a particular situation. These are listed below with descriptions, explanations and comments.

Flexible liners

Flexible pool liners are supplied in large flat sheets from a roll and are considered to be the most convenient method of forming a pool, especially one that is informally shaped. A formal pool can also be made with a flexible liner provided the excavated sides, if perpendicular, are given some support. This is achieved with side walls of concrete blocks, bricks or planking. In formal situations, unless one is using a 'tailor-made' liner made to fit the pool excavation exactly, there will be problems, especially where internal corners occur. The closer to 90°, the greater the problem (this is inevitable when endeavouring to fit any flat sheet into a box shape). Creasing is bound to happen at the corners where there will be material surplus to requirements. Where there is an external angle, such as would exist in an 'L'-shaped pool, for example, the problem is exacerbated and serious creasing will result as the angle pushes the liner forward. Whichever type of corner, internal or external, it pays to take a great deal of trouble to fold the excess material and make it as unobtrusive as possible.

To install a flexible liner, a set and precise sequence of events must be followed to ensure success. To begin with, the top proposed edging level should be established and judged against other features, beds, paving, etc., with which it will be associated. The outline of the pool can then be marked out using string and canes, or a hosepipe if the pool is to be informally shaped. If formal, pegs, profiles and lines can be used to establish the more precise shape, not forgetting to make an allowance for any internal side-supporting walls which may be necessary. Excavation can then commence to the required depth. If it is intended to keep fish in the pool, this means going down to a minimum of 450 mm (18 in). The sides will be shaped according to the style of pool, perhaps incorporating underwater shelves for aquatic plant pots and containers. In formal situations the excavated sides will most probably be perpendicular; if informal, they will be sloping. If the latter, it is best to keep the angle below 30° as this will encourage detritus to settle on the slopes. A far more realistic look will then result, resembling the sediment one would expect to see at the bottom of a natural pool.

When the excavation is complete it should be raked over to become smooth. Some soils are fine or sandy but others are stony, and in areas of flint this could mean really sharp edges exposed at the soil surface. An unprotected liner could, on contact with such sharp edges and subjected to water pressure, readily become lacerated and then leak. To prevent this, the excavation should be entirely covered (including the sides) with either a 50 mm (2 in) layer of soft sand, or a geo-textile material (Biddim or Terram for example) to form a protective barrier. Within a formal pool where supporting walls have to be built (in the usual way with a foundation and mortar) it would not be possible to take sand up such straight vertical walls, so make sure any wall face is as flat and as smooth as possible.

When all is ready the liner is then very carefully placed into the prepared excavation. Since liner material is extremely heavy, this is best done by either an unrolling process or by seeking help from others so that it might be lifted into place. Dragging a liner across the excavation and peripheral edging can cause damage to the liner, and even collapse of the side at the excavation. At this point, it is worth mentioning that if you intend to lift the liner into place, it will need unrolling first at the side of the pool excavation to get it as flat as possible, and to establish who is going to hold and lift which corner. The flattening process should be done as quickly as possible, especially in summer. The reason for such urgency is that the liner, which is usually black, absorbs heat from the sun's rays to the extent that any grass underneath will be literally cooked. On a really hot day this can take place within 15 minutes. If there is a likely delay,

then cold water must be constantly played onto the liner surface.

The liner, when carefully lifted or rolled into place, within the excavation, is then smoothed out as far as possible, and at the corners excess material carefully and neatly folded. If the pool is too large for this operation to be carried out from the sides, it will mean climbing in and walking over the lined base. If this is the situation, shoes and boots ought to be removed and substituted with smooth-bottomed footwear like slippers or even stockinged feet to prevent any possibility of damage.

When the liner is finally in place the water is then introduced by hose and the pond filled; and depending upon size, this might take from several hours to days – volume is generally underestimated on these occasions! On filling, the water pressure presses the liner against every undulation and profile of the excavation, causing the liner to move and adjust itself. It is for this good reason that edgings and finishing to flexible liner pools are always put into place after filling. If done before, and in conjunction with the weight of the water, tensions and stretching of the liner will result, as will the formation of voids between the liner and excavation – all potential danger points which make the liner far more likely to split or be cut by sharp objects. This settling in of a liner has even been known to drag a prematurely laid edge into the pool. Although black liners are known and used to enhance the light-reflecting properties of the water surface – so making the pool appear bottomless – some might prefer gravel, pebbles or even soil instead at the bottom of their pool. If this is so, as an extra precaution against damage, a geo-textile layer could be placed beneath the gravel and over the flexible liner.

When entirely filled, the pool will need to be edged in some way and for different reasons, for example to protect the liner edge; to provide an area for marginal planting; create a firm edge where grass is brought right up to the water or as a mowing edge; and finally as a paved surface for sitting or walking.

The liner should never be left exposed above the water line. This is both ugly and completely unnecessary. Which particular edge treatment is chosen will depend on pool style and situation. It is very likely that at one side of a pool there will be a different treatment given than at another. Where a paving edge is chosen this should ideally oversail (i.e. project over) the liner slightly, both to disguise it and to create an interesting shadow line. The oversail should be approximately 25 mm (1 in) – more could make the edging unstable since there would be insufficient support, and less would allow the liner to be readily seen. If the edge is to be given a grass mowing edge (Fig. 9.6), this could be of flat brick or stone. On the other hand, you might want the grass to go to the very water edge (Fig. 9.7), in which case there would be no hard edge visible. Both are fairly easily achieved as the illustrations show.

When marginal planting is required, soil is brought over the edge of the liner and into the water itself. Under these circumstances an underwater ridge will need to be incorporated to retain the soil and prevent it from migrating to the pool bottom. Where water and soil out-side of the pool are linked, some water loss must be expected since the soil will act as a wick in dry weather.

Stepping stones are very popular as a means of walking across pools, and less difficult to install than you might think (Fig. 9.8). If step-ping stones are to be included, this must be known from the outset because the individual concrete foundations (approximately 100 mm 4 in deep), to support the stepping stones, will need to be put in their place, in the pool formation before the liner is positioned. When set, a layer of geo-textile material should be placed over the concrete surface to prevent the puncturing of the liner by small sharp stones. After laying in the liner more geo-textile is placed over the liner to coincide with the foundations beneath. Over this a hollow column of concrete block or brick is built up, to equate in height with the proposed water level. The stepping stone is then firmly mortared into place, oversailing the pier all round by approximately 25 mm (1 in). This creates a shadow line. The pier itself would normally be painted with a bitumastic paint or proprietary brand sealant to make it less con-spicuous beneath the water.

Liner materials The materials used for the manufacture of flexible liners are either butyl or PVC. Butyl, which is a synthetic rubber material, is the most often used and is available

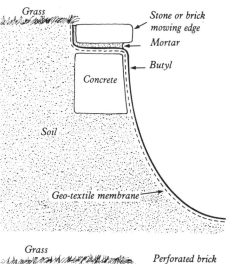

Fig. 9.6 Grass mowing edge.

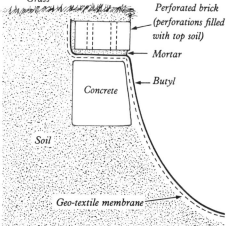

Fig. 9.7 Grass taken to pool edge.

Fig. 9.8 Typical cross section of stepping stone construction.

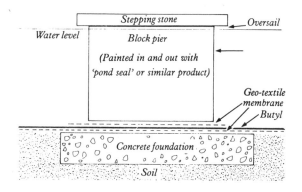

113

in several thicknesses. It is immensely strong, flexible and will stretch substantially before tearing. For garden use, a thickness of 0.75 mm is the norm. It is black in colour and can be jointed and vulcanized on site when large sheets are required, although this process must be carried out by specialists with special equipment.

Polyvinyl chloride (PVC) This too is black, but the surface is generally more glossy than for butyl. PVC liners are reinforced with nylon or a similar webbing, this is compressed between two outer leaves of PVC. It is a stiffer, less flexible material and tends to crease where butyl will bend. Neither is it considered by some to be as strong as butyl. However it is less expensive and for smaller pools does as well.

When ordering either butyl or PVC from stockists it is important that the sheets are large enough to cover the base and sides of the proposed pool, plus approximately 300 mm (1 ft) to 450 mm (18 in) all round. This is needed to tuck in beneath surrounding edging materials, including soil. Sheet sizes are very easy to underestimate, especially when the liner has to be ordered in advance of the pool excavation. Sticking accurately to the pool surface area plan and the proposed cross-sectioned measurements will help to avoid this and so save having to make last-minute adjustments.

Concrete Concrete is generally more expensive to use as a pool liner than butyl or PVC., but nevertheless has its uses, especially in formal situations. A concrete pool can be precise or geometrical, with none of the worries of creasing and folding associated with flexible liners. To be absolutely waterproof, concrete needs to be 15 mm (6 in) thick and very dense. This can, at times, prove to be a very expensive or inconvenient alternative where such a thickness is necessary for reasons of strength. Thinner concrete will, at 100 mm (4 in) minimum, suffice for very small pools. At such thickness it must also be made waterproof, either using waterproof paints, rendering or bitumen on the interior.

Where the pool design calls for vertical sides, they should never actually be so! A gentle outwards batter (slope) is recommened at 1 in 10 (10 mm in 100 mm) or 1 in 12 (1 in in 12 in). This will ensure that in winter, ice is allowed to move harmlessly upwards as its volume

increases. If the ice is confined within truly vertical walls, it will still expand and may crack the pool walls in the process. A concrete pool bottom should not be truly level either; rather, it ought to slope gently with a small depression in the centre. This will allow the last vestige of water to be more easily removed when cleaning-out time comes.

As for constructing a formal concrete pool, this can be done either by installing a concrete slab, then pouring concrete behind shuttering to form the sides; or alternatively laying the concrete slab and forming the walls with concrete blocks. The latter, being solid or hollow, would need to be reinforced and the hollow filled with concrete. If concrete blocks are used to build the pool sides, they will never be as waterproof as dense-poured concrete and will doubtless need to be lined in some way to make them so. In an informal situation the initial procedure is almost the same as that for laying a flexible liner: a hole is excavated to accept the pool edges, but in this instance an allowance must be made during excavation to allow for the depth of concrete which will obviously be much thicker – perhaps 150 mm (6 in) than butyl or PVC.

The first rule in making informally shaped pools of concrete is not to create a situation where varying water depths create weight differentials (Fig. 9.9). So whatever the superficial shape, the cross-sectioned shape should resemble a dish or saucer. This will ensure water pressures that are evenly distributed and so prevent the pool breaking its own back, so to speak. It is vitally important in formal, but especially informal pool construction that the concrete liner is of equal thickness throughout (Fig. 9.10). This is usually achieved by pushing timber pegs or metal bars into the excavation-formation sides and bottom, all protruding by the same amount as depth gauges and equivalent to the proposed concrete thickness. On having laid sufficient concrete to reach the top of the pegs or bars, these are removed and the hole immediately filled with concrete. It is important to remember to remove all the pegs or bars, which would otherwise rot in time and cause the pool to leak.

Planting shelves can be created in concrete using the same principle as a flexible liner

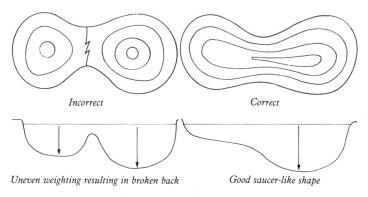

Incorrect   *Correct*

Uneven weighting resulting in broken back   *Good saucer-like shape*

Fig. 9.9 Avoiding weight differentials within informal concrete pools.

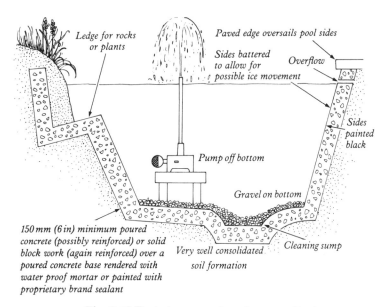

Fig. 9.10 Typical cross section of concrete lined pool – either formal or informal.

pool. Dummy shelves are cut into the ground, then covered with concrete. An alternative method is to build retaining walls on the pool's concrete floor and then backfill with soil.

Ideally, concrete should be sealed with a proprietary brand sealant on completion of work. Alternatively the first water in the pool should be allowed to mature to the extent that alga grows on the pool bottom and sides. This water should then be replaced with fresh water, but without 'cleaning' the sides. The reason for sealing or maturing a concrete-lined pool before introducing plants and fish is to prevent damage to aquatic animal or plant life, as untreated concrete releases detrimental chemicals into the water.

The upper peripheral edges of a concrete pool are fairly easily dealt with, especially where paving is adjoining. The pool sides being adequately strong to retain the water should be strong enough also to support the formal oversailing edges of paving. Grass too can be taken right to the edge of a concrete-lined pool without fear of collapse or sinkage,

115

as might be experienced with an unedged flexible liner. If the quality or stability of the soil beneath the pool is suspect, it will be as well to introduce some reinforcement into the concrete base and sides. Where concrete blocks are used with which to build the sides, this is almost obligatory. A suitable mix for a concrete pool would be $1:1\frac{1}{2}:3$ (cement:sand: aggregate) to which has been added as a precaution, a proprietary water-proofing agent.

Brick pools Pools could also be built of brick in or out of the ground, but either would need to be lined in some way. Even if the bricks themselves are impervious, it is unlikely the joints would be, and there would also be the question of thermal movement differentials between brick sides and the necessary concrete base. The lining could be flexible (e.g. butyl or PVC) although these might present a fixing problem. A waterproof sand/cement render or *in-situ* GRP (Glass-reinforced plastic or fibre glass) lining would likely be the most efficient and effective means.

Rigid pre-formed or fibre glass pools (GRP) These 'off the peg' rigid liners are a convenient means of installing a pool in the patio garden as they are both light and impervious. They are available in many shapes and forms resembling rocky pools to very formal geometric squares and circles. Provided they relate to the overall design of the garden they could well be con-sidered as an option. Unfortunately their interiors are mostly coloured either light grey or blue and occasionally printed as pebbles. These surfaces are readily seen through the water and make the pool appear shallow; whereas a dark interior would ensure light reflection from the water surface, making the pool appear deep. Also the installation of a pre-formed rigid pool liner is not quite so easy as it might first appear because the excavated hole in which the liner is placed must be precisely the same as the underside of the liner, added to which it is vital that it is level. While this of course goes for any pool, with the rigid liner it is particularly difficult to achieve, and any dis-crepancies will be exaggerated when the level water surface is so readily compared with the top of the liner.

Rigid liners are, like flexible liners, laid over soft sand for protection, and precise excavation must be allowed for. When making a formal pond, rigid liners are set sufficiently down into the ground to permit paving being taken over and beyond the pool edges to disguise them. Waterfalls kits and 'rocks' of fibre glass are sold in conjunction with rigid liners.

In-situ fibre glass Fibre glass (GRP – Glass reinforced plastic) is infrequently used as an *in-situ* pool liner. This is a little puzzling as it is excellent for the purpose. It is thin, light and comparatively flexible. For this reason it is used mostly for reparation and reproofing old and leaking concrete pools. It is exactly the same material from which modern canoes and boats are made and with similar techniques, the only difference being that for pool pur-poses the idea is to keep water in and not out.

The process involves excavating a hole in the soil and then providing a clean surface inside, over which to lay the fibre glass. In a formal situation the sides might be of concrete blocks which, it goes without saying, should be strong enough to withstand sideways water pressure, but not needing in themselves to be water-proof. If set directly onto the soil (which should be smooth) as in an informal situation, overlapping brown paper sheets will do, which are just slightly dampened so that they adhere one to another. Fibre glass kits can then be pur-chased from specialist shops from which to make the actual liner.

For reparation work, all surfaces need to be scrupulously clean. After filling an *in-situ* fibre glass pool, make sure the water matures to the extent that algae grows at the sides before emptying and then refilling for plants and fish to be introduced. Fibre glass can be coloured, so a water surface light reflecting the black interior can be included if desired.

Overflows

Most pools of whatever material they are made, will need an overflow so that a pool does not spill over after heavy rain. This might result in a deterioration of the pool edging during frosty weather, including the lifting of copings by ice, a 'natural' pool surround becoming very muddy, and in some if rare instances, water pouring between the liner and the ground beneath. This could cause a section of liner to be pushed above the water level – often referred to as 'the hippopotamus syndrome'. When a pool is at ground level i.e. not raised, the water from the overflow should be conducted away to the nearest rainwater outlet. The overflow pipe will take the form of a fixed pipe at one corner of a ground-level pool at a height which is calculated to be the highest permissible water level. The diameter will depend on the size of the pool, ranging from 20 mm ($\frac{3}{4}$ in) to 75 mm (3 in). It is always a good idea to stuff the end of a pipe with either a nylon pot scrubber or a ball of chicken wire in the case of a larger pipe. This will allow water to enter whilst keeping objects such as leaves at bay, which might otherwise block it. Where a pool is raised, the overflow pipe – which could be a piece of electrical conduit pipe sawn to an appropriate length – is positioned just beneath any coping or capping, and similarly dealt with to keep leaves, etc., out. In winter besides the overflow pipes, extra precaution can be taken especially in the case of formal pools to prevent damage to the sides from the pressures of ice. A couple of floating tennis balls or some expanded polystyrene blocks will act as 'safety valves' and absorb some of the pressures.

Waterfalls, streams and cascades

To many, a patio garden would not be complete without a waterfall and cascade. Extreme restraint is recommended in their use, however, as the concept of a patio garden which is often inherently formal can be at odds with that of a rock and water cascade which must be inherently informal! To bring the two together in harmony takes a great deal of design skill. If the style of a patio garden is generally formal, then so should be any falls or cascades within it to avoid a conflict of ideas. If informal, then the fall and cascade should be informal too.

Streams, cascades and waterfalls may be made of the same materials of which the main pools are made. Where concrete is used to form 'streams' this should be achieved by overlapping units, the reason being that set concrete – being so rigid a material – may crack by virtue of the weight differentials and thermal movement, especially if laid as long and comparatively narrow sections.

It is never a good idea to mix materials when making streams, cascades and waterfalls – for example, natural stone with concrete or butyl and concrete. They can never be properly joined or sealed due to different expansion and contraction rates. It is better to make the main water course of one material or another, and thereby make it entirely waterproof. Then, add the different materials as required for cascades, edging etc, and to provide the character.

So that your man-made stream does not become dry when the water pump is turned off, rather than make it slope from the upper to the lower level, you could construct a series of stepping, shallow, minor ponds. This way, there will always be water visible.

Other water features

Pools are by no means the only way that water may be introduced into a patio garden. Indeed where there are young children pools can be potentially dangerous, and some other safe way of introducing water might have to be found. Fortunately there are several options.

Wall mounted fountains Wall fountains are probably the most convenient; they consist of a bowl which is waterproof, a tiny electrically driven submersible pump, which pushes the water through the pipe (normally positioned at the rear of the wall fountain) to re-appear higher up. From there the water falls back into the bowl, then back up the pipe again as a continuous process. Wall-mounted fountains are available in many styles, materials and sizes. They make excellent focal points and are effective in the very tiniest garden.

Mill stone fountains This is a general name given to the type of fountain which originally made use of redundant mill stones. Modern materials such as GRP (glass reinforced plastic) have not exactly replaced the real thing but their high cost and rarity have made the GRP imitations a better option. Some of the later editions do not even imitate mill stones and have evolved into sculptures. In essence the mill stone fountain is a low, textured cylinder with a hole at its upper centre from which water bubbles. The water then covers the upper surface, moves down the sides and disappears through the surrounding pebbles and gravel. Beneath the mill stone is an unseen chamber, acting as a reservoir which collects the water and in which there is an electrically driven, submersible pump. The pump pushes the water back up through the mill stone to commence its journey again. This is an extremely safe and effective way of having water, and is extremely useful for the smallest patio since the mill stone units are available in many sizes, textures and colours, all resembling natural stone.

Bowls and container pools Small attractive pools can be made utilizing plant bowls and other containers, and this is especially useful where space is at an absolute premium. Containers such as these would need to be waterproofed (see page 114).

Fountains are an excellent way of bringing movement and light play to a pool; additionally they introduce oxygen into the water, benefitting both plant and animal life. Styles of fountain can range from nothing more than the simplest surface 'gurgle' to extremely complicated, multi-tier, moving arrangements. However, the style will obviously need to reflect that of the style of the host pool. A very ornate fountain for example, in the middle of what is supposed to be a natural pond, will immediately look and be out of place. Fountains need not simply be displays of water either, they might be formed by water pouring or spraying from a piece of sculpture or any other suitable objects – boulders or pebbles for example. Fountains can be within the pool or at the side depending upon the desired effect.

Fountains should be of a size, width and height relative to the water surface area of a pool. If too wide, water will spill over on surrounding surfaces. If too high, wind blown droplets may also fall outside the pool area, deplete it and waste water. The unfortunate effects of this may be compounded as most surfaces of surrounding materials should be laid so as to gently slope away from a pool surface. This is done to prevent dust and leaves washing into the pool itself.

Pumps and planning

To benefit from the sights and sounds of moving water and for purposes of oxygenating in what will be an artificial environment, some source of power will be necessary to move the water. In a natural situation water moves by gravity, the water source most likely being surrounding higher ground or other areas upon which rain or snow has fallen. In urban situations the water is gathered and supplied via the Local Water Authority through a tap. Under normal circumstances it is against the law to use water to operate fountains, waterfalls, etc., and then run to waste. If a meter has been installed, you would soon find it an extremely expensive proposition. A circulating pump is therefore the logical answer. This will make use of the same body of water by moving it around. Only loss through evaporation need then be made up from mains water, which is permissible, or perhaps through other available means.

Where water is to be moved from one place to another to fill artificial streams for example or to make waterfalls or cascades, it will be necessary to take the water from somewhere. This will almost invariably be the lowermost pool in the system, which in effect will be acting as a reservoir too. However this reservoir should be sufficiently large and of sufficient volume to be able to have water taken from it, yet not appear depleted.

This is far easier to achieve if the bottom pool is informal with sloping sides. In formal situations the falling water level may be gauged against surrounding edging, so exaggerating the amount of loss. When designing a pool, from which it is known that water will be removed to supply and fill ancilliary features, an allowance must then be made. The precise allowance will only apply to a particular water system, but some idea can be gained by calculating the entire water area (outside of the lower and main pool area) and multiplying by 25 mm (1 in) to 50 mm (2 in). This approximation will indicate the volume of depletion in the lower pool, since it represents the volume of water in transit. 25–50 mm (1–2 in) is the amount that the water needs to rise to activate a waterfall and cascade. Where there are several minor pools or just one other in a system, they should never amount in volume to be greater than the bottom pool. A pump is nearly always placed in a lower pool and this could mean that in order to fill the others and possibly a stream and cascade as well, the lower pool could conceivably be pumped dry in an attempt to fill the others, and to the detriment of the submersible pump. Any system should therefore be designed and calculated as a series of 'balanced' volumes.

Rockeries

Rockeries seem to follow on naturally as a topic from pools as very often the one is used in association with the other. Rockeries are extremely popular, creating an environment and conditions where plants of quite a different type to that found in beds and borders may be grown. Because the concept of a patio garden is an entirely artificial one and a good rockery emulates nature, the two concepts must be brought together very harmoniously indeed. This might mean going away from what is generally accepted as a rockery and using stones and pebbles in a different way, but nevertheless, creating a suitable environment for rockery plants.

Rockeries in the accepted form were, if not invented by the Victorians, certainly popularized by them. These took the form of artificial outcrops or rock faces built with natural stone pieces. Their purpose was to accommodate and display collections of alpine and associated plants. The Victorian legacy remains and rockeries are still very popular.

In the past rockeries were, it appears, treated as separate entities and to many it did not matter that they did not harmonize with the garden as a whole. Unfortunately, this is still true today and some rockeries appear 'plonked' into corners, regardless of their surroundings. For a rockery to work on an aesthetic level, an attempt at least should be made to make it appear that nature has had a hand in it. In this respect associated structures will have a great

bearing on their success or failure. A heap of stones and soil pushed into a brick wall corner will never be more than exactly that. The same heap of stones and soil arranged well with a backdrop of appropriate planting, for example, to soften or even screen the walls, will at least give the idea a chance.

Where rocks or rockeries are included in a garden, it is always a good idea if several similar rocks are repeated elsewhere. This ensures visual continuity and gives the impression of the rocks occurring naturally. Rockeries are best if placed in a mainly sunny situation, since there are many more plants which enjoy this position rather than shade. Some shade-loving alpines, though, are very beautiful and it should not be too difficult to accommodate these too.

In very formal situations where a conventional rockery may appear incongruous, it is worth considering a rock wall instead, where some or all joints can be filled with soil. In this situation the plants should be put in whilst the wall is still under construction, to ensure that the roots are in contact with the soil core, or in the case of a stone retaining wall, with the soil at the rear.

Conventional rockeries need to be weeded regularly to prevent strong-growing weeds sending their roots well into the soil and around the rocks, making eradication difficult. This could mean dismantling at least part of the rockery and then starting again.

Rockeries can be put together in various ways, each having a distinct style. The best known imitates a 'fault' or escarpment where rocks are arranged to appear stratified (Fig.

Fig. 9.11
Rockery stone laid suggesting natural stratification with plateaux
(*a*) Elevation
(*b*) Cross section.

Fig. 9.12
Boulder stone
arrangement.
(*a*) Elevation
(*b*) Cross section.

Fig. 9.13
Pavement
rockery.
(*a*) Elevation
(*b*) Cross section.

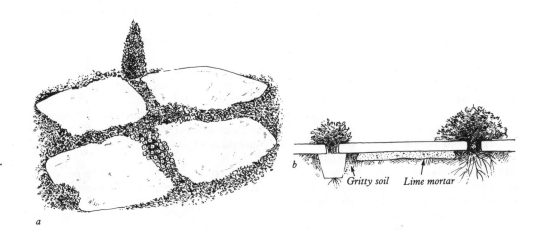

Gritty soil   *Lime mortar*

Fig. 9.14
A scree garden.
(*a*) Elevation
(*b*) Cross section.

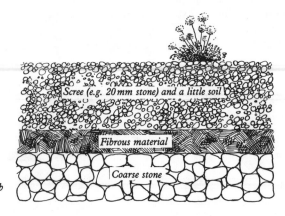

Scree (e.g. 20 mm stone) and a little soil

Fibrous material

Coarse stone

9.11). Cracks filled with soil and earth plateaux facilitate planting. This should appear as natural as possible, avoiding the spotted 'burial mound' look.

The second technique uses stones, rocks or boulders in an almost sculptural way (Fig. 9.12), often free standing, with plants growing between. Two distinctly different appearances can be achieved depending upon the types of plants chosen. On the one hand, grasses, phormiums and yuccas, etc. will produce a 'desert' look. Lush planting on the other hand (hostas, rodgersias, rheums) will give a moist 'boggy' look.

Rock plants and alpines are also grown between natural flat stones, and this is called 'pavement rockery' (Fig. 9.13); and for real enthusiasts, a scree garden provides a challenge (Fig. 9.14). A scree is a mixture of stone debris mixed with very little soil, such as would be found at the base of a disintegrating rock outcrop. This calls for a very specialized and fascinating group of plants.

Stone types for rockeries

Where a natural stone occurs locally it is probably best to use this (provided it will not disintegrate in frost). There will then be an immediate link between the rockery and any adjacent stone walls, etc. It will look 'at home', especially if the garden soil has resulted from the same rock type, having been broken down over millions of years. Where stones have to be imported they should preferably have been 'weathered'; this will ensure that any flaking or cracking due to the vagaries of the weather will have previously taken place.

The softer the stone, the more immediately they will become covered in algae, moss or lichen, as such stones tend to be more water absorbent and the texture provides an easier foothold for them. Coarse sand stones and lime stones such as Cotswold are examples. Hard stones like Westmoreland or Cheddar stone, which are carboniferous lime stones are still suitable, but take much longer to weather. This process can be accelerated by painting rockery stones (and any other masonry for that matter) with a soot and cow dung slurry. Some advocate painting with milk, but this method is not quite so instant in effect.

When constructing rockwork, good building principles should not be abandoned, as a collapsing rock bank could be potentially dangerous. For this purpose conventional rockeries should be well founded into the soil with the largest stones set well in. Subsequent layers should be angled back and firmly set into the supporting soil so that no movement takes place when trodden on. Not only will this ensure stability, it will also direct rainwater from the rock faces and ledges towards the plant roots. The soil will need to be rammed around each stone.

A conventional rockery is usually more stable if the stones are large. Also a rockery of a smaller number of large stones looks much better than one of a greater number of small stones. Of course, the size of stone may ultimately be dictated by not only the source, but by access to the site.

For purposes of ordering materials and building, it takes one man about a day to put one tonne of rocks together properly, and a cubic metre of rock pieces with voids (i.e. not solid) will weigh approximately $1\frac{1}{2}$ tonnes. Rockery building needs a good 'eye' if it is to be convincing.

Lighting

Lighting adds an exciting dimension to any patio and extends interest and enjoyment of the garden far into the evening during both summer and winter. When designing a lighting scheme, the size of the patio garden will affect lighting unit positions and their numbers. If the patio garden is small then the lighting effects will be seen mostly from either within or just outside the house. If the patio garden is larger, then the lighting must be more than just 'stage' lighting. People will be moving through the patio garden and the effects of the lights will then be seen to be constantly changing, appropriate to specific areas and features.

Light fittings will be chosen on two bases: for lighting effect only, or for the contribution the light fitting itself makes to the overall garden design. In other words some light fittings are made to be totally unobtrusive and intended to be hidden between plants or to blend in with architecture, or indeed made to be recessed into walls and steps; whilst others are made to be ornamental – wall and standard lamps for example. Spotlights, on the other hand, send out well-defined directional beams of light, whilst other types result in diffused or soft effects. So, for example, a focal point that requires emphasis at night time, this could be achieved with a directional beam or spotlight to give the best results; whereas a soft light might be more appropriate where, for safety's sake, steps need to be illuminated or a curve in a path, etc.

Different light types can be mixed and positioned to create different moods. Light fittings can be positioned at ground level for horizontal or upwardly pointing lighting or at varying heights. Should there be a main viewing point in a garden, and there usually is, bright lights should preferably not be positioned so as to shine back into people's eyes, or even from the sides. This is both unsettling and irritating.

A carefully designed lighting scheme can create practically any mood.

Garden lighting equipment should be expressly made for the purpose and be rust or corrosion resistant; for this purpose aluminium alloys, bronze, stainless steel and plastics are mostly used. Lights of sculptured form are popular also and the fitting and bulbs are then placed in timber, terracotta, or bronze housings, some of which are extremely beautiful and ornamental. All mains garden lighting must be earthed, especially if manufactured of metal.

The illumination of water both above and below the surface seems literally to transform a whole patio at night, bringing excitement and delight, especially if the pool has a fountain. In the daytime a pool may still be interesting but will be seen in context with other elements, whilst at night, darkness makes a foil and the whole concentration will be on the water. Very special scaled lighting units and fittings are available for underwater purposes, even if only for use at the sides of a pool! Colour filters are also available for pool lights and when used with discretion are very effective indeeds.

Most floating or submersible power supplies are low voltage and any associated sockets and plugs must be totally waterproof. Most lighting operates on one of three voltage levels, i.e. 12 to 24 volts, 110 volts and 240 volts. Transformers are needed to achieve the first two and a 110-volt transformer needs to be directly tapped to earth to improve the safety factor.

Electricity

There are few patio gardens that will not benefit from at least one electrical power point. Power is needed for many purposes: for lighting, water pumps, security (e.g. automatic gates), barbecue rotisseries, mowers and other maintenance equipment, as well as conservatory and glasshouse heating.

Electricity in any form must be treated with the greatest of respect and its installation must, without question, be left to a qualified electrician. He or she can advise on the most suitable types of fittings. It goes without saying that all external sockets must be weather-proof and strong. A 'circuit breaker' plug or socket is recommended when mowers or, for that matter, any hand equipment is used externally. For specific advice, or for a list of registered electricians, consult your local electricity office; they might even help to design the system as well as recommend someone to install it. Some firms specialize in designing and installing garden lighting.

Garden Furniture

If a patio can be considered to be an outdoor room, then it will require furniture to make it both purposeful and useful. The furniture will mainly consist of seats and a table or tables, which will take one of two forms. It will either be built in and therefore fixed, or portable for moving from one position to another. Built-in furniture will be less versatile, but might be needed for other purposes i.e. to be decorative or to act as a focal point for example. Tables and chairs may be selected for quite different purposes and their style may reflect this. For example, a chair required for lounging will therefore probably be low and able to adjust to a horizontal position. On the other hand, another might simply be for sitting up at a table for dining. Similarly, tables might be needed for different purposes, placing drinks upon, for example, or for pot and plant displays, or again for dining. It is important that sufficient space is provided on the patio not only to accommodate such items of furniture, but to permit easy access to and around them (see page 23). This is, unfortunately, often underestimated. Exterior furniture, like interior furniture, is very much a matter of personal choice.

As happens indoors, styles and colours will be chosen to relate to their surroundings and the general decor; and so they should outdoors! The design and style of furniture can 'grow out' of the materials from which it is made, some examples are listed below:

Timber
Timber is very versatile indeed and can be used to make both formal and rustic styles. Either smooth and planed or occasionally even retaining bark. Some tables and chairs are highly ornamented, whilst others are beautiful because of their clean uncomplicated lines. The choice of soft woods or hard woods will in turn affect the textures and finishes of a table.

Metal
Metal furniture tends to be longer lasting than timber although much depends on the quality of maintenance given. Cast iron was a favourite outdoor table material in Victorian times, chosen for its strength and weight which gives stability. Aluminium alloys have largely replaced cast iron by imitation, being much lighter yet sufficiently stable. It is far less costly to produce and does not rust, so the degree of maintenance required is also less. Real wrought-iron tables and chairs are still obtainable but high production costs make them expensive – those that are available tend to be antiques. Imitations made from spot welded iron strips are obtainable just about everywhere, but unless treated with an anti-corrosive coating will, rather like wrought iron, be vulnerable to rust, because of the large number of nooks and crannies. Non-ferrous metals like aluminium alloys and bronze are superior, although bronze is, if anything, more expensive than wrought iron. Aluminium and steel furniture is occasionally covered with a protective plastic covering, or is enamelled.

Plastics and GRP
(glass re-inforced plastic/fibre glass)
The cheapest varieties are very readily available and from just about every retail outlet, including garage forecourts. These are light, flexible and reasonably long lasting, but only if they incorporate ultra-violet light inhibitors. Without these, they can become dangerously brittle. There are, of course, as with most other things, varying qualities and some plastic furniture is extremely well designed, strong and long lasting, but naturally this will be reflected in the price. Plastic or GRP furniture tends to have a smooth surface but textures can and are easily introduced. Colours are very wide-ranging but white is probably the most common. This type of furniture is extremely easy to clean.

Stone
Stone tables and seats would almost inevitably be fixtures, not least because moving them around would be difficult indeed on account of their weight. The stone would need to be durable and frost-proof and the table top cambered, although as gentle as possible, in order to shed rainwater. This principle would need to apply to the seats as well and for the same reason, except here the seat will slope. Stone seats are available in many design styles and sizes, being entire or made up of linked units. The quality of stone would need to be of a type that responds well to being cut, tooled and finished. This probably means a finely grained stone, such as Portland or slate.

Concrete
Concrete for making garden furniture will, like many other garden features, be a result of pouring the mixture whilst still fluid, into a mould, or alternatively comprise reconstituted stone units. The costs of making up moulds on site for poured concrete, unless the design is simple in the extreme, will amount to more than building with 'off the peg' reconstituted stone units. If special finishes are required this will send costs even higher. Nevertheless, there are occasions, especially where 'built-in' seats are required, where it might be a simpler and more cost effective proposition. Reconstituted stone would in all respects be treated as real stone.

The alternative to the above is to buy ready-made concrete furniture. This is readily available from most garden centres and is found in all manner of styles and finishes. The drawback with concrete furniture is that it is extremely heavy.

Glazed ceramics or terracotta

This type of furniture is becoming very popular and much of the glazed ceramic styles are imported from China and said to be frost proof. Nevertheless, always check with the supplier. The seats normally take the form of hollow barrels, or have a flat-headed mushroom appearance, including the tables. Some are extremely beautiful with intricate designs, and others quite plain. Because they are hollow, they are easily moved around. Terracotta has, on the other hand, been a traditional material for furniture but of fairly simple design due to problems of moulding and firing. Not all terracotta is frost proof and therefore may have to be taken indoors in winter.

Basketwork

Basket-weave furniture, being made of natural willow and other similar materials is very light, flexible and attractive. It is not a good idea to leave basket-weave furniture out in the open unprotected in inclement weather, especially over winter, since it will deteriorate quickly. The colours will either be those of the natural woven materials or the result of varnishing, dyeing or lacquering. It is not unusual for different colours to be introduced in the same piece of furniture. Where used as a table the woven upper surface is not suitable upon which to stand glasses or bottles since it will be uneven. A smooth flat surface can be provided by utilizing a sheet of toughened glass. This also permits sight of the tabletop underneath. Its design can still then be enjoyed.

Combinations

Much of the garden furniture available is made up of a combination of materials, especially where tables are concerned. Already basket weave and glass have been mentioned but there are many other combinations: wrought iron and glass, brick and timber, plastic-coated metals, etc.

Mobile furniture

Some seats, loungers and tables have wheels attached and occasionally handles to enable them to be moved about from one place to another. This is a very convenient means of following the sun (or shade) around the patio.

Soft furnishing

Soft furnishing for garden seats, chairs and loungers make sitting far more comfortable. Cushions and mattresses are either sold as part and parcel of a chair or suite, or separately. The soft furnishing of some swing seats is an integrated part, supported with sprung wires. It is suggested by some manufacturers that their soft furnishings are made to be left outside, whilst others recommend theirs to be taken indoors during winter or inclement weather. It is advisable, however, to take them all indoors during winter, as this way they will last much longer and remain cleaner. Even those designed for permanent outdoor use will attract algae and even moss if detritus is trapped in piping or seams. Light too, will affect the material even if waterproofed, to cause fading and degradation.

The quality and materials used for patio soft furnishing will vary as much as for indoor use and this will be reflected in the price. Patterns of material will be a matter of personal choice, ranging from strong geometrical and bold floral patterns to plain pastel colours, and from glazed material to textured cloths. With regard to patterns and especially if a patio is small, bold floral patterns may clash horribly with nearby plants and flowers, each distracting from the other. In such instances plain and striped materials might be a better choice in neutral colours.

Any metal work supporting soft furnishing in the form of steel spring, wires or straps will need to be regularly maintained and if necessary lightly oiled. This is necessary, because even if coated with an anti-corrosive film or paint, stretching and rubbing together in use might wear the coatings away, leaving unprotected surfaces.

Large items of furniture, for example swing hammocks, with cushions and padded backs are sometimes too big to be stored indoors and there will be no choice other than to leave them outdoors. Here, a flexible waterproof cover is a worthwhile investment. Again though, if it will be seen in conjunction with plants or flowers, indeed any other garden element perhaps for weeks on end, the choice of a colour or pattern which is neutral is recommended. It might otherwise make an unwanted focal point.

CHAPTER 10

Decorating the Patio

Focal Points

Focal points are in most cases chosen and positioned simply as objects of beauty, of interest or as conversation pieces. This is all very well but in many instances they are required to play more than just this single role. Their presence is an important and essential part of the patio garden's design, bringing either a sense of movement or terminating a view at a pre-determined point for example.

The same focal point is likely to be part of a carefully thought out scheme whereby the patio garden's designer has worked out a specific route that the visitor is encouraged to follow. In this instance the focal point or points are positioned at strategic places so that in being drawn to one, on arrival another hoves into view and so on.

Another reason to include a focal point is to act as a distraction or draw the eye away from some other object or element which may be unattractive – an ugly building for example. Lastly, focal points might be employed as the termination point of an axis or axes, or occasionally to mark where two lines of axes cross. The latter is an example of an 'intermediate' focal point or a place from where various patio elements appear to revolve or evolve.

Focal points can comprise of practically anything provided it has an appropriate foil to emphasize it. Most commonly it will be some object which is man-made.

This list is almost endless but objects which spring most readily to mind are statuary and vases. Other objects may be needed to perform a dual role, such as seats or other furniture, summer houses, gazebos, planters, sun dials, bird baths, etc. Seats make particularly useful focal points since they offer rest and repose on arrival – in a way a reward for making the journey. Summer houses, being very architectural, provide shelter or shade; planters of course host plants; sun dials tell the time; and bird baths attract birds. These are in this context, secondary but very important roles.

Focal points can be created from natural objects too. Weeping trees suggest tranquillity, whilst an upward thrusting conifer is in the nature of an exclamation mark, strongly commanding attention. Between these two extremes lie a vast host of tree shapes, one being appropriate for a particular set of circumstances. Some shrubs or plants are textured, coloured, or cut in such a way as to make excellent focal points.

Topiary has long been appreciated for its value in this respect. Here their clipped forms almost demand attention. Rocks or boulders arranged singly or in groups have also been used for centuries as eye catchers, sometimes in association with plants, or not where extreme simplicity is called for, as exemplified in some Japanese temple gardens.

No one could argue that water makes a most if not *the* most effective focal point. Seen in a completely natural setting, or in a formal setting, there is little else that is so attractive and eye catching. In a state of stillness its reflective properties are quite magical. When moving, what is lost in reflection is more than adequately compensated for by sound. In the smallest patio garden water can usually be incorporated if only as a simple wall-mounted fountain. Even so its impact will be significant.

Some focal points, can, perhaps strangely, lie outside the patio garden and in someone else's property. These are known as borrowed focal points. A distant view, 'windows' in a wall, or a wrought-iron gate, permitting a view beyond, will all be effective. Occasionally a borrowed focal point can be so eye catching and dramatic as to distract from the garden itself. When this happens little can be done except perhaps to arrest the eye momentarily with an intermediate focal point. Otherwise the best idea is to frame the borrowed focal point with perhaps some trees, so incorporating it into the general view.

As a rule, where more than one focal point is employed it is not a good idea to be able to see them together. This will lead to visual confusion, even confliction, with one point vying for attention with the other. That is not to say that a group of carefully selected and positioned objects will not work together as a composition. They can and do so very well, tables and chairs beneath a shady tree for example. Focal points then should be chosen not only for their particular and individual appearance but for their appropriateness to role and position. With the latter, scale is an important consideration. The objects must be of an appropriate size in the context of its setting. It is no use whatsoever if an object is so small as to be insignificant when viewed from the other end of the patio; and conversely, not so large as to dominate everything around it. This could result in making a small area appear even smaller. Style, material and colour too are important considerations.

An object selected, again without consideration to its proposed context, can result in the most awful confusion. The obvious example of the wrong style is the ubiquitous Greek statue placed in a garden of modern design where new and precisely shaped materials are used in the construction. Materials from which focal points are made also need to be in harmony with their surroundings, obviously the focal point needs to make a statement but it's all a question of degree.

Colour choice too is extremely important, and the colour of the chosen object – no doubt brought about by the material from which it was made – will visually succeed or not by virtue of the background. The background will act as a foil and so make the focal point stand out and be more visible. But even here harmony should prevail. We know that certain colours do not always go well together and this is as true when grouping focal points with background as with anything else. The greens of plants in a garden are accepted as being neutral in colour and consequently are very effective as background for most objects. The shade of green, however, should still be chosen with care in conjunction with the desired focal point. Good harmony of greens is exemplified by using patinated bronze against the dark green of yew; whilst a contrast of terracotta against shiny green beech leaves is stimulating. What is not good is where the background is making its own statement. Most varigated plants therefore are not usually suitable for this reason.

Contrasting textures are another matter for consideration, although it is true that this concept is a little obscure. Nevertheless a focal point chosen without reference to its own texture in comparison with the texture of the proposed background can bring disappointment. Here again direct contrasts do not always work, especially where one man-made object is placed against another – a very smooth and white classical statue, for example, against a very rough and rustic stone wall. Contrasts like this can sometimes be too great. The concept of contrasting textures must include shade lines; by this is meant the dominating patterns of shade caused by the sun or artificial light striking an object or feature. This results in the shadows appearing as predominantly vertical, horizontal or oblique lines. Sunshine striking a brick wall for example will create mainly horizontal shadow lines. A statue of a standing human figure has predominantly vertical shadow lines, as would a strictly fastigiate tree. It can be imagined then that an object having predominantly vertical shadow lines will be thrown into greatest contrast with a background having horizontal shadow lines. This phenomenon can work for or against, depending upon which effect is desired. Finely textured backgrounds such as brushed concrete walls or dense small-leaved evergreen shrubs are appropriate for most situations. However, any focal point forming part of a patio garden's structure should be strong enough visually to do so and be seen against an appropriate background. Any other adjacent features may be considered as decorations or furnishings, but should never actually compete with the focal point. To make an analogy, if the patio were a room, the plants, paving and walling materials, etc. are the carpets and wall paper. Each makes a unique contribution to the whole – yet never distracts from the focal point which in this context is the fireplace.

Sculpture

It must be said at once that the choice of

sculpture is a very personal thing: 'Beauty is in the eye of the beholder' is as true here as anywhere. Nevertheless principles of good design should prevail. The right choice will not only give pleasure on a visual and intellectual level but make a contribution to the whole. This way the 'clashes of culture' so often witnessed in patio and other gardens can be avoided. Immense care must be taken if various pieces of sculpture are used together, more especially so should these pieces derive from different ages and cultures. The problem can be exacerbated if other characteristics like colours or materials also differ. Rather than run such a risk, pieces of sculpture are best placed so that they may be appreciated individually. This might mean giving each its own space or back-drop, or be positioned away from the other, where they cannot be immediately compared.

Occasionally statuary or sculptures are arranged so as to be seen together, perhaps as a pair or even in rows. Yet it will be noted that on these occasions there is usually some harmonizing factor. They might all be of the same material or part of a theme – the seasons, for example. The style or atmosphere of a patio garden will best determine the nature of the sculpture or sculptures. Classical pieces do not always work well in modern settings where the style of that setting is obviously apparent, in other words where the sculpture cannot be visually separated from it. Curiously the reverse is not necessarily true. The most modern and abstract works can look at home in traditional settings, indeed in completely natural surroundings they really come into their own.

The types and styles of sculptures are very numerous indeed. The choice is perhaps too great, especially where imitations and reproductions are concerned, although this should not be interpreted as a criticism. The existence of reproductions means that beautiful (and not so beautiful) sculptures are available to all. Original works would of course be preferred but are often unaffordable.

Sculptures will be chosen on several bases, firstly appealing to the eye and to the intellect, although most people have a distinct and predetermined preference. The style of a sculpture will be a product of a culture or a fashion in its place in time. As most sculptural styles change dramatically over the years, the choice is vast and will continue to be. Within different cultures there were and are different 'schools' producing sculptures of greatly differing styles. Abstract sculptures appear to be more popular than ever but impressionistic and realistic pieces still account for the greatest number of sales. The material from which a piece is cast or made will be another basis of choice. Some might have a preference for bronze, others stone or one of the many available materials. The material of which the sculpture is made will also help to determine the style of a sculpture, depending on how practical it is to be moulded, cast or carved. Sculptural materials include stones, such as granite, portland and marble, each one of these requiring different tooling techniques.

By definition sculptures made from real stone are original. The quality of the stone must be of the very best, more especially so if the work is to be subjected to the elements. For this reason marble is not a suitable material for the patio garden within or near industrial areas, or where very low winter temperatures are experienced. This is also true of some other stones, like Bath or Cotswold stone for example. These are oolitic lime stones which are not impervious to water, making frost damage a real danger and like marble, likely to break down more quickly in polluted atmospheres.

Terracotta
A material often used for sculptures. The originals are moulded by hand, using special clay of flexible type. On completion the work is dried then fired in extremely hot ovens. A very skilled operation indeed from start to finish. Terracotta should always be checked for frost-proofness at the place of purchase, but by no means is it always. It would be upsetting indeed if an expensive terracotta sculpture shattered in the first hard frost, but terracotta brought home from warmer climates is often suspect in this regard.

Colours of terracotta sculptures vary from a light biscuit colour to the deepest red. This will depend on the source of the clay and the firing techniques. Occasionally terracotta will be glazed. This takes the form of a colour glaze or a clear glaze. Unique pieces may be commissioned, although generally a mould is made from an original to produce a number of replicas.

Concrete

Sometimes made respectable by calling it reconstituted stone. It probably accounts for the majority of garden statuary made today.

Unfortunately, in its new and raw state concrete does not have much appeal. It can take a considerable time to 'weather' and even then not entirely successfully. Concrete which has been cast in a wet state produces a smooth surface which does not encourage the growth of mosses or lichens. To make these items easier on the eye, they sometimes go through an 'antiquing', process, but unfortunately because of the obvious way it is usually done, it does little to improve the appearance. When concrete statuary has been made by the semi-dry method it is on the whole more successful as it looks like real stone. This is particularly so if the aggregates have been selected from the same source as the natural stone it is imitating. It is preferable to cast concrete in another way also, so that the finished surfaces are less smooth, especially where sand stone and lime stone aggregates are used. These 'weather' far more quickly. Concrete is rarely used as a sculpture medium in its raw state, that is, when it is not imitating something else.

Metals

Metals account for much of the material used for modern sculptural work, with bronze probably accounting for most because of its resistance to the elements, its good colour, patinated or anodized, its strength and malleability. Lead was used extensively in the past but less so now. This is no doubt due to its high cost and weight.

Copper left untreated takes on a coating of beautiful *verde gris* but does not have the strength or durability of bronze.

Cast iron is not much used today as moulding, and casting is very expensive and difficult. Its inflexibility can cause cracking and unless treated will rust steadily.

Wood

Wood is not often used for sculptures intended to remain permanently outside, especially in temperate climates, unless it is carved from very hard woods like oak. Even so, this will never have the durability of hard stone or metal. Preservatives can of course be applied and in some instances paint, but this would need to be applied on a regular basis.

Topiary Shapes in Containers

Plants have been used as living sculptures for possibly thousands of years. During the Middle Ages the use of topiary reached its peak. Clipping and cutting usually small-leaved evergreens into all manner of forms representing ships, birds, chess pieces, animals, even geometric shapes (cones, balls, cubes and so on), reached a high state of art. Latterly the clipping of topiary has generally been found to be too time-consuming for the busy garden owner and also takes too long to establish, yet clipped box balls and similar shapes still continue to be used to announce entrances, flights of steps, and so on.

Plants shaped into clipped balls or any other of the traditional shapes are still very popular as patio decorations when grown in pots. These can be moved about, make splendid winter features and add a degree of sophistication. The topiary shapes work best of course in a patio garden which is generally formal.

Whereas topiary results from clipping, some other plants have their stems and branches trained into fantastic shapes. Trained plants make most fascinating additions. Probably the most familiar are bay trees. These may be planted with more than one tree in a container, making it possible to ornamentally entwine their stems like ropes. Mature bay trees are usually imported from Holland, Belgium or Italy and are expensive.

Other Ornaments

Other ornaments include bird baths and sun dials. Birds baths attracting the local bird population will bring pleasure to birds and humans alike. What could be more decorative?

Other items of decoration are not only chosen for visual effect – some emit sound! Wind chimes for example: these most likely originated from the Far East, and what a delightful addition to any patio garden. Mostly

Concrete 'setts' (Blanc de Bierges), bricks and tiles harmonize well to bring warmth and light to this very tiny patio garden, whilst steps create interest (Robin Williams' design).

This curving brick
path disappears
intriguingly from
view, the steps denote
a change in level and
beg the question
'What lies beyond?'
The pergola frames
this beautiful picture.

Left:
'Mill Stone' fountains make attractive water features without the risks associated with pools – especially where the very young and the elderly are concerned.

Below:
Rustic furniture looks well in an appropriate setting. Here it links visually with the screen behind, but an alternative screen, yew for example, would show it off rather better.

Buff concrete pavers crisply define this formal pool
and act as effective 'stepping' stones too.

Reproduction furniture, here in a Victorian style,
brings elegance to this patio.

Focal points need a
good foil or
framework to work
well. This wall and
bust make an
excellent composite
focal point in this
very tiny patio
garden.

Nightlighting not only extends the useful life of a garden but dramatically affects its appearance in a most exciting way.

Using contrasting leaf
form, size, shape and
texture to create
interest in this cool
corner of the patio.

these are made from sections of hollowed wood or pieces of bamboo, each having a different musical pitch. Hung together, they gently tap each other in the breeze to produce sounds suggestive of wooden percussion instruments. Aerolian harps are also enjoying a revival and it would be possible to incorporate one of these. When the breezes blow they pass through the harp strings, to cause them to vibrate and emit sounds that can only be described as ethereal. The varying strength of the wind causes the harmonious notes to alter.

Not musical but nevertheless wind activated are patio 'toys'. These are sometimes home-made but may be purchased from garden centres. Tiny, brightly coloured men may be seen pedalling bicycles, chopping wood, turning grind stones, and all manner of activities at speeds according to the wind's strength. They do need to be fairly high from the ground, though, to catch the wind.

Planting Containers

Think of a rigid material and it is likely that there will be a container made from it. The material from which a container is made will also have a bearing on or even determine its design.

The planting of containers is discussed in detail in Chapters 12 and 13 (see page 157, but their mention in regard to arrangement and grouping is appropriate and important here. Shape, size and form of plant containers will depend entirely on the materials from which they are made and the method of manufacture or construction. What is important in this context is that they should be appropriate to the area in which they are placed. When built *in situ*, incorporation is not such a problem as they may be made in the style or material of surrounding architecture, boundary walls or fences. Where individual containers are chosen, however, there is a call for greater imagination, a thinking ahead as to how the container or containers will appear in the patio rather than in the garden centre with hundreds of others. A few measurements taken of the patio to estimate which sizes are best to fill or stand in a particular area will be very helpful. Try also to imagine the amount of additional space that will be taken up when the container

is full and overflowing with plants. Additionally, the choice of appropriate style, colour, material and so on, must be made.

It is better to ask yourself the questions and more importantly to get answers before going to the garden centre. This way you will get what is appropriate and what is in scale to your patio. Impulsive buying rarely works, although we all succumb to it occasionally. Contrasting styles or materials must be used together with extreme care. This is not to say it never works, just that it often does not.

Container grouping

Groups of containers, especially pots, look well particularly when arranged in odd numbers of three, five and so on. This is an old and well-tested theory, although slavish adherence to it may not be appropriate in all situations. There are occasionally times when an even number will look more pleasing. When used informally, varying sizes of the same style of pot can be really attractive, especially when stepping down in height with the taller ones at the rear. What the rear is, will of course, depend on the point from which the group will be viewed. Should the group be approachable from any direction, then the view which is more often taken (in other words, the main view), will determine their relative positions.

Such problems will not exist if the container group is situated against a wall, fence or, for that matter, any object not permitting a 'rear' approach or view. Using the same style of pot or container will bring a sense of continuity even when there is a different group of plants in each.

When the same plants are used in all the pots or planters of a particular grouping, the effect can be stunning. Containers and pots used and planted in this way does call for a degree of self discipline since most of us like to see as great a variety of plants as possible, especially if our patio is small. It must be stressed however that too many different plants in various containers and seen together will look confused and spotty, possibly making an area look smaller.

Pots and containers of individual design tend to be used more often in groups than those of the same style. This more often than not

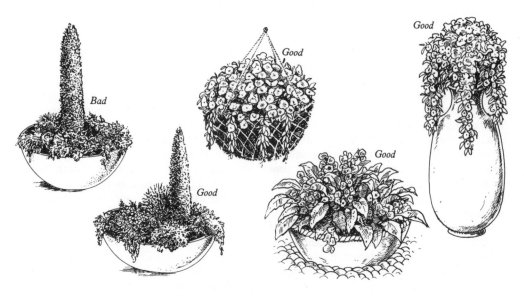

Fig. 10.1 Examples of plantings relative to their containers in terms of harmony.

results from separate purchases over perhaps many years. If a really attractive pot or container is seen, then naturally one wants to buy it as a work of art as much as an object in which to put a plant. In this way quite a collection can be built up but the problem is in arranging different styles, materials and colours harmoniously. In extreme cases the plants growing within them can solve the problem. For example, by choosing the same or similar plants for all of the pots or containers. Occasionally pots or containers are used without being planted and are placed to be admired for their individual beauty or interest. Indeed, in some instances planting may be a positive distraction. An example of a container often used as sculptural form is the terracotta jar or urn. Their original use was to hold olive oil or wine. Such jars incidentally make excellent focal points if of an appropriate size.

Where a container or pot is used for the purpose of planting up, the shape of the pot or container should be envisaged in terms of the whole, that is the overall appearance of container and plants together. In combination the two entities should be harmonious, pleasing and entire.

Examples of planting combinations relative to pot or container shapes are illustrated in Fig. 10.1. As a rule of thumb, the overall planting shape should reflect the shape of the container or pot, or at least be in balance with it. It is probably easier to give bad examples rather than good. A shallow dish shape should not have a vertical plant growing within it as its centre, such as a fastigiate conifer. Here the basic forms and associated shadow lines – horizontal and vertical – are opposite and therefore at variance. Similarly, a tall vase needs to have planting of a cascading nature. To continue the vertical line with a tall plant will produce a rather strange looking, rigid combination.

Containers which were originally intended for plants can often be adapted to make small water features and fountains. In the majority of cases these containers will not have been made impervious but rather the reverse, as they will have drainage holes in the base. Where individual planters are not waterproof the means of making them so will depend on the materials used in their manufacture. In the case of terracotta, this will mean blocking up the drainage holes with mastic then coating the interior with a proprietary brand of 'pond seal'; alternatively, an application of tar or bitumen. Porous concrete can also be sealed in this way. An interior which is black is by far the best colour, especially if the container is shallow. This will reflect the light from the water surface, making the water appear deeper. Large saucer shapes are best for small fountains to reduce any water loss caused by drifting water spray. Very tiny submersible pumps to operate a fountain are obtainable. Used in this way water can be delightfully introduced into a garden where no other opportunity may exist. See also pp. 110–118.

Window Boxes

Window boxes have a very strong unifying effect between the house architecture and the patio garden. This is particularly useful where the house architecture is informal. The unifying effect is heightened if all the planting within them is the same. Window boxes should, like other elements, be in keeping with the associated architecture of house and patio. What could be more incongruous than, for example, rustic bark clad window boxes beneath the windows of a beautifully proportioned Georgian house? The choice of plants for the window box should not ignore the style of the window box itself or the architecture with which it is associated. Rustic or informal situations call differently for the appropriate planting. Formal situations call for formal planting and this means making a positive statement in keeping with the 'strength' of the architecture. Here, plantings

of exactly the same plants or flower colour in every window box would achieve the greater effect.

The colour combination of both window boxes and the plants within them should blend with the associated walls for maximum effect. Window boxes are made in practically all the same materials as the other containers: timber, rigid plastic, fibre glass, terracotta and various metals. All should be frost proof and durable.

It is always best to fix a window box firmly by means of non-ferrous or stainless steel screws and wire, or a series of purpose-made brackets either to the window ledge or to the wall, whichever is appropriate, for reasons of safety. Even a small window box can, when filled with damp soil and plants, be considerably weighty. One falling from several floors up could result in dire consequences.

Window boxes will only succeed when used in conjunction with good horticultural practice. This means adequate drainage, fresh compost and the plants being regularly fed and watered. It is not unusual for plants in a window box to be a little crowded but since in the main they are used for seasonal planting displays, it does not present too much of a problem.

Types and Styles of Containers

As we know, when water freezes its volume increases and when composts or soils are saturated naturally the same thing happens

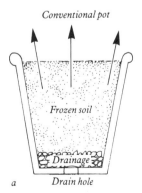

Conventional pot

Frozen soil

Drainage

a   Drain hole

Unsuitable pot

Waterlogged frozen soil

b   *Poor or no drainage*

Fig. 10.2 The effects of frost bound soil in planting containers. Besides being frost proof the shape of the pot or container itself is important. Shapes to avoid – especially if no proper drainage is incorporated – are pots or containers which are narrower at the top than at the bottom and which are filled with soil. (a) This shape allows the frozen soil (larger in volume) to move up. (b) This shape won't allow the frozen soil to move upwards – pressures are outwards and pot breaks.

(Fig. 10.2). If the pot or container is of a restricting shape and made from an inflexible material such as terracotta, upon freezing the pot will shatter as the soil or compost expands – the force is considerable. Besides this, other damage may occur to the container itself if it is not frost proof, and it may crack even when it is unfilled. It is always wise to check frost proofness at the point of purchase. If the origin of the pot or container is uncertain, or if it has been brought home from a place where frosts or very low temperatures are not experienced, do err on the side of caution and keep them indoors during the winter months.

Pots and containers left permanently outside gain some protection by being well drained, so ensuring the contents do not become waterlogged, then to become frozen. As an extra precaution, choose a shape that will allow the planting medium to expand on freezing – something which is internally smaller at the bottom than at the top and preferably with a smooth interior, allowing the upward movement of the contents as its volume increases. This is an important reason for using traditional clay pots as they have the perfect shape in this respect. Shapes similar to an oil jar, having a narrow neck, are not as suitable, particularly so if filled to the very top. It is essential that this type be very well drained or left entirely empty during the winter.

Materials used for containers

The plan made of the patio should ideally include both the intended container types and their positions. Containers will fall into two basic categories: those which are permanent or fixed, and those which can be moved about.

Fixed or permanent containers are either built or constructed *in situ* or are of such a size and weight that they may be considered permanent. Permanent container designs will take account of the surrounding architecture. Therefore if the house is of brick for example, then bricks of a similar type used to build the container will produce the most aesthetically pleasing result. The house or other nearby walls may, on the other hand, be 'rendered' or pebble-dashed, and here again a container of matching finish will be the best choice.

Bricks

The most popular material for permanent plant containers is brick. Bricks may be manufactured from clay, concrete or a sand lime mixture. Most are suitable but must be of an exterior quality.

Concrete bricks

The best quality concrete bricks have low absorption rates so do not normally require a damp proof course when used for building plant containers. They do not, as a general rule, look as good as their clay counterparts but are less expensive.

Sand/lime bricks

Where appropriate sand/lime may be used for building a plant container but only the very hardest quality. Even then they would need to be fully protected against frost by incorporating top and bottom dpc's and tanking within.

Concrete blocks and reconstituted stone

Concrete blocks or reconstituted stone, if good quality, will generally resist frosts.

Stone

Stone, like brick and reconstituted stone, can be used to build permanent containers, but must be of a durable type.

Timber

When used to make permanent containers, timber will need to be durable and of cross-sectional sizes that have adequate strength. The larger the container the greater the soil or compost pressures, especially when wet. The two main forms in which timber is used to make containers are either as boards or framed sheets. In board form, according to the design these might be positioned vertically, diagonally or horizontally with supporting rails at the rear. If positioned vertically, some form of timber 'coping' will be necessary to prevent rainwater from entering the exposed end grain which might otherwise cause rapid deterioration. Depending on the desired effect, boards may be finished 'sawn' (a textured finish) or 'planed' (a smooth finish) and treated with a preservative either before or after construction. If treated after construction it is sometimes difficult to be sure that all joints and corners are reached. Pre-treated timbers, available from most timber outlets, are the best option of all.

When using ply, this must be of an exterior quality and is commonly known as 'marine ply'. Remembering that it is likely to be almost constantly damp, in use, ply must be treated with preservative. Otherwise moisture will be able to penetrate fully what is after all a comparatively thin sheet. Ply thicknesses of 10 mm or 20 mm are the most appropriate but would need to be framed additionally with strong timbers, depending on the size of the container. Should the container be very long or wide, say 1 m (3¼ ft) in any direction, it might well call for an internal brace or braces passing through the planting medium from one side of the container to the other and by some means fixed to the sides or the framing. This ensures stability and reduces the risk of the sides bulging outwards from internal pressures. Ply can be rebated and stained to resemble boards, externally.

Old railway sleepers are sometimes still available and it is possible to construct plant containers from them. They can be fixed together either horizontally or vertically.

All permanent plant containers benefit from not having a base – in other words, the planting medium is in contact with the native soil, to which has been added some drainage material. There are circumstances where there is no native soil beneath, indeed the whole area may have been previously paved or concreted over. This is of course where raised permanent containers come into their own, providing the opportunity for bold planting, but would need a drainage layer beneath the planting medium. A sheet of geo-textile matting (e.g. Terram or Biddim) is useful laid over the drainage medium, allowing only water to pass through but not fine soil particles. These would otherwise block up the drainage layer over a period of time or at least make it less efficient.

Even when a container is made from pre-treated timbers its life can be extended further if the interior of the container is made more or less water-proof. This can be achieved in several ways: by lining out the interior with heavy duty polythene, coating the interior with bitumastic paint or by lining it with fibre-glass. In all cases good drainage will still be necessary.

Movable Containers and Planters

Timber

Containers which are made simply by joining the timber together with nails, should be avoided; Screws and joints are best. Check too the quality of the wood and that it has been adequately treated with preservative, especially on the inside where damp soil or compost will be in contact with it. Lastly look to see if it has drainage holes and are the insides of the holes treated with preservative? A choice can be made from a great many styles, from a sophisticated Versailles planter, complete with boarded panels, moulded framing and ball finial feet, to a rude framing to which has been nailed slices of tree bark. Half barrels are very popular and an excellent example of recycling, although the suspicion is that they are now made specifically to hold plants. As with their permanent counterparts the same principles apply. It is a good idea to inspect carefully any timber container at the point of purchase to ensure it is strongly made with good joints, or well fixed with non-rusting screws.

Terracotta pots and containers

Terracotta probably accounts for the largest proportion of the total numbers of containers sold. The reason being that terracotta is perhaps the best material of all. It feels good and the colours ranging from biscuit to deep red seem at home in any position, indoors or out. It 'breathes' since it is porous, so moderating the soil temperatures within. At the same time terracotta absorbs water then gradually releases it, initiating a more even moisture distribution over a longer period. There are a few plants however that do not benefit from growing in terracotta pots. This is when efflorescence (various salts and trace elements in or added to the soil) build up on the pots interior to such concentration as to become harmful, and this is especially true of old pots. Some plants such as azaleas for example can actually benefit from this situation, providing the planting medium is 'acid' which converts the efflorescence salts into a soluble form, making it then available to the plants.

Terracotta pots are either moulded by hand or machine, producing a range of styles from the simplest to the highly decorative. Sizes vary from the literally minute (approximately 25 mm/1 in) to giants of 1 m ($3\frac{1}{4}$ ft) or more. Heights vary too but not necessarily in proportion to the diameter. A terracotta pot will therefore be available somewhere to meet any need, visual and functional.

Antique terracotta vases can be obtained but these are extremely expensive.

Terracotta is sometimes glazed internally, which extends sometimes over the lip. Others are glazed both inside and outside in various colours.

Metal containers

Metals are not used so frequently to make planters as they once were. This is probably due to the high cost of materials and manufacturing processes. As with terracotta, old metal containers, vases and planters command very high prices indeed. Historically cast iron, bronze and lead were the most popular metals for containers but these are not mainly replicated by other metallic materials. Even so modern bronze, brass and copper containers are still occasionally used outdoors. Depending upon the desired appearance metals may be anodized or coated in some way to prevent tarnish or alternatively deliberately left to tarnish.

Tarnished bronze and copper both look extremely attractive in their bright green livery. One word of warning though – most plants, if not all, find any copper salts poisonous and 'green' stems leaves and roots in direct contact with copper could prove fatal to the whole plant.

In a garden setting plain aluminium is not visually acceptable to most people and is normally disguised to look like some other metal. Metal containers tend to be heavy anyway and become even more so when filled with soil and plants. This may be a contributing factor to a lack of popularity when compared with containers made from other materials.

Concrete (reconstructed stone) containers

Concrete planters and pots may be seen just about everywhere. Their quality varies from excellent to very poor indeed. In its pure form, concrete, as far as container-making is con-

cerned, is shunned by most people. Given some imaginative exterior treatment however, concrete containers can be made to be very attractive.

Glass-reinforced cement (GRC)

Glass-reinforced cement is used to provide, in the main, modern looking planters, cuboid, cylindrical and many other simple forms.

Glass-reinforced plastic/rigid plastic containers (GRP)

These are a fairly recent introduction. To begin with no one could argue they were attractive but latterly, by using new techniques, they have become far more acceptable. Here again GRP materials are normally employed to imitate just about all the other container materials, even stone.

Container watering (irrigation)

The amount of water needing to be applied to a container will depend upon four things:

1. The number, type and size of plants growing within a container, relative to its size.
2. The nature of the planting medium.
3. The position the container occupies.
4. The ambient temperature.

To take the first instance, if small annuals are growing in a large volume of container compost or soil then the uptake of water will be far, far less than the same volume supporting shrubs or perennials. Additionally, some plants demand much more moisture than others, in accordance with their original and natural habitat. Impatiens (buzy lizzy) or azaleas require a higher moisture content in the compost than would aubrieta or an evergreen euonymus for example. For this reason it will pay to research individually the groups of plants if the first intention is to plant them together in a single container. Their moisture requirements could be significantly different, so making their watering quite a problem. An alternative planting scheme may then have to be drawn up with plants of a compatible watering need planted together.

Ultimate plant sizes must also be taken into account as overplanting can easily take place, bringing its own problems. On the other hand a slight overplanting of annuals is generally accepted, as their life is short. It is the permanent subjects which need careful consideration. Not only is the choice of the planting medium in terms of nutrients, minerals and pH important but so is its structure. When it comes to working out a watering programme some plants insist on growing in a freely draining compost, others prefer one that it is retentive. Open and sandy are examples of freely draining soils, whilst clayey soils are not. Where larger containers are filled with the local soil, this may cause problems in one direction or another unless the soil type can be established and the watering system adjusted accordingly. Fortunately the drainability of most soil types can be adjusted to suit. If too freely draining, by adding very fine humus. Coarse humus may exacerbate the problem by making it even more freely draining! With poorly drained clay soils the well known treatment of adding lime and coarse organic material works well. Should you intend to grow ericaceous or other lime-hating plants then this treatment is not advised. Instead it might mean completely filling the container with a lime-free compost. The nature of the soil or compost then, will have a direct bearing on the degree to which it is watered. This will need to be ascertained over a period of time to get the water application just right. A calibrated moisture recorder can be very useful in this respect and fortunately is not expensive.

The position of the container is another factor in the watering equation. Quite obviously if it is in a position where hot sun shines all day then much of the moisture in the container will be lost through evaporation. Under such circumstances the plants will naturally be making extra demands too, so in combination the drying out process will be greatly accelerated. Constant watering will be essential in summer, meaning at least once a day.

In open situations, where wind is a problem, the amount of evaporation will increase. Similarly affected are patio gardens near the sea and in town where surrounding high buildings may cause wind funnelling. In summer either the ambient temperature or direct sunlight will heat up a container and its entire contents, including soil and plant roots. In winter this will be reversed and in very low temperatures might result in the whole being turned into a block of ice. Neither situation is good for the plants which would otherwise be growing naturally in soil at ground level without perhaps such extreme temperature fluctuations. In conclusion then, in summer copious watering, and in winter probably none at all since most plants growing in containers hate to be cold and wet at the same time.

Manual watering

Of the three basic methods for container watering, the first to be considered is the use of a watering can. Unfortunately this method can be a bit hit and miss in terms of amount and timing. Another problem also arises where there are a large number of containers, making the operation both inconvenient and time consuming. Apart from this, there is the question of where and when to use the watering can and should it be used with or without the rose attached. Some plants, like fine leaved acers, resent very much having their leaves made wet when the sun is shining and will respond by curling up and turning brown, whilst other plants do not mind their leaves becoming wet. A mixed planting will restrict watering to late evening and night times only, which may not be convenient to the owner.

Watering cans are available in a vast range of shapes and sizes, but not all have capacity indicators, an important feature if watering is to be carried out scientifically. Watering cans are sometimes decorative to the point of being ornaments. Others are basic and functional. According to the specific job in hand they will have short or curved spouts, whilst others have very long spouts for watering hanging baskets and the like – although the latter may not be of the conventional shape – perhaps more like a bottle on a pole. Some have only coarse roses others fine, or adjustable. In some instances the rose is removed altogether to direct water to the plant roots. For example, the previously mentioned fine-leaved acer could be watered in this way, so keeping the leaves dry.

Some watering cans are in essence hand-operated pumps with a reservoir designed to produce a spray or jet of water. Attached to a pole and hose this type best answers the watering problem of high window boxes and hanging baskets.

Plastic watering cans have now more or less replaced metal, because they are lighter and less expensive. Where appearance is considered to be as important as function, brass, copper and ceramic watering cans are available.

Self-watering systems
Self-watering containers are extremely convenient, but generally have to be made for the purpose. This somewhat limits the choice in terms of shape and style. It is possible to adapt some other vessel to become self watering but it will require a degree of ingenuity. In basic terms a self-watering container comprises an outer shell, which acts as a reservoir within which is suspended a second compost filled vessel (rather like a porringer). The compost in the vessel is thereby kept separate except for a linking wick. As the plants take up water from the compost or as evaporation takes place, water is drawn from the reservoir into the compost via the wick and at a naturally controlled rate. This means that the plants are never either over- or under-watered as long as the reservoir is regularly replenished. A visual indicator is normally incorporated to ascertain when more water is needed.

Watering trays and saucers
Standing any container (providing it has drain holes at the base) in a water-filled saucer or tray will supply water at a more or less controlled rate as it is taken in at the bottom and distributed by means of capillary action to the root areas. The amount of water must be carefully controlled, as overwatering can result, especially when water retentive composts are used in the container.

Positioning of Containers
The positioning of containers on the patio depends on a wide range of considerations. The first group of considerations are based on practical problems for the users of the patio, where the containers should be located in places where they do not obstruct a main route through the garden, or can be used to divert people to other areas. The second group of considerations are aesthetic ones, the use of containers as an integral part of the design of the patio. The third group of considerations relate to the wellbeing of the plants in the containers, and how the position affects the choice of plants.

Positioning in relation to patio use
It is important that containers on the patio are positioned in such a way that they can be enjoyed without obstructing the use of the patio, or being dangerous. Containers in well trafficked areas should be well balanced and stable, with plants that maintain the physical stability and balance of the container, and do not prickle or catch on clothing. The rim of the containers should be smooth, and at such a height that grazed shins are not a problem. Containers should never obstruct a pathway, or create a hazard to people passing by.

Containers can be strategically located on the patio so that they intentionally compel the users of the area to walk around them, or draw towards them. In this simple way, attention can be taken away from a patio level window, or a little privacy can be given to certain rooms in the house.

In a similar manner, window boxes should never stick out so far that they become a danger, with sharp corners catching clothing or prickly plants scratching the unsuspecting individual. Street facing window boxes should not stick out so far that pedestrians are forced to walk in the road, and window boxes of all sorts should always be very securely fixed, remembering that a fully planted and watered window box is very heavy when cantilevered out from a building.

Hanging baskets should be hung above head height, or in a position away from busy areas, and again they should not contain prickly plants. The use of special fittings to enable the baskets to be raised and lowered for watering and tending is of great advantage for baskets hung in busy and awkward places.

Positioning in relation to the design of the patio
The design of the patio can depend on the use of containers to make it work, with special

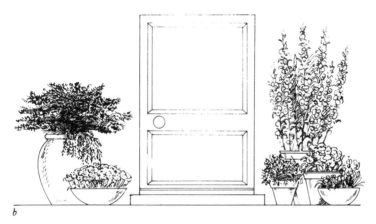

Fig. 10.3
Positioning of containers.
(*a*) Group of containers flanking a flight of steps.
(*b*) Group of containers beside a doorway.

features enhanced by the use of containers, or containers themselves becoming the focal points. Topiary can be well used in this situation, with a well tailored evergreen plant as the focal point within a garden of bright flowers. A false entrance can be made to look very real by hanging baskets either side of the doorway, and maybe placing a large container to one side.

Certain features of the patio can be given emphasis by the use of containers, such as placing an upright specimen plant either side of a flight of steps, or a group of containers at the side of a doorway (Fig. 10.3).

Positioning in relation to the plants
When positioning containers on the patio, it is very important to take into consideration the effects of the elements on the plants and the containers, how the sun, shade, wind, and aspect affects them, and how a group of plants benefit from the microclimate created by their grouping.

Sun and shade
These affect the choice of plants to grow in the containers, how much care they need, how vulnerable they are to drying out.

Containers located in full sun will tend to dry out very fast, and will need to be watered at least twice each day in sunny weather. In winter they will still need regular watering, and will be more prone to the drying effects of wind. These containers will also be vulnerable to overheating, when the moist soil in the containers becomes very hot and 'steams' the plants living in the containers. Containers made of a dark coloured material, such as terracotta, will absorb the sunlight and make the problems seem worse.

Containers located in the shade will have different problems and advantages. In hot weather they will not dry out so fast, the plants will not be under such stress from bright sunlight, overheating and the need for frequent watering. In cool weather and in winter, the plants will grow noticeably slower as the soil will take longer to warm up, and will not achieve such high temperatures. If they become frozen, containers located in shade will take longer to thaw out, which can be an advantage for the plants.

Suitably chosen, many plants will thrive in a container in a shady spot without becoming too drawn and leggy. The containers can be turned round at regular intervals to avoid this happening, but with the right choice of plant, it should not always be necessary. Sometimes a shady position is also a very sheltered position, and gives the opportunity to grow a tender plant that it would not normally be possible to grow.

Some plants thrive in full sun, revelling in the extremely hot conditions that it creates for container grown plants, and put on their finest show under these conditions. Other plants dislike full sun intensely, and their performance will be poor, yet the same plants will often thrive in shady positions. When choosing plants for containers, the position in relation to sun and shade is an important consideration, to ensure that the right plants are chosen.

Wind

Wind is another important consideration when positioning containers. Sometimes a position appears to be ideal from many aspects, but only when a container is placed in that position does a problem with wind become evident. Testing a position with a child's paper windmill can save a lot of problems with moving heavy containers full of plants at a later date. A draughty spot will cause windburn and scorching to the plants, making them unhappy although all the other conditions may appear ideal. Wind will also increase the effects of frost and cold, making the effects of a light frost much more serious.

Some plants are quite happy in a draughty spot, and will flourish without complaint. Many other plants will resent wind in any form and grow stunted and misshapen. The problems of wind can be reduced by suitable screening, either with a commercial netting which is usually obtrusive and ugly, or by planting to break the wind. In a new garden it may be necessary to use a combination of the two methods, using netting until the permanent shelter planting has established. The only other answer to a serious wind problem is to remove containers from any draughty position.

Aspect

This is the relation of the container to the points of the compass, and is the indication as to what weather conditions the plants can expect. Containers in an east-facing position will get the early morning sun and very little sun after noon. This aspect can be very damaging for plants such as *Camellia spp*, where early morning sun following a frost will seriously damage any flowers and flower buds. An east-facing aspect is also a poor choice where plants are prone to windburn, such as *Mahonia* × 'Charity', as easterly winds tend to be cold and biting, and cause a great deal of damage.

A north-facing aspect is greatly appreciated by some plants, where the lack of direct sunlight is no problem and the cold winter winds are appreciated as the forerunner to spring. The climbing hydrangea, *Hydrangea petiolaris* enjoys both a north and an east aspect and resents a coveted south facing position. Many clematis, often thought of as plants for a sunny position, enjoy a north aspect. Many roses also flourish in this position. Both *Garrya elliptica*, with its showy catkins in winter, and *Pyracantha coccinea*, with its white spring blossom and red berries will brighten a north facing aspect.

Both the south- and west-facing positions receive somewhat more gentle weather conditions. These aspects tend to be damper but warmer, catching the prevailing south westerly winds in most parts of the country. Because these aspects catch more sun, containers located in these positions will tend to dry out faster, and occasionally to overheat. The plants will be more prone to battering by wet winds, but also will receive more rain. Many plants will enjoy the warmer location of the south and west aspects, and it will be possible to grow many slightly more tender plants in a south-facing position.

Grouping of containers to create microclimates

Within a plant community, the climatic variations can be considerable, even within a small community such as a group of containers full of plants. Differences will exist in light penetration, temperature, humidity and wind effects that will be of importance to the plants growing in the containers. The sizes of the plants will also have an effect, as that will determine how much of the heat of the sun actually reaches the soil in the container, and so limit how warm it becomes.

Within a plant community of a group of containers, the outer plants will take the full force of the weather conditions, sheltering and protecting those plants towards the centre of the group. The taller plants will receive much of the sunlight, sheltering and shading the smaller plants beneath their leaf canopy. The humidity will be greater towards the centre of the group, and this can benefit the plants, or cause a problem with mildew under the right weather conditions.

Most important of all, a group of plants, whether or not in containers, creates a small community. They share each other's company as well as microclimate, and can support each other by growing close and intermeshing. If the principles of companion planting are followed, then within a group of plants there can be ones chosen for their ability to control certain pests, and this can reinforce the benefits of the community. Like with any community, if it is broken up, possibly with the removal of the plant containers, then the members will miss each other's company as well as the benefits of the microclimate created by the community, and will possibly not grow so well for some time as they adjust to the new physical and social conditions.

Children in the Patio Garden

Children often like to have a part of the patio garden for their own. Maybe a grassy area could be made exclusively for play, perhaps near or amongst some shrubs, creating a secret place for a little tent or a Wendy house. A very popular addition would of course be a swing. For younger children (provided they are in sight of the house) a small paddling pool and sand pit will bring hours of pleasure.

Undoubtedly, the swing is a very popular feature with most children and will get a great deal of use. Its frame must be firmly fixed into the ground, so that it is not in danger of toppling over. If it has ropes, as opposed to chains, these should be inspected regularly for signs of fraying or rotting. If there is a shortage of space, the swing can be attached to the pergola and be included as almost a decorative feature within the patio garden, provided it can be hooked up out of the way when not in use.

If a sand pit is to be a permanent feature it is best sunk into the ground. This will facilitate the sand being easily swept back into it when the children have finished their play. The bottom of the sand pit should be filled with rubble, for drainage, then covered with a fairly deep layer of sand. A wooden or net cover is essential to keep cats and dogs out. Even so the sand should be changed regularly. When the children have outgrown the sand pit, it can then be incorporated into the general garden plan by conversion into an ornamental pool or flower bed.

The type of grass chosen in the area intended for children's play, should be of a tough variety – a dwarf rye grass, for example – or it will wear away very quickly.

A paddling pool purchased from a toy shop will be made of plastic in either a rigid or inflatable form. These types are probably the most convenient, since they may easily be kept clean and stored out of sight when not in use. If a permanent paddling pool is installed it should be very shallow indeed, for safety's sake. The construction will be similar to one of the rigid types described under the section dealing with patio pools.

One of the advantages of reserving specific parts of the garden for the children is that they are less likely to trample the flower beds or meddle with the vegetable patch. Apart from the features mentioned previously, to facilitate play, it is well known that many children are keen to grow their own flowers and vegetables. With this in mind, perhaps a small patch of soil could be set aside to encourage this interest.

139

PART VI

PLANTING THE PATIO AND CONTAINER GARDEN

CHAPTER 11
Planting Design

Design Theory

Now that the variations of size, shape and material of the patio, and size, shape and material of containers, and the choice of plants have been considered, it is time to look in closer detail at those design principles which remain constant, although their application may change dramatically.

Unity

Unity is achieved by limitation of materials and by strength of purpose to express one over-ruling idea through the garden, resulting in a coherent style.

Within the very restricted space of a patio, it is essential that every element in the garden forms part of the scheme. Generally the site imposes a unifying influence on the garden, the basic landform uniting it with the surrounding countryside, but a patio is often visually far removed from the influence of the land and must have its own distinct style.

Unity is often achieved by the repetition of some design element both in terms of planting and the partio 'hardware'. The use, say, of round-shaped containers on a circular patio with a circular pond and a curved seat following the lines of the paving will give a positive theme of round shapes and unify the whole garden scheme. The circular theme could then be continued into any grassed areas, and into the shapes of any borders, letting the eye and the brain subconsciously appreciate the homogeneity of the design (Fig. 11.1).

The design of the patio may be imposed by a dominant feature to which all the other elements are subordinate. This may be a view out or through the garden, when the design of the patio and the use of containers is used to frame and enhance the view, but not so that the detail of the patio detracts and distracts from the dominant feature. The dominant feature may be a building or part of a building, where the style and shapes should be echoed in the style and shapes used in the patio and

containers. The repetition of shapes in both the vertical and horizontal planes is a very simple and satisfying way of unifying the area without it feeling at all contrived, and the subsequent planting can be designed to enhance the theme (Fig. 11.2).

In a small inward-looking garden, the main interest must be supplied from within its own boundaries. A good specimen tree or unusual piece of sculpture can form the focal point around which the design revolves. The peace and restfulness created by a unified design is essential in a small restricted area such as a patio, and is especially important if the garden consists of little more than a sitting area and the surrounding plants.

Patio gardens are often designed around a central open space, where the garden has the function of an outdoor room that needs as much sun as possible. In such a restricted area, a garden that does not have a unifying theme will become just a collection of plants and containers around a bit of paving, looking as though no thought has been given to it.

Scale

Scale and proportion are both attributes of unity, for without them there can be no harmony of design. Within the landscape, the scale is defined by the expanse of sky and horizon, but within the patio garden, the scale is defined by the boundaries of this lesser space. Despite this more restricted space, a more generous scale is needed than within a building, for the garden is a place of leisure, expansion and release.

Within the garden, everything must relate to the human proportions. The parts should either fit together to make one indivisible whole, or one element should dominate over all the others. The relationships between all the parts of the garden relate to the human users of the garden and must allow for freedom of movement and comfort. It is better that a

Fig. 11.1 Diagram showing unity using circles.

Fig. 11.2 Diagram showing unity using the horizon as a dominant feature.

Fig. 11.3 Diagram to show the importance of correct scale in the use of containers.

few substantial-sized containers are used on the patio than a whole mass of small pots, which will not only look messy, but will also be difficult to maintain. The collection of small pots will be much more appropriate at the foot of the greenhouse, where the scale of the building relates better to the scale of the pots (Fig. 11.3).

Planting scale can be used to create a *trompe l'oeil*, and in the right place, this can be very effective on a patio to give a feeling of increased spaciousness. If used badly, it can create more problems than it solves, and become a nasty mess and visual jumble. The subtle use of a mirror in a small enclosed area of a patio garden can also change the scale and give a feeling of openness.

False perspective is again the manipulation in the use of scale in the garden. It is of little use in the restricted area of the patio, as the scale of the area is too small for the true perspective to be evident, and the imposition of a false perspective only muddles the senses.

Division of space

The patio and its surrounding area is usually considered as one space, but both plants and planted containers can be used to subdivide this space to good effect. The space need not be divided with a solid barrier, but a group of

pots, or a large plant leaning softly across the paving can give the feeling of partly dividing the area into spaces with different uses. Containers can also be used to delineate a division of space by creating a narrow point or passageway leading into another area (Fig. 11.4). Placing a matching pair of pots at the top or bottom of a set of steps states very clearly that a different part of the garden is being entered, and so gives the opportunity to introduce a different style of garden.

Division of space is necessary to retain the human scale of the patio area, to make the space an area in which one can relax comfortably.

Light and shade

The use of light and shade is also about division of space, the relationship of mass to open area, and the use of rhythm and repetition in volumes. Light and shade gives us contrast, the shaded sitting area with the light open area, the rose bower to the open patio. The contrast of light and shade gives interest to the spaces and an understanding of their content, and a pleasure in looking or passing from one to the other.

The same plants in a shady area will appear different in a sunlit area, for the light plays differently on their leaves and flowers, shining

Fig. 11.4 The use of containers to divide and delineate space.

through their winter coloured twigs and creating ever changing patterns. The growth habits of the plants will be different in light and shade, and so will be the overall effect of the plants.

Rhythm and repetition

Even in a small area such as a patio, rhythm and repetition are an essential ingredient of the unity within the space. The repetition of a design feature, the echoing of a shape both in the paving and the walling, gives an integrity and homogeneity not achieved in other ways. The repetition of a plant or group of plants gives a continuity within the garden when other things alter. Whether on a small or large scale, the repetition of a design element or a particular plant or tree helps create a continuity throughout the area.

Tone and texture

Textural variations are important in the choice and use of materials within the garden. Different textures can be used to achieve certain effects and moods, and can add or detract from the overall harmony of the garden. The careful use of texture is a technique particularly suited to small intimate areas, where all the elements of the design are seen at close quarters.

Tone is an important consideration in the use of colour in the garden. Other than in a garden too small to have a lawn, all colours used in a garden relate to the green of the grass. The colours themselves are muted and softened by the grey of the English skies and the mellow tones of stonework and brickwork. The colours used in the planting need also to be mellow to maintain the harmony within the design. In the bright sunlight of a Mediterranean or Californian sun, the soft colours appropriate to the English climate look faded and washed out. Strong bright colours reflect back the strong sunlight, and compete well with the contrasts of the bright skies and the harsher modelling of the surfaces. Conversely, the strong bright colours that look so right in the gardens of France and Italy look brash and vulgar in our English gardens, and can only be used with great care and the skill of a trained artist.

Simplicity

Within a small area such as a patio and its surroundings, as within a larger area, the aim should be for simplicity of style and intent in planting. It requires a certain boldness to reduce the number of elements in a garden, whether it is the number of different paving materials, or the number of different plants, but too many different elements will create a restless 'busy' atmosphere.

A patio area, whether used for entertaining and play, or as a retreat for sitting and unwinding from the day, is too small an area to clutter up with a myriad of different shapes, colours, tones and textures. The choice of containers should echo the shapes and materials of the patio, and their content should add, not detract, from the overall effect. Containers should be bold without being excessive, and a few well placed pots will have a much greater impact than a large number of small pots.

The planting of the patio should be as simple as possible, as any extra fillip can be given to the planting by altering the contents of the containers. Planting around the patio should set off and enhance the area, and not aim to be dominant in its own right. Only in this way can one create the atmosphere of gentleness and peacefulness found only in simplicity.

Focal points

Plants as focal points are just as important in the restricted area of a patio as they are in the expanses of a large garden. Without a focal point, a patio becomes just an open space without meaning. A focal point does not need to be anything complicated. A single simple pot correctly located, or a specimen tree or shrub will give a focus to the views through the patio. A focal point is needed to feature when looking onto the patio from the house or adjacent building, or when entering the area of the garden containing the patio. For the patio itself does not need to be next to a house or other building; it can be located in another part of the garden and still perform its function of providing an outdoor living space.

Contrast

Contrast is fundamental to all things, including garden design. Light and shade, sunlight and gloom, control and bedlam, the yin-yang complement is almost an intuitive ingredient that is recognizable immediately.

The use of contrast in the planting of the patio and containers adds interest and variety to the area. Contrasting the shape and colour of the foliage of a group of plants is a simple way of maintaining the interest of the planting long

after the flowers are gone over. In a similar manner, the colour of the plant flowers can be contrasted, or the shape and habit of the plants, or the winter colours of their twigs.

Care must be taken not to contrast too many of the attributes of the plants at any one time, otherwise the whole area of planting will become fussy, appearing restless and cluttered. It is best to maintain the harmony within a group of plants and contrast only one feature at a time, whether it is the leaf shape, or colour of flowers, or just the scale of the plants.

Style

The particular style of the patio and surrounding garden is immaterial. No one particular style is any better or worse than any other – it is all a matter of personal preference, and appropriateness to the site. A patio and surrounding area in a modern freeform style will look out of place outside a Georgian-style conservatory, as none of the principles of unity will have been adhered to. Conversely, a very formal and classical style patio (terrace) would be unsuitable for some small modern semi-detached house on a large housing estate.

Within these constraints, the style of patio depends on the requirements for its use, its location, and also on the available budget when constructed. The important thing is to maintain the unity of style throughout the whole of that area of the garden, keeping it spacious and simple.

Plant Attributes

Habit

The habit of a plant is the characteristic shape or form that it makes as it grows and matures. A plant may, for instance, have a weeping habit, like certain willows, but the distinctive form may not be apparent until the plant reaches a certain age or maturity. Generally, the habit of the plant is evident from an early age, and is a distinctive characteristic that influences its location and choice of companions in any planting scheme (Figs. 11.5–11.7).

Foliage texture – visual

Foliage texture is the effect created by the foliage of a plant. The texture may be soft, as

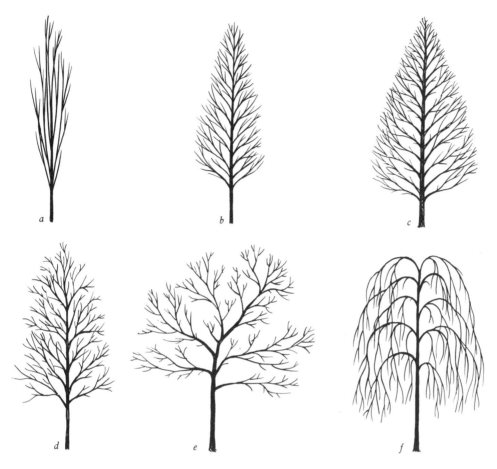

with many soft-leaved plants like *Stachys lanata* (lamb's ears) and *Salvia officinalis* (sage), or it may be hard, as with many hard leafed plants such as roses and most cotoneasters. The affect that the plant has in a planting scheme depends on the foliage texture as well as the colour; small dark reflective leaves such as those of *Ilex* spp (holly) will make the plant appear closer than the small dull leaves of *Philadelphus*. Large shiny leaves seem the closest of all, and so not to muddle the design visually, it is best to plant such plants, for instance, *Bergenia cordifolia*, near to the observer.

The effects of plant foliage texture can be utilized in the patio to give the area a feel of spaciousness. By planting larger leafed plants in the foreground and smaller leafed plants further away, shiny leaves close and dull leaves in the background, an air of comfort and space can be achieved without the viewer being aware that it has been done intentionally.

The use of a large number of large leafed and architectural plants can give an impression of exuberance and lushness, almost of domesticated jungle. This sort of effect must be used with care otherwise it becomes overpowering and the plants appear to dominate the patio area without leaving any space for people.

Foliage texture – tactile

Sight is not the only sense used when enjoying a garden; hearing, smell, touch and occasionally taste are all important ways of experiencing plants. Foliage texture should be felt as well as seen. The tactile properties of foliage

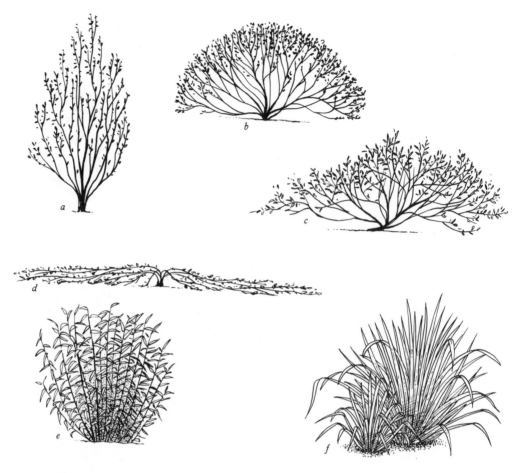

Fig. 11.6 Shrubs.

(a) Upright *Berberis thunbergii 'Erecta'*

(b) Rounded *Hebe rakaiensis*

(c) Spreading *Viburnum plicatum 'Lanarth'*

(d) Prostrate *Ceanothus thyrsiflorus repens*

(e) Grasslike *Arundinaria viridistriata*

(f) Archtectural *Phormium tenax.*

texture are a very important factor to consider when planning the planting for tubs, pots and other containers. Containers are raised up and the plants are generally at finger height, easily available to touch and appreciate. The soft velvet of *Stachys lanata* contrasts with the leather-rough texture of *Mahonia aquifolium* 'Smaragd', the prickly smoothness of holly with the warm lacework of *Tanacetum densum*, and the small leafed texture of *Thymus serpyllum* contrasts with the fleshiness of *Sedum spurium*.

Plants for patios and containers should be chosen particularly for their tactile properties, as touch is something that we all appreciate,

but rarely admit to enjoying, and so seldom design gardens with touch in mind.

Some examples of tactile plants:

Artemesia spp
Eucalyptus gunnii
Ilex aquifolium 'Ferox Argentea'
Lavandula spica
Mahonia aquifolium 'Smaragd'
Myrrhis odorata
Myrtus communis
Rhus typhina
Sedum spp
Stachys lanata
Tanacetum densum
Thymus serpyllum

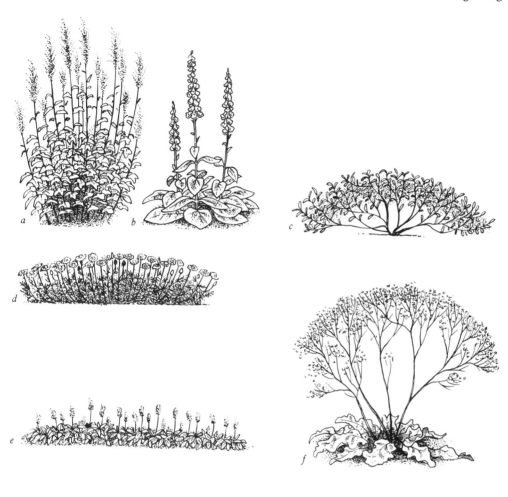

Fig. 11.7 Perennials.

(a) Tall upright *Macleyea cordata*
(b) Small upright *Digitalis mertonensis*
(c) Bushy *Ballota pseudodictamnus*

(d) Spreading *Anthemis cupaniana*
(e) Prostrate *Lamium maculatum*
(f) Architectural *Crambe cordifolia.*

Foliage smell

Hand in hand with foliage texture goes foliage smell as another plant quality to consider when planning any planting. Each time a plant is touched, whether deliberately or unintentionally, its surface is disturbed and smells are released. Some plant foliage smells are similar to the flower smell, some are different but complementary, and some a total contrast. Some foliage smells are pleasant, some a positive feature in themselves, such as the smell of the Mexican orange blossom, *Choisya ternata.*

Some smells are very pungent, almost medicinal and definitely culinary, such as the smell of the leaves of herbs like thyme, sage and marjoram. Many herbs contain the volatile oils used in medicines, such as thymol in thyme, and it is these oils that make the foliage of herbs so pungent.

Herbs often release their smells at the slightest disturbance, a light brush with the hand or a mere breath of wind on a warm balmy night can be sufficient to set free those images of long Mediterranean evenings and happy holidays past.

Some examples of plants with fragrant foliage:

Artemesia spp
Choisya ternata
Eucalyptus gunnii
Lavandula spica
Myrrhis odorata
Myrtus communis
Salvia officinalis
Thymus serpyllum

Foliage colour

Foliage colour varies through every shade and tint of green, from the yellow greens of *Robinia pseudoacacia* 'Frisia', the fresh new green of emerging beech leaves, through the blue greens of *Euphorbia wulfenii* and the prostrate juniper, *Juniperus* 'Blue Carpet'. At one end of the spectrum of greens are the distinctly blue foliage plants blending into the greys of *Salvia officinalis* (sage) and *Ruta graveolens* (rue), *Lavandula spica* (lavender) and *Dianthus* spp (pinks). Grey leafed plants often have marvellous smells, too, as many of them are culinary or medicinal herbs. At the other end of the spectrum there are the yellow leafed plants, bright and demanding, giving delight on the dullest of days, plants such as *Ligustrum ovalifolium* 'Aureum' (golden privet), *Alchemilla mollis* (ladies mantle) and *Origanum vulgare* 'Aureum' (golden marjoram).

There are many plants, too, with purple leaves, or green with a distinct purple tinge, purple sage, the smoke tree, *Cotinus coggygria* 'Royal Purple', and some of the purple-leaved flowering cherries. All of these plants are very difficult to place well, as the purple colour absorbs the light, and on a dull day creates a visual hole in the composition of plants. Used with discretion, purple-leaved plants associate well with yellows and greens, where an interesting, if slightly restless composition of colours can be developed. The purple-leaved plants also associate well with those with grey leaves, using blue and pink flowers to give a little cheer and lift.

When combining plants with different colour foliage, at least half the plants should have green leaves, otherwise the whole group becomes far too demanding on the eye and brain, too restless, and creates an atmosphere that is not congenial to relaxation. As relaxation and pleasure are the major requirements of a patio, plants with different colour foliage should be used with discretion. If there is any doubt as to whether a plant with coloured leaves should be used in a scheme, then use the green form, as it will be easier to associate with other plants.

Variegated leaves come in many forms, often yellow and green, or white and green. The detailing of the leaves can be very beautiful, with marbling, edging, stripes, blotches of either colour, and even tinges of pink, usually found in green and white variegation.

Variegation in plant leaves is often the result of a viral infection at some point in the history of the plant, a feature that has then been developed and refined to produce an interesting and desirable garden plant. Again, plants with variegated leaves should be used with discretion. Excessive use of variegated plants will create a very restless planting scheme, and the whole garden area will seem as if it has been infected with some nasty disease. Used with discretion, variegated plants can add a lightness and brightness to a planting scheme in a way that cannot be achieved with flowers or other sorts of foliage.

Examples of plants with yellow and gold-coloured leaves:

Alchemilla mollis
Ligustrum ovalifolium 'Aureum'
Origanum vulgare 'Aureum'
Spirea × bumalda 'Goldflame'

Examples of plants with purple foliage:

Berberis thunbergii 'Atropurpurea'
Cotinus coggygria 'Royal Purple'
Rosa glauca
Salvia officinalis 'Purpurescens'

Examples of plants with variegated leaves:

Aralia elata 'Aureovariegata'
Brunnera macrophylla 'Variegata'
Cornus alba 'Elegantissima'
Euonymus fortunei 'Emerald Gaiety'

Autumn colour

Plants that colour well in autumn are precious in a garden, as the autumn is often a time of rain and drab grey days and any bright leaf colour is always welcome and cheering, as if the plants were bidding farewell to the summer gone. Good autumn colour in a plant increases its value in a garden, and especially in a small restricted area such as a patio garden where every plant must earn its keep and contribute to the garden in more than one way.

Some examples of plants with good autumn colour:

Amelanchier canadensis
Hosta 'Thomas Hogg'
Kolkwitzia amabilis
Sorbus 'Joseph Rock'

Flower colour

The colour of the flowers of a plant is one of its most important attributes, but for many plants the flowers are over and gone in a very short space of time, leaving the foliage to continue the effect of the plant's presence. Flower colour needs to be considered in conjunction with foliage colour, so that it works in with any theme or colour scheme, and that whatever the season, all the flower and colour associations are right for the location.

A great deal of work has been undertaken over the years on the theories of colour associations, and many complicated rules have been developed, most of which are inappropriate for our small patio area with its containers of plants. There is one simple rule in colour combining when planting, and if adhered to, will always produce a satisfying colour scheme.

All plant colour, whether of the flower or foliage, contains either yellow or blue as its basic colour. Even red colours contain either yellow (creating the orange-reds) or blue (creating the magenta-reds). When planting, keep all the blue based colours together, and do not try to mix them with the yellow-based colours, which should also all be kept together. In this way a planting scheme will always be harmonious and satisfying.

Flower colour can also affect the perceived size of the patio. Vibrant colours, the bright reds and yellows, always appear closer than the more muted blues, greys and whites. To give the feeling of spaciousness on the patio, the effects of the different colours are utilized, with the bright and vibrant colours planted close to areas of activity and the gentle cooler muted colours planted further away.

White flowers, and some blue flowers, have the effect of glowing when the light levels are low, at dusk. A patio that is used in the evenings can be enhanced and the pleasure of the garden can be prolonged by the careful planting of white flowers, especially night scented white flowers, near to the patio and in the containers.

Flower shape and effects

The shape of the flowers on a plant affects the way it looks, of course, and this can be used to advantage at certain times. The flat lacecap shape of the flowers of *Viburnum plicatum* 'Lanarth' gives the shrub an effect of layers of frothing lace when it is in full bloom. Likewise, the elegant upward facing goblets of the flowers of *Magnolia campbellii* give the tree a look and feeling of elegance and class not seen in any other plant.

The overall effects of a large shrub covered in a myriad of tiny white flowers, such as *Amelanchier lamarkii*, can be totally breathtaking, but have a totally different visual effect in a planting scheme to *Viburnum opulus* 'Sterile', whose large snowball flowers can be equally, but differently, breathtaking.

Flower smell

The smell of flowers is of course one of the most important considerations in designing a planting scheme and choosing plants. In the restricted area of a patio, flowers must smell as well as look good, and if possible continue to produce more flowers throughout the whole season. Smell is a sense that cannot be closed off and so the smell receptors work all the time. It is important, then, that the garden always smells good, whatever the time of year.

Berries and fruit

Berries and fruit are another important consideration, as they provide colour and interest in the garden throughout the autumn and winter, as well as food for the birds and other wildlife.

The colour of the fruit or berries can be another consideration in the planting design, and can contribute significantly to the colour scheme in autumn and winter. The addition of bright red berries or yellow fruit can add seasonal cheer for man and beast alike.

There are two major considerations when planting trees and shrubs with fruit and berries. Some fruit and berries are exceedingly poisonous and should not be grown where there is a chance that they may be eaten by children, or even uninformed adults. The other consideration is that when fruit and berries fall to the ground, they tend to make paved surfaces slippery and dangerous. It is advisable, then, to plant fruiting trees and shrubs a distance away from well used areas of the patio, and to ensure the paving is well cleared of fallen fruit and berries, as well as leaves.

Some examples of plants with good fruits and berries:

> *Euonymus europaeus* 'Red Cascade'
> *Malus* 'John Downie'
> *Pyracantha* 'Mohave'
> *Skimmia japonica*
> *Sorbus* 'Joseph Rock

Bark and twigs

The effect of the bark and twigs of a plant can extend the seasonal interest through the winter. For instance, the humble silver birch, *Betula pendula*, looks as equally magnificent in her unclothed form in winter, when her fine white stem can be enjoyed without a modest covering of leaves. The paperbark maple, *Acer griseum*, with its cinnamon coloured peeling bark, adds both warmth and interest to the winter garden, as well as being a small tree very suitable for patio and container planting. The golden ash, *Fraxinus excelsior* 'Jaspidea' adds a cheerfulness to the winter garden with its yellow twigs, best seen in the thin winter sunshine of a frosty morning.

Some examples of plants with interesting bark:

> *Acer davidii*
> *Acer griseum*
> *Betula pendula*
> *Eucalyptus gunnii*

Some examples of plants with coloured twigs:

> *Cornus* spp
> *Fraxinus excelsior* 'Jaspidea'
> *Genista* 'Lydia'
> *Kerria japonica*

Wind tolerance

Patios are notoriously draughty places, located often beside a large building which creates wind turbulence and draughts from unexpected quarters. Containers located on patios are even more susceptible to the effects of wind, as their root run and hence their stability and grip on the world is very restricted. Plants that stand up well to the effects of wind and draught are exceedingly useful in maintaining a good display throughout the year.

Some examples of plants that are relatively wind tolerant:

> *Berberis* spp.
> *Betula* spp.
> *Buddleia* spp.
> *Cotoneaster* spp.
> *Crataegus* spp.
> *Spirea* spp.

Salt tolerance

Some plants withstand the effects of salt spray much better than others, and the range of plants available for planting in a seaside garden can be very limited. Surprisingly, there are a large number of plants that do withstand salt, and it is always worth experimenting to widen ones own range.

Some examples of plants that will withstand salt and sea air:

> *Buddleia* spp
> *Fuchsia magellanica*
> *Hydrangea macrophylla*
> *Hypericum* spp.
> *Olearia macrodonta*

Withstands frequent clipping

Some plants, especially certain evergreens, withstand and appear to enjoy and thrive on frequent clipping or pruning. These plants are ideal for use on a patio and in containers, either as formally trained specimens, or just as large plants that are subtly restrained for living in confined spaces. The use of these plants means that height and volume can be achieved without the plants encroaching on the smaller shrubs and plants and pushing them over.

The use of formally trained specimen plants in containers on a patio can add or reinforce a very positive style within the garden and is a very simple way of adding interest.

Some examples of plants that withstand clipping and pruning:

Buxus sempervirens
Laurus nobilis
Pyracantha spp.
Rosmarinus officinalis
Santolina chamaecyparissus
Viburnum tinus

Shade tolerance

Shade tolerance is another important attribute of plants chosen for patio and container gardens. Often the space available is limited by hedges, walls and buildings, all of which create pockets of shade for much of the day, often for all of the day in winter. Plants that thrive under these conditions are valuable, especially if they will also tolerate a certain level of frost. Often in winter a shady area of the garden will not thaw out in the course of the day, and will possibly remain frost bound for several days, until the air temperature rises enough for the ground to thaw.

Some examples of plants that will withstand some shade:

Berberis spp.
Bergenia cordifolia
Lamium maculatum
Mahonia spp.
Viburnum tinus

Lime-free requirements

Most plants are very tolerant of the acidity or alkalinity (pH) of the soil in which they grow, and will thrive given the correct nutrients, adequate water and an appropriate position. However, there are a few plants that are very fussy about their soil, and inevitably these plants are always desired by those people with completely wrong site conditions. Most alkaline or chalk-loving plants will grow equally as well on acid soil, but many acid-loving plants just curl up and die on an alkaline soil. Acid-loving plants not only care about the soil that they are planted in, but also about the

water that they receive. It is quite possible to grow azaleas or camellias in acid soil in containers on a patio in the Cotswolds, but never ever water them with tapwater, as this will be their kiss of death. Water them only with rainwater, or stand back and watch them die a slow painful death.

As a matter of ecological policy and good common sense, it does not seem right to attempt to keep plants and keep them healthy under alien conditions. A great deal of hard work is created by keeping any plants in conditions that need to be continually maintained against nature. It is better to work hand in hand with the natural forces, to grow the plants that enjoy the environment that they are in, and to enjoy the plants that cannot be grown under these conditions in their native or natural homes. So, go to the Sussex Weald to enjoy rhododendrons, azaleas and camellias in their full glory of flowering, enjoy the *Viburnum lantana* with its white lacecap flowers and red berries in August in the hedgerows on the Salisbury Plain, and grow in the garden those plants that will thrive there.

Plants for wildlife

Even in the small area available in a patio garden or purely in a container garden, some allowance should be made to encourage the other creatures that share and enjoy the space and make it come alive. Insects, bees, butterflies, birds and small mammals have their place in the garden, sharing it, caring for it and making their life and living from it. The enjoyment of the garden is considerably increased to know that it is providing a home and habitat for many other creatures other than man.

Other creatures living in the garden add to its beauty in many ways. Many of the creatures themselves, especially the birds and the butterflies, are very beautiful and enhance the planting with their colours and their song. Many of the insects, not only the bees, help with the pollination of the flowers to create the fruit and berries for which many of the plants are grown. Many of the insects, birds and small mammals scavenge, eat and so control many of the insect pests in the garden, and so allow the plants to grow into their full beauty.

Books have been written on the benefit of worms in the garden, but here let it be sufficient to say that worms are the quiet unsung workers of the garden. They dispose of old leaves and other organic matter, taking it down into the soil to be broken down further by the soil organisms, and in so doing they aerate the soil and improve it for the benefit of plants and other living creatures. Without the worms, the soil would degenerate into a hard solid mass of mineral matter without the life to grow any plants at all.

In a well-balanced garden of any size, all creatures have an equal right to exist and enjoy its facilities, and if any one creature becomes a problem, it is an indication that the garden has fallen out of balance. Restoration of the balance is important, for if it is out of balance for any one creature, it will be out of balance for all the occupants, including man.

Certain plants are obvious choices for encouraging wildlife in the garden, and there are many others, too. Encouraging wildlife also needs an approach to the garden that is flexible and adaptive. For instance, if a plant becomes a little unruly in its manner of growth, it is not immediately trimmed back at the expense, say, of a small birds nest. The plant can be left a little rampant until the fledglings have flown from home. A certain small element of chaos in the garden, where the planting is not made to toe the corporation line, is conducive to wildlife, providing habitats for nesting and feeding, but this need not be at the expense of good hygiene and care. Again, a happy balance is needed.

The following plants are easy to grow and provide a good nectar source for insects:

Alyssum maritimum	(alyssum)
Aubrieta deltoides	(aubretia)
Buddleia davidii	(butterfly bush)
Caryopteris × clandonensis	
Convulvulus tricolor	
Daphne odora	(daphne)
Dianthus barbatus	(sweet william)
Hebe spp	(shrubby veronica)
Hyssopus officinalis	(hyssop)
Lavandula angustifolia	(lavender)
Lunaria annua	(honesty)
Myosotis spp.	(forget-me-not)
Origanum onites	(marjoram)
Petunia × hybrida	(petunia)
Reseda odorata	(mignonette)

Sedum spectabile	(ice plant)
Skimmia japonica	
Spirea × bumalda	(bridal wreath)
Syringa spp.	(lilac)
Thymus serpyllum	(creeping thyme)

The following plants produce fruit, nuts and berries, providing valuable food for wildlife during the winter:

Berberis × stenophylla	(berberis)
Corylus avallana	(hazel)
Cotoneaster horizontalis	(fishbone cotoneaster)
Crataegus monagyna	(hawthorn)
Euonymus europaeus	(spindle)
Hedera helix	(ivy)
Ilex aquifolium	(holly)
Lonicera periclymen	(honeysuckle)
Malus 'John Downie'	(crab apple)
Pyracantha coccinea	(firethorn)
Sorbus aucuparia	(rowan)
Viburnum lantana	(wayfaring tree)
Viburnum opulus	(guelder rose)
Vitis vinifera 'Brandt'	(grape vine)

Types of plants not recommended

A patio is generally an area of intensive domestic use, with people passing to and fro, sitting and relaxing at times, using a barbecue and other patio furniture and enjoying a safe area for pleasure activities. Bearing this in mind, certain types and families of plants are inappropriate for use on the patio.

Prickly plants, especially those of a vicious nature should be avoided, or at least planted with great care and thought given to their location. All berberis and pyracantha plants are exceedingly spiny, as are most chaenomeles, and should be located away from positions where people will brush past. These positions, usually close to paths and paving, are best utilized by plants of a sensuous nature, where the texture of their foliage and the perfume of their flowers can be appreciated at close quarters.

Roses can be difficult plants to position successfully, as many are very prickly, but also have wonderfully scented flowers. Care needs to be taken in positioning roses so that their beauty and scent can be enjoyed without any danger to the users of the patio.

Holly and gorse are also very prickly plants and need great care in their siting. They shed their leaves and spines throughout the whole year, leaving a very prickly layer of litter beneath the plant that should be handled only with great care. The prickly leaves and spines are dropped during all the months of the year, not just during specific seasons, so the problem always exists.

Some plants are particularly poisonous in some or all of their parts, and their use is not recommended where they might be eaten by children or animals. Included in this category are the trees and shrubs *Laburnum, Taxus* (yew), *Buxus* (box), *Prunus laurocerasus* (cherry laurel), *Cotoneaster, Hedera* (ivy), *Daphne mezereum,* the perennials *Lupinus, Aquilegia, Iris, Digitalis* (foxglove), *Helleborus, Pulsatilla, Polygonatum* (Solomons seal), *Aconitum* (monkshood) and the bulbs and corms of *Narcissus, Eranthus* and *Cyclamen.*

Criteria for the Choice of Plants for Containers

The following criteria are to be considered when choosing plants for containers and patios. These criteria are very important over and above the other plant attributes already listed, as the planting scheme chosen may be both functional and beautiful in concept, but will be of no use at all if the plants are not happy in their chosen places.

Drought tolerance

Plants grown in containers are totally dependent upon their human carers to provide food, water, good growing media and an appropriate position in which to grow. Deficiency in any one of these items will cause severe stress in the plant, but lack of water causes such a rapid response the results can be observed in a matter of a few hours. It is important, then, that any plant growing in a container should have a certain level of drought tolerance, to enable it to survive in good form at times when neither rain nor tap water are forthcoming.

All round general tolerance

Unless you are a dedicated gardener with an infinite supply of time and patience, there are bound to be times when your plants in containers take a lower priority to other important items. It is essential then that your containers are full of plants that do not depend on a twice-daily molly-coddle to keep them in best form. To that end the general all-round tolerance of the plants is another factor to be taken into consideration when choosing plants to live in containers.

Hardiness

Hardiness is an important factor in the choice of plants for container growing. Unless it is intentional that the tubs are moved for the winter into a sheltered place or greenhouse, any permanent planting should be hardy. Nothing looks worse than an attractive container located in a prominent position, wrapped up with bracken and string to keep the cold out, like some misplaced children's joke. Remember that the container is on show for 365 days of the year, and should look good every one of those days. Container-grown plants are particularly susceptible to root damage in frosty weather and the choice of plants should reflect this.

Every plant must earn its keep

When planting in a restricted area, such as a patio and the containers placed on it, every plant used must have an element of interest for every season of the year, in other words, every plant must earn its keep.

The ideal deciduous plant starts the spring with long lasting scented flowers, breaking into leaf with an unusual colour developing into light feathery summer foliage, seeing autumn out in a blaze of fiery colour, and passing through winter with a lacework of filigree twigs and patterned bark that glows in the low winter sun, with masses of long lasting fruit that is gradually eaten by the birds.

The ideal evergreen plant is tolerant to regular pruning to keep it in good shape, starts the year with a long lasting blaze of scented flowers, produces new foliage of a soft contrast to last year's leaves which gradually tones down as the summer progresses, and is covered in a multitude of bright berries which the birds devour during the course of the winter.

Inevitably, there are no plants that can be everything at all times, but when choosing a

155

plant for the patio area, it is essential to consider its effect out of season. For instance, *Syringa vulgaris* (lilac) has magnificent scented blowsy flowers for about three weeks of the year, but its foliage is generally rather dull, its form and habit of growth is not endearing, as it throws up a mass of suckers from its roots, and its branch pattern and bark have nothing to recommend them. Lilac, then, is at best a plant used at the back of a large shrub border in a large garden, and is not very appropriate for our patio environment.

A small tree suitable for patio and container planting is a *Betula pendula* (silver birch). With its beautiful bark which provides interest through twelve months of the year, and its light feathery foliage, opening to a delicious light green and finally falling in the autumn in a blaze of buttercup yellow, the birch is one of the most hardy and tolerant of trees.

CHAPTER 12
Successful Planting Schemes

Plant Combinations in Relation to the Site

The spirit of the landscape

No garden, however enclosed and private, is totally insulated and detached from the landscape that surrounds it. Landscape is not only the hills and plains, the forests and water courses, but also the towns and villages, the streets and housing estates in which the gardens are situated. A garden is an integral part of this very variable landscape, and the layout and planting within it are a small part of a very large whole.

If the layout and planting of the patio garden are to be successful, they must accept that they are part of a much larger 'garden', and work accordingly. For a planting scheme to be successful, it must take its spirit from the surrounding land and adapt the details and specifics to the individual garden. A garden, especially a patio garden, must not mimic nature or slavishly copy her, but should work in the spirit that she intended.

The soil of the garden will define the types of plant that can be grown, whether it is acid or alkaline soil, very sandy and well draining, or very heavy and fertile with clay. Because of this, the planting within the garden will relate to the planting in the outside landscape. The cultivation of plants that do not easily grow on the local soil creates a great deal of work and heartbreak for the gardener, and a successful garden will be full of plants that love the soil in which they are growing.

Plants growing in containers are different, in as much as the gardener can control and determine the type of soil in which the plants are growing. All the choices of plant appear to be open to the container gardener, but even in containers the plants are affected by their surroundings, the soil that is in the ground, and by the water they drink. Of course acid loving plants can be grown in areas of alkaline soil, within containers, but they feel and look out of context. A heather and conifer garden can make an interesting contrast to the viburnums and cotoneasters that grow so well on chalk and limestone, but it will look painfully out of place growing in the soil, and should be grown in a container to look its best.

The use of contrast in the choice of plants can add to the interest in the garden, but the plants should be used in a way that states quite clearly where they belong, and no attempt should be made to integrate them into the main planting of the garden if they are out of context. Used with discretion in containers, plants that contrast with the natural landscape can look very good, and can be given the care and attention that they deserve to help them thrive.

Colour

Plants must always relate to the area in which they are growing, in terms of shape, style, colour, size and the location of the containers. Patio planting must relate also to the materials of the patio, the materials of any adjacent buildings, sometimes to the historical context of those buildings, and of course to the use of the buildings.

The colours of the materials used for the paving and walling will have an important influence on the choice of foliage and of flower colour. The warm reds and orange of terracotta and of some bricks contrast beautifully with the blues and greys of herbs and grey-leaved plants. White, pink and blue flowers blend well here, where strong orange and red flowers compete with the brickwork for attention.

The hard blue-greys of slate and granite create a gentle calm atmosphere when planted with grey, silver, green and blue foliage and flowering plants, but make a good contrast and background to strong yellow, orange and red flowers, calming them down and reducing their aggression to warmth. In any planting scheme, the use of foliage is very important, and green, silver and grey foliage should be used generously, to set off the cooler colours and to tone down the brighter colours.

Care should be taken with the use of strong bright flower colours. Many of these plants look good in the hot sun and clear blue skies of a southern or Mediterranean climate, where the light is much stronger and clearer. These bright colours can look good in well chosen positions on the patio, especially in containers, but can clash with the colour of the buildings and the surrounding plants. The soft English sunlight is ideal to bring out the best in the pastel shades of flower colours, which tone well with the muted brick and stone colours of the buildings. The strong bright colours are best planted in containers, where their beauty can be appreciated and used as focal points, and for emphasis and contrast.

Site use and the choice of plants

The choice of plants for use in containers depends also on the expected and actual use of the patio, or area where the container is located. For instance, the choice of plants for containers on a swimming pool surround would be different to the choice of plants for a container on a shaded front door step. The swimming pool will usually be in use in the daytime and early evenings in hot weather in the summer months, and the plants for those containers will need to look their best at those times. A container on a shaded front door step will be on view for twelve months of the year and will need to look good for every day of those twelve months.

For a family that always takes a six-week holiday in the middle of the summer, the containers will need to contain good spring planting and late summer and autumn planting, so that they can be appreciated at their peak of beauty, rather than past their best at the end of a summer. A patio and barbecue area that is used for evening entertaining will be enhanced with a planting of *Mathiola bicornis* (night scented stocks) and *Nicotiana affinis* (tobacco plant), both of which have a strong fragrance in the evenings.

The correct choice of plants for containers and patio planting is important, so that the area can be enjoyed to its full potential and used as another room of the house.

Planting in relation to site aspect

The aspect of the patio, and the position and aspect of the pots on the patio influences the choice of plants to grow there. Many plants are very tolerant as to where they grow, provided that their main requirements are catered for, but some plants can be very choosy as to their location and aspect, flourishing in adverse conditions and resenting what one would consider a choice location.

It is best always to grow plants that enjoy the aspect chosen for them, and not to attempt to grow plants that will not thrive in a particular position. It is not enough to rely on the micro-climate formed by a group of plants to try to grow a plant that dislikes a particular aspect; all the plants within a group should be suitable for the position. In a patio garden with damp areas, it is best to choose plants that enjoy the damp conditions, and to continue the theme into the planting in the containers. In this way the continuity and harmony of the design is maintained in the planting.

The same approach applies to a windy spot on the patio, or to a particularly shady or sunny position. Choose the plants that enjoy and thrive in these locations, whether or not they are grown in containers, and the results will be much more rewarding.

Using annual and biennial plants in containers gives the opportunity to experiment with plants and colour schemes at not too great a cost in time and money, to find out which plants do well under certain conditions. This is one way to find out which plants are the most appropriate to the individual site, and to then develop the idea, if desired, with the use of perennial plants and even shrubs.

Designing with Plants and Containers

Choosing containers

The choice of container is crucial to the whole effect of the patio, the garden and the planting. Not only should the container be appropriate and blend with its surroundings, but it should also be compatible with others in a group, and if it is to be used as a focal point, it should be large and bold enough to play the part chosen for it.

Practical considerations will influence the choice of container, such as the size and depth of soil needed for the plants and the space available on the patio or the chosen position. It is also important to consider the use of that part of the garden, so that a highly decorated terracotta container is not placed where it is likely to be hit with children's bicycles, for instance.

Choosing the plants

The choice of plants for use in containers is very wide, as almost any plant can be grown in a container, given the right conditions of good suitable compost, the right position, an appropriate size of container and the right companion plants. As the choice is so wide, it is easy for a planting scheme to fail from being too fussy.

Start the choice of plants by considering the position and aspect of the container. Then consider the intention of the design. Is it to bring a mass of bright colour close to the house to supplement the restrained planting of the patio just for the summer, or is it to be a permanent feature of the garden? Is the planting needed to break the wind or to screen a bad view? In these situations the function can limit the choice of plants.

The number of plants in a container is of course limited by the size of the container. If too many different species of plant are included in the container, the scheme will become 'busy' and restless. It is important too that all the plants in a container need the same growing conditions and type of soil.

Each plant has many different attributes that commend its use in a particular position or for a special effect. Whether it is the shape or colour of its foliage, or its textured bark, or berries, or the colour of the flowers, or its use as a foil to the colours of other plants, each of these things has to be considered in relation to the other plants, and to the container.

Suiting the plant to the container

Wherever a container is situated, whether it is on a patio, on some steps, hung from a bracket, fixed to a wall or buried in a mass of planting,

its character will determine its suitability for plants of different kinds. Sometimes the container is almost incidental to the planting, where the plants just cascade out of the container and smother it in foliage or flowers and virtually conceal the container itself.

Often, however, the container will influence the planting very strongly, and should be allowed to do so to bring out the beauty in both the container and the plants. There is an obvious compatibility between low growing succulents and alpines growing in a stone trough, and between brighly coloured trailing varieties of annuals in a hanging basket, where the style of container is enhanced and enhances the plants growing in it.

Hanging baskets need low bushy and trailing plants (Fig. 12.1). Bold containers, whether old

Fig. 12.1 A hanging basket with plants.

Fig. 12.2 A bold container with plant.

Fig. 12.3 A tall container with plants.

Fig. 12.4 A simple concrete container with plants.

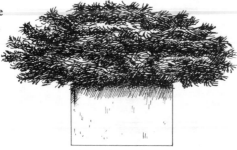

Fig. 12.5 A square box with planting.

or new, need strong dramatic planting (Fig. 12.2). Tall pots and urns look good with pendulous bushy plants that can tumble and twist down their sides like flowing locks of hair (Fig. 12.3).

Traditional terracotta pots and concrete containers in simple shapes are ideal for more subtle compositions and groupings, their unassuming outlines setting off the detail of an interesting plant grouping (Fig. 12.4). Square boxes are good for low bushy shrubs (Fig. 12.5). Wide shallow containers are best for plants that are bushy and spreading, with a little height as well as width (Fig. 12.6).

Parsley pots, strawberry pots and other containers designed specially for a purpose look best with the plants that they were designed for, although they can look good with a mixture of plants, for instance, different herbs (Fig. 12.7). It is important to remember that growing conditions in a container are rarely ideal, with overcrowding and drying out being obvious problems encountered. The larger and more rampant species of plant need a reasonable depth of soil to grow well, and so the larger free-standing containers really come into their own when planted with larger shrubs and small trees. They then have enough room to develop a good root system, and can look good enough to be used alone. Annuals often look best in mixed groups and bulbs are most effective when a single species is massed.

Grouping plants and containers

Not only the choice of plants, but also their arrangement in the container will be defined and depend on the shape and style of the container. Generally, plants can be classified into three groups when they are considered for planting, (upright, bushy and trailing), and any planting scheme can contain a combination of one or all of the groups.

A wall pot, for instance, would possibly contain upright plants at the back, close to the wall, bushy plants in the centre, and trailing plants around the front edge. A wide free-standing container could have the same combination of plants, but the tall upright plants in the centre surrounded by bushy plants, with trailing plants around the rim. Trailing plants really come into their own when used in window boxes, hanging baskets,

Fig. 12.6 A wide shallow container with planting.

Fig. 12.7 A parsley pot and a strawberry barrel.

urns on a plinth and any pot on the edge of a wall or balcony.

This idea of three tiers of planting applies not only to annuals, but also to perennials, and to shrubs and trees. All that we are doing is copying nature, because any woodland contains different tiers of planting, the trees, then the shrub layer, then the herb layer with the perennials, and then finally the ground cover layer on the floor of the woodland. All successful gardens are planted on this principle, with trees, shrubs, perennials and annuals mixed to form the different layers, and the same principle applies equally well to planting in containers.

The different tiers of planting need not be symmetrical, as many containers are not symmetrical, and are not located in a position where symmetry would be appropriate. A window box, for instance, could be planted asymmetrically, with taller plants at one end and low growing plants at the other end, and so

allow for the window to be opened without damaging the plants (Fig. 12.8).

Successful Planting Schemes

Successful planting schemes depend on many factors, as previously outlined, but the one essential item so far not mentioned is that planting schemes always depend on the imagination and enthusiasm of the gardener. No scheme is too outrageous or unusual, and just might be totally stunning in its effect. If it is not suitable for one reason or another, the plants can usually be used elsewhere and a new scheme can be worked out.

The following schemes are only suggestions and ideas for further development. All the schemes illustrated here have been planted and grown. No quantities of plants are given, as the size of the container will define the space available and limit the number of plants. Plant generously, especially with annuals and bulbs, and give permanent perennial and shrub

Fig. 12.8 An asymmetrically planted window box with an open window.

planting plenty of space to grow and develop over several years.

Ideas for window boxes

Spring scheme
Spring is a season of gold, white and blue, and this scheme combines the three colours in a stunning spring display of flowers. After flowering, all the plants should be removed from the box and used elsewhere in the garden.
   Plants used:

> *Narcissus cyclamineus* 'February Silver'
> *Narcissus jonquilla* 'Waterperry'
> *Primula vulgaris*
> *Scilla sibirica* 'Spring Beauty'

Summer scheme
This combination of summer flowers thrives in a sunny position, but will also give a good show in partial shade. A white window box will set the plants off to show their best, the solidity of the pelargoniums contrasting with the airy lightness of the lobelias. Dead-head the pelargoniums regularly.
   Plants used:

> *Lobelia erinus* 'Crystal Palace'
> ivy-leaved *Pelargonium* 'Rouletta'

Year-round scheme
This window box is planted for the contrast of the foliage colours and textures. The colour scheme is in green and silver, with white flowers from the *Hebe rakaiensis* picking up the same theme, and the little gold button flowers of the *Helichrysum plicatum* adding a little colour in late summer, if it is allowed to flower. If desired, annual plants can be added in the spring and summer to give some colour, but the scheme is calm and pleasing throughout the whole year.
   Plants used:

> *Chamaecyparis lawsoniana* 'Ellwoodii'
> *Euonymus fortunei* 'Silver Pillar'
> *Hedera helix* 'Adam'
> *Hebe rakaiensis*
> *Helichrysum plicatum*

North-facing scheme
Begonia × tuberhybrida are good window box plants, and will give a show for the whole summer on a north-facing window. *Lobelia erinus* is equally obliging, and will provide a trailing effect. This scheme can be given continuity and can become the basis for a permanent show by adding the evergreen fern, *Polypodium vulgare* 'Elegantissimum' and the

trailing ivy, *Hedera helix* 'Little Diamond', and adding suitable plants for a winter and spring display. A white or terracotta window box sets these plants off to their best.

Plants used:

Begonia × tuberhybrida (non-stop pink)
Hedera helix 'Little Diamond'
Lobelia erinus 'Blue Cascade'
Polypodium vulgare 'Elegantissimum'

South-facing scheme

This group of plants need a south-facing aspect and plenty of sun to bring out the best in the plants. The gazanias can be brought through the winter if stored in frost free conditions, but otherwise this must be considered an annual scheme.

Plants used:

Gazania × hybrida (mixed colours)
Mesembryanthemum criniflorum (mixed)

Ideas for hanging baskets

Spring scheme

Although bulbs do not trail and hang down from a hanging basket, they can be used to provide a little height, and by careful positioning when the basket is planted, they can be encouraged to grow out of the sides. Several of the primulas should also be planted to grow around the sides of the basket. The scheme is in spring colours of white, yellow and blue, and if desired the primroses can be replaced with winter flowering pansies.

Plants used:

mixed crocus in white, yellow and blue
Hedera helix 'Glacier'
Hedera helix 'Goldheart'
mixed primulas in white and yellow

Summer scheme

This is a very traditional hanging basket, using low arching fuchsias with trailing lobelia. The dainty lobelia flowers set off the heavier flounced flowers of the fuchsia, to give a display that will last all summer to the frosts.

Plants used:

Fuchsia × hybrida 'Lena' or 'Ballerina'
Lobelia erinus 'White Fountains'

Herb basket

Herb plants can thrive in hanging baskets, as they enjoy well drained soil and plenty of sun. All these herbs are perennials and shrubs, and so the basket can be used for several years. Purple-leaved annual basil, *Ocimum basilicum* 'Dark Opal' can be added to the basket to give height and to continue the colour theme of silver, gold, purple and green. The marjorams, thyme and variegated apple mint can be planted through the sides of the basket.

Plants used:

Chrysanthemum parthenium 'Aureum'
Helichrysum angustifolium
Mentha rotundifolia 'Variegata'
Origanum vulgare
Origanum vulgare 'Aureum'
Salvia officinalis 'Purpurescens'
Thymus serpyllum lanuginosus

Perennial basket

This basket uses the grace, elegance and hardiness of *Alchemilla mollis* to good effect. Very few plants are needed, as alchemilla will grow quite large in only one season, and several should be planted through the sides of the basket. A smaller but similar basket can also be made using *Alchemilla alpina*, and the height of the basket means that the silken undersides of the leaves can be fully appreciated. Suitably cared for, fed, watered and overwintered, this basket will last for several seasons before the plants grow too large and need repotting. It will look its best in the summer through to the frosts.

Plants used:

Alchemilla mollis

Year-round basket

This basket is based on the different colours of the foliage of the *Ajuga reptans*, with a little height given by the black grass *Ophiopogon planiscapus* 'Nigrescens'. The bugle is fairly vigorous, and the runners will trail down. They can be planted back into the basket gradually. A variation of this basket can be made using the cream and grey green form of variegated bugle, *Ajuga reptans* 'Variegata' and creeping Jenny, *Lysimachia nummularia*, which has round green leaves and bright

yellow flowers all summer and is evergreen.
Plants used:

Ajuga reptans 'Burgundy Glow'
Ajuga reptans 'Rainbow'
Ajuga reptans 'Variegata'
Ophiopogon planiscapus 'Nigrescens'

Ideas for wall pots

Spring scheme
This simple spring collection of plants has a colour theme of yellow and gold, and so its location must be chosen with care, as not all walls are the best backdrop for a gold colour scheme. A variation suitable for use on a very orange coloured wall would be to substitute the ivy for *Hedera helix* 'Adam', the alyssum for *Arabis caucasica* and the miniature daffodils for *Narcissus cyclamineus* 'February Silver'. *Aubrieta deltoidea* 'Dr Mules', a deep purple form of aubrieta can also be added to the wall pot. All of these plants can be retained in the wall pot, or can be used elsewhere in the garden.
Plants used:

Alyssum saxatile
Hedera helix 'Goldheart'
Narcissus cyclamineus 'Tete-a-tete'

Summer scheme
Trailing tradescantias are generally used as indoor plants, but they can be used to good effect outside in a sheltered spot, such as in a wall pot. Both the lobelia and the tradescantia will grow up as well as down, and will climb into the foliage of the pelargonium, softening it a little.
Plants used:

Lobelia erinus 'Cambridge Blue'
Regal pelargonium 'Applause'
Tradescantia albiflora

Year-round scheme
This scheme gives a combination of grey and green foliage, with the dianthus giving a little height and colour for most of the summer, and the ivy picking up the shades of pink in the winter. The wall pot will look good for at least two seasons before the plants become overcrowded.

Plants used:

Dianthus × allwoodii 'Doris'
Hedera helix 'Glacier'
Iberis sempervirens

Ideas for troughs

Spring and summer scheme
This is a very simple scheme, with the *Anthemis cupaniana* forming an evergreen grey carpet with yellow centred white daisy flowers at the same time that the tulips are in bloom. The anthemis will continue to flower throughout the summer if regularly dead headed, and the tulips could be replaced with a yellow summer bedding plant, such as *Coreopsis* 'Early Sunrise' to continue the show into the summer.
Plants used:

Anthemis cupaniana
Coreopsis 'Early Sunrise'
Tulipa 'Sunkist'

Year-round scheme
This scheme for a trough uses the effects of the foliage to look good for the whole year. In summer, the little yellow flowers of the rue pick up the yellow in the variegated periwinkle. This scheme is also very tolerant of aspect, and will thrive for many years if cut back hard in late spring.
Plants used:

Ruta graveolens 'Jackman's Blue'
Vinca major 'Variegata'

North-facing scheme
This scheme is based predominantly on foliage, with the busy lizzies, *Impatiens wallerana* 'Futura' adding colour for the summer. A little height is provided by the irises, which also add colour in the winter with their bright orange-red berries that last most of the winter.
Plants used:

Hedera helix 'Adam'
Impatiens wallerana 'Futura'
Iris foetidissima
Salvia officinalis
Santolina chamaecyparis

South-facing scheme

Pelargoniums thrive on a south-facing aspect, and this scheme fills the trough full in shades of pink and white, upright and trailing, with the ageratum complementing the scheme in a mid blue. The pelargoniums should be lifted and removed before the first frosts, but if cuttings have been taken, or the plants are not needed for the following year, then the display flower can be left to late October.

Plants used:

Ageratum houstonianum (mid blue)
Cineraria maritima
zonal *Pelargonium* 'Modesty' (double white)
zonal *Pelargonium* 'Regina' (pink)
ivy-leaved *Pelargonium* 'Sybil Holmes' (pink)

Edible scheme

This scheme, suitable for a large trough, combines both edible and decorative plants in flower shades of red, blue and white. It is best placed where support can be given to the climbers, possibly against a fence or wall with wire supports. Vertical canes would work well, but would visually detract from the plants. The tomatoes and runner beans should be picked and eaten as they ripen, the rhubarb chard leaves should be picked regularly to remove the older leaves and expose the deep red of the new leaves, and the carrots should be thinned with great care to retain a good display of the feathery foliage.

Plants used:

Beta vulgaris 'Rhubarb Chard'
Daucus carota 'Favourite'
Ipomoea tricolor
Lobelia erinus 'Cambridge Blue'
Lycopersicon lycopersicum 'Tumbler'
Phaseolus coccineus 'Scarlet Emperor'

Ideas for urns and tall containers

Spring scheme

An urn or a tall container needs planting that will both trail down and grow upward. In this scheme, the holly-leaved, variegated *Osmanthus* provides a solid evergreen framework for the clematis to climb. The candytuft is also evergreen, with white flowers appearing at the same time as the clematis, and will itself trail a little.

Plants used:

Clematis alpina
Iberis sempervirens
Osmanthus heterophyllus 'Variegatus'

Summer scheme

This combination of ornamental cabbage and busy lizzie is both unusual and stunning. The cabbage provides foliage colour for the whole summer, and when removed at the end of the season, it can be eaten! The busy lizzie will soften the roundness of the cabbage and echo its frills.

Plants used:

Brassica oleracea (pink and green)
Impatiens wallerana (double soft pink)

Year-round scheme

The central plant of this scheme is bold, architectural in form, and provides the colours with which the accompanying plants associate and blend. As the verbena are tender and probably will not survive the winter, cuttings can be taken for the following year, or they can be replaced with *Aubrieta deltoidea* 'Bressingham Pink' for spring colour, and a bright pink pelargonium, such as 'Clorinda'.

Plants used:

Ballotta pseudodictamnus
Phormium tenax 'Sundowner'
Helianthemum nummularium 'Wisley Pink'
Verbena × hybrida 'Sissinghurst'

Single plant

A single plant can look effective in an urn or tall container, but it needs to have both height and width, and to trail downwards to an extent. The shrub rose can be regularly pinched out and gently trained to produce the required effect, and will look good for all the summer. 'Cornelia' has a sweet pervasive scent and is repeat flowering through to the frosts.

Plants used:

Hybrid musk *Rosa* 'Cornelia'

Ideas for large free-standing containers

Spring scheme

Height and colour are provided in this scheme

by the golden form of silver birch, whose leaves open gold and stay that way all summer. The gold colour is picked up in all the other plants, and the white of the birch stem is echoed in the white crocuses. This container of plants will give pleasure all year, especially with the addition of *Lillium candidum, Lillium* 'Bellona' and *Anemone × hybrida* 'Honorine Jobert', for summer and autumn flowers.

Plants used:

Betula alba 'Golden Cloud'
Crocus tomasinianus (yellow and white)
Euonymus fortunei 'Emerald and Gold'
Euphorbia polychroma

Summer scheme

This is a flamboyant scheme in shades of yellow and gold, with a wide contrast of leaf shapes and plant habit. Height is provided by the lilies, and later in the season by the abutilon.

Plants used:

Abutilon 'Canary Bird'
Agave americana 'Variegata'
Chrysanthemum frutescens 'Jamaica Primrose'
Helichrysum petiolare 'Limelight'
Hosta plantaginea
Lillium 'Citronella Strain'

Year-round scheme

This combination of perennial plant and shrub starts early in the season with the new leaves on the potentilla, and once in flower, will continue throughout the summer and autumn. The catmint will flow gently over the edge of the container, as well as climbing up through the potentilla. Continuity is provided through the winter with the ivy, and then the snowdrops, whose foliage will die down and disappear as the catmint starts to grow in the spring.

Plants used:

Galanthus nivalis
Hedera helix 'Glacier'
Nepeta × faassenii
Potentilla 'Daydawn'

Single plant

The single plant in a large container needs to look good for all 52 weeks of the year, and to have continuing interest. *Pieris* 'Forest Flame' does just this, as it is evergreen, with new leaves appearing brilliant red, then fading pink to cream then green, with long drooping inflorescences of scented flowers. It is an acid loving plant and will not thrive in areas of hard water on chalk or limestone. *Choisya ternata* will grow well in these areas, with fragrant apple green leaves and scented flowers for the whole summer.

Plants used:

Choisya ternata
Pieris 'Forest Flame', or

Edible scheme

All the plants in this scheme are edible, except for the black-eyed Susan. The colour scheme is of yellow, with a touch of purple from the climbing French bean.

If the container is free-standing, support for the beans and black-eyed Susan should be given. A pyramid of 2 m (6 ft) canes, tied at the top would be functional, but a permanent decorative pyramid, made of white painted timber and reaching a height of about 2 m (6 ft) would look stunning in the right position (Fig. 12.9). As the golden zuccini plant will be very vigorous, it should be omitted in all but very large containers.

Plants used:

Beta vulgaris 'Burpees Golden'
Cucurbita pepo 'Golden Zuccini'
Lycopersicon lycopersicum 'Golden Sunrise'
Phaseolus vulgaris 'Purple podded climbing French bean'
Thunbergia alata 'Susie'

North-facing scheme

This scheme is of evergreen plants and will brighten up a north-facing position. The colours are in dark green and white, with a touch of purple in the summer provided by the lavender and the stachys. Fragrance is provided in the winter by the sarcococcus, and in summer by the lavender, and the lauristinus is winter flowering. This is a quiet tasteful scheme and not for those who hanker for bright colours.

Plants used:

Euonymus fortunei 'Emerald Gaity'

Iberis sempervirens
Lavandula angustifolia 'Hidcote'
Pittosporum garnettii
Sarcococca humilis
Stachys lanata
Viburnum tinus 'Eve Price'

South-facing scheme

This is a scheme of sun-loving shrubs and perennials, gradually building up through the summer months to give an unusual and subtle display of silvers, blues and purples in late summer and autumn. Suitably fed and watered, this collection of plants will not need to be disturbed for several years, and will look better each season. The caryopteris, fuchsia and perovskia will all need to be pruned very hard in late spring.

Plants used:

Caryopteris × clandonensis 'Kew Blue'
Fuchsia 'Mrs Popple'
Hebe pinguifolia 'Pagei'
Heuchera 'Palace Purple'
Perovskia atriplicifolia
Phormium tenax 'Purpureum'
Salvia officinalis 'Purpurescens'

Ideas for wide shallow containers

Spring scheme

This spring scheme in red and blue is designed for a wide shallow container at ground level, where the flowers are appreciated from above. The rue gives permanent height and structure, with the forget-me-nots using the blue theme to provide a base for the red of the two types of tulip. The plants should be removed when they have finished flowering; the rue could be retained for part of the summer planting, and the tulip bulbs can be naturalized in a border, or heeled in to the ground to die down for use another year.

Plants used:

Myosotis sylvatica 'Royal Blue'
Ruta graveolens 'Jackman's Blue'
Tulipa 'Flying Dutchman'
Tulipa greigii 'Red Riding Hood'

Summer scheme

The tree mallow will put on a show of bright pink flowers for the whole summer, and will grow vigorously to a maximum of about 2 m (6 ft) unless regularly pinched out to make it

Fig. 12.9 Diagram of –
(*a*) Temporary plant support made of canes
(*b*) A permanent structure made of painted timber.

more bushy. The hosta and the rose will give colour earlier in the summer, while the mallow is still fairly restrained in size.

Plants used:

Hosta undulata 'Variegata'
Lavatera olbia 'Rosea'
Rosa 'Nozomi'

Year-round scheme

This scheme uses the year round effects of the foliage, and is suitable for sun or part shade. The hosta adds another element of colour in the autumn when its leaves turn bright yellow before dying down. The space left by the hosta leaves can be planted with crocuses for early spring colour.

Plants used:

Crocus tomasinianus (yellow and white)
Heuchera 'Palace Purple'
Hosta 'Thomas Hogg'
Iris pallida 'Variegata'
Tolmiea menziesii

Edible scheme

This scheme is centred round a standard bay tree, and all the planting is low, using the different colours and textures of the foliage to create interest. The container will provide interesting salads all through the summer if a wide range of lettuce varieties are planted.

Plants used:

Allium cepa (grow from sets)
Daucus carota 'Favourite'
Lactuca sativa (mixed varieties)
Laurus nobilis (standard mop head)
Portulaca oleracea

North-facing scheme

This scheme will brighten a north-facing position for all seasons of the year, in a theme of green, silver and gold. Many of the plants are evergreen, with plenty of winter interest with yellow mahonia flowers and red berries of the iris.

Plants used:

Alchemilla mollis
Crocus tomasinianus (white and yellow)
Iris foetidissima
Mahonia aquifolium

Philadelphus coronarius 'Aureus'
Phlomis fruiticosa
Vinca major 'Variegata'

South-facing scheme

This is a fragrant long-flowering scheme, as permanent as any container planting when well cared for, fed and watered. Each winter or spring, before the buds break, the roses should be checked over for dead wood and pruned very lightly to help them maintain their shape. The cotinus should be pruned back hard each year to give a good display of its rich-coloured foliage. *Helichrysum petiolare* and *Verbena* 'Loveliness' would be good additions for the summer.

Plants used:

Cineraria maritima
Cotinus coggygria 'Royal Purple'
Rosa 'Cardinal Hume'
Rosa 'Sea Foam'
Rosa 'The Fairy'
Salvia officinalis 'Purpurescens'
Senecio 'Sunshine'

Ideas for small containers

Spring scheme

One of the best effects to be achieved with a small container for a spring display is to fill it full to bursting with spring flowering bulbs or corms. For an early display, try snowdrops, maybe the double snowdrop, *Galanthus nivalis* 'Flore Pleno'. Any of the other smaller bulbs and corms will also do well in a small container, such as crocus, scilla, chionadoxa or one of the miniature narcissi such as *Narcissus cyclamineus* 'Jack Snipe', 'Tete-a-Tete' or 'Jenny'.

For an unusual spring display, plant *Pulmonaria saccharata*, with its spotted leaves and flowers opening pink and turning blue. There are white and red forms available, if needed for a colour scheme. Combined with low growing spring-flowering bulbs in toning colours, the effect is both interesting and long lasting.

Plants used:

Crocus tomasinianus (white and blue)
Pulmonaria saccharata

Summer scheme
This scheme fills a small pot full of a traditional houseplant and the black grass to give an unusual effect. The pot would look good on its own, or accompanying a larger pot planted in pink, silver and green.
Plants used:

Begonia rex (pink and silver)
Ophiopogon planiscapens 'Nigrescens'

Perennial scheme
Hostas make unusual and good container plants, and to keep the plant in scale with the container a smaller leafed variety has been used. It will be interesting from the days in spring when the points of the leaves just start to poke up through the soil right through to the autumn when the leaves turn gold with frost.
Plants used:

Hosta 'Groundmaster'

Ideas for unusual containers

Chimney pots
Chimney pots are often unusual and distinctive in their shape, and lend themselves to strong, architectural planting. Due to their depth, it is best to choose a flower pot that will fit inside the chimney pot, and plant into this. The planting will tend to dry out rapidly, especially in hot weather, and plants should be chosen accordingly, or the chimney pot located in a shady spot.

Chimney pots seem very appropriate next to a door, and bold interesting planting can turn a wait on a doorstep into a real pleasure. It seems almost a shame and a lost opportunity to use a chimney pot for an arrangement of annual plants when it could be used for one bold plant to create a dramatic effect. A large-leaved *Begonia haageana*, usually grown as a house plant, suits the shape of a chimney pot perfectly, but for a slightly less tender scheme, a bold fuchsia will look good, with a little more height provided by marguerites. This combination of plants will tend to be thirsty and need frequent watering.
Plants used:

Chrysanthemum frutescens
Fuchsia 'Swingtime' (double red and white)

Barrels
Barrels are good containers for water gardens on a patio or within a restricted area. Of course a barrel must be made suitably watertight, and the planting must be small, simple and effective. This scheme is suitable for a small half barrel; a larger container increases the numbers of plants that can be considered, but care must be taken not to choose vigorous varieties that will tend to take over the available space!
Plants used:

Acorus calamus
Aponogeton distachyos
Butomus umbellatus
Myosotis palustris
Nymphea odorata 'Rosea'

Oil jar
Oil jars are difficult to plant and are generally best left empty as a focal point. Any planting needs to be both striking and subtle, and must not detract from the shape of the jar.

This low-growing Japanese acer and the hebe form a classic purple and grey colour combination, enhanced only by another container of contrasting shape, low and shallow, at the foot of the oil jar and planted with low annual plants such a dwarf verbena, and crocuses in the spring. This planting will benefit from winter protection in a frost free and wind free position, although the plants are hardy.
Plants used:

Acer palmatum 'Dissectum Atropurpureum'
Hebe 'Quicksilver'

Built-in containers
This combination of plants gives interest all through the year, starting with the crocuses in spring, followed by the cotoneaster with its leaves unfurling, then coming into flower, and finally the autumn leaf colours and the red berries with the Kaffir lilies. This group of plants works best next to a wall, so that the cotoneaster can be encouraged to grow upwards rather than outwards.
Plants used:

Cotoneaster horizontalis
Crocus mixed
Schizostylis coccinea

CHAPTER 13
Plants and Planting

Planting in Paving

Planting in paving is a method of planting that needs a good helping hand from Nature, and the cooperation of the plants themselves. Much planting in paving is random self seeding by plants that thrive in the situation, and its randomness is part of its charm. Too much planning of paving planting creates a stiff and formal area that tries too hard to seem casual and uncontrolled and so never looks quite right.

The principles of planting in paving are very simple. First, choose the plants that enjoy the conditions provided in paving, i.e. a very restricted root run, open exposure to all weathers and an ability to withstand the fierce conditions, limited water supply at very intermittent intervals, and the possibility of being walked or trampled on at any time. Luckily, some plants survive and even thrive under these conditions.

For the most vigorous growth of paving plants, the paving should be laid loose on sand, with sand brushed into the joints. This allows plants to seed themselves in the sand and their roots to gradually make their way into the soil below. The drawback of this arrangement is that weeds seed themselves equally as well in sand, especially the ones with long tap roots such as dock and cow parsley, and are exceedingly difficult to remove without removing part of the paving at the same time.

Paving that is laid to last, with a good hardcore base below the concrete and the joints fully pointed with cement, is less conducive to the survival and growth of plants. Given time, usually about ten years, some plants are persistent enough to seed themselves and grow in the cracks of the paving, often rooting in the debris collected and rotted in the corners of the patio. The persistence of plants is to be marvelled at; *Buddleia*, *Verbascum* (mullein), *Digitalis* (foxglove) and *Rumex* (dock) are very often seen growing in the gutters of busy main roads, on the roofs of derelict buildings and on virtually sheer cliff faces, and are usually amongst the first to colonize a paved area.

To integrate good quality paving with plants, it is necessary to specifically allow for the planting. Holes should be left in the jointing of the paving, raking out the layer of concrete below. This enables plants to grow in compost or soil in the resulting gaps, rooting into the layers below the patio without disturbing other parts of the paving.

Another more positive way to integrate the planting into the paving of the patio is to remove the occasional paving unit (and its supporting concrete) so that the resulting gap is large enough to accommodate several small plants or a larger shrub. The soil in the hole should then be dug thoroughly, any stones, brickbats and lumps of concrete should be removed, and well rotted compost or manure dug well in, making sure that the soil is broken up at the furthest depth of digging to ensure adequate drainage. Appropriate plants can then be planted, with of course the addition of bonemeal to the soil at the time of planting as a long term, slow release fertilizer.

Plants in this sort of situation will suffer from similar problems to those planted in containers, as a hole in paving is nothing more than a ground level container on a large scale. Waterlogging and drying out are the two major problems suffered by plants growing in paving, and occasionally the heat from the paving in a hot summer can scorch the plants. Plants in this position will need regular feeding after a year, maybe two years, as their food supply will be very limited. For many plants, a regular winter mulch of manure or well rotted compost will both feed the plants and protect them from the worst.

From a design point of view, the plain surface of the paving sets off the leaves and flowers of paving plants in all their variety, and the leaves and flowers of the plants soften the harsh surface. The plants provide a visual link between the more formally planted areas of border and containers, the green surface uniformity of lawn, and the hard surface of the paving.

Most plants suitable for growing in paving are low growing. As well as the conditions listed above, other criteria for the choice of paving plants include the fact that taller plants would get in the way of the human occupants of the patio, most domestic paved areas being rather small. Larger plants, especially those with bold foliage, are more effective as well as being easier to control if planted on the margins of the paved areas.

Plants that grow well in paving

The list of plants below is a collection of plants of all types that are known to grow well in the difficult conditions created by paving. The list is not exclusive, as many other plants can grow well in the situation, but the following are generally very cooperative and will put on a good display if treated well. It is always worth experimenting with plants in different positions, and planting in paving is no exception; if a particular plant does not appear on the list but has many attributes to make it a good paving plant, then try it.

Bulbs and other similar plants have not been included in the list, as their dying foliage looks very unsightly, especially as spring flowering bulbs die down during the late spring and early summer, a time when the patio is in regular use and should look good. The smaller bulbs, such as *Crocus* (crocus), *Chionodoxa* (glory of the snow), and the small *Narcissus* (daffodils) can be grown in association with other plants that will grow and hide the dying foliage of the bulbs.

Many of the alpines look very good on a patio, but are very inconvenient to grow in a well trafficked area, as they require protection from winter wet.

The plants listed below are also variable in their ability to withstand being walked upon regularly, let alone having garden furniture placed upon them. Some, such as *Arenaria balerica* and *Anthemis nobilis 'Treneague'* (chamomile), will withstand moderate wear and tear quite satisfactorily, but others will curl up and die at the thought of a heavy foot misplaced.

Ajuga reptans
Alchemilla alpina
Alchemilla mollis
Alyssum maritimum
Alyssum saxatile
Anthemis nobilis
Arenaria balearica
Armeria maritima
Aubrieta deltoidea
Campanula portenschlagiana
Cotoneaster [prostrate and low-growing varieties] spp.
Dianthus deltoides
Euphorbia myrsinites
Hedera [small-leaved varieties] spp.
Helianthemum nummularium
Hypericum polyphyllum
Iberis sempervirens
Lamium maculatum
Limnanthes douglasii
Lithospermum diffusum
Lysimachia nummularia
Myosotis sylvatica
Nepeta faassenii
Origanum vulgare 'Aureum'
Origanum vulgare
Phlox amoena
Phlox douglasii
Phlox subulata
Pulsatilla vulgaris
Saponaria ocymoides
Saxifraga spp.
Sedum spurium
Stachys lanata
Thymus serpyllum
Verbena hybrids
Veronica prostrata
Viola cornuta

Planting in Containers

Large containers

Large containers are likely to remain in place in the patio for the whole year, possibly being brought in to a frost-free environment during a severe winter. They can be potted up with permanent planting, or the planting can be changed with the season. Whether the planting is permanent or temporary, the same principles of planting design apply.

Permanent planting can consist of combinations of trees, evergreen shrubs, deciduous shrubs, perennial plants and bulbs, corms and tubers, maybe in the form of a container herb garden, a container 'herbaceous border', a water garden or a topiary feature. Almost any combination of plants can be used, and the grouping and combining of plants for effects is discussed elsewhere.

Temporary planting can consist of a container vegetable garden, a temporary screen of annual climbers, or just the desire to keep all the planting options open and change the colour scheme and style of planting with the season.

Permanent planting is always planted directly into the compost in the container. Temporary planting can either be planted directly into the compost in the container, or can be retained in the pot liners in which the plants are grown, and the liners are then planted in the container. This method makes the changing of winter and summer bedding plants very quick and easy. The use of pot liners is very effective in troughs and window boxes, but is less efficient in the use of space in large round containers, as the plants cannot be set very close together.

To plant up a permanently planted container, first ensure that the container is clean and structurally sound, free from cracks and flaws that will break under the strain of the first frost. Then the container is 'crocked' by placing a layer of crocks or broken pots over the holes in the base of the pot. A layer of small stones or gravel is then spread over the crocks, followed by a layer of leaf mould or peat to act as a reservoir. The container is then filled to within 50 mm of the rim with a good quality loam based potting compost mixed with two or three handfuls of bonemeal (Fig. 13.1). If the compost is very dry, it should be watered thoroughly and left to stand and drain for 24 hours.

Once the design for the planting has been worked out, the final positions of the plants are located and holes of the appropriate size are made in the compost. The plants should be well watered and drained before removing them from their pots. Set the plants in their holes one at the time, at the same height or a fraction lower in the soil, and then firm the compost around the plant roots.

Once all the plants are in position and planted, the container should be mulched, either with gravel chippings or with pulverized bark, whichever is more appropriate. The whole contiiner should then be gently and thoroughly watered.

Window boxes

There is a very definite art to the planting of window boxes, for window boxes are containers with a difference – they are viewed mostly from one side. Usually located outside a window, the occupants of the room will look past the window box to the view outside, but will be able to enjoy the planting at close quarters. The maintenance is also usually undertaken from the inside of the building, rather than from outside. The overall effect of

Fig. 13.1 Cross section of large container.

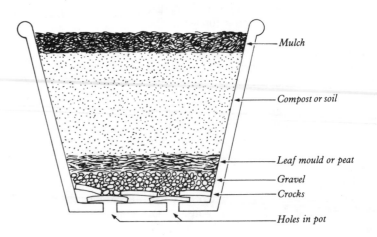

- Mulch

- Compost or soil

- Leaf mould or peat
- Gravel
- Crocks

- Holes in pot

the planting will be seen and appreciated by those outside the building, whether passers by on the pavement or road, or the occupants of a patio.

Window boxes can be constructed of a wide variety of materials in a wider variety of styles. Many window boxes are purely containers to hold plants outside a window, other window boxes are works of art in their own right. There is such fun in livening up a quiet corner with a window box designed, for instance, as a recumbent cat, painted in bold tiger stripes on the wooden construction, and planted with *Doronicum columnae* (leopard's bane), *Antennaria doica* (pussy toes), and *Puschkinia scilloides* (striped squill) for spring flowering, and *Nepeta nervosa* (small leaved catmint), *Catananche coerulea* (cupids dart) and *Lilium tigrinum* (tiger lily) for summer effects.

The style of window box, and its size, should be appropriate and in proportion to the building itself. A large, white painted timber container with decorated iron brackets will look totally out of place on a small suburban semi-detached house. Conversely, a simple, small self-watering window box would be totally lost and inappropriate on the front of a large Georgian mansion. Any container used for plants should be generous in size, and window boxes are no exception, because actively growing plants always spread further than originally anticipated, and in doing so give a warm relaxed feel to relieve the hardness of the walls of the building.

The colour of the window box is also an important factor to consider. Should the box blend with the house walls and allow the plants to be the most important feature, or should the window box be a feature in its own right? A window box should not stand out and dominate the scene with an aggressive colour and poor style, but can be a work of art in its own right.

When maintaining window boxes, the points to remember are that window boxes are nothing more than plant containers, generally quite shallow and not holding much soil, located in vulnerable positions in the air, and subject to all the problems that beset all other plant containers, problems of exposure to the sun, high winds, frost and freezing winds, lack of water, too much water and in some instances, pollution from vehicles of fumes, carbon monoxide, lead, and dirt.

Watering
The problems of watering and maintaining the window box in a suitable condition for the growth of plants can be overcome by ensuring that the drainage facilities are good, and providing an automatic watering system. The need for water exists throughout the whole year, as the proximity of the box to the house means that it will be within the rain shadow created by the roof, and so will be watered by rain only when the wind is in that quarter, and then probably not in an adequate quantity. Controlled watering is essential, as over-watering can cause a mud slurry to run down the wall of the house, looking unsightly and causing untold problems to the structure of the building, as well as all the other problems caused to the plants by waterlogging of their growing medium.

Adequate drainage is usually provided by the use of a layer of drainage material or 'crocks' at the bottom of the window box, beneath the soil. It is recommended that a layer of geotextile material (e.g. Terram or Biddim) is used to separate the soil from the drainage material and so prevent the drainage becoming clogged and ineffective.

If the window box is designed to be self watering, then the manufacturer's instructions should be followed when the box is installed, to ensure that the drainage works correctly. The use of the self watering system should also be in accordance with the manufacturer's instructions.

If the window box has to be watered manually, then it should be checked daily in dull weather, and more frequently in sunny weather, especially if the box is located so that it catches the sun or wind. The window box should never be allowed to dry out, as it will be very difficult to re-wet the soil, but conversely, the soil should never be allowed to become waterlogged due to over-enthusiastic watering or poor drainage.

Composts and mulches
The compost used in a window box should always be water retentive, so that the problems created by the position of the window box are

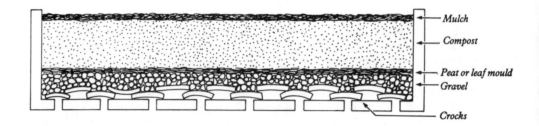

Fig. 13.2 Cross section of a window box.

mitigated a little by the growing medium. As the compost will be the life source for the plants growing in the window box, and will not be replaced unless it becomes totally lifeless, poisoned or is of the wrong pH for any new planting, then the best quality should always be used. Either a peat-based compost or a loam-based John Innes compost can be used in a window box.

Water-retaining polymers are now available on the domestic market and they are suitable for use in window boxes. These polymers come in the form of granules, but when water is added they swell up to many times their original size, absorbing vast quantities of water and then looking like lumps of jelly. These polymers will absorb up to fifty times their weight in water, and hold it in a form that is easily accessible to the plants as they grow and need it. Although the polymers can be very useful, especially used in a window box that is located in a particularly stressful position such as full sun, they are no substitute for daily care and regular watering of a window box.

Once planted, window boxes should always be mulched. The mulch could consist of a 20 mm layer of washed gravel, or a 50 mm layer of a fine grade bark mulch, or any other mulch that is clean and good to look at (Fig. 13.2). The use of a mulch will slow down the rate that the compost dries out and will maintain the moisture levels in the window box, so reducing the need for continual watering. With time, the mulch will gradually be absorbed into the soil and will improve it. A mulch will also reduce the compaction of the soil caused by continual watering.

Feeding

As with any place where plants are grown, the soil that they are growing in must be maintained in good heart to ensure healthy happy plants and a good display of flowers and foliage. If the plants were growing in the ground, an annual mulch of well rotted manure would be the preferred means of feeding both the soil and the plants. This method is not very suitable for window boxes, as manure is messy, with a pungent smell, and would probably need to be applied from within the building. Also, window boxes do not usually contain enough, if any, earthworms to integrate the manure into the soil, and the lack of regular rain would result in the manure forming a hard unsightly crust on the surface of the soil.

There are several other means of caring for the soil in a window box, the least preferred of which is to continually water the plants with a liquid chemical feed. This method gives good results in the short term, but does nothing to maintain the texture and life in the soil. In the longer term, the soil will become hard, impoverished and lifeless, and no amount of further chemical feeding will improve the health of either the plants or the soil. The window box will then need to be emptied of soil, thoroughly cleaned out, and refilled with good quality water retentive potting compost. This sort of task is time consuming and messy, and should be avoided whenever possible.

On the small scale of a window box, a compromise is needed between the use of chemical fertilizers and the organic method of feeding the plants and soil. During the

174

growing season, from late Spring through to late summer, the fast growth of the plants and the production of flowers can be helped with regular feeding with a good all-round liquid organic fertilizer, possibly of a seaweed origin. The production of fruit, flowers and strong hardwood can be encouraged with a fertilizer high in phosphorus and potassium, using a liquid feed that is balanced for such a purpose. These are especially useful for annual and perennial plants.

At the end of the main flowering season, when the window box is cleared, tidied and possibly replanted for winter, then a generous amount of a dehydrated organic manure should be added to the soil. These dehydrated organic manures are available bagged in small quantities, and are clean to handle, although there is a slight smell for the first few days of use. The dehydrated manure should be incorporated thoroughly into the soil and watered well in, but without disturbing the roots of any permanent planting. In the following spring, a small amount of 'Growmore' should be incorporated with any spring bedding plants. Where the window box contains predominantly permanent planting, a generous amount of bonemeal should be added to the soil when the planting is originally undertaken, and more should be added each autumn, with the dehydrated organic manure.

Maintenance

Window box planting needs regular maintenance without fail, as in such a small area any minor problem quickly becomes very visible. Remember, though, that regular maintenance does not mean cutting every plant back to a neat little mound that never touches another plant. On the contrary, a little controlled chaos is very attractive in a window box, as long as it does not get out of hand to the detriment of the health and looks of the plants. Pruning of plants follows the same regime as with plants in other containers and in the ground, but if the choice of plants was good in the first place, then very little pruning should be necessary.

Control of pests and diseases

Plants that are well tended, fed and cared for will generally be fit and healthy, especially if their location is considered with care and the correct plants chosen for that position. A full breakdown of appropriate treatments for various pest and disease problems is given elsewhere in this book. The use of chemicals should be avoided whenever possible, and it is feasible and sometimes much more practical to use simple remedies in such a small area of planting. For instance, an infestation of greenfly can be treated by washing the plant with a dilute detergent, easily applied using a sponge. This action also washes off the greenfly. This small scale gentle treatment of the plants is much easier to undertake than mixing up messy and smelly chemicals, as it is not essential to wear protective clothing and can be done at a moment's notice, as soon as the problem is observed. It also means that the plants receive some personal handling and care.

Other window box problems

Frost is not so much a problem with window boxes as with free-standing containers. Window boxes gain a lot of protection and warmth from the building to which they are attached, and will rarely be affected by any other than a very hard frost. However, window boxes are very vulnerable to the effects of freezing winds, as their location, raised up above the ground but attached to a building, means that they are very exposed to wind but do not have the benefit of other plants around for shelter. Freezing winds will burn the new growths of deciduous plants and the leaves of evergreen plants, and often the damage is not evident until some months later, when the plants start growing again after their winter dormancy. As many plants will happily withstand frost, the best form of protection for a planted window box is to provide enough shelter to protect the plants from the wind.

Window boxes, as they are exposed to the wind, are very vulnerable to drying out. Once having dried out, it is difficult to effectively re-wet the soil in the box, especially as the box cannot usually be easily removed from the building and soaked in water. Drying out of the soil imposes all sorts of stress on the plants, and affects their growth for the rest of their life. The wind itself will also affect the choice of plants, as some plants otherwise ideal for window box culture are very sensitive to the

Fig. 13.3 Drawing of window box plants trailing down house wall.

wind and will grow in a raised exposed position.

Some window boxes will be very exposed to forms of pollution, especially if they are located near a busy road. Dirt, fumes and lead deposit will all affect the growth of the plants, and the choice of plants. For instance, it is not advisable to eat any vegetables of herbs grown in a window box by a busy road, due to contamination by petrol fumes, lead and dirt. The same pollutants will also affect the occupants of the room opening out onto the window box.

Any window box fronting onto a street will have a risk of being affected by vandalism in some form, whether it is the picking of flowers, stealing of plants, or the wanton destruction of the whole window box. But it is worth keeping a street-facing window box in good condition, as a neglected box is far more likely to suffer from vandalism than a well tended box.

Window boxes as part of the patio design
The design of a patio can be considerably enhanced by the installation of window boxes, if they are appropriate to the style of the house and the garden, and suitable for the lifestyle of the occupants. Window boxes themselves can reflect the style of the patio and increase the potential of the design. The planting can echo

and augment the ground level planting, and give scope to increase the potential of the area with planting that trails down the walls of the house from a high level, as well as plants that climb up the walls from a low level. The subtle use of window boxes can create a vertical garden to complement the horizontal garden (Fig.13.3).

Planting design for window boxes
The most effective planting for a window box is to limit the choice of plants to simply one or two species, and allow them to grow to fill the window box to the point of spilling out over the sides. It does not matter whether the choice of plants are annuals, biennials, perennials, small growing shrubs or climbers, the impact of a simple design is much more than with a collection of different plants. As window boxes are generally viewed from a distance, it is the overall impact that matters, rather than the details.

Window boxes can also be planted with a theme. The theme could be one of colour of flowers and foliage, or of different textures, or even of edible plants, or healing plants. For instance, a window box with a selection of herbs outside a kitchen window will be both useful and decorative, as well as smelling good and, depending on the choice of herbs, have colour and interest for most of the year.

As with all planting design, all the aspects of the plants will need to be considered, such as leaf colour, leaf texture, flower colour, time of flowering, shape of plant and its habit, and of course cultural requirements. All the design principles of harmony and contrast will need to be considered, even on the small scale of a window box, and in relation to the rest of the patio.

Suggested plants suitable for window boxes
  Permanent planting
    All low growing herbs
    Anthemis cupaniana
    Berberis thunbergii 'Atropurpurea nana'
    Clematis spp and hybrids
    Erica (heather) varieties
    Euonymus fortunei cvs especially 'Emerald Gaiety' 'Silver Pillar'
    Grasses such as *Carex morrowii* 'Evergold' and *Festuca glauca*
    Hebe 'Carl Teschner'
    Hebe pinguifolia 'Pagei'
    Hedera (ivy) varieties
    Jasmine spp
    Juniperus communis 'Compressa'
    Miniature roses
    Ophiopogon planiscapus nigrescens
    Vinca spp. (especially *Vinca minor*)

  Temporary planting – annuals, biennials and tender shrubs
    Alyssum maritima
    Begonias, both fibrous-rooted and tuberous-rooted
    Convolvulus 'Tricolor'
    Dianthus, annual
    Fuchsias
    Helichrysum petiolarum
    Impatiens
    Lobelia erinus
    Pansies and *Violas*
    Pelargoniums, especially trailing varieties
    Petunia × hybrida
    Tropaeolum majus nanum

Bonsai

Bonsai is the specialized art of growing plants in containers, and there are many books available which explore the art, and the philosophy from which it stems, in great depth.

The idea beneath the cultivation of bonsai plants is the creation and enjoyment of the landscape in miniature. The word 'bonsai' means literally 'plant in a tray'. It is a technique by which any tree or shrub can be turned into a dwarf specimen by restricting its growth, and by pruning its roots and branches. It is in the skilled pruning that the art lies, being able to see the potential adult tree in a miniature form in a seedling, and being able to train and develop the seedling to create this miniature adult.

The technique was developed by the Japanese and Chinese, and was applied mainly to hardy trees and shrubs of all kinds, such as *Betula* (birch), *Acer* (maple), *Pinus* (pine), *Larix* (larch) and *Fagus* (beech). As these types of plant are totally hardy, they spend most of their time outdoors, being brought into a warm house only for a few days at a time.

The containers used for bonsai plants are very distinctive, usually shallow earthenware dishes, glazed on the outside with a deep lustre glaze, and with large drainage holes in the base. As the dishes are very shallow and the water demand of the plants is quite great, they need very frequent watering, especially in warm weather.

The aim of regular pruning and root pruning is to gradually develop a plant of character that looks like a miniature version of the same plant found in the wild. The regular pruning and restricted root run in the shallow dish will slow the growth rate down and help the plant to produce small leaves in scale with its size.

As the plants grow they can be trained into very complex shapes and can be made to look very weatherworn and gnarled. Plants can seem to be of great age and character when they are only a few years old, but as with trees and shrubs that they really are, bonsai trees can live to a great age.

Bonsai plants can be used to decorate the patio in many ways. As a focal point, a bonsai tree is restrained and cautious, inviting a closer look at its detail and complexities, and is best placed on its own. Any other plant too close will alter the relative size relationships and make the bonsai tree just seem like a stunted weed by altering the scale of the miniature landscape. But if the plants near the bonsai are

177

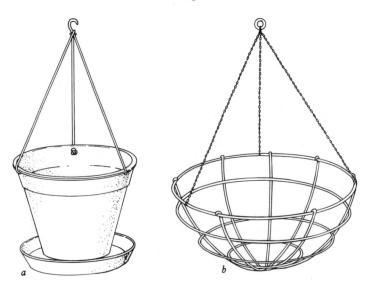

Fig. 13.4 Two types of hanging basket.
(a) Self watering
(b) Wire.

chosen with care, they can continue the effect created by the bonsai and extend the miniature landscape into the garden.

Plants suitable for growing as Bonsai

Trees:
Acer palmatum
Betula pendula
Fagus sylvatica
Larix decidua
Pinus nigra

Shrubs:
Cotoneaster horizontalis
Eleagnus × ebbingei

Hanging baskets and other containers

Hanging baskets are often used to decorate the outside of buildings, and the domestic patio area is another place where they can be used to good effect. Hanging containers add another dimension to the planting of a patio and are generally an underused feature with a lot of potential for the imaginative gardener.

Hanging and wall-mounted containers can add height to planting schemes, and are very valuable to use in small spaces. When planted, they should look good from below as well as from the side and above.

Types and styles of hanging baskets

Self-watering hanging baskets resemble hanging flower pots with a built-in dish beneath the pot, usually made of plastic (Fig. 13.4(a)). These containers should be crocked and filled with compost like any ordinary flower pot, and then planted with plants suitable for the pot shape, colour and location.

The traditional wire basket, often made of plastic coated wire, has much more potential and scope in its use and planting than the self-watering type of container, despite the problems of dripping after watering and drying out (Fig. 13.4(b)). Plants chosen should be able to withstand a certain amount of drying out, as this will be a problem however conscientiously the watering is undertaken.

Composts

Composts used in hanging baskets should always be free-draining but water retentive. Peat-based composts are more water retentive than loam-based composts, but are more difficult to re-wet once they have dried out. Water-retaining polymers are useful to mix with the potting soil to greatly increase the water retentive properties of the compost, but they do occupy a noticeable amount of space in the pot or basket, so reducing the amount of available nutrients for the plants.

Watering

Watering of hanging baskets is achieved in one of two ways: either the water is taken to the basket, or the basket is taken to the water. When baskets are hung at a high level, it is difficult to water them from a watering can or hand held hose. One simple method to overcome this problem is to tie a length of hose to a bamboo cane about 1 m ($3\frac{1}{4}$ ft) long and use it as an extension hose from the hosepipe. In this way the basket can be watered more accurately, less water is spilled and wasted, and the watering can all be done from ground level without straining. A similar idea is to use a purpose made attachment connected to a large garden sprayer, only to use water in the container, not pesticide!

To take the basket to the water, the basket should be hung on a hook attached to a rope and pulley, so that the basket can be lowered and raised at will, and so then becomes easier to maintain and water. There are mechanical devices available from specialist shops which allow one to raise and lower the hanging basket just by pulling it down and pushing it back into place again, similar to a rise-and-fall light fitting.

Regular watering is the essence of a good hanging basket. As the whole of the basket is exposed to the elements, it will dry out very fast, especially in hot weather. The basket should be watered at least once a day, at least twice in hot weather, and checked at regular intervals. In times of a heatwave, then it is best to move the basket out of direct sunlight into a shady spot.

Feeding

As a hanging basket needs to be watered so frequently, it is essential that it is fed regularly. Each time the basket is watered, some nutrients are washed through the soil and are lost with the excess water. To keep the basket planting healthy, it is necessary to feed the plants regularly, probably once each week. A good all round liquid feed is recommended, preferably one that is high in potassium and phosphorus to stimulate the flowering of the plants, rather than a fertilizer that is high in nitrogen, which will stimulate lush green leafy growth at the expense of flowers.

Maintenance

The most important items of maintenance for a hanging basket are watering and deadheading. Regular deadheading of plants prolongs their flowering season, as the removal of dead flower heads allows space for new flowers to grow and open. Some plants will continue to flower through the whole summer without any deadheading, but many appreciate the removal of spent flowers and the general tidying that this incurs. Regular pinching out of the growing tips of some plants will encourage them to produce bushy new growth, and the removal of dead flower heads prevents the production of seeds, and allows that energy to be spent in the production of more flowers.

Towards the end of the season, the removal of any annual plants that have died or are dying will give the space for the other plants to grow for the final part of the season, and put on a show until the basket is emptied.

It is recommended that the baskets are removed for the winter months, as they are very vulnerable to the effects of frost and wind. A hanging basket has no natural protection for the plant roots, and frost can easily get into the root systems of the plants and kill them outright. Wind, too, can have devastating effects by drying out the basket in a matter of a few hours, and combined with frost, can rapidly kill a marvellous hanging display.

Location

Traditionally, hanging baskets are hung either side of a doorway or porch in a domestic situation. In municipal and commercial locations, they are often hung on posts purpose made for the job, but with little if any relationship to a building or other planting in the area.

As hanging baskets are by nature temporary features, they can be located almost anywhere. The restrictions on their location are both practical and aesthetic, as a hanging basket needs somewhere from which to hang, and it must look good once hung there. It is important that the chosen hanging place is amenable to plant life, even if it does entail a commitment in terms of watering and maintenance.

Hanging baskets can be used in all sorts of locations where normally no other plant would survive, for the same reasons that make them difficult to maintain. Because hanging baskets always needs regular watering, they can be hung in places where they will never receive any natural rainfall, such as inside a porch or verandah, or under a loggia. They can be used to brighten a shady corner, because they can be turned round easily to stop the plants growing leggy, or can be regularly exchanged with hanging baskets growing in full sun, thus giving each group of plants a respite from that set of inhospitable conditions.

The final bonus of a hanging basket is that it is temporary. If the planting scheme is not good or does not fit with other planting, or if for some reason the basket dries out beyond redemption and the plants die, or for any other reason, horticultural, aesthetic or otherwise, the hanging basket can just be removed and emptied, without leaving bare soil to stare recriminatingly after the deed has been done. Similarly, the planting scheme can be altered each year if so desired, and many different combinations and colours can be used, without great expense or permanent commitment.

Planting design
As a hanging basket is such a small container compared with the rest of the garden, one of the most important considerations when planting is scale. Scale is to be considered in the choice of plants, the arrangement of the plants, and especially in the location of the hanging basket.

Hanging baskets look best when they are planted with small-leafed plants, where the size of leaf and size of container relate to each other. A basket planted with large-leafed plants will be swamped under the sheer enormity of the leaves, and it will not take many large leaves to fill the basket. Large leaves will also give the impression of the basket being very close, and will probably cause people to duck their heads unnecessarily!

The choice of plants is determined not only by scale, but also by many other factors. The location of the hanging basket is important, as to whether it will be hung in a cold, draughty corner, or hung in a sheltered nook in a wall which will enable the contents to gently cook,

even in a damp grey summer. Although a hanging basket is very adaptable, it is best to start with the most appropriate plants for the location.

The arrangement of the plants will to an extent be determined by how close the hanging basket will be looked at. The best effects and impacts are achieved by planting the basket with solely one species of plant, allowing it to spill over the sides and planting it to grow through the bottom so the mature effect is of a ball of flowers and foliage. For a hanging basket that is going to be seen at close quarters, a mixture of planting that coordinates with the planting of the surrounding area can raise the planting scheme to eye level and above and the hanging basket marries into the whole area as if it was always intended to be there. To create a hanging basket that is a focal point of the area of planting, the basket should be planted boldly, with a few different plants as possible, in as very strong tone of one colour used in that area of the garden.

When planting a basket of mixed species of plants, consideration must be given to the major design principles of scale, harmony, contrast, etc. Contrast is particularly useful to use in such a small container, where the plants are very close together and their leaves grow almost intermeshed, the contrast of foliage colour and texture, of size and shape, and of flower size, shape and colour create an unusual and interesting planting.

Planting up a hanging basket
Wire hanging baskets need lining to stop the soil and plants falling out, and either a natural lining of sphagnum moss or a synthetic lining of green foam will work well. It is easier to work with the basket supported on a large pot or a bucket, to keep it stable and safe during filling. Sphagnum moss should be living, and well dampened before use, planted green side outwards and held in place with a little potting compost.

Plants can be planted through the side of the basket, through the moss and into the soil in the basket. Using a foam liner, plants can be planted through the slits as the basket is filled with compost. In this way the basket will look good from below as well as from the side and above.

Fig. 13.5 Planting a hanging basket.
(b) Support basket on large pot or bucket. Start to line basket with moss
(b) Hold moss in place with compost
(c) Plant trailing plants through sides of basket while filling

(d) Continue filling and planting basket
(e) Mulch planted basket with moss, leaving room to water.

The basket is gradually lined with moss and filled with potting compost, and more plants are planted in the top of the basket. The tallest plants should be planted in the centre of the basket, and any trailing plants should be planted at the edges. The top level of compost should come to about 20 mm ($\frac{3}{4}$ in) below the top of the basket, to allow enough space for a topping of moss around the plants that will act like a mulch, and to still leave a space for water, so that it does not all run off the top surface

without having time or space to soak into the compost (Fig. 13.5).

Wall containers and baskets should be planted up in a similar manner, but with the taller plants to the back of the container, against the wall.

After planting, the basket should be watered gently but thoroughly. If the potting compost is very dry, the basket can be soaked for a while in a bowl of water until it is thoroughly moistened. If the compost is not completely damp at this point, the plants will not become established and thrive, and the basket will never look good.

Suitable plants for hanging baskets:

Annuals such as:
Alyssum
Begonia
Dianthus
Helichrysum petiolarum
Impatiens
Lobelia
Petunia

Perennials such as:
Alchemilla mollis
Aubrieta
Campanula
Iberis sempervirens
Nepeta alpina
Violas and *pansies*

Tender shrubs such as:
Fuchsia with trailing habits
Pelargonium

Shrubs such as:
Euonymus fortunei with low growing trailing habits
Hebe

Strawberry barrels and parsley pots

Tall pots and barrels with holes in the sides for plants enable large crops to be grown in a small space, but this form of intensive growing needs extra care and attention.

The traditional earthenware parsley pot is made of terracotta and has numerous holes for plants above its 'waistline'. Parsley pots do not always need a central drainage and watering column, but one can be made from a tube 75 mm diameter of chicken wire filled with gravel. The drainage column should finish about 150 mm below the surface of the soil. Strawberry barrels are often made of plastic, are self assembly, and are straight sided with a central drainage column. These barrels can often house as many as thirty plants, and are a very intense form of cultivation.

When full of compost, strawberry barrels and parsley pots are very heavy to manoeuvre, so before planting up they should be located in their final position, preferably on castors or a movable base, so that they can be turned at regular intervals to ensure that each plant receives some sunshine. The barrel or pot should also be as level as possible and slightly raised up, to ensure that all the plants receive an adequate amount of water, and that the excess drains away (Fig. 13.6).

Planting up

Plant up a strawberry barrel or parsley pot on a calm, dull day. With the pot or barrel on a level surface as above, cover any large drainage holes with crocks and put in a layer of large gravel and small pebbles at the bottom for drainage. Then if you want a drainage column up the centre of the pot, put it in now and start to fill it up with gravel, whilst filling up the rest of the pot with compost. Put a flower pot upside down over the top of the drainage column once it is full of gravel to stop any compost and roots growing into it. Plant the required plants at the appropriate places as the level of each hole is reached, firming the compost gently as it is added. Finish filling the pot about 75 mm ($2\frac{1}{2}$ in) below the rim, and plant up to the top. Finally, water the plants well.

General care of strawberry barrels and parsley pots is similar to that of other containers, with regular efficient watering as the first priority. Regular feeding with a liquid organic feed is essential, especially once any fruit has started to form, as the large number of plants will soon deplete the available nutrients in the potting compost. The pot or barrel will also need to be turned regularly, to ensure that all the plants receive some sunshine and do not become leggy.

Plants for strawberry barrels and parsley pots:
annual plants, trailing
Fragaria × ananassa (strawberry)
Pelargoniums, especially trailing geraniums
Petroselinum crispum (parsley)
Salvia officinalis (sage)
Thymus spp. (thyme)
other low growing herbs

Potato barrels

Worthwhile crops of potatoes can be grown in a very small space using a potato barrel. Potato barrels are similar to strawberry barrels but without the side holes for plants to grow out of,

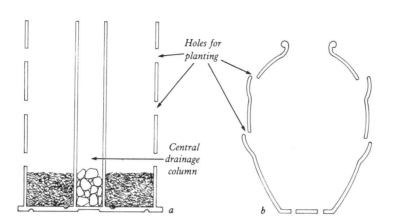

Fig. 13.6 Cross section of (a) Strawberry barrel (b) Parsley pot.

Holes for planting

Central drainage column

a

b

usually about 750 mm (2 ft 6 in) high and 600 mm (2 ft) wide (Fig. 13.7).

First a layer of drainage material or crocks is placed in the bottom of the barrel, and then about 100 mm (4 in) of potting compost is added. Lay four or five sprouted seed potatoes evenly on the soil, with the sprouts upwards, and cover with another 100 mm (4 in) of potting soil, firm and water well. The potato plants will grow fast through the soil, and when they have reached about 200 mm (8 in), add another 150 mm (6 in) of potting compost. Each time the plant stems have grown 150–200 mm (6–8 in) above the soil level, add 100–150 mm (4–6 in) more potting compost.

Add a final layer of compost to bring the soil level up to 50 mm (2 in) below the rim of the barrel, and allow the plants to grow normally, watering well as necessary throughout all the growing period. Check the size of the developing potatoes by feeling for them under the soil; harvest early varieties when the plants flower, maincrop potatoes when the leaves start to die down.

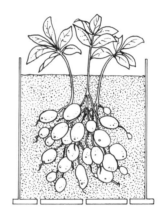

Fig. 13.7 Cross section of a potato barrel.

Sinks

Sinks are shallow containers, made either of glazed china or of stone, that are usually used for the cultivation of alpine plants.

Glazed china sinks are often discards from old fashioned kitchens, unceremoniously disposed of after a long life of domestic duties.

Fig. 13.8 Sink garden planted and mulched with gravel.

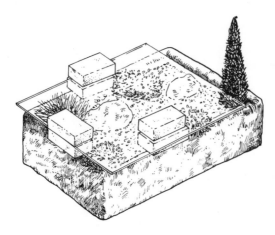

Fig. 13.9 Sink garden with winter protection.

The sink should be planted using appropriate alpine plants, well spaced to display them well. The surface of the sink should be mulched with gravel, possibly with the addition of one or two larger stones to give the feel of a miniature mountain landscape (Fig. 13.8).

It is not usually necessary to move alpine sinks into a sheltered place for winter, but it is essential that they are kept free draining and protected from accumulating excess rainfall. The plants in the sink can be protected from the worst of the rain by covering the sink over with a piece of glass raised on bricks, and weighted down with bricks to prevent the wind lifting and breaking the glass (Fig. 13.9). This protection should be removed in spring to allow the plants the full warmth of the sunlight.

Plants Types

The best patio planting consists of a mixture of established trees and shrubs, with climbers, perennials, biennials, annuals, bulbs, ferns, herbs, fruit, vegetables, topiary and water plants growing in appropriate places within the framework. The aim of the patio planting is to provide a backdrop of interesting plants that creates a simple, virtually self maintaining picture against which the containers can be placed, their planting used to enhance and augment the patio planting, or used to provide colour, contrast and bright seasonal interest.

The choice of plants for patio and container planting can be overwhelming, but the options are immediately reduced once the practical constraints are taken into consideration. Excesses or deficiencies of light or shade, shelter or wind, and the actual physical location of the plants will reduce the choice for any particular location, as will the type and acidity or alkalinity of the soil.

The choice of plants will definitely be determined by aesthetic considerations, using the rules of design to contrast the leaf shapes, to blend flower colours, to create rhythm and repetition with the shapes of the plants, the shape of leaves, colour of foliage and flowers and to harmonize with paving, walling and any adjacent buildings.

It is important to remember that a plant is a

They can be very simply converted for garden use and the white glazed surfaces can be disguised if desired with a simple mixture plastered on the outside to give the appearance of volcanic rock or rough cut stone.

To disguise a glazed sink, first sand the surface very thoroughly with a very coarse sandpaper, to give a key to the covering mixture. Then make a mixture of coarse sand, peat and cement, adding just enough water so that it adheres to the china. This mixture is then plastered thickly to the sides and top edges of the sink, working it down the inside so that the finished article looks as though it has been water worn out of rock. The outside of the sink can be built up to give a naturalistic look to the container. The sink must be left to 'go off' for several days before any attempt is made to move it.

If a sink is to be planted with alpines, then alpine conditions must be created. Although alpines will withstand great depths of snow and freezing cold weather, they will not tolerate damp conditions around their roots. Good drainage must be provided with plenty of crocks or stones in the bottom of the sink, and the plug hole must be left open to drain any surplus water away fast. Any good quality potting compost will be suitable for alpine plants, but it should be mixed with some fine gravel and silver sand to provide very good drainage conditions.

living and growing being, and will often become much larger than the knee-high bunches of leafless twigs that was bought in the preceding winter. Always check the eventual size of the plants, as a rapidly growing and eventually very large shrub will completely alter the scale of the planting, and possibly overwhelm a small patio area. Conversely, a plant that will never ever grow higher than waist high is a poor choice for privacy and screening.

It is very difficult to give the potential size of plants in precise figures, as there are many factors that govern the ultimate size of a plant, and these factors often interact. The quality of the soil is important, as an impoverished soil will only allow poor plant growth and poor plant health. It is essential that the soil is improved with well rotted manure and good compost before any plants are planted, and that the improvement of the soil continues every season. Soil improvement, though, must be undertaken with the plants in mind, as some plants actually enjoy a slightly impoverished soil and will grow smaller and more compact, and better able to withstand the cold and wind.

The physical elevation of the garden will also affect the potential size of a plant. A high altitude garden will have a shorter growing season, and so a plant will take longer to reach its ultimate size. Also, at high altitudes, the effects of wind are more telling.

Other factors affecting the size of plants include latitude, the height of the water table, the presence of available water, soil temperature, and the amount of shade to which the plant is subjected. All these factors are interrelated; for instance, the soil in a shady position will be cooler than the soil in a sunny position, and will dry out at a slower rate, leaving more available water.

Another important aspect of establishing a successful patio and container garden is the hardiness of the plants that are used. The concept of hardiness can present a great problem, but it is basically the ability of the plant to survive. Hardiness depends on two factors – air temperature and wind speed. The greater the wind speed, the greater the cooling effect will be on the plant. So the effect of a strong breeze on a light ground frost is to make it seem much harder and colder. Any wind will dry soil out quickly, and will evaporate more moisture through the leaves of a plant, causing a greater water demand on the soil. A plant that will happily survive a frost say of $-5°C$ ($23°F$) might well not tolerate the same temperature with a wind of Force 5.

Hardiness is not an absolute phenomenon. A shrub might well be very hardy after a long, hot summer and a cool, dry autumn, which are perfect conditions for woody stems to ripen. The same shrub, though, may well succumb to a light frost after a wet summer and a warm, wet autumn, where the new growth of wood has not had a chance to ripen and harden, and is still very soft.

Proximity to the sea is another factor affecting hardiness, as the sea air will mitigate the effect of frost, and allow less hardy plants to be grown. But the sea air will stunt and distort the growth of some plants and other plants will die at a hint of salt on the breeze.

The distinction between hardy and half-hardy plants depends to a great extent on local climate and microclimate. Some plants traditionally grown as half-hardy annuals are suitable for sowing outside after all danger of frost has past, especially in warmer more sheltered areas. Many plants grown as tender perennials will withstand a certain amount of frost, especially if they are sheltered from the wind.

Finally, the choice of plants used in the patio and container garden will depend on what is available. Garden centres and nurseries only stock a limited range of plants, garden centres especially selling only plants that sell well. The customer is then limited to only being able to buy what the garden centres stock, unless an effort is made to seek out the more specialist nurseries to obtain some of the less common plants.

Sadly, many garden centres and nurseries do not look after their plant stock as well as they should, and it is essential to choose the plants fastidiously, buying only those that are healthy and vigorous and will grow on quickly. Size is no indication of vigour, and it is better to chose a plant with three or four short but strong, sturdy shoots than a plant with one long spindly shoot that has been struggling to reach the light. The bark and leaves should be of a good, fresh colour with no obvious blemishes that could be the signs of a pest or disease attack. Large numbers of weed seedlings in the pot indicate neglect, and the plant will probably have suffered similarly.

If a plant appears to be superficially satisfactory, do not hestitate to knock it out of its pot to check its roots. A good plant should have a well developed root system that permeates and holds on to much of the compost in the pot. It should, though, not have spent so long in its pot that the roots have wound themselves around the inside of the pot walls and become 'pot-bound'. If there is no alternative to a pot-bound plant, the roots should be carefully teased out before planting. If a plant is so pot bound that there is little compost left in the pot to act as a water reservoir, and the leaves have started to wilt and yellow, then it should not be bought under any circumstances, as it will not become established and thrive.

If, when you knock a plant out of its pot, all the compost falls away leaving a shrub with a small root ball, it is highly likely that it was not grown in the container and has been recently potted up from open ground. Again, unless there is no other option, a shrub like this should not be bought, as it will not grow away well once planted, and will need vast quantities of water to become established.

Evergreen Trees and Shrubs

A shrub is a woody plant that does not die down to the ground in the winter, but retains its woody stems. An evergreen shrub also keeps its leaves throughout the winter. A tree has a single woody stem unbranched to about half or more of its height, and the same species of plant can be trained to grow either as a tree or a shrub. This section covers evergreen trees and shrubs that are not conifers, which are discussed elsewhere.

Naturally small and medium sized shrubs are the easiest to grow in containers, but many larger size trees and shrubs can be grown, provided the roots can be annually pruned to restrict the growth.

The care of trees and shrubs in containers and on patios is straight forward, provided several points are remembered. Trees and shrubs are designed by nature to grow in much larger areas, where they can spread their roots and canopies. When growing in containers and on a patio, their roots are restricted, and so their ability to forage for food and water is drastically curtailed. To ensure that the plants grow and stay healthy, they need regular watering, feeding, and care of their soil.

Evergreen trees and shrubs need water all the year round, as they do not lose their leaves and continue to transpire through the winter as well as through the summer. Ensuring an adequate water supply in winter can be difficult at times, when a hard frost freezes the soil and the plant roots cannot take up any water. Plants grown in containers should be moved into sheltered, preferably frostfree areas for the winter months. Those evergreen plants growing in the ground have a much greater chance of survival in frosty weather as their roots are insulated by the surrounding soil. The greatest stress is placed on evergreen plants when there is a freezing wind that causes the plants to use more water, but the ground is frozen, making the water unavailable.

Evergreen trees and shrubs grown in pots need regular care to their soil to thrive. One method of care is to repot the plants annually, removing all the old soil from around the plant roots and repotting the plant in fresh compost in a larger size pot, or in the same size pot if it has reached the required size. The plant roots can be pruned to restrict the size of the plant, especially a strong growing shrub, but this is a difficult job to do successfully. Another method of care is to feed the plant regularly throughout the summer with a liquid organic feed, and to mulch the soil thickly in the winter with a well rotted compost. The soil can be replaced every few years if so desired, but with regular feeding, watering and general care and attention, this should rarely be necessary.

Evergreen trees and shrubs grown in pots and in the limited confines of the patio need regular pruning to keep them relatively compact and in good shape. For most plants, all that is needed is the removal of dead stems and small branches that spoil the overall shape, and the shortening back of any very long growth. Many of the grey leafed evergreen shrubs need cutting back hard in the late spring to encourage fresh new growth in the summer, and to allow the plant the protection of this new growth in the winter.

Deciduous Trees and Shrubs

Deciduous trees and shrubs all lose their leaves at some point in the year, usually autumn, and sometimes in a blaze of colour, but all retain their woody stems above the soil surface. There are also a few conifers that are deciduous, but all of them are forest trees and are potentially far too large for patios or container culture!

Deciduous trees and shrubs give a changing interest to the garden and show the beauty of the seasons in the wide variety of leaves, flowers, bark and twigs, habit and form, fruit and berry. They are generally very easy to grow, and many are tolerant of adverse conditions. Some, such as roses, have a wonderful fragrance in the flowers as well as beauty. They make good plants for container culture, with a wide variety to choose from to suit any and every situation. In the restricted area of the patio and containers, all the plants grown must have several attributes that make them desirable, because there is not a great deal of space for the type of plant that has one brief magnificent moment of glory and is then very boring for the rest of the season. All the plants included in the list below are desirable for at least two attributes that will give interest in the garden.

Because this group of trees and shrubs are deciduous, they are dormant for several months of the year and so make less demand on their environment in terms of food and water. Despite this, they can still suffer a great deal during frosty weather, and often the damage is not evident until well into the growing season in the following year. Deciduous trees and shrubs grown in containers should therefore be moved into a sheltered, frost free place for the winter, or otherwise protected against the frost by wrapping the container in insulating material. Deciduous trees and shrubs growing in the ground are naturally protected by the soil and by the proximity of other plants and buildings.

General care of deciduous trees and shrubs is similar to that of other plants, that is, water well, feed well, mulch well, prune appropriately and care carefully for the plants. Most plants grown in containers thrive in any good potting compost, whether peat based or loam based. General soil care can consist of an annual top dressing of fresh compost in spring and regular liquid feeding in the summer, with repotting of the plants every two or three years combined with pruning of the roots, or the plant container can be mulched well with well rotted manure and fed with a liquid organic feed in the summer. Plants growing directly in the soil around the patio will just need a good annual mulch of well rotted manure. In all cases it is essential that no plant ever suffers from lack of water.

There are many ways of pruning deciduous trees and shrubs, and there are many that need no pruning other than the removal of dead and crossing over wood, and the removal of straying growth. Generally, the rule of thumb is that a shrub is pruned after flowering, and that the old wood that has flowered is removed. Spring flowering shrubs like forsythia and weigela are pruned in early summer, and late flowering shrubs like hydrangea are pruned in spring.

Conifers

Conifers are cone-bearing trees, many of forest origin and consequently of potentially a great size. Conifers for use in containers must be chosen with care to ensure that their container homes are large enough for several years' growth and that the species used will not outgrow its position too rapidly.

Conifers grow well in containers, as they tolerate root restrictions, and need much less food from the soil than other larger leafed plants, especially deciduous plants and perennials. A very few conifers are deciduous, and these are very large, fast growing trees which are totally inappropriate to grow in containers, other than as bonsai trees.

Conifers are available in a very wide variety of shape, ultimate size and colour. Shapes very from very low growing spreading plants like *Juniperus horizontalis* 'Glauca' (blue juniper) to very distinctly upright plants, such as *Juniperus virginiana* 'Sky Rocket', with variations and permutations of globes, cones, vases and spires. Colours vary from the bronze golds of *Thuja occidentalis* 'Rheingold' in winter through yellow greens, greens, blue greens to the silvery blue foliage of *Juniperus squamata* 'Blue Carpet'.

Ultimate size is important when choosing conifers for patio and container culture, as it gives an indication of the rate of growth. A fast growing conifer will soon grow out of its space, and a conifer that is destined to grow to 36 m (120 ft) will inevitably have a fast growth rate, and so will not be recommended for growing in a container. Other conifers lose their distinctive shapes or foliage with age, sometimes becoming open and leggy, or gaining a totally different character and style. Some conifers, sold as miniature or dwarf conifers, are not so much miniature or dwarf, but are just slower growing than others; there is no reason why these should not be planted in containers for a few years until they grow too large, when they can be planted out in the garden.

Conifers look best grown singly as specimen plants in tubs. Spaces in the containers can be used for small bulbs or sometimes annuals, but conifers are distinct and handsome without the need for a supporting cast.

Conifers are easy to grow in containers, providing attention is paid to their basic requirements. Most are tolerant of any soil, although a few are very specific about their needs for an acid soil. They should be top dressed each year with fresh potting soil, or in alternate years use the addition of a slow release fertilizer, such as bonemeal, forked lightly into the top surface of the soil, to replenish the soil.

Pruning is generally not necessary, except to remove any dead or dying wood, or to remove any parts of the plant that may have reverted in leaf form, or in habit.

The most important consideration for growing conifers in containers is that they must never be allowed to dry out. The need for water continues for twelve months of the year, and it is important to ensure that the conifer is always watered when there is the need, even in the middle of winter. The middle of winter is in fact extremely important, as conifers generally do not lose their leaves, and so continue to use a substantial amount of water every day. Windy weather increases the plant's water demand, and frosty weather inhibits the uptake of water from the soil, so a combination of wind and frost can be disastrous for conifers. Adequate available water is essential in such adverse conditions to the life of the container grown conifer.

Climbers and Wall Shrubs

Many houses have exterior walls that benefit from the interest and colour provided by climbing plants and wall trained shrubs. In the limited living area provided by the patio garden, climbing plants provide an extension of the garden into the vertical plane, and a whole new area to consider.

Climbers cling to their supports in several different ways, and these influence the choice of plants. Some climbers are self supporting, clinging to the walls of a building with adapted roots that form small suction pads; this category includes all *Hedera* species (ivies). *Hydrangea petiolaris* (climbing hydrangea), *Euonymus fortunei* forms and *Parthenocissus* forms (Virginia creepers). These climbers do not need support once established, and they can all, except the *Euonymus fortunei* forms, eventually become very large plants, almost to the point of nuisance.

The other major group of climbers is the one of plants that twine, their whole stems twisting around the supports, or around their own stems. Into this category fall the *Lonicera* spp (honeysuckle), *Passiflora* (passionflower), *Polygonum baldschuanicum* (Russian vine), *Vitis* (grape vine) and wisteria.

A third, smaller group of climbing plants consists of those that cling by means of tendrils; this category includes most of the clematis species and cultivars, as well as *Lathyrus* (sweet peas).

Supports for those climbers that twine or have tendrils should be strong, and much larger than is originally anticipated. Climbing plants tend to grow faster and larger than the sizes given in many books, and often need much more support than originally expected. Smaller supports for small climbers can often be pushed into the containers, but larger more vigorous climbers and wall shrubs need strong permanent support. Galvanized wires fixed to the walls with vine eyes are ideal, with the wires spaced at about 45 cm (18 in) apart, but heavy duty netting or trellis, securely fixed, will also work well. Where the supporting wall is rendered or painted, the plant supports should be attached so that they can be hinged down from the wall, so that any maintenance work to the house can be undertaken without severe damage to the plants.

General care of climbers and wall shrubs is the same as for all container and patio grown plants, where the operative words are care and attention. Pruning will vary according to the plant, (there is a section on general care and plant maintenance to follow), but the general rule of thumb is to prune deciduous plants after flowering, and to prune evergreen plants in late spring. Sometimes the very vigorous plants like lonicera, clematis and jasmine can provide problems when they have been allowed to become very bushy, to the point of forming a tangled thicket. In these instances, the best method of pruning is often the most drastic – to cut the plant down very hard and allow it to grow up again from the base. Generally, the easiest climbing plants to manage are the self clinging climbers, as they rarely need little more than trimming away from doorways and windows when they start to invade.

Perennials

Hardy perennials are often overlooked as suitable plants for container culture, but generally respond well to the conditions imposed, and many flourish and show their best when container grown. Chosen with care, perennials can provide colour and interest for most of the year, both in flower and foliage.

Unlike the annuals and biennials, perennial plants do not need replacing each year or two years. Once a plant is established in its container, it only needs a regular top dressing of compost each year, mulching with well rotted manure in the autumn, and possibly liquid feeding in the summer and autumn, depending on the time of the main growth and flowering of the plant. When a plant eventually becomes congested in its container, it should be lifted and divided, and the healthiest section replanted in fresh soil, and then mulched as before.

Winter treatment of container grown perennials is the same as for any container

grown plant, that is, to protect the whole container from frost. When the plants are grown in the ground, there is a thick layer of soil over and around the root system and this insulates it from the frosts. A container can easily freeze solid and seriously damage both the root system and any dormant growth buds.

Perennials fall into two major groups, the herbaceous plants that lose all their leaves and top growth in the winter and die back to a ground level clump of dormant buds, and the evergreen perennials that keep most of their leaves through the winter. These evergreen perennials, such as some *Helleborus*, *Bergenia cordifolia* and *Pulmonaria saccharata*, are particularly valuable in the patio area and in containers, as many of them also flower in the winter months as well as having decorative foliage.

The true herbaceous perennials generally flower from early summer onwards, giving a good summer and autumn showing of flowers, and can be successfully planted with spring flowering bulbs, and with evergreen perennials.

To appreciate the overall shape and texture of the plants, rather than the massed colour effect that the flowers give, the best way to plant a perennial plant is as a single specimen plant in its own container. A single wooden tub full to the brim and overflowing with the foliage of acanthus or hosta will add distinction to any planting and cheer any patio with its effectiveness and simplicity. Provided the plant chosen is of low maintenance requirements, then there need be very little work in maintaining a simply planted container other than watering regularly, feeding regularly and removing dead leaves and flowers as and when this becomes necessary.

Container and patio gardening provides the ideal cultural conditions for cultivating the less hardy perennials, such as agapanthus. The patio area tends to be sheltered, and maintain its own temperate microclimate, and containers can be moved into frost free areas, so giving the opportunity to grow slightly tender plants.

Any good quality potting compost can be used to grow perennials in containers, but a loam-based compost is recommended. All composts should be regularly watered and fed in the growing season and mulched in winter.

Perennial plants have a wide variety of habits of growth, types and colour of foliage, and flowering habits. Some create great clumps of plant in time, some spread by underground roots to gradually colonize an ever increasing area, and some form dense mats of ground-covering foliage. For some perennials, the foliage is the essence of the plant, and the flowers slightly more than incidental, such as with hostas and bergenias. For other plants, the flowers make a nondescript clump of foliage into a memorable plant, such as rudbeckia and doronicum. The plants that spread by means of underground roots are ideal for container culture because their spread is limited by the container they are growing in, whereas it is not advisable to grow these spreading plants around the patio as they might well swamp everything else growing near them.

Annuals and Biennials
Of all the plants available for planting in containers, annuals and biennials are the most adaptable and accommodating. They are very fast to grow, either flowering in their first season (annuals) or in their second season (biennials), and as they are generally grown from seed, the capital outlay to produce a beautiful display of flowers is minimal. Due to their ephemeral nature, their beauty lasting only one or two seasons, annuals and biennials are indispensable in the garden.

Annuals are particularly useful to fill temporary gaps in shrub planting, where the shrubs are newly planted with large spaces between them to allow for growth. Annuals will fill gaps left by the dying leaves of spring bulbs, or can be used as a temporary expedient when a gap is left by a plant death or move. Used in containers, they allow colour schemes to be changed each year, as desired, and allow for dense planting to give a massive show of colour.

Annuals grow from seed, flower in the same year and then die, all in the same growing season. They can be sown where they are to flower, but for use in containers, it is best to start them in smaller pots or trays and plant

them out once the previous bedding plants have been removed, and once the threat of frost has passed (for half hardy annuals). Some hardy annuals can be sown in the early autumn to flower the following spring, so providing some winter greenery as well as flowering earlier than spring grown plants.

Biennials are also plants that are good for filling gaps in borders and containers. They grow vigorously one year and become established in root and leaf, then flower the following year. This can cause problems if they are to be used in containers, as room will be limited and biennials produce no display until the second year. As their seeds must be sown in early summer, and the plants grown on until the following spring, biennials are usually grown on somewhere else until they can be moved into their final homes.

Some plants, such as wallflowers, are technically perennials, but are treated as biennials as they flower best in their first and second years.

To get the best results from annuals and biennials, a good well balanced soil or potting compost should be used, either peat based or loam based. Annuals grow very fast in a short space of time, so a regular and adequate water supply is essential. If they are allowed to dry out at any time, growth will be severely checked and flowering reduced and delayed. A liquid feed should be applied once the flower buds are visible.

General maintenance other than feeding and watering consists of regular deadheading, to remove the unsightly dead flower heads, prevent the formation of seeds (unless required) and allow the other flowers to come on and prolong the display.

The general principles of planting design apply as much to annuals and biennials as to any other grouping of plants, and this must be borne in mind when planting for the next season. Often a container or area of patio garden looks much better planted with a mass of the same type of plants, rather than a mixed jumble of species.

Annuals are ideal plants for use in hanging baskets, as their ephemeral nature means that they can be thrown away at the end of the season. Again, mass planting of one species alone in a hanging basket is very much more effective and eye catching than a mixed lot of species that is so often seen.

Bulbs, Corms and Tubers

Bulbs, corms and tubers are specially adapted leaves that store food, to enable the plant to safely overwinter and to survive dry summers, and to be ready to grow and flower when the season arrives. They are all very suitable for container culture, as they rarely take more than one season to produce leaves and often flowers, and are generally very easy to cultivate.

In a temperate climate, the most popular bulbs are those that are planted in the autumn and flower in the following spring, growing rapidly with the increasing warmth of the new year. Some of the most welcome of these bulbs actually flower in the winter, such as *Eranthus hyemalis* (winter aconite), *Galanthus nivalis* (snowdrop) and many crocus species.

With careful planning, there can be colour in the garden throughout the whole year from the use of bulbs, corms and tubers. From the early winter and spring flowering bulbs, through the summer flowering *Leucojum aestivum* (summer snowflake) and *Gladiolus × hortulanus* (gladioli) to the autumn flowering *Nerine bowdenii* and *Schizostylis coccinae* (kaffir lily), with varieties of cyclamen flowering from autumn to spring.

One of the many advantages of the use of bulbs is that the foliage generally dies down and disappears after the plant has flowered and set seed, allowing space for other bulbs and herbaceous plants to follow on, or for deciduous plants to come into leaf and flower.

Bulbs can be planted very close together, to give a massed show of colour when in flower, but once the display is over, it is best either to remove the bulbs, or to have other planting to take the attention away from the dying foliage. As each bulb contains its own food supply for one season only, close massed planting will not be very good in the second year, unless the bulbs are directly in the earth, where they will benefit from the feeding of the other plants.

All the bulbs, tubers and corms grow well in a standard potting mix. Some will need lifting and drying after flowering, others can be left in the same position for several years.

Permanently planted bulbs will benefit from an annual top dressing of bonemeal in autumn.

Ferns

Ferns are very adaptable plants, hardy and tolerant of adverse conditions, and many of them are ideal for patio and container gardening. Some can cope with sunless corners, dry and draughty spots, and the right species will flourish in the most inhospitable position.

There is an astonishing variety of foliage amongst the different species of fern, from finely cut fronds to still leathery leaves. Habits also vary from large clump forming ferns to small spreading carpet forming plants. Most forms are flowerless, reproducing by spreading, or by sexual means with spores.

Used in mixed planting, ferns make a wonderful foil for many other flowering plants, and make good ground cover in both damp and dry areas. They can be used to good effect in dry walls, rock gardens, and peat beds. Ferns are very adaptable plants, and will grow well in containers in any standard potting mixture.

The easiest way to propagate ferns is to divide them in spring or early autumn; growing ferns from spores is a difficult specialized job. Despite this, ferns are a joy to grow and plant, and their wide variety are an under-exploited garden resource.

Herbs

Many of the culinary herbs have traditionally been grown in containers on window sills and patios for hundreds of years, and they respond well to container culture. Most are aromatic, with attractive flowers, and some are evergreen, with interesting foliage throughout the year. Herbs vary in size from very low ground-hugging plants like *Mentha pulegium* (pennyroyal) to the statuesque *Angelica archangelica* (angelica), and have an equally wide range of leaf size, colour and texture.

Generally, herbs enjoy a well-drained site, not necessarily very fertile. They need regular watering, especially in summer, when grown in containers, but resent waterlogged soil. They are happy growing in any general potting mixture, and many thrive in a chalky soil.

Some herbs are particularly invasive, such as

the various *Mentha* spp. (mints), and should always be planted separately in their own containers. An old bucket sunk in the soil is often not adequate, as the plants will spread by falling over and layering themselves along the ground. Some other herbs are annuals and biennials, and will need re-sowing each year, if they have not already seeded themselves in every odd corner imaginable.

Herbs also associate well with other ornamental plants, especially those herbs with coloured leaves like *Salvia officinalis* 'Purpurescens' (purple sage) and *Oreganum vulgare* 'Aureum' (golden marjoram). Some make effective ground cover plants, such as *Thymus serpyllum* (creeping thyme) and *Symphytum grandiflorum* (dwarf comfrey), and others make good accent plants and focal points, such as *Foeniculum vulgare* 'Bronze' (bronze fennel) and *Angelica archangelica* (angelica).

Where space is limited, or an unusual effect is desired, a single container with holes in its side can be used to grow a variety of herbs in a small space. Known as 'parsley pot' or 'strawberry pot', these containers are very distinctive, and can be planted with a wide range of herbs, or a large quantity of just one of two plants, to create a distinctive feature in the garden.

Vegetables

Most vegetable plants are annuals, and those that are not are often treated as such for convenience, especially when planted in containers. The time taken from sowing to harvesting the vegetables can be as short as three weeks or as long as five months.

Vegetables can be grown in any type of container, provided there is a minimum depth of soil of 23 cm (9 in), and the compost is rich and nutritious. Ordinary garden soil can be used, but the risk is run then of introducing pests and disease into the containers. Because the vegetable plants make fairly large demands on the soil in terms of nutrients, they appreciate a regular liquid feed, particularly the slower growing plants. The soil should never be allowed to dry out either, as this will set the plants back in their growth and they will never produce crops to their potential.

Most vegetables do best in a sunny position, particularly in the earlier part of the growing season, as this will encourage fast early growth and earlier cropping. Later in the season, some vegetables will appreciate a certain amount of shade, especially in the heat of the day. Avoid placing vegetables in windy or draughty places, as many do not stand up well to exposure, and trailing and climbing plants will need supports.

It is most economical to grow vegetables from seed, but some plants are easily available as young plants in spring, generally cucumber and tomatoes. Other vegetables are best planted in the place where they are to grow and mature, and the excess seedlings are thinned out. Again, some of the more tender plants are best started indoors and then planted out into the containers or their place in the ground as soon as the risk of frost is past. Generally, the instructions on the seed packets are very clear and the advice is sensible and appropriate.

Vegetables can be used as ornamental plants to good effect, as some have very interesting foliage and flowers. Carrots have bright green feathery leaves that contrast well with the other vegetables, and with large leafed perennials like *Bergenia cordifolia* (elephant's ears). Lettuce comes in a wide variety of leaf shapes and colours, and Swiss chard, with its white stems and green leaves, harmonizes well with some variegated plants. Rhubarb chard has deep red stems and large red tinged green leaves, and beetroot itself has deep red-green foliage.

For a fast growing and showy annual climbing plant, there is nothing to beat the runner bean, with its many little red flowers all through late summer to the first frosts. Climbing French beans make a good contrast, and those with dark blue pods add extra interest. Climbing plants should always be well supported, either on a purpose built timber pyramid, or on a pyramid shape structure made of strong canes.

Because vegetables are annual plants, they can be used like summer bedding plants, planted for the season to give extra colour and texture to the garden, and then removed after they have served their useful design purpose. But unlike bedding plants, the plants can be

The beautiful
variegated leaves of
Cornus alba
'Elegantissima' turn
bright colours in the
autumn and fall to
reveal the glowing
red colour of the new
twigs.

The feathery golden foliage of *Sambucus racemosa* 'Plumosa aurea' softens the hard lines formed by the squared trellis.

The large white
margined leaves of
the *Hosta* 'Thomas
Hogg' soften the edge
of a planted area.
This *Hosta* also
makes a good
container plant.

Detail showing the
attractive peeling
cinnamon coloured
bark of *Acer griseum*,
giving interest
through all seasons.

A small border using
blue flowering plants
to create harmony
amongst the
contrasting flower
and foliage shapes.

A border using
yellow flowering
plants to give
harmony to
contrasting flower
and foliage shapes.

Sorbus 'Joseph Rock' has persistent yellow berries in autumn and winter, and the leaves turn fiery colours before falling.

The flat pink flowers of *Sedum spectabile* contrast well
with the soft grey leaves of *Stachys olympica* and
provide a source of food for butterflies.

Alpines can be effectively grown in modern shallow
concrete containers and used as an unusual feature.

eaten in some way, and so serve another useful purpose, as well as the debris being recycled via the compost heap!

Fruit

Most fruit-producing plants are trees and shrubs, and these days many of them are so highly bred that they bear little resemblance to the original wild plants from which they are derived. Fruiting plants may be grown in containers for many years, providing that they are well fed and cared for, and that attention is paid to improving their soil with composts and mulches.

Top fruit includes apples, pears, plums, peaches and apricots, trees belonging to the *Malus* and *Prunus* families, as well as the mulberry, *Morus nigra*, and the fig, *Ficus carica*. Soft fruit includes raspberries, gooseberries, all the various currants, blackberry, loganberry and all the new hybrids, and the only herbaceous perennial fruit plant, strawberry. There are a few plants that do not fall into any of the categories, the grape vine being one of them, as it produces climbing stems known as rods.

General care of soft fruit and top fruit grown in containers consists of feeding and watering the plants throughout the growing season until the early autumn, and then just keeping them damp enough to stop the compost drying out during the winter months. Any good quality loam based potting mix will provide a good medium for the plants to grow in, and the containers should be generous in size. Plants should be moved into a frost free area in severe winters.

Plants should be well mulched in winter with a well rotted manure or compost, which will act as a source of food for the plant as well as a soil improver and a blanket to insulate the soil surface of the container. Feeding in the spring and summer should be weekly or fortnightly, with a liquid manure or a seaweed extract.

Each type of plant has its own specific pruning regime that relates to the habit of the plant and to the manner of fruit production. Despite this, the general principles of remedial pruning apply, those of removing all dead or diseased wood and weak or crossing stems.

Support of fruit laden plants is important, because when they are grown in containers their root systems are restricted and the plants do not have the ability to hold onto the soil so tightly and could fall over with the weight of fruit.

Harvesting of fruit takes place over several weeks and is determined by local climate conditions, the type of weather experienced throughout the summer and the variety of fruit that is being grown. Each type of fruit has pests and diseases specific to it, but the general principles of plant care apply under all circumstances. A well manured and cared for plant is less vulnerable to pest and disease problems than a plant under stress, and should it become infected, it will have much more resistance to the problem and will be able to fight it off better. Birds can be a real problem to fruit growing, as they are indiscriminate and often destructive, so it is best to keep ripening fruit trees and bushes netted until the fruit is harvested. Soft fruit is particularly vulnerable to attack from birds.

When considering the use of fruit in the patio garden or in containers, it is important to consider the importance of freshly picked fruit against the shape and habit of the plants, and the space that they occupy. As this part of the garden is usually very restricted in space, it is essential that the plants grown look good or are productive for more than just one short season. In this way, the selection of appropriate plants is simplified. For instance, apple and pear trees have blossom in the spring, as well as producing a crop of fruit that is decorative as well as useful. Figs, too, are wall shrubs with impressive foliage, making a wonderful feature even at times when there is little or no crop. Conversely, raspberry canes have little to recommend them in terms of decorative plants, as they are awkward and stiff, need tying in at about 1.2 m (4 ft) above ground, and are not good value in a small garden.

Water-garden Plants

Chosen with care for their size and lack of aggressiveness, water plants are well suited to container growing. Some of the plants need to be permanently growing in water, others need to be in permanently moist soil, but whatever the requirements, they provide no problems of watering!

Almost any watertight container can be used for a water garden, although half barrels are the most useful and pleasing, and of good proportions of depth to surface area. Concrete containers and even old sinks, suitably treated, can be utilized to good effect as water-garden containers.

There are two main types of water-loving plants – marginal plants and aquatic plants. Aquatic plants live and grow under the water, needing at least 30 cm (12 in) depth of water to live and grow. Some aquatic plants, such as *Nymphaea* species and cultivars (water lilies), have floating leaves, and most have flowers that stand proud above the water. Marginal plants inhabit the zone of wet soil at the water-line edge of a pond or stream, and so can be grown in normal potting soil that is kept very wet.

To plant aquatic plants, start with an empty watertight container suitable for a water garden, and place a 15 cm (6 in) layer of good quality loam based potting compost at the bottom, well fertilized with a generous handful of bonemeal for every 9 litres or so of loam. The aquatic plants are then planted into this loam, and mulched with a layer of clean gravel. The gravel helps to prevent the soil becoming cloudy when the water is added. Water is then very gently added to the container, preferably from a watering can with as fine a rose as possible, to try and avoid the cloudiness that is the outcome of turbulent water.

Marginal plants are often grown in plastic baskets or pots designed specifically for the purpose. These baskets are first lined with a fine mesh gauze, paper or even moss, to prevent the soil running out into the water, then filled with loam and the marginal plant. They are then planted at the appropriate points in the water garden container.

Planting of both marginal and aquatic plants is best undertaken in spring, as the plants are breaking from their dormancy. The water garden container is best located in partial shade, as full sun can easily warm the relatively small quantity of water and can encourage the growth of various algae, especially the smothering green blanket weed. The marginal plants should be taken out and repotted every two or three years, and the aquatic plants should be split every three or four years. Failure to do this will result in the container water garden becoming an overgrown swamp jungle where only the strongest plants survive.

In winter, the water level of the garden should be reduced, possibly down to soil level, and the container stored away from frost. In milder areas, any ice that forms on the container should be broken, and a piece of polystyrene or soft wood should be floated on the surface of the water, to take up the pressure from any ice, and prevent cracking of the container.

There is such a wide variety of aquatic and marginal plants that a complete water garden can be designed in a container, a garden within a garden that incorporates all the principles of design to make an interesting and pleasing feature on the patio.

Tender Perennial Plants

Many of this small group of plants are the traditional plants for use in containers and window boxes. They are very showy in flower and in leaf, often giving a brilliant display from late spring until the first frosts.

They are generally very easy to propagate from cuttings, and this is the common method of overwintering fuchsias, pelargoniums and helichrysum, in a greenhouse or on a domestic window sill. Cuttings are taken in late summer, and after ensuring that they are established, the cuttings are overwintered and the parent plants are left in place in the containers until the first frosts destroy the display, and they need to be removed.

Tuberous begonias will need to be lifted from their summer homes for the winter, dried off and stored in a frost free place. Fibrous-rooted begonias, impatiens and coleus will also need to be moved indoors, and can be successfully used as houseplants. Datura, too, will need to be brought indoors for the winter.

The advantage of this slightly more labour intensive method of care of these plants is that when the season is right for them to be planted outside, the plants are fairly mature and a good display of flowers is produced in a short time.

Topiary

Topiary is the art of training and sculpting plants, often into free-standing shapes and images. Topiary can be permanent or temporary, evergreen or deciduous, serious or fun. A wide variety of plants can be used. Do not be tied by convention when experimenting with other plants as topiary specimens, as there are many other plants that grow well as topiary specimens.

Most of the plants listed have small leaves, and will break and grow from old wood when pruned. Because of this, the plants can be encouraged to form dense shapes which are very effective as specimen plants.

Training of topiary can be approached in several ways, and whichever way is chosen, it requires patience and an image of the finished effect, as well as strong canes, string, wires and good quality secateurs. Start with a plant that already has a shape that looks promising for the final sculpture, and gently shape it using a mixture of careful pruning, tying in and wiring of branches. Power hedge trimmers can be used on more mature topiary specimens, but the best effects are achieved with hand shears and secateurs. Always use secateurs for shaping specimens with large leaves such as *Laurus nobilis* (bay) and *Ilex aquifolium* (holly), to avoid unsightly cut leaves.

For climbing plants such as *Hedera helix* (ivy) and all its various cultivars, a mesh support is needed for the plant to climb up. The support can be made in the desired shape of chicken wire, and should be filled with sphagnum moss, and the climbing plant can be trained up the support. The growing shoots should be pinched out regularly to encourage the plant to produce lateral shoots, and so cover the mesh support quickly. For a quick effect, use several climbing plants, of the same species of course, and train them over the frame, tying them in when necessary and pinching them out regularly.

Mop-headed standards are trained by growing the plant up a single stem, gradually rubbing off the side shoots as the stem becomes longer. Some plants, such as *Taxus baccata* (yew) and *Buxus sempervirens* (box) will take some years to reach the desired height, and will need a strong support for the stem until it thickens enough with age to be self supporting. Other plants, such as *Chrysanthemum frutescens* (marguerite), will only take one or two seasons for the main stem to reach a good height, with about 45 cm of stem.

Topiary specimens are eminently suitable for container cultivation, as their requirements for frequent and regular care coincide with the needs of container growing. The less hardy plants can easily be moved indoors for the winter and will continue to give pleasure at times when the patio is less used. Hardy topiary plants can be kept outside during the winter, provided the usual protections are given to the plants and their pots in times of severe weather.

Topiary specimen plants make excellent focal points on the patio, their clipped or pruned shapes making a simple statement about their nature of being. Evergreen topiary plants are particularly effective in winter, when their bold green outline contrasts with the greys and buffs of the deciduous stems, and they are particularly handsome in frost and snow. In summer, their uncompromising shapes contrast well with blowsy annual planting. Flowering topiary specimens, *Fuchsia* spp (fuchsia) and *Chrysanthemum frutescens* (marguerites), are a wonderful feature on their own.

PART VII

CARE AND CULTIVATION OF THE PATIO AND CONTAINER
GARDEN

CHAPTER 14

Tools and Equipment

Basic Requirements

The patio and container gardener needs only a few tools, but these few should always be of good quality and should last for many years if well cared for. Many of the new and gimmicky tools should be avoided, unless they have been tried and tested and shown to be of positive use in the garden. Otherwise, the long tried and proven traditional tools are the best.

Before buying any tools, always try them out to make sure that the handles are comfortable, they are light enough for ease of handling, and that their balance is right.

Spades

The spade is one of the most important garden tools, and is available in a wide range of sizes, weights and shapes of blade. The most useful spades for the patio gardener are a digging spade for normal work in the ground, and a border spade for large work in containers as well as lighter work in the ground.

A digging spade has a straight edge to the blade, for cutting into the soil easily and so it is an essential tool for jobs such as digging holes for trees and moving large established plants. A border spade has a curved edge to the blade, which makes it less likely to catch on other plants, and it is noticeably smaller and lighter than a digging spade.

Forks

Forks also come in a wide range of shapes and sizes, but the two most useful to the patio gardener are the digging fork and the smaller, lighter weight border fork. For handling manure, compost, prunings and fallen leaves, a muck fork with long round curved tines is indispensable.

Hoes

Hoes are also several and various. The Dutch hoe has a D-shaped blade, and is operated walking backwards, sliding the blade too and fro just below the soil surface to cut off the weed stems. The draw hoe usually has its blade at right angles to the handle and is operated with a chopping or drawing motion working forwards.

The most useful hoe type tool for use in the patio garden is a combination of the two types of hoe, called a 'swoe'. It has a double edged blade on a swan neck stem, on a long handle, and is operated with a drawing motion. It is very manoeuvrable and is ideal for simple weeding work around and underneath shrubs, and will work in tight corners without any trouble (Fig. 14.1).

Rakes

Rakes, too, come in a wide variety of shapes and sizes, from wide wooden hay rakes, narrow garden rakes to springy metal rakes for leaf collecting (Fig. 14.2). For working in the restricted area of a patio, a rubber bladed rake is indispensable for removing fallen leaves from on top of and between closely planted shrubs and perennials, as well as from paved areas and paths. The rubber tines are flexible and so do not pull and damage plants if used with care. An ordinary metal garden rake is useful for general garden work such as breaking down the lumps in dug soil and raking it to a suitable tilth for planting.

Broom

Another essential tool for the patio gardener is a good broom or two. The very nature of working on a patio or with containers means that soil and other debris will be spilt on the paved area, and a broom is needed to clear the mess after working. An old dustpan and brush can also be useful when clearing up in a tight corner.

Trowel and hand fork

Essential for every patio and container gardener is at least one trowel and hand fork. Two trowels are recommended, one with a

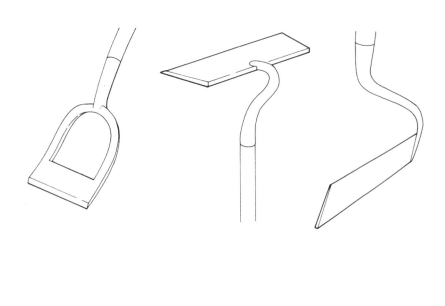

Fig. 14.1 Hoes.
(a) Dutch hoe
(b) Draw hoe and
(c) 'Swoe'

Fig. 14.2 Rakes.
(a) Garden rake
(b) Rubber rake and
(c) Springy metal
rake (leaf rake).

conventional wide blade and rounded end for top dressing and planting, the other with a narrow pointed blade for bulbs, seedlings and small plants. A hand fork is essential for weeding and general cultivation work in containers and around the patio, for loosening the soil surface and for planting.

Both trowel and hand forks are available with long handles and mid-length handles to make garden work easier for those less able to bend to work, but the usual length of handle is 150 to 200 mm (6–8 in). They should be strong, with a curved shank, and made of stainless steel if it can be afforded.

Secateurs

Good secateurs are essential for work on plants, whether it is skilled pruning or just simply deadheading. Secateurs can be of two types. Anvil type secateurs have two blades, one that chops against the flat plate of the other blade. This type of secateur is strong, easy to obtain and easy to maintain. The double cut scissor type of secateurs are more expensive than the anvil type, but the slicing scissor-like action eliminates any rough tears and bruises. They need regular maintenance to keep the blades clean and cutting well, and are available in both right-handed and left-handed forms.

It is important that secateurs are tried out before they are purchased, as unsuitable ones will make your hands sore, as well as damage the plants. Under no circumstances should secateurs be used for cutting string and tie fix, as this will blunt and notch the blades.

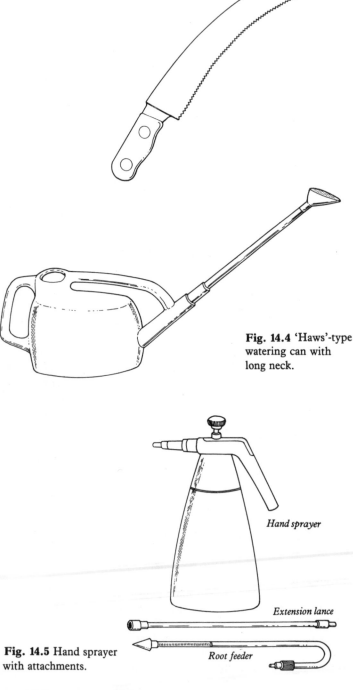

Fig. 14.3 Curved blade pruning saw.

Fig. 14.4 'Haws'-type watering can with long neck.

Hand sprayer

Extension lance

Root feeder

Fig. 14.5 Hand sprayer with attachments.

Loppers

Loppers or long handled pruners are useful for pruning small trees and large established shrubs. It is better to use loppers than to damage secateurs by trying to cut through branches that are too thick for them. Like secateurs, there are two types of loppers available, anvil and double cut type, working in the same way as before.

Garden knife

A garden knife is essential for some pruning operations, such as removing the growing tip of a plant, removing suckers, and taking cuttings, as well as for cutting string and tie fix, and opening bags of compost. Choose a knife with a high quality carbon or tungsten steel blade, and always keep it impeccably sharp. The blade should be retractable or fold away for safety reasons.

Pruning saw

A pruning saw with a curved blade (Fig. 14.3) is invaluable for many pruning operations where it is not possible to use loppers or an ordinary bow saw. A pruning saw should have a curved tapered blade, and cut on both the push and pull strokes, enabling the user to cut very neatly in awkward spaces, for instance, when cutting old wood out of the base of a shrub. Some pruning saws have blades that fold away into the handle, but the fixed blade types are to be preferred.

Watering can

Another essential for the patio and container gardener is at least one good watering can. The best style is one with a long neck, as it is more manoeuvrable amongst plants and allows water to be put where needed (Fig. 14.4). Plastic cans are much lighter to handle than metal cans, but may split if left out in the frost. Various rose attachments are available, fine spray for watering seedlings and a coarser spray for established plants. A full watering can should not be heavy to handle, and the preferred size is 4.5 litres (1 gal).

Garden sprayer

A garden sprayer is a useful tool for the application of foliar feeds, pesticides and for washing plants in very dry and dusty weather. Sprayers containing 1.5 or 3 litres (2.5 or 5 UK pints) are the most convenient sizes for patio and container gardening. An adjustable nozzle and a squeeze trigger control that will hold in the 'on' position are useful refinements. The liquid is generally held in a pressurized container, from which the nozzle and trigger control unscrew; an extension lance and root feeder attachments are usually available to fit (Fig. 14.5).

Regular and thorough cleaning of the sprayer will prolong its life, as well as stop any cross contamination of feeds, and other chemicals. Generally, the little rubber 'O' ring in the pressure plunger perishes after a few years, but replacements and other spare parts are usually available from the manufacturer and some garden centres.

Sundries

A carrying sheet of canvas or hessian with handles at each corner, usually about 1.2 m (4 ft) square, is useful for moving soil, pruning debris and plants.

A strong plastic bucket is another all round piece of equipment, useful for carrying weeds and other debris, tools, plants and other bits essential for good gardening, as well as for baling out the water butt, soaking small containers and impromptu watering of large plants.

Green garden string, fillis string and tar twine all have their individual uses in the efficient running of the garden. Tar twine is the strongest and longest lasting of the three, and is useful for tying in large climbing plants such as roses. Plastic tie fix is also useful, and can be reused several times before it disintegrates, but it tends to cut into fleshy stems and so must be used with discretion.

Any labels used should be the white plastic type, where the pencil writing can be washed off and the label can be reused. Wooden lolly sticks look much better than white plastic labels, but fade and rot in the soil very quickly.

A small wheelbarrow is also useful for moving soil, debris and even pots and other containers, but is not essential, depending on the size of the patio garden.

Storage of Tools

Good quality tools are an investment that should last a lifetime, provided that they are always thoroughly cleaned, well cared for and stored in a suitable place. A dry storage area is essential, and the larger it is the better it will be. A garden shed with a potting bench and room to store composts and fertilizers, tools, seedboxes and plant pots is ideal if space in the garden permits.

Many patio and container gardeners, however, do not have space for this sort of luxury and end up with a compromise situation, possibly using a corner of the garage, or part of a utility room or storeroom as a storage area for gardening tools and equipment. Provided that the area can be kept dry with a little room to manoeuvre, the location of the storage area is irrelevant.

Tools are best stored hung up, rather than propped in a corner ready to fall over at a moment's notice, when the bottommost item is needed in a hurry. It is also safer for children and adults alike, as those who have been unfortunate enough to be hit on the head with a rake will testify; and sharp edges to spades and other tools are less likely to get damaged this way.

A high shelf is useful, to keep ordinary garden sundries out of the way, in an easy to find place and out of reach for prying little fingers. Secateurs, watering cans, string, wire, bonemeal, dustpan and brush and even the oil can could live up on this shelf.

Any chemicals, especially anything potentially poisonous, should always be kept in a locked cupboard, with every bottle and container clearly labelled with the name of the product and the fact that it is poisonous, and the antidote if it is known. Protective clothing should always be worn when handling and using chemicals, and this should be stored near to the locked cupboard. Strong rubber gauntlet style gloves, a facemask to protect against breathing in any spray, safety goggles, a strong pair of wellington boots and a pair of overalls form the basic protective clothing.

201

Maintenance of Tools

It is worth buying high quality, well finished tools, preferably with stainless steel blades. Although very expensive, stainless steel tools will repay the investment with long years of service, but to do so they must be kept in good order and treated with care. Ordinary forged steel tools will also last many years given the same careful treatment.

After use, any soil should be thoroughly scraped off. The tool should then be washed if necessary to remove any final remnants of soil, then carefully dried. Any moving parts should be oiled, and all blades wiped over with an oily rag to leave a thin protective coating which will inhibit rust. Tools can be stored wrapped in oily rags if they are not regularly used.

Maintenance of electrically driven tools is a specialist job only to be undertaken by a qualified electrician. Day to day maintenance of electric equipment is the same as with any other tool, that is, clean thoroughly and oil moving parts as necessary. Any maintenance of electrical equipment should only be undertaken with the tool disconnected from the power supply.

In the winter, when the outdoor demands of the garden are reduced, some time should be spent indoors repairing and maintaining tools. This is the time to replace the handle on the spade which was broken the previous summer whilst moving paving slabs, or to sharpen the blades on the shears. Some garden centres offer a blade sharpening service to their customers, and it is worth having the blades of a cyclinder lawn mower professionally sharpened and set. Digging tools such as spades, half moon irons and turfing irons should be sharpened occasionally so that they cut through the earth more efficiently.

Winter time is also the time to clean out the storage area and sort it out ready for the onslaught of the new season. Hygiene and good housekeeping are essential for healthy plants, and this starts before the seeds are even planted. Seed trays and pots should all be cleaned of last season's debris and washed to remove any overwintering creatures. The storage area itself should also be cleaned out and any broken tools should be repaired. Odd leftovers of any chemical should be disposed of safely, labels can be washed clean, the hose

checked for leaks and even the rubbish bin emptied!

Specialist Tools

Occasionally the situation arises when there is a job to be done that needs a specialist or unusual tool. There is a decision then to be made as to whether to try and borrow the tool, buy it or hire it.

Hiring tools

Hiring tools as they are needed is an inexpensive and reliable way of having the full unlimited use of a tool of which one cannot justify the purchase. If the tool is to be used regularly over many years, then the purchase can be justified, but for a brief spell of intensive use on a 'one off' job, then it is better to hire.

Whilst constructing the patio, the use of a small electric cement mixer can save a lot of time and effort in mixing cement, and a slab cutter can prevent a lot of wastage of broken slabs when cutting paving, and give a very much neater finish. But after the patio laying is completed, there is little need for the use of a cement mixer or a slab cutter, and they are best returned for further hiring.

Buying tools

The purchase of some tools can be a big investment that cannot always be justified in terms of their use, but because they are used intermittently throughout the year, it can be a big advantage to have them to hand at very short notice.

Sack truck

If the patio has a large number of large plant containers with shrubs and plants that are not reliably hardy, then the purchase of a small sack truck will make moving the pots to a sheltered or protected spot for the winter a simple task. Some sack trucks have a second, removable pair of handles to enable a second person to assist in moving the load through awkward places and up and down steps (Fig. 14.6). Once bought, a thousand and one other tasks will be found for a sack truck, from moving bags of potting compost without straining the back, through to moving the washing machine to clean behind it!

Fig. 14.6 The use of sack barrow with extra handles to move a large container.

Fig. 14.7 Long arm pruners.

Long arm pruners

Long arm pruners are remote control secateurs at the end of a long pole or wooden handle. They are usually used for pruning branches that are out of reach of long handled loppers, even from a set of steps. Long arm pruners can be up to 2.4 m (8 ft) long, and are difficult to store easily. Their advantage as a pruning tool is that the cutting blades are like a curved pair of scissors, so that the branch to be cut can be held at the same time, until the cut is made (Fig. 14.7).

CHAPTER 15
Growing Media

Composts

Growing plants in containers has many drawbacks in terms of the work involved, but it has several big advantages. The main advantage to consider here is that the container gardener has almost total control over the contents of those containers. If the soil balance is right in the first place, it will provide a good and appropriate home for the chosen plants.

The planting medium used in containers should crumble easily but hold together when squeezed; it should retain moisture without becoming waterlogged; it should permit free drainage and circulation of air, since plant roots need oxygen; and it should have the right balance of nutrients and the correct level of lime or acid according to which plants have been chosen to grow in the container.

Many gardeners use 'potting compost' as the planting medium in containers (not to be confused with 'garden compost' that results from the rotting of organic matter). There is a series of compost formulations devised by the John Innes Horticultural Institute which are based on loam, i.e. good quality soil. These loam based composts are recommended for the container gardener. Despite the fact that they are heavier and not so clean to handle as peat based soilless composts, they provide a much better root hold and support for the plants.

The John Innes composts are made by several different manufacturers, as the name refers only to the recipe of ingredients and is not a trade name. It is better to buy a reputable brand of John Innes composts, as a little known cheap brand may not be properly balanced or disease free. As the mixes have a short shelf life, varying from three weeks to a year, it is best to buy from a supplier with a fast turnover of stock. Store them in a frost free place in closed plastic bags, and do not keep them for too long. If the compost is cold when it is needed for use, bring it indoors or into a heated greenhouse to warm up for several days.

Each John Innes compost mix has been formulated for a specific range of plants. The seed compost is for starting seeds and the cutting compost is for starting cuttings. For established plants, there are the composts numbered 1, 2 and 3, each with a different level of nutrient content – no.3 being the strongest with the highest nutrient content.

Standard John Innes compost no.1 should be used for fine rooted, slow growing plants like young heathers and alpines. It is also used for sickly plants, and for tiny seedlings in spring.

Standard John Innes compost no.2 is a multipurpose compost, and is used for any plant of average vigour, except for acid loving ericaceous plants.

Standard John Innes compost mix no.3 is used for quick growing and vigorous plants, especially those that need to gain height, like tomatoes and sweet peas.

Modified composts are available for acid loving ericaceous plants. The season also influences the choice of John Innes compost. It is better to use a weaker formula in spring for young and slow growing plants, and to use a stronger formula later in the year for vigorous plants.

Other composts

There is a wide range of 'soilless' composts available, that is, composts that are not based on loam. Many are based on peat, mixed to specific formulae and are marketed under many brand names. They are cleaner to use, are cheaper, and weigh less than loam based composts, all of which are important to the container gardener. They can fluctuate easily between being very wet and very dry and dusty, a noticeable problem in areas of high rainfall. Neither do they provide as good a roothold for the plants as soil based potting mixes, which is an important consideration for containers used on the patio, especially in exposed and windy situations.

Soilless composts come in a variety of

John Innes compost formulations

It is generally cheaper and less time and space consuming to buy the John Innes composts ready made, but they can easily be made up by using the following recipes.

The basic John Innes soil mixture:

7 parts (by bulk) sterilized loam
3 parts coarse, dust free, undecomposed moss peat
2 parts sharp washed sand

The John Innes base can either be bought or made as follows:

2 parts (by weight) hoof and horn
2 parts calcium phosphate (superphosphate of lime)
1 part potassium sulphate (sulphate of potash)

To make John Innes no.1:

36 litres basic soil mixture
112 g John Innes Base
21 g powdered chalk

To make John Innes no.2:

36 litres basic soil mixture
224 g John Innes Base
42 g powdered chalk

To make John Innes no.3:

36 litres basic soil mixture
336 g John Innes Base
63 g powdered chalk

To make John Innes seed compost:

2 parts (by bulk) sterilized loam
1 part moss peat
1 part sharp sand

to 36 litres of this mixture add

42 g calcium phosphate (superphosphate of lime)
21 g powdered chalk.

To make John Innes cuttings compost:

1 part (by bulk) sterilized loam
2 parts moss peat
7 parts sharp sand
no fertilizer

To make up composts:

Sift the loam on to a large plastic sheet over a flat surface. Moisten the peat with a watering can, and mix the two together with a spade. Keep the chalk and the base separate, then mix them together with some of the sand and add this to the loam and peat with the rest of the sand. Mix very thoroughly.

---

strengths and types, including ericaceous composts for acid loving plants like azaleas and pieris, which like the peat.

Some composts are 'bark fibre' based, with usually a mixture of peat and bark as the base. They are best avoided by the container gardener, as they provide problems of feeding, watering and anchorage.

It is better to use an approved potting mix than garden soil, especially soil from a town garden. Garden soil will contain weed seeds, stones, disease spores and the by-products of other chemical and fertilizer treatments, not to mention any other deposits left by the local cats (one of the less desirable forms of organic fertilizer)! Garden soil may be of poor quality, even nearly inert through mistreatment and neglect, and soil from a town garden could contain contaminants from pollution, and could be acid from soot and sulphur.

'Grow Bags' are made of plastic and contain mostly peat, sometimes a little pulverized tree bark, and added nutrients. They are often used for fast growing plants such as tomatoes, but will grow many other plants like lettuce, strawberries, beans and summer flowering annuals. Once they have been used for the first crop, they can be used again, either the following season to grow a less demanding crop like basil, or the contents can be used in the garden as a soil improver or planting medium.

Grow bags are not suitable for growing deep rooted plants like beetroot and carrot.

Fig. 15.1 Grow bag in a tray.

Although they are clean to use they do present a few problems. They are difficult to keep well watered, as they tend to dry out very quickly, being so shallow and with such a wide open soil area. One solution is to put each grow bag into a tray with a layer of gravel beneath it, and make a number of slits in the plastic bag, so that any excess water flows out of the bag and into the tray (Fig. 15.1). The bag can also be fed and watered by filling the tray with an appropriate liquid feed and allowing it to be absorbed by the peat in the bag.

Another problem of grow bags is that they are very difficult to move safely once they have been planted up, other than when they are placed on a tray. Neither do they look attractive, however they are disguised. They are purely functional containers for growing crops, without any aesthetic appeal. As they are shallow, it is very difficult to stake the plants securely. Special frames and structures can be bought that surround the grow bag with a metal frame and provide anchorage points for any canes or other supports, but again they look unsightly, although functional.

Soil testing

A correctly chosen potting mix eliminates the need for soil testing, as it will be at the correct acidity or alkalinity (pH) according to the mix. After some time, it may be necessary to check the pH of the mix, possibly because a plant looks sickly, or that the water in the area is excessively alkaline.

Simple soil-testing kits are generally available from garden centres, and they will show the acidity of the soil with a simple colour comparison. A sample of soil is taken, placed in a test tube, some chemical is poured in, and the tube is stoppered and shaken. Once the contents have settled, the colour of the liquid is compared with a colour chart that relates the colour to the pH value. In this way, an assessment is made of the chemical balance of the soil before any chemical fertilizers are added.

Soils

Topsoil and subsoil

What goes on underground, whether it is under the soil or within a container, should be the constant concern of every gardener, even the most amateur one. Earth is the mother of all, and her children's health depends on her own. For a good garden, however small and humble, it is essential to understand your soil and to keep it in good heart, for the quality of the soil affects every plant and creature in it, affects the quality of everything it produces, the flavour and size of the edible crops, the herbs, the salads, and even the flowers, trees and shrubs.

Topsoil consists of a very thin film over the surface of parts of the earth, compounded partly of pulverized rock surfaces and partly of the decayed vegetable and animal wastes of countless centuries. It is very thin in comparison to the size of the earth, and is not inert, but teeming with tiny organisms like bacteria, yeasts and fungi. These million myriads of organisms transmute the chemicals in the soil into forms usable by plant life, living themselves on the nature of the soil. Hence the soil itself is alive, a living organism to be cared for and cherished, for upon it all life depends.

To retain the fertility in the soil, food and air are needed in a form usable to the plant life. Regular, careful digging is one method of aerating the soil, and replenishing the humus with well rotted manure is one method of feeding the soil. Artificial and chemical fertilizers merely feed the plants, so giving a quick return in terms of plant growth, but allow the soil to gradually die.

Below this thin film of topsoil is the subsoil. It may only just be below the surface, as on a chalky down, or it may be several feet below. It is relatively stolid and inert, and its lighter colour indicates its lack of organic matter. Subsoil should never be brought to the surface unless someone knows how to treat it to make it fertile. Builders are notorious for removing the topsoil from housing sites, leaving only subsoil for the unsuspecting householder to use for a garden.

Subsoil can be made fertile by creating the conditions conducive to life by soil organisms. Aerating and feeding by digging in quantities of organic matter will gradually convert the subsoil into a reasonable growing medium, and the help given by other small creatures like worms must not be overlooked, as they aerate the soil by tunnelling and digesting the organic matter to convert it into a form usable by the smaller soil organisms.

Compaction of top soil occurs when the soil has been abused by trying to work it under the wrong conditions, or by frequent use of heavy machinery, or by the persistent weight of people walking over it. Compaction drives out all the air from within the soil and leaves it in a state similar to subsoil, but with a little more organic matter. Compaction can only be remedied by ceasing the practice that caused the problem originally, and by adding air in some form, whether by digging, or spiking and aerating, or by blowing compressed air into the soil below ground to loosen all the soil particles.

Types of soil

The main constituents of soil are sand, clay, chalk or lime, and humus, bound together of course with air and water. To be useful to man, at least two of these main ingredients must be bound together. Thus chalk and clay make marl, and sand, clay and humus make loam, the type of soil needed for nearly all crops.

Sand

This is composed of relatively large particles of silica, rough and loose, which holds lots of air and so becomes warm easily, but which holds no water. It makes a soil light and easily workable, but has no food value. Soils with too much sand are easily workable, but are 'hungry', needing frequent feeding with organic matter. Sharp sand is the type of sand best for gardeners' use.

Clay

Clay is a tight bound mass of tiny particles, and there are many types. It holds water all too well, obstructing the passage of air, and making it cold, stiff and sticky. When dry it becomes solid and bricklike, and shrinks and cracks. It is chemically active because the particles are so small, and provides many plant nutrients. Together, sand and clay balance and correct each other's faults.

Lime

Important in maintaining the acidity/alkalinity of the soil, and in making it easier to work. A pure chalk soil is also a very 'hungry soil' and requires a large quantity of humus to bring it into all round fertility.

Humus

A precious element, elusive of definition, that is the product of the decomposition of vegetable and animal matter. It contains the life of the soil, the living energy without which the soil would be purely a heap of lifeless mineral particles. Humus darkens and warms the soil, but there can be excess of it, and a few plants prefer to be short of it.

Other vegetable matter commonly added to soils are peat and tree bark. Peat is vegetable matter long decayed in waterlogged conditions, and tends to be acidic in nature. It is useful in the cultivation of plants that dislike lime, but is not the only form of acid soil. It holds water in the same manner as a sponge, without clogging the air spaces, and is a good conditioner of clay soil, providing an easy root run for plants. It is a major ingredient of potting composts.

The alternative to peat is a by-product of another industry, coir, which does not deplete natural resources in the same way as peat. Harvesting peat is destructive to the environment, as it removes certain rare habitats, and it is preferable to avoid its wholesale use as an all-round soil conditioner because of this.

Tree bark is also a by-product, of the forestry industry in this case. The bark is removed from the timber prior to sawing, and it is ground up and composted. It is useful as a substitute for peat for some uses, and it is often used as a mulch. It is essential that the bark is well composted, otherwise it will deplete the available nitrogen in the soil as it rots down, before it can add its own contribution to the level of humus.

All types of soil require ample humus, and the best type of soil is a well balanced loam, preferably full of the fibres of old decaying roots, as of old rotted turf.

Chemical elements in soil

The principle chemical elements and their compounds in soil are nitrogen, potassium, phosphorus, and calcium. There are many other elements in the soil essential for plant life, but these four are the only ones that need constant renewal in cultivated soil.

Nitrogen

This improves foliage, making the plant large, leafy and green. It is particularly good for plants grown for their foliage, both edible and decorative, and good for the young growing period of a plant. It is easily soluble in the water in the soil, and so is apt to be deficient in regions of heavy rainfall.

Phosphates

Particularly useful for root development, and so is good for root crops, and for the ripening of seed.

Potash

Particularly noted for its effect both on fruit and foliage. In shrubs it helps to ripen and harden the wood, and promotes the formation of flower buds.

Calcium

The element found in limestone and chalk. It is a plant food, promotes the decomposition of vegetable matter, and helps strengthen the structure of woody plants and trees.

The important thing to consider is the balance of these various elements in the soil or compost. An excess of one of these elements is just as harmful as a deficiency in another, whether it is caused naturally, as when there is a lack of lime on an acid soil, or may be caused by the exhaustion of the soil elements by a particular crop.

The chief method by which nature herself corrects any deficiencies in the chemical balance of the soil is by leaf fall and other forms of decay, by returning to the soil what came out of it.

Chemical fertilizers have their place in the range of chemicals available to gardeners, but the basis of all good plant feeding is the feeding of the soil by the liberal return of large amounts of organic waste.

Organic foods

Organic foods are slow in action but enduring in their effect. Most have a physical or structural use in the soil, as humus and in aeration, as well as their chemical value. The most outstanding and easily obtainable ones for general use are well rotted manure, old turves, garden compost, leaf mould, and the commercially prepared products like bonemeal, hoof and horn, fish blood and bone, and dried blood.

Manure

Manure generally means animal dung. The best are cow, horse and pig, but the droppings of poultry, sheep, goats and rabbits are also valuable. The quality of a particular manure varies as to what the animals have been fed on, and it will also contain weed seeds, insect pests, grubs and, of course, a pungent smell!

Animal manures should contain short straw or other litter, and should be partially rotted. This removes the excess of acids that are harmful to plant life, and reduces the nitrogen demand on the soil as the manure rots down.

Animal manures should not be left to stand in the open for any length of time, as their vitality will be washed out by the rain and evaporated by the sun. They can also be composted, by themselves or mixed with other organic refuse.

Good animal manure can be difficult to obtain, and once obtained it is bulky and a little smelly to store. A reasonable substitute is a commercially produced dehydrated and composted animal manure, available in bags like potting compost. For the patio and container gardener, this product is to be recommended, as it is less bulky, clean to handle, and in presealed packs for easy carrying, which solves the problems of handling fresh manure.

Dried blood

A highly nitrogenous fertilizer, quick acting and effective. It is best reserved for the more precious plants, as it is not a cheap commodity.

Hoof and horn

A naturally slow release form of nitrogen. Like dried blood and bonemeal, it is a by-product of the slaughterhouse and so an animal waste.

Fish, blood and bone

A high nitrogen fertilizer with some of the long term benefits of slowly released phosphates from the bone. It is a good all round general fertilizer.

Bonemeal

A good all round slow release fertilizer, very high in phosphates. It is good for almost everything, but does contain some lime. Always add bonemeal when planting trees and shrubs.

Compost

In this context compost refers to the vegetable and animal wastes that have rotted down to make humus. This is done on the domestic scale in a compost heap. The heap should be big enough to generate enough heat to rot the refuse and kill any weed seeds. It should hold a certain amount of air and not be too well compacted, otherwise anaerobic decomposition occurs, methane and other undesirable gases are produced, and the whole heap turns into a slimy smelly mess. Under optimum conditions, the time taken to make humus in a compost heap is about three to four months.

There are many styles and shapes of compost bins, most of which work fairly well. The optimum size bin is about 1 m sq (3¼ ft sq) and about 1 m (3¼ ft) high, with a removable front panel for access to the compost. The whole bin should have a removable cover to protect the heap from rain and wind, to keep the heat in, and to allow more refuse to be easily put on the heap (Fig. 15.2).

It is best to have at least two compost heaps, so that the second one can be building up whilst the first is left to mature. Three heaps would be ideal, with one to use, one to stand, and one to build.

Making compost is important in that the waste materials of the garden are returned from whence they came, in a form that can be used in the soil for the benefit of the other living creatures. Not to return one's waste to the land is to squander the resources of the earth and to deplete it for one's children.

The only drawback to making compost for the patio and container gardener is the amount of space that a compost bin occupies. Most patio areas are very restricted in size, and a compost bin will take up a substantial amount of space in this limited area.

If it is possible to fit in by means of making compost, then do so, as it is a very convenient way to dispose of garden and kitchen waste to good long term effect.

Leaf mould

This is nature's own way of feeding plants with naturally made compost, and a gardener can do no better. Leaves are slower to compost than garden and kitchen waste, and so must have their own compost bin. Oak, beech and hawthorn are the best leaves to use; chestnut, sycamore and ash take much longer to decompose. Conifer leaves are useless to compost, as are tough leaves like holly, laurel and rhododendron, and leaves of roses and fruit trees should always be burnt to prevent any spread of disease.

Fig. 15.2 A compost bin.

Inorganic foods

The majority of inorganic foods are artificial or chemical fertilizers. They are quick acting, easy to handle, carry no pests, and can be adjusted to the needs of the particular plant or crop. The effect of these chemicals is not enduring, as they feed only the plant and not the soil, and their long term continual use can lead to depletion and finally death of the living soil. Many are caustic and should not touch any portion of the plant, and should not be applied on a windy day.

As these chemical foods are very strong, they should only be added little and often, in the spring and summer, and just pricked into the surface of the soil with a fork or hoe. They should always be stored in a dry place, in a securely locked cupboard up off the ground.

The chief artificial fertilizers are *sulphate of ammonia*, which provides nitrogen, *super phosphate of lime*, which provides phosphates, and *sulphate of potash*, which provides potash. There are many other chemical fertilizers for use in the garden, but they are not necessary to the patio or container gardener. A well tended soil full of humus, well cared for and well watered as necessary, will give a good healthy display of flowers or crop of salad vegetables.

For general use, a reputable 'complete' or balanced fertilizer is best. 'National Growmore', although devised for vegetables, is good for flowers and shrubs, all except ericaceous plants, but should be applied with care as it will burn the foliage if applied too generously. 'Phostrogen' is a good liquid feed, excellent for short term use for annuals in containers and hanging baskets. There are also preparations for special purposes, such as 'Tomorite' for tomatoes, and 'Top Rose' for roses.

The need for lime

Lime is a naturally occurring inorganic fertilizer with many uses in the garden, including the patio garden. It has both organic and chemical properties, and must be used with discretion.

Lime has a marked physical effect on the structure of heavy soils, helping to break them down. It promotes the decomposition of organic matter, and helps break sticky clay down to loose crumbs. In decomposing organic matter, it encourages worms and helps to provide plant food, as well as being a plant food itself. It cures clubroot in cabbages and allied plants, like wallflowers and stocks. In excess its effects are harmful, and to a wide range of ericaceous plants, it can be lethal. Its chief uses are for vegetables and fruits, but it is also enjoyed by carnations, irises, clematis and many other flowers.

The need for lime depends on the acidity or alkalinity of the soil. Acidity and alkalinity are measured on a scale of pH. A neutral soil has a pH of 7; and acid soil has a pH below 7, say 6.5 for a slightly acid soil; and an alkaline or chalky soil has a pH above 7, say 8 for a garden on shallow chalk downs. A pH of 5.5 indicates a very acid soil, sour and unpleasant smelling, and in this situation a very heavy dressing of lime is needed.

The pH of the soil can easily be measured with a simple soil testing kit, available from most garden centres. It is best to test several samples from different parts of the garden, as there may well be variations, even in a small garden. Bear in mind that builder's rubble is often very alkaline, due to the cement and lime that is used in building, and so that to test the garden soil just after a patio has been built may well give an incorrect reading.

Unless the soil is so acid that it is sour and unusable, it is best to bear with the nature of the garden and enjoy the soil as it is meant to be. Many plants thrive on acid soils, and many plants thrive on alkaline soils. Many plants that thrive on a chalky alkaline soil will also grow well on an acid soil, but rarely will an acid loving (ericaceous) plant do well on an alkaline soil. To attempt to grow ericaceous plants on an alkaline soil is a recipe for disaster, a lot of hard work to no effect, and to little avail. However big the hole is dug, however much peat is added to the soil, it will always be alkaline, and the ground water will also be alkaline. Ericaceous plants grown in these conditions may grow for a very few years, but will gradually curl up and die. It is best to use lime only to condition and improve the soil, not to try and alter the nature of the soil.

Hydroponics

One particularly interesting system of growing plants in containers is the greenhouse method of ring culture, or hydroponics. Ring culture derives its name from the use of open ended or bottomless pots or rings, which are filled with a growing medium and stood on a bed of moist gravel. The plant growing in the ring, usually a tomato plant, forms two sets of roots, one set in the compost for nutrient absorption and the other set of roots in the gravel, for water absorption.

Used in the greenhouse, this is an alternative to grow bags, producing a carefully controlled environment in which the plants can crop efficiently. Very little soil is used to grow a substantial crop, and ring culture has none of the pest and disease problems of using greenhouse soil to grow the plants. At the end of the season, the ring culture bed can be flushed out with a disinfectant such as Jeyes fluid or potassium permanganate, and is then ready for the next season (Fig. 15.3).

In many ways this represents the extreme in terms of ecological abuse of growing plants in containers. The plants are totally dependent on man to provide food, water and care, and without man the plants would die. Both the crops and the plants grown in this manner look very healthy, and at any sign of a mineral deficiency, the balance of chemicals in the liquid feed can be altered. Essential trace elements and even systemic insecticides can be given to the plants this way, as a form of force feeding! But the plants and the crop contain no living energy that is obtained from growing with roots grounded in the living soil, and there is little benefit in growing crops in this manner to eat, despite their healthy looks.

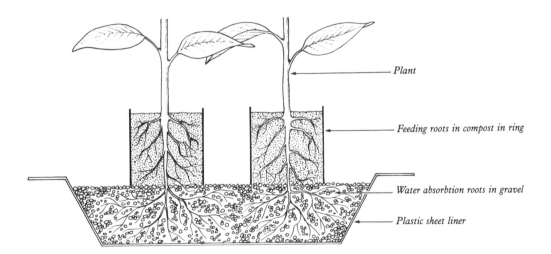

Plant

Feeding roots in compost in ring

Water absorbtion roots in gravel

Plastic sheet liner

Fig. 15.3 Cross section of ring culture pots and bed.

CHAPTER 16

General Plant Maintenance

Watering

All watering of plants must be both gentle and thorough. To be gentle, always use a watering can with a rose, or a fine sprinkler (Fig. 16.1). If it is essential to use a hose, then it must only be with a spray attachment, or a rain or mist forming attachment.

Plants watered by hand need long thorough watering as if they had been stood outside on a long rainy day. A prolonged soaking will do a great deal more good than just playing around making the surface of the soil damp, which only serves to draw the fine rootlets of the plant to the surface and leave it vulnerable to excessive drying out at times of hot sunny weather.

Plants in containers especially need sensitive and sensible watering. As they are particularly vulnerable to drying out, regular and efficient watering is essential. The plants should be watered gently with a watering can with a spray rose, and should be watered so that the water reaches the rim of the pot and is allowed to gently soak through the compost and to drain away. This should be done at least on a daily basis in summer, and twice daily in hot weather. Remember that watering is still necessary in winter at times when there is little rain. When the plant foliage covers all the soil in the container and does not allow rain to penetrate the soil, then water is needed all year round.

If the container has been allowed to dry out, the compost will shrink away from the sides of the container, and any water will just run around the outside of the compost and flow away down the gap between the compost and the container. The only effective way of rewetting the compost so that it expands again and absorbs the water is to sit the container in a bucket or sink of water and allow it to gently soak up the moisture.

If this is not possible due to the size of the container, then it will be necessary to try and rewet the compost manually. Make several thin deep holes into the compost with a thin cane or pencil, and water the container every hour, to allow the water to penetrate the compost through the holes. Making the holes in the compost can damage the plant roots, but it is the only effective way in allowing the water to wet the compost, and to give the plants a chance of living. The moral of this is not to let the container dry out in the first place!

As a patio area is usually paved and located to create a much needed sun trap in this cool English climate, it is by definition a warm space, and containers of plants will dry out rapidly. Plants growing in the ground around the patio will also dry out very rapidly, as they too suffer from restricted root runs and the effects of the warmth of the paving. Attention must be paid to their water requirements, and the easiest way to do this without a large time and effort commitment is to install an automatic watering system. It also makes sense to grow those plants that enjoy the dryer conditions and will thrive without vast quantities of mollycoddling.

Some plants, such as hydrangeas and rhododendrons, need to be kept moist even when planted in the ground, especially in dry weather. Sweet peas, garden peas and beans dislike cold tap water and should be watered with rain water; if none is available, a large tub

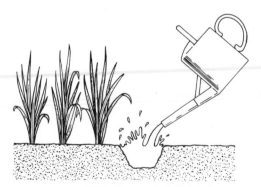

Fig. 16.1 How not to water.

of tap water can be left to stand for at least twenty four hours in sunlight, and this can be used as a substitute for rain water. Rainwater is, of course, preferable for all watering operations whenever possible.

Weeding

However well kept the garden, whether patio garden or container garden, weeds will always appear. Nature abhors bare soil, and if it is not covered by a mulch, something will grow. If it is a plant that is not needed in that position, it will be called a weed.

Weeds are usually fast growing and compete with existing plants for water, light and food. As they grow so fast, they soon swamp the other plants and win the competition for light, and often for water. Weeds are generally prolific seeders, making sure that their progeny continue their life's mission. It is not without good reason that there is a saying 'one year's seeds is seven years' weeds'. Weeds are best removed before they seed in an attempt to reduce the numbers of the next generation of weeds.

Removal of weeds by hand is best. Using a small hand fork for slightly more stubborn weeds, thoroughly remove the offending plants complete with roots to prevent regrowth. Larger weeds, such as dock, thistles and cow parsley, are best removed with a large garden fork if they have become established, as they have a very long tap root. If the tap root is not removed completely, it will regrow and the plant will reappear.

Hoeing is another way of removing weeds, but the conditions must be right for it to be effective. If the soil is dry and the weather is warm, fibrous rooted weeds that have not flowered can be hoed and left to wither on the surface of the soil. If the weeds have flowered or seeded, they must be raked off and composted or burnt. Hoeing is not appropriate if the ground has been mulched as it will just disturb the mulch unnecessarily. It is easiest to hand weed on mulched soil, as there will be very few weeds and they will be easy to pull out.

Some weeds defy all but the most persistent gardener. Couch grass (twitch) can be removed by continual digging out and following the roots to their end, taking care not to break a root, as it will immediately sprout afresh and start a new colony of couch grass. If it is essential to use a weed-killer, Dalapon is designed solely for couch grass.

Bindweed can be removed in time with persistent digging out of every tiny piece of root to be found. The same approach applies to ground elder and coltsfoot, a strange medicinal plant that flowers early in spring with small yellow composite flowers and produces its leaves in the summer. Persistent removal of the leaves and as much root as possible will eventually kill these weeds from the lack of food they need from the air and sunlight. If it is essential to use a weed-killer, then a hormone weed-killer painted on to the leaves will eventually kill the plants. A systemic weed-killer, used persistently, will also eventually kill the weeds. Failing all this, the ground should be cleared of all shrubs and perennial plants, the soil dug through very thoroughly, the weed roots untangled from the roots of the shrubs and perennials, and only then should the area be replanted.

A patio will at times be vulnerable to weeds, especially if the paving has not been laid with all the care it was due and so perennial weeds have seeded and grown in the cracks and joints. The most effective way of removing these weeds is to get down on hands and knees and remove them using an old kitchen knife. Tap roots should be painted with a systemic weed-killer or sodium chlorate to prevent regrowth, if desired, but read and act on the instructions with the chemicals, and always wear protective clothing and store the chemicals, well labelled, in a locked cupboard. If weeds are going to regrow due to poor quality pointing of the paving, then the pointing should be raked out and redone.

If using weed-killers in the patio area, take extra precautions to avoid the chemicals running off the paved surface on to the planted areas next to the paving. Any damage will not be immediately obvious, only showing up in the following season and possibly looking like a mineral deficiency until the full extent of the damage is seen.

Generally, it is best to avoid the use of chemicals and to rely on efficient soil preparation and continual care to keep the patio and containers free of weeds.

Mulching

Mulching is the process of spreading a thick layer of matter, usually organic matter, on the surface of the soil. The mulch can be organic matter like bark chippings, leaves, leaf mould, manure, mushroom compost, peat or grass cuttings, or it can be inorganic matter like gravel, limestone or granite chippings.

A mulch serves many purposes in the garden, and has many advantages over leaving the soil bare. The soil beneath the mulch will be retained in the same state as when the mulch was applied, as the mulch acts like a thick blanket and insulates the ground. So if the ground was warm and damp when the mulch was applied, it will stay warm and damp when beneath the mulch. Conversely, if there was frost in the ground when the mulch was applied, the ground beneath will tend to stay cold and hard beneath.

Because the mulch insulates the soil, it will insulate the roots of the plants growing in the soil, and so help slightly tender plants to survive a bad winter. In a very hot dry summer, a thick mulch will also conserve water, by not allowing the surface of the soil to be exposed and so dry out. The soil will remain workable, instead of drying out and cracking, and any weeds will still be removable.

A thick mulch over the soil will also deter most weeds, and those weeds that manage to make it through the mulch will be spindly and weak, easy to remove. The only weeds that are not suppressed by a mulch are the very aggressive perennial weeds like bindweed, couch grass and ground elder.

Organic mulches like grass cuttings, manure and bark chippings will eventually rot down and add to the humus in the soil, possibly adding some nutrients as well. Grass cuttings will rot down very fast, and care must be taken not to locate them too close to shrubs, as they will burn the stems with the heat and organic reactions taking place. They will also tend to deplete the soil of nitrogen for a time before they add to the nitrogen in the soil.

Manure, particularly if it is well rotted, makes a very good mulch. It may not look very pretty, especially if it is full of straw, but it is an excellent insulator, and feeds the soil and the plants long after it seems to have disappeared. It is one of the best mulches to use in an established garden, even a patio garden, as it gives so much benefit.

Bark chippings are the right mulch to use in decorative plantings, as they look good whatever the season. They have all the benefits of an organic mulch, but take anything up to ten years to rot away, depending on the size of bark chippings used. They can be used, with great care, around most perennial plants.

Gravel chippings also make a good mulch, but without the property of rotting down to add to the humus in the soil. They do, however, help to open up the soil surface and allow the absorption of rain water into what could be a hard solid mass of soil. They also make a good surface to 'scree' gardens, where the stones are used as the main feature and the plants are mostly alpines needing very good drainage, which is provided by the stones on the surface and in the soil.

Gravel and chippings can be used to cover extensive areas of soil, and plants can be allowed to seed themselves. This treatment can be used to make a very informal patio area, and any unwanted plants or weeds can be easily removed from the gravel.

Mulching gives a good finish to the soil and makes the garden look good and cared for. Weeds can easily be removed from the mulch, and so the time commitment in maintaining the garden is reduced.

The original depth of mulch will determine how effective it is. For the best effect, most organic mulches should be at least 100 mm (4 in) thick. Even on the surface of planted containers, a minimum of 50 mm (2 in) is needed to have any benefit at all, and the deeper it is, the better. Gravel should be at least 50 mm (2 in) thick, and again will be more effective if it is deeper.

Mulches need topping up at regular intervals to maintain their long term benefits. Mushroom compost, peat and manure will need topping up annually; fine bark chippings will need topping up every two or three years, and gravel will need topping up about every five years.

Staking

Staking is necessary for taller, non-rigid plants, in order to prevent damage by wind and rain. It is a regular garden maintenance job, and although it may appear tedious, it is part of caring for the garden and has many benefits.

The main benefit of regularly staking plants is that they get checked over, untangled, sorted out and cared for. Any other problems come to light, such as damage by insects or animals, and the general health of the plants can be assessed. Then any other action can be taken if necessary. It also gives the opportunity to appreciate the plants close at hand, as well as admiring them from an arm's reach away, and this appreciation gives an understanding of the care that is needed.

Delphiniums, gaillardias, peas and sweet peas, carnations and a few other plants need staking very early in their growth, but generally the right time to stake is when the plant has made about three quarters of its growth. Staking must be thorough and tidy, each plant cared for individually. A large clump of chrysanthemums tied with a single piece of string to one stake is a horticultural horror to be avoided under all circumstances.

For general work, the easiest and least conspicuous supports are twiggy pea sticks. They should be trimmed to an appropriate height and planted firmly in the ground so that they completely surround the plants, with one or two extra in the middle. The fast growing foliage will soon hide the sticks, and the support will be effective and natural.

Bamboo canes can be used instead, several to a plant, with green gardening string or raffia tied round at intervals to support the plants. For tall growing plants such as delphiniums, each individual flower spike should have its own support. Never tie up plants by bunching them together with one piece of string tied to a solitary cane. There are now available commercial systems of metal stakes that link together to give a comprehensive support to plants, to provide a framework through which the plants can grow. These systems, like any other method of plant support, are only effective if they are in place before needed. If the plants are already flopping, then no method of support will be adequate (Fig. 16.2).

Trees should be staked with a low stake, about 200 mm (8 in) high, held to the tree with a special tree tie to prevent chafing. Staking at this low level will allow the tree to develop its own stability and holding roots, but will give enough support to avoid wind rock and loosening of the soil (Fig. 16.3).

If it is necessary to use a longer stake, then make sure that the tree is secured well with a special tree tie to prevent chafing. Check the tie regularly and gradually move it down the stake to allow the tree to learn to stand by itself, so that by the third or fourth year stake and tie can be removed.

Planting

Poor and slovenly planting is the cause of many a fine healthy young plant growing into a straggly, malformed weakling. It is essential that a plant is started off well in its new home, because it affects the whole of the rest of its life.

The general requirements are simple: a good, friable, well-worked soil that is not sodden or crumbly dry; a hole dug generously large enough, slightly deeper and wider than seems necessary, to accommodate the plant with its roots spread comfortably well down, not scrunched up, crowded or twisted; a handful of bonemeal at the bottom of the hole for trees, shrubs, perennials and some bulbs; a gentle but firm backfilling of soil and pressing down, possibly treading carefully to firm it in; and a good watering in with rainwater, if available. The other essential for any garden work, particularly planting, is the right state of mind. There is no point planting at a time when one resents the job; it is best done with a happy heart, because then it will be done well and the plants will thrive.

Planting should only take place in 'open' weather, when the ground is neither frostbound nor saturated. When planting in a dry spell or in the summer, soak the ground thoroughly the night before with the hose for a big job, and water the plants in extra well. Pour some water in the hole just before the plant is put in, and water well after backfilling.

Trees should always have their stake, long or short, planted before the tree is put in the hole, to avoid damaging the roots. Make sure the stake is straight before planting the tree.

The depth of planting is important. Trees and shrubs should be planted to the depth of the old soil mark. Carnations and rhododendrons should be planted shallow, phlox rather deep. Each plant has its own individual requirements.

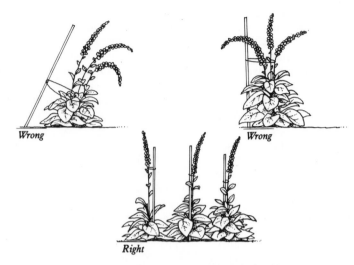

Fig. 16.2 Right and wrong ways of staking plants.

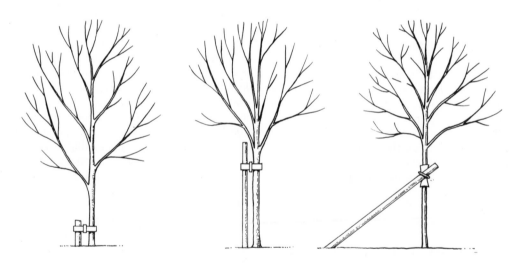

Fig. 16.3 Different methods of staking trees.

When planting in heavy clay, work some peat or spent grow bag potting compost around the roots of the tree or shrub, to give them an easy start. Be gentle with the firming in, as otherwise compaction will occur.

Plants are available container grown, so planting can take place at any time of the year. It is more sensible not to plant in the middle of a hot summer, as a great deal of work with watering will be needed to keep the new plants alive. Likewise, do not plant in the middle of a hard winter. Think about the plant requirements, and plant accordingly.

Container-grown plants can often be 'pot bound', having the pot full of a mass of coiled roots. Having removed the plant from the pot, give the rootball a gentle squeeze to loosen the soil and gently tease out the roots. Cut them back if they are excessively long, rather than wind them round inside the hole. Plant and water with care, as these plants may take a little longer to become established.

Plant any plants as soon as possible, rather than leave them to sit around in their pots. If a delay is unavoidable, heel in a bare rooted plants in a spare piece of ground and water well. Pots can be treated in a similar manner, as planting the pot in the ground on a temporary basis will give it support in the wind, protect it from frost and reduce the rate of drying out. At times of frost when it is not possible to heel in the plants, they can be stored in a frost free shed for a few days, provided that the foliage and roots are kept moist. The main cause of death and disability to a plant at this stage is lack of water and dehydration.

Planting in containers follows the same basic procedure, whatever the type of plant. First prepare the container, making sure that it is thoroughly clean. Place a layer of crocks at the bottom of the container to act as a drainage medium, and to stop the soil gradually being washed out of the holes in the bottom of the pot. Fill the container to within about 3 mm of the rim with the appropriate potting compost or soil mix and firm gently. Work out the planting design and the position of the various elements of the contents of the container by setting the plants on the soil surface. Then, with a trowel, make holes and plant each plant in turn, starting with the central plant or the tallest plants. Firm in each plant gently, and water well.

Mulch the container with either bark chippings or gravel as desired. For a temporary planting of annual plants, fresh green moss can also be used as a mulch.

Pruning

Pruning trees and shrubs is overrated as a problem garden task. It is straight forward, an enjoyable challenge, provided that it is approached with gentleness, the right tools well sharpened, a knowledge of the plant and its habits, and an aim or reason for undertaking the pruning in the first place.

Why prune?

The main reason for pruning can be any one of the following, or a combination of any of the reasons:

1. the shrub has become too large for its allotted space and one is loth to dig it out and replace it;
2. you wish to encourage its flowering;
3. it is full of dead wood and you wish to clean it up and rejuvenate it;
4. you wish to stimulate new growth for the foliage effects, or for the effects of the coloured bark of the new stems;
5. the neighbours have complained about the quantity of jungle that is trying to escape from your patio garden;
6. the plant has grown too big for its pot but you do not want to use a larger size container.

Once the reason for undertaking the pruning has been defined, then the approach is clear and the method is a matter of enlightened common sense. It is essential to know the plant and its habits, whether it is spring or summer flowering, whether it flowers on old wood or new wood, whether it will grow or 'break' from old wood, and so on. All this information is gleaned from observing the plant through the seasons.

Basic remedial pruning of established plants involves the cutting out of dead wood, and the removal of branches that cross over. This will let light and air into the plant, both essential requirements for life. Any branches should be cut as close to their origin as possible, so as not to leave any awkward snags that look ugly and let in any disease to the plant. When finished, the plant should look as if it had originally grown in that way (Fig. 16.4).

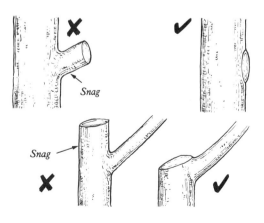

Snag

Snag

Fig. 16.4 Correct and incorrect methods of pruning showing snags.

217

Fig. 16.5 Pruning out spent flowering wood
(*a*) Light pruning results in several new shoots
(*b*) Hard pruning gives two or more long strong shoots e.g. *Forsythia*.

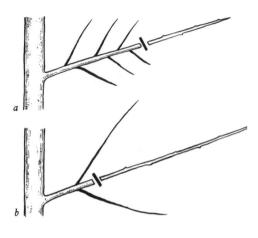

Fig. 16.6 Pruning to three buds from base.

Remember when pruning, look at the problem many times, make a decision and act on it with confidence. If necessary, cut back a little at a time; mistakes cannot be stuck back on!

To rejuvenate an established shrub, if it is one such as laurel or willow that will 'break' from old wood, cut it back hard at the base, leaving little more than a stump. It will then grow new wood from the base, and within a few seasons will have grown back to a reasonable size shrub. This method is just the garden form of coppicing. It will depend on the type of shrub as to when this is done, but only cut

evergreen shrubs in late spring and early summer, to allow any new growth to season and harden before the next winter.

To encourage a plant to flower, it is fundamental to know what time of year it flowers, and whether it is on old or new wood. Shrubs that flower on old wood usually flower in the spring and early summer, spending the rest of the growing season growing wood to flower in the following spring. These shrubs should be pruned just after flowering, in early summer, so that the energies of the plant can be used to build new wood, rather than forming the seeds that follow the flowers. The old wood that has flowered should be cut away, to encourage the growth of new wood. Sometimes this seems very drastic, especially if the shrub has flowered very well and so there is a lot to cut out. Examples of shrubs needing this type of pruning are philadelphus, weigela and forsythia (Fig. 16.5).

Shrubs that flower on new wood usually flower in late summer and autumn, having grown the wood, formed the flower buds and grown them into flower all in that season. Pruning should then be undertaken in the autumn and winter, ready to give the plant a head start in the spring. Examples of this type of pruning are hydrangea, buddleia and some forms of clematis.

Plants that bloom on both old and new wood can be approached in whichever way suits the gardener, remembering the principles of removing dead wood, crossing branches and encouraging new growth.

Inevitably there are a few exceptions to this. Some trees bleed profusely when cut, so they should be pruned only if essential, and in late summer or early autumn when the sap is no longer rising. Evergreen trees and shrubs should be pruned only in late spring, and only if essential to the health of the plants.

To prune to stimulate new growth for foliage effects, for plants such as catalpa and cotinus, prune each branch hard to three buds above its base. Do this in winter or spring, ready for the plant when it breaks into the new season's growth. For plants that are grown for the winter effect of their coloured twigs, such as some willows and dogwoods, pruning is undertaken just before buds burst in the spring (Fig. 16.6).

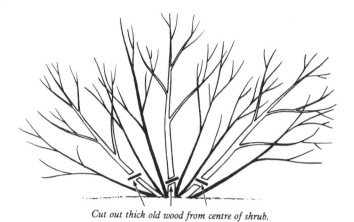

Cut out thick old wood from centre of shrub.

Fig. 16.7 Thinning an established shrub.

If the intention of the pruning is to reduce the size of the plant but to keep its shape and overall effect, then the approach is different. This sort of pruning is often needed when the neighbours complain about being swamped by some plant growing from the other side of the boundary, but where it is still necessary to maintain a foliage screen for privacy. Often it is evergreen shrubs that need this treatment.

Rather than just cutting the shrub back hard without any method, the structure of the shrub is considered, and old and very large wood is removed from inside the plant. All the cut branches are then hidden by the remaining foliage, which is less dense and considerably more contained than at the start of the job (Fig. 16.7).

If a container grown plant has grown too big for its pot, but it needs to be retained in that particular size container, then both the foliage and the roots need pruning. Pruning should take place when the plant is repotted, usually just before it starts into growth in the spring.

When the plant is removed from the pot, the roots should be teased out and the very long ones cut back to a joint, in a similar manner to cutting back a branch to a joint. In this way the mass of roots are reduced, but most of the fine feeding roots are retained.

The upper part of the plant is pruned by removing dead wood and crossing branches, and then the plant is carefully thinned by removing some of the larger older branches to allow the new growth plenty of light and air. This should be done after the plant has been repotted.

How to prune

There are a few general principles that apply to all forms and manner of pruning trees and shrubs. Pruning of fruit trees and bushes, clematis and roses are specialist jobs with a slightly different approach, but these principles still apply.

First, if in doubt, don't! A bit cut off by mistake cannot be stuck back on.

Always cut out dead wood, diseased wood, and feeble spindly growths.

Cut back into clean healthy wood that shows no discolouration or scar.

Remove spent flowers and seed pods immediately after flowering, if possible, except on hydrangeas and plants grown for their berries or fruit.

Where branches cross, keep the one that will most help to make a shapely plant, and cut out the other branch or part of it. This applies especially to open habit plants, roses and fruit, not so much to a dense habit plant like a berberis.

Use only sharp clean tools, and make clean smooth cuts. Never break the branch of a hard wooded plant.

Always cut just above a new bud, or flush

Fig. 16.8 Hard pruning of santolina.

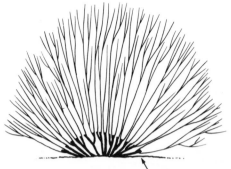

Cut all long growth back hard to form a dense dome.

with the junction with another branch. Never leave a snag or stub end. Choose a bud that is pointing in the direction that the new shoot is needed to grow, usually outward.

Cuts should always be sloping or vertical, never horizontal, so that any water runs off.

Remember that pruning is a way of adapting the natural shape and habit of the plant to a particular need. The method of pruning and the final result must not contradict the natural form, but be an adaptation of it. This will then avoid the stubby amputated branches of badly pruned trees and the rounded domes of the 'corporation clip' that is so often done to shrubs in municipal care. The pruning should bring out the best in a plant, whether it is flower, berry, fruit or foliage.

Remember also that many plants do not need pruning at all.

Grey-leaved plants

Grey and silver-leaved plants are usually aromatic, often evergreen, originating in Mediterranean regions where the climate is hot for much of the year and the ground is often of limestone. These plants make very good patio and container plants, as they will tolerate a relatively poor alkaline soil with good drainage, plenty of strong sunshine and drought. Rich moist soil and the shade will make them sulk, even rot and die. Grey-leaved plants need a different pruning regime to most other plants. In late spring, usually towards the middle of April, just when they are beginning to show signs of growth, they should be cut back very hard. Some, like santolina, should be cut back to make a small dome of old branches which will then produce fresh new growth for the coming year (Fig. 16.8). *Salvia officinalis* (sage), *Ruta graveolens* (rue), some artemesias, perovskia, caryopteris, *Athemis cupaniana*, helichrysums (including curry plants) and *Senecio 'Sunshine'* can all be treated this way, to give a dense mound of new growth that will look good all summer and through the autumn and winter. Marrubium (horehound), ballota and phlomis (Jerusalen sage) can also be cut back, possibly not quite so hard, in spring.

Using this regime for grey and silver-leaved plants means that they are tidy and controlled in the early part of the growing season. As the summer progresses, they grow larger and flower, generally with little yellow daisy flowers (which should be removed if the effect of the silver foliage is to be retained). The final size and shape of the plants is retained throughout the whole winter, giving structure and form, colour and brightness to the winter garden.

220

CHAPTER 17

Organic Container Gardening

The Principles of Organic Gardening

An organic gardener is one that does not use any chemical fertilizers, pesticides, fungicides, and herbicides. Some gardeners have always gardened in this way, others have given up the addiction to chemicals on ethical grounds, such as to stop pollution harmful to birds, bees and man. Some have given up the use of chemicals for purely financial reasons, as with any addiction, the continuing use of chemicals is a costly and on-going expense.

The difference between organic and inorganic fertilizers is based on the way that plants feed. Inorganic fertilizers provide the chemicals that the plant needs, in a form that is easily absorbed into the sap flow of the plant and can be extracted as required. Hence inorganic fertilizers feed only the plant. They feed the plant very fast, but wastefully, as they soon wash out of the sap-stream and are lost to the plant.

Organic fertilizers feed not only the plant, but also the soil. The soil is full of micro-organisms that continually work, breaking down organic matter in the soil and converting it into a form that is of use to all living matter. The cycle of life and death of soil organisms produces nutrients for use by other living creatures of the soil, including plants. In feeding the soil its whole fertility is improved and one of the many benefits is healthy well grown plants.

If the soil is exploited in using a large input of chemicals to increase the yield of crops, then there is a gradual breakdown of soil structure, and the soil loses its vitality. The end result over several years is a gradual decrease in yield. The loss of a viable soil structure is accelerated by constant inputs of a vast range of insecticides, herbicides and fungicides whose residues actually destroy the microorganisms that are essential for a living soil.

The chemicals used to make fertilizers are either obtained from natural deposits, of which there are only a few and are rapidly running out, or they are manufactured in a process using about five times as much fuel as fertilizer produced. Much of this fertilizer is then applied to land that already has more than plenty already in the soil, and a high proportion of it is washed through the rivers to the sea, polluting and damaging the ecological balance in passing.

Many of the chemicals used in pesticides, herbicides and fungicides are complicated synthetic substances, their molecules differing from naturally occurring ones in as much that nature cannot easily break them down and take them apart for recycling into other harmless and beneficial substances. These chemicals break down very slowly and the by-products, often poisonous, gradually accumulate in the liver and body fat of other creatures, subjecting them to a slow and painful death by poisoning.

Virtually any weed, disease or insect pest can develop the ability to survive the application of chemical treatment which was once effective in its control. In this way, chemical treatments are continually fighting nature and repeatedly losing the battle, and new chemical treatments then need to be developed to maintain control. A more sympathetic and obvious approach is to use nature to maintain the balance, and never let the plants and soil deteriorate into the state where the use of chemicals is thought to be necessary to 'bring things under control'.

Organic growing is much more efficient than inorganic growing because it utilizes the natural cycle of returning waste matter to the soil. Returning the waste products from growing trees, shrubs, fruit, vegetables and flowers continues a cycle that started in time immemorial.

Compost and manure are then the lynch pins of organic growing, as they are the simple way of returning waste products to the soil for recycling. The composting process is very simple and easily done on a garden scale, even a small patio garden, and more details are found in the section on soils (see page 206) in this book. The general and regular use of well rotted compost and manure feeds the soil with a wide range of nutrients, as well as improving its texture, aeration and water holding capacity by increasing the amount of humus.

Some plants, usually those of the legume family, have a very special relationship with a group of soil organisms known as nitrogen-fixing bacteria. These bacteria live in specially adapted parts of the plant roots, nodules, and convert the nitrogen in the soil and air into a form that can be utilized by the plants. By growing members of the legume family (peas, beans, clover), nitrogen can be added to the soil without the application of chemical fertilizers. The plants can be grown for their crops, for their decorative value and for their use as a green manure.

Green manuring is a process where a very fast growing crop is grown and then dug back into the soil to rot down and become a manure. In this way the soil is enriched by the addition of undecomposed plant material, which holds the soil nutrients through the winter. These are then returned to the soil in the spring, when the crop is dug in, and as a consequence the soil is improved by both the crop and the digging. Excellent though this method is, it is not very relevant for patio and container gardens.

Crop rotation is important if vegetables are grown organically, even on a container scale. Certain groups of vegetables take particular nutrients out of the soil, and others add to it. Some vegetables are particularly prone to certain insect infestations and to infection by certain diseases. To minimize the effects of high nutrient demand by some plants, and to stop a build-up of disease in the soil, the same crop should never be grown in the same soil for two consecutive seasons. This applies equally well to container grown vegtable crops; either the soil in a container should be completely changed before planting the same crop again, or a different container should be used.

Crop rotation is not only of benefit to the plants, it can also save work for the gardener.

Leguminous plants, such as peas and beans, put nitrogen back into the soil and so should be followed by a crop with a high nitrogen demand, like the cabbages and quick growing catch crops of lettuce and radish. Then brassicas are followed by potatoes and some late maturing root crops, the fast growing root vegetables like carrots, beetroot and parsnips being grown with the beans. Manuring and a rich soil is needed for the legumes, and brassicas should not be grown in freshly manured soil, so the rotation order cuts down a little work for the gardener in the amount of manure to be used.

Pests and diseases are controlled by this method of crop rotation, as they are never allowed to build up in the soil over the years. The practice of monoculture, that is growing the same crop in the same soil repeatedly, allows a build up of disease organisms in the soil, and the reduction of soil vitality over these years leaves plants particularly susceptible to infections and infestations. Growing disease resistant varieties of crops also helps to reduce the incidence of pest and disease problems, but these varieties are only disease resistant, not disease proof. The use of disease resistant varieties is only a help in maintaining a healthy garden, and is not a complete answer to problems of disease.

Methods of Organic Patio Gardening

Although organic methods are not always totally applicable to patio and container gardening, the general principles can still be applied with great success.

Soils and composts

Soil improvement should be undertaken as a matter of course, using domestic compost if possible, supplemented by the use of well rotted animal manures, or, if this is not feasible, by the use of dehydrated prepacked animal manures, compost or sewage sludge. A very good compost for use in containers can also be made from a combination of garden soil, silver sand and leaf mould, well rotted compost, well rotted manure or even dehydrated manure. The aim is to produce a rich and nourishing soil for the container plants that will not run out of nutrients in the middle of the season, or become very compacted with continual watering through the summer. A good healthy soil will also withstand frosts much better than a soil that has become heavy and compacted, and of course the plants will be fit to withstand a large amount of inclement weather without any pampering.

Compost and manure can be used to very good effect in the areas around the patio, which are often poor soil with vast quantities of builder's rubble, concrete foundations and other undesirable debris. Thorough digging is necessary before any planting is undertaken, to remove any brick bats, stones, and other household treasures, as well as to aerate the soil, and of course to remove all annual and perennial weeds. It is at this point that compost or manure should be incorporated into the soil, as deeply as possible, and in very generous quantities. After the beds and borders have been planted up, they should be mulched with an appropriate mulch to conserve water and warmth in the soil.

If the soil has been thoroughly prepared before planting is undertaken, then there should be no need for further digging in the borders. Further additions of manure can be made annually in the autumn, laid on the soil as a mulch whilst the soil is still warm from the summer. It will gradually rot down and be taken into the soil by the worms in the course of the year, and need topping up in the following autumn.

Organic pest control

The most fundamental principle of organic pest control is that a healthy soil grows healthy plants that are less susceptible to problems of pests and diseases. Regrettably, from time to time the natural balance of the garden slips, and problems of pests or disease occur.

Organic pest controls tackle these problems from several different angles, using a range of different approaches. One way is to take a conventional approach of spraying with some toxic chemical to kill the problem, but to use an organic chemical that has no lingering effects in the soil and is relatively harmless to other wildlife. There is a wide range to select from, with derris, pyrethrum, quassia and nicotine being the most easily obtainable.

However, both derris and pyrethrum will kill a wide range of insects, including desirable ones like hoverflies, ladybirds, bees and butterflies. Homemade sprays can also be used, made from nettles, elder, comfrey, rhubarb and wormwood with a soft soap solution to ensure a good coverage.

Another simple and popular approach is to encourage natural predators. Hoverflies, both adults and larvae, eat vast quantities of aphids, and can be actively encouraged in the garden by planting *Convolvulus tricolor*, an annual related to the perennial bindweed. The hoverflies will feed on the nectar of the convolvulus for the first few weeks of their lives, refueling each morning ready for a hard day of hunting aphids. *Convolvulus tricolor* can be used as a decorative hardy annual in borders as an edging plant, or as a good plant for containers.

Hedgehogs should also be encouraged in a garden, as they are great consumers of slugs, cutworms, millipedes and caterpillars. The only destructive damage that hedgehogs have been known to do is to eat strawberries while searching for slugs! Hedgehogs can be encouraged by putting out diluted milk in an untippable bowl, but only at night when there is no competition from birds. Bread, bacon rind and any fish based tinned cat food is good for hedgehogs, who can become very tame and live in the garden for many years.

Birds are great consumers of all sorts of insect pests, the most obvious one being the consumption of snails by thrushes. All kinds of tits, mostly blue, coal and great tits are great consumers of aphids, especially greenfly. By hanging a small piece of bacon fat with just enough room for three birds, about 30 cm (1ft) above a rose bed, the birds will queue to get to the fat and while they wait they will search for greenfly eggs on the bark of the bushes. Fat hung for birds in a similar manner amongst viburnum and euonymus shrubs will help keep down the problem of blackfly, for these bushes are their winter quarters.

Robins are regular scavengers of soil for insects, larvae and tiny pupae. Allotment areas can be forked over gently twice in the course of the winter to allow the robins to pick out all the food organisms.

Biological controls can also be used, utilizing

the predatory effects of certain insects and fungi on particular problem creatures such as whitefly, red spider mite, mealy bug and caterpillars. These methods of control can be very effective and are best utilized in the closed environment of the greenhouse, and for serious growing of vegetable crops.

Companion Planting

Companion planting is the domestic form of symbiosis in plants, that is the living together in harmony to the mutual benefit of all concerned. Some plants very definitely thrive in each other's company, whereas other plants hate each other to death. Very little research has been done on this subject, and most of it on the companion planting of vegetables.

Tradition has it that garlic and other strong smelling members of the onion family will reduce the amount of blackfly and greenfly on roses. From an ornamental point of view, there are many beautiful decorative alliums that associate well with roses, and if they help to control aphids by natural means, then this is to the advantage of the organic gardener.

Amongst the other ornamental plant combinations, the planting of *Nicotiana affinis*, the ornamental tobacco plant, will reduce a problem with whitefly, and the English marigold, *Calendula officinalis*, will also reduce insect infestations, as well as being a useful culinary and medicinal herb. Mexican or African marigolds, *Tagetes erecta*, when planted thickly, will control certain pernicious weeds like ground elder, ground ivy and bindweed, as well as help with insect control. The common nasturtium, *Tropaeolum majus*, will also help control whitefly, especially on brassicas.

Certain shrubs will also act as control mechanisms, for various reasons. *Ligustrum ovalifolium*, the semi-evergreen oval leafed privet, is a very greedy feeder, and will make the soil around it very barren. *Sambucus niger*, the common elderberry, poisons the soil around it and so very few plants will grow in its company. This is due to the high level of hydrocyanic acid in the plant, a feature that can be used to advantage in making an insecticidal spray from its leaves. Rhubarb associates well with the brassica family, the cabbages both ornamental and edible, as its

high level of oxalic acid is a good deterrent to clubroot.

Certain agricultural research can be of use to the patio and container gardener when it comes to companion planting. Many of the so called 'weeds' that farmers take great pride in eliminating from their crops are in fact of benefit to them. A field of wheat will grow much better with a light sprinkling of ox-eye daisies, and rye needs a few cornflowers to thrive. Other plants usually considered as noxious and troublesome weeds, such as ragweed, purslane and nettles, bring up minerals from the subsoil to supplement a depleted top soil, and are an excellent indicator of soil conditions. As companion crops, they not only provide a home and food for bees and butterflies, they help domestic plants to get their roots down to food which would otherwise be beyond their reach.

Bio-dynamic Gardening

One of the fundamental ideas underlying the bio-dynamic approach to gardening is that the earth is a living organism in its own right. The earth breathes; it has a pulse, a circulatory system, it is sensitive and it has a skin. It breathes out during the morning hours, in during the afternoon and rests during the night. Its circulatory system is provided by the water cycle as it evaporates from the oceans, falls as rain and flows back to the sea; its pulse is the changing of the seasons, with an expansive outpouring in the spring and summer and a contraction in the autumn and winter. The soil and plant complex acts as a skin, a sensitive skin, where wounds are quickly healed by a covering of plants.

One of the other fundamental ideas underlying the bio-dynamic approach is that the earth is an integral part of the cosmos, a satellite around the star called Sol, our sun. The earth is subject to all the influences of the cosmos, and so all its occupants, whether human, animal, insect, plant or rock, are all subject to the influence of the cosmos. The obvious influence is that of the sun, which affects the length of day according to the season, the temperature of each part of the earth, the growth and well being of plants and animals, and of course the growth and well being of man. There is no small part of day to

Above:
An interesting and unusual container planted permanently and simply with a purple-leaved Japanese maple (*Acer palmatum* 'Dissectum Atropurpureum').

Left:
An unusual tall terracotta container flowing over with a mixture of *Verbena* and *Artemesia*.

A variety of herbs
and aromatic paving
plants softens and
adds interest to a
large expanse of
paving. The raised
beds give height and
can be planted with
alpines or with low-
growing bedding
plants.

A small patio with
Thymus growing in
the paving to create a
fragrant walk and
sitting area.

A window box with
seasonal planting of
Pelargonium,
Helichrysum petiolare
and *Argyranthemum
fruitescens* added to
structural planting of
Hedera helix 'Adam'
and a small
Phormium.

A window box with zonal and trailing pelargoniums, using a narrow range of colours for visual impact. The colours are set off well by the neutral colour of the brickwork and white-painted wood of the window and window box.

Below:
Bark mulch is used to retain moisture in the soil, to suppress weeds and improve soil fertility. It also looks good.

Right:
The dry conditions in a hanging basket can provide the right conditions for growing a wide variety of herbs.

xxx

Ivy leaved trailing
pelargoniums thrive
in the dry conditions
of large containers
and provide a
stunning show of
flowers.

A sink with alpines used as part of the layout and colour scheme of the whole of the patio garden.

day life that is not directly influenced by the sun in some way.

The next most important influence is that of the moon, as it affects all things that contain water, and all living creatures consist of 80%–90% water. In the same way that the moon gives us the tides in both the oceans and the inland seas, it influences all water within plants and animals. The relationship of the sun and the moon influences the earth, and the stars also have their effect on the earth.

It must be acknowledged that the human race is part of this whole system, affected by cosmic influences, and part of the living ecosystem of earth. Man is not just an onlooker, manipulating nature to suit his personal ends. The food we eat, the water we drink, the air we breathe all bind us inseparably to the biosphere. It is necessary to think in terms of participation with nature, appreciating the size of the forces and influences and to work our gardens, our farms and our lives as a cooperative and mutually beneficial partnership.

To bring this philosophical approach to the earth into practical everyday terms for the gardener, it is necessary to understand that everything is part of the living balance of nature, and that our every action affects this balance. Conversely, we can use all these cosmic influences, and the natural balance and cycles of the living earth to our own advantage in the garden.

As the garden is a small part of the living skin of the earth, then the care of the soil is essential. As with organic gardening, the use of good quality compost and manure in the garden is of vital importance, to maintain the humus and life in the soil. A living healthy soil is essential for healthy plants, especially for those grown in containers and in the restricted space of a patio garden. The bio-dynamic approach to gardening uses several specific organic preparations to assist the making of compost and to improve the life of the soil. Mulching is also another good way of caring for the soil and the plants growing in it.

Problems with pests are considered to be influenced by a change in the balance of the garden, either naturally caused or caused by man. A naturally caused imbalance could occur in a cold spring, when the aphids emerge late, but where early sunshine has tempted out the ladybirds and hoverflies too soon, and they have been lost in a sharp frost. The resulting aphid infestation then has no effective natural controls until the predator population has built up again. A man-made imbalance could occur when the host plants have grown too fleshy and sappy, providing ideal conditions for an aphid infestation, possibly due to an unsuitable rotation, or the application of raw manure or a soluble fertilizer. In either case it is a weakening of the constitution of the plant that has allowed the infection to occur.

Very often the use of a foliar spray will bring the problem under control until the natural balance is restored. An organic spray prepared from nettles and soft soap is simple and effective, especially when applied in the evening to prevent the sun scorching it on the leaves, and when the earth is in the contraction part of the cycle before rest for the night. As a last resort, derris or pyrethrum can be used, both naturally obtained insecticides. They are best applied with great care, at dusk, when the bees have gone to bed.

In general, the approach to bio-dynamic gardening is very similar to that of organic gardening, but with the added refinements of some special fertilizers and composting preparations, and working not only with the sun, as in conventional horticulture, but also with the moon and the stars.

CHAPTER 18

Plant Health

Container problems

Drought and drying out

Drying out can happen at any time, usually in the summer months and at times of very limited rainfall. It can be aggravated by the type and style of container, whether it absorbs heat or is porous and dries out through the fabric of the container, not just through the soil. The problem is worse with intermittent watering with a hose, where the water falls with force onto the soil and tends to run off, leaving the soil scarcely moistened. The soil will shrink away from the sides of the pot and any water will run down between the soil and the pot and run out through the drainage holes at the bottom. Rain is generally much more gentle and soaks in better than tap water.

Soil in containers will dry out rapidly again once having been allowed to dry out, as it then becomes difficult to rewet. The only way to effectively rewet the soil is to stand the container in a bath of water for some hours until the soil is thoroughly moist. This is difficult with a large container!

Shape in relation to drying out
Containers with wide tops and narrow bases offer a large soil surface to the elements without providing a large volume of soil to act as a reservoir, so they dry out fast in the wind and sun. This can be compounded with the container being made of a porous material such

as terracotta. Containers with a large volume of soil and relatively small surface area dry out much more slowly (Fig. 18.1).

Location in relation to drying out
Sun, wind and frost are the main causes of drying out. Locate pots in sheltered spots where they are not in full sun all day. Avoid exposed windy positions. Where unavoidable, choose containers of a reasonably non-porous material with a shape that holds a large quantity of soil in relation to the exposed surface area. Water well and regularly and never allow to dry out. Plant with plants that will withstand the conditions.

Overheating

Overheating will occur at any time of year, where the container is located in a sunny, sheltered spot. The problem is worse if the container is of a dark colour and absorbs the heat. The soil becomes hot as any moisture within the container heats up, and the plant roots are 'steam cooked'.

Overheating can be avoided by locating the container in a position where it is not in full sun all day, and by ensuring soil is thoroughly moist, full of humus and able to retain water. The container should be well planted and the soil should be covered with a mulch, which

Fig. 18.1 Different shapes of containers.
Containers A and B will dry out much faster than containers C and D.

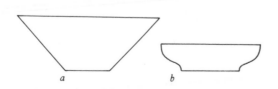
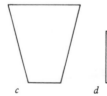

a   *b*   *c*   *d*

will act as a blanket to help the container maintain a steady temperature. Changing the style of container for one of a different colour or material can help.

A certain amount of soil warming can be beneficial to plant growth, but it must be treated with caution, because the benefit is rapidly lost if the pot overheats.

Waterlogging

Waterlogging occurs when there is too much water in a plant container for too long a time and the plant roots start to suffer and rot from lack of air. Adequate air is needed around the roots of a plant to enable it to breathe and grow, and an excess of water drowns the roots and the plant slowly dies from the base upwards. Milder symptoms include premature leaf fall, chlorosis and colour changes in the leaves.

Waterlogging can also occur even in times of drought, when the container is being watered regularly with a hose but the drainage of the container is inadequate for the sudden inflow of water, and the plants are left waterlogged.

Waterlogging can be exacerbated by the location of the container. A container located in full sun will dry out faster than a container in part shade. If the container is waterlogged, the plants will be sitting in the shade with their roots in water for a longer time and so hasten the process of deterioration.

To prevent waterlogging, check all containers regularly for adequate drainage. Terracotta pots require crocks (bits of broken pot) at the bottom of the pot to ensure that the drainage hole does not get blocked with soil. Other styles of container require checking at regular intervals for efficiency of drainage.

Any container without drainage holes should be used only with great caution. A thick layer of stones and crocks should be at the bottom of the container, separated from the soil with a water permeable fabric such as Terram, to allow the water to run to the bottom of the pot without leaching all the soil with it. Above the fabric layer should be a layer of peat or similar water holding material to act as a reservoir for the plants in the soil above (Fig. 18.2).

Frost

Frost can cause drying out and desiccation of

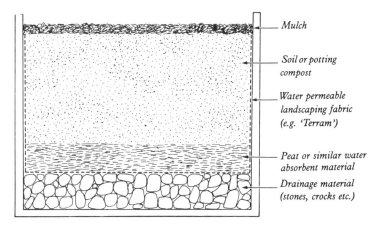

Mulch

Soil or potting compost

Water permeable landscaping fabric (e.g. 'Terram')

Peat or similar water absorbent material

Drainage material (stones, crocks etc.)

Fig. 18.2 Cross section of a container without drainage holes.

plants, especially in cold windy weather with a weak winter sun. Frost on wet soil causes expansion of the soil and will crack, even break a container, leaving the roots of the plant exposed to further damage. Frost can gradually damage a terracotta container by causing it to spall (flake) off in layers, destroying both the looks of the container and its effectiveness as a safe and secure home for plants.

Frost and wind will cause dessication due to fast evaporation of available water, and the plant's inability to absorb more water from the frozen soil. All parts of the plant above and below ground will be damaged.

Reduce and avoid damage by protecting pots and containers against frost and freezing winds by moving them into a sheltered spot that does not catch the early morning sun. If a container catches the early sun, it will thaw out much quicker than the soil and die from lack of available water and repeated freezing and thawing. If the space is available, pots can be moved into a sheltered protected place such as a cold frame or unheated greenhouse.

Containers can be left *in situ* and protected with straw or bracken tied in a thick layer around the container to protect the roots, and a thinner loose layer around the plant to give protection but to allow the free flow of air around the plant.

Wind burn and scorch

Wind burn and scorching is caused by locating the container in a draughty position, giving rapid drying of the soil and the plants.

227

To prevent problems of windburn and scorch, containers should be moved into a less exposed position, or permanent shelter with a screen of netting or other shrubby plants should be provided.

Problems of wind burn and draughts can occur at any time of the year, not just in the winter, and they can also occur in the least expected places. A simple test for draughts at a particular point in the garden is to use a child's paper windmill and to observe it working. It will move when little else is stirring if placed in a draughty spot.

Ageing of containers

Some containers, especially wooden containers, deteriorate with age and eventually collapse, leaving the plant roots exposed to the elements. Terracotta containers will break up after severe frost, especially when waterlogged, as they have little natural elasticity to accommodate the expansion of the soil on freezing.

Plant containers should be checked regularly for signs of deterioration, and the plants should be repotted into a new container before the problem becomes serious, and before what is a routine job becomes an emergency.

Infestations

Pots and containers can become infested with various creatures that generally do no harm or are even of benefit in the garden, but an infestation of them in a pot can cause untold damage.

Worms

These are generally beneficial for the soil, as they consume organic matter such as dead leaves and break it down into a usable form for plants. They also aerate the soil with their tunnelling, providing valuable air spaces. An infestation of worms is a problem as the large numbers create a lattice of holes in the soil and leave many of the plant roots exposed to the air, which can give a slow malingering death to the plants.

The only effective remedy for an infestation of worms is to empty the container completely, refill it with new soil and replant the plants. The old soil from the container can be used with great benefit in another part of the garden, to introduce the worms back into the garden soil.

Ants

These can be a problem in a similar way to worms. By constructing a nest within a container, ants disturb and damage the roots of the plants, reduce their vigour and cause premature death.

Again, the only effective way of dealing with an infestation of ants is to empty the container and refill it with fresh new compost, having first killed the ants with a proprietary ant killer or boiling water. Before replacing the container in its original position, check the surrounding area for more ants, and deal with them appropriately, otherwise they will rapidly reinfest the container.

Woodlice

These are scavenging creatures that clear up the debris of garden life. Often they will infest the drainage hole area of a container, but although unsightly and unpleasing, they rarely cause any problems.

Plant Problems
Hygiene

Basic hygiene is essential for healthy plants, whether on the patio or in containers. The few basic rules that apply to all forms of gardening are:

1. Always remove and compost any rubbish, dead leaves, weeds, prunings and any other waste material.
2. Always use clean tools, so always clean tools after use and oil them when necessary.
3. Always remove and burn any diseased or infected plant material. Do not compost it.
4. Check plants over regularly for any sign of problems, whether pests, diseases, or signs of any other form of stress.

Starvation and feeding

Plants, like all other living creatures, require nutrients to grow, and care and attention to grow well. The soil that they are growing in should contain a wide range of nutrients and plenty of humus to keep the texture open, and to rot down and provide more nutrients for growth.

Plants growing on and near patios will have a restricted root run due to foundations for the paving and any walls, and so will have their ability to forage for food with their roots severely curtailed. Plants in pots by definition have a limited root run and a limited food store in the container.

Plants both in containers and near the patio will have a tendency to dry out and so will need regular watering in all but the wettest of years. This regular watering, whether with watering can, bucket, hose or sprinkler, will tend to leach many of the nutrients needed for health and vigour out of the soil, and the plants will show signs of various mineral deficiencies after a while. Dropping leaves, yellowing or mottling of leaves, small straggly growth and malformed flowers all indicate the need for a balanced diet.

Feeding can consist of proprietary liquid fertilizer (Maxicrop, Phostrogen, Tomorite, Liquinure etc.), proprietary granular fertilizer (Growmore), fertilizer consisting of dehydrated animal manure (6X, DUG), mass produced organic fertilizers (bonemeal, fish blood and bone) or home made organic fertilizers (well rotted compost, well rotted farmyard manure, comfrey liquid, nettle liquid).

Application of fertilizers, as with watering, should be regular, and should consider the needs of the plants. Instructions for the application of proprietary makes of fertilizer should be adhered to, as the plants will not benefit from an overdose of enthusiasm for feeding. Home made fertilizers should be applied generously, but with discretion. Fertilizers with a high proportion of humus in them will feed the soil as well as the plants, and will have a much greater long term benefit.

Fertilizers should generally be applied early in the growing season, especially on trees and shrubs, so that any new growth has time to harden before the winter. Any soft lush growth will otherwise be damaged by frost and wind in winter. Annual plants will need to be fed regularly, usually once a week, once they have started to show signs of setting flowers.

Some proprietary fertilizers are designed for specific purposes, with a high proportion of magnesium or potash to encourage flowering or fruiting. These products should be used with discretion, and always comply with the manufacturer's instructions.

Intermittent watering

Intermittent and irregular watering will cause a large amount of stress in plants, especially those that are already potentially stressed by their place of growing, i.e. in a container or location with a restricted root run. Plants will put on growth during times of adequate watering, only to wilt, lose their leaves and flower buds, and sometimes become scorched around their leaf margins in times of deprivation. The compost in the container will dry out and shrink away from the sides of the container, become difficult to rewet, and so damage the plants' roots. This sort of plant treatment will leave the plants vulnerable to infection with diseases and infestation with insects such as aphids and red spider mite, and without the health and vigour to fight off the problems.

Overcrowding

Too many plants in a container will leave them straggly and leggy in their struggle to gain adequate light. They will consume soil nutrients very rapidly. Plants can be thickly planted in a container to good effect, as long as adequate care is taken. The plants must be well fed from a very early stage, and must be pinched out regularly to encourage bushy growth.

Plants can also be thickly planted around a patio, provided that the same general rules are complied with i.e. feed well and prune well and regularly. The effect will be very good at the start, but in the long term overcrowding of permanent planting is not recommended. It becomes very expensive and heartbreaking when the extra plants must be dug out and possibly thrown away to give the remaining plants room to grow and thrive.

Poor pruning

Poor and insensitive pruning can result in straggly misshapen plants, or plants that are so grown together and dense that they cannot breathe and grow well. Pruning should always be done with care and sensitivity, with the health and vigour of the plant in mind (see page 231).

Careless use of chemicals

Sometimes problems will occur with plants, and if after all other possibilities have been eliminated, then check on the use of chemicals in the vicinity of the plant. Spray will drift a long way from the original source and intended point of application, and can have devastating effects on plant growth. Plant symptoms can include rapid growth with severe distortion of the plant and a gradual malingering death, or leaf burn and scorch at times when wind burn or sun scorch are very unlikely. Each of these possibly indicates the use of weed-killers too close to other plants.

Inorganic chemical fertilizers can also cause problems. Excess of a product such as Grow-more can cause a sudden flush of fleshy growth, and can cause burning and scorch of the leaves. Fungicides generally do not cause noticeable problems, but these and all other chemicals should be only used with great care, only when all the simple remedies fail, and in strict accordance with the manufacturers' instructions.

Climatic conditions

Plants in containers are very vulnerable to all sorts of severe climatic conditions and protective measures should be taken to minimize any damage and suffering.

Heavy rain and hail

A heavy downpour will damage young plants very seriously; hail will cut soft growth and leaves to shreds and damage flower buds to the point that no flowers are produced. Snow will collect on branches, weigh them down, pushing the plant out of shape, and even break them. Plants can be protected with fine netting, forming a tunnel structure over the plants or wrapping the netting around the narrow columnar plants, or by the simple expedient of moving the plants in their containers under cover.

Frost

So often unpredictable, an overnight frost will damage roots, scorch leaves, shoots, buds, and flowers, and will damage and break containers. A frost combined with an east wind will do untold damage to even the hardiest plants, by drying them out in a very short length of time,

causing dessication and early death, especially if the plants are thawed by the early morning sun. To avoid this sort of damage, move containers of plants into a north facing sheltered spot by a wall or building for the duration of the bad weather, or bring all the containers under cover for the winter if their contents are particularly vulnerable.

Winds and draughts

Exposure will cause wilting of plants due to rapid evaporation of water, scorching, browning and leaf loss. The stress induced in a plant due to wind is very great, and to site a plant container in a draughty spot is asking for trouble for the plants. In a draughty spot, plants will not thrive; they will become distorted and bent, sculpted by the wind, and will probably die.

If there is no option but to locate a container in a draughty position, then it is essential to be aware of the situation, to turn the container daily so that the wind hits a different part of the plant each day, and to remove the container of plants to a sheltered spot to 'convalesce' at regular intervals.

Problems with wind and draught apply from the moment the plants are transported from their original nursery; a journey in an open vehicle at 40 mph is the equivalent to a wind of 40 mph even on a calm day, which is a strong wind for a plant under stress to withstand, and will cause windburn and scorching. Plants should only be moved in closed vehicles, or if this is not possible, they should be very well wrapped up to minimize the deleterious effects of wind.

Strong sun

Wilting and scorching of plant leaves is common, especially if they are covered with water droplets from rain or watering. The water droplets will act as small lenses and magnify the effects of the sun's rays, causing small brown scorch marks on the leaves. Strong sun will also cause porous pots to dry out rapidly and so causing the plant to wilt. This can be minimized by only using terracotta pots in shadier spots, or by standing them inside a larger non-porous pot and filling up the space between the two pots with wet peat, kept moist by regular watering.

Repotting

Some plants enjoy the stressful conditions within a pot or plant container, and thrive, producing masses of roots. Other plants grow slowly under the restricted conditions of the patio or container and take several years to outgrow their location. However fast a plant grows, the time will come when it should be repotted. This time is usually indicated by a large number of roots growing out of the bottom of the pot in the search for food, when the food supply within the pot has been exhausted.

Some plants will only flower when they are totally pot-bound, when the restricted food supply implies that they must flower and produce seed to survive. If these plants are vital for the design of the patio, then at least two pots of them should be available, so that one potful can be repotted with the consequent loss of flowers for that year and possibly the next, while the other pot is left to bloom. The plants can then be repotted alternate years, or alternate two years, and so maintain continuity of flowering.

Marauders

Birds

Can cause a great deal of damage to container plants by picking off new shoots and flower buds, and so stopping all growth and flowering. They will also pick over the soil or mulch in the top of the pot and throw it out, making a continual unremitting mess and exposing plant roots.

There is no simple solution to bird damage; sometimes the careful use of black sewing thread strung carefully between the plants is enough to deter further visits, and at other times even the most elaborate bird scarers have no effect.

Slugs and snails

Slugs and snails are herbivores with a vengeance, always eating the best young shoots, leaving holes in the most visible leaves, and leaving their slimy trails across everything in sight. In a single midnight feast they can completely strip a container full of small new plants or devastate a mature hosta.

Again there is no simple solution to damage by slugs and snails. A gritty mulch on the soil surface of a plant container can help to dissuade them, and proprietary treatments, usually of methaldehyde, can be used with care, but often to little effect.

Pets

Can cause serious damage to plant containers and their contents. The acidity of a dog's urine can damage terracotta pots and alter the acidity of the soil inside the pots. Cats often dig up the fresh new soil in a large pot, throw the mulch and the soil out onto the surrounding paving, and expose the plant roots while looking for somewhere to scratch and squat. Again, their urine, in any quantity, can alter the acid balance of the soil and so damage the plants.

Pests and diseases

General plant health

The main aim when cultivating plants in containers and on patios is to grow healthy thriving plants that look good and give pleasure to the users of the patio. Healthy plants suffer very little from pest and disease problems, so the challenge is to keep the plants healthy and thriving, rather than to treat pests and diseases in sick plants.

Illness, including infestation by pests, can be seen as a symptom of an imbalance in the equilibrium of the living being, whether animal, vegetable or mineral. This imbalance renders the plant (in this instance) susceptible and vulnerable to infection or infestation by any organism that can take advantage of the situation. Many pests and diseases are naturally occurring in the environment and in the soil, awaiting a suitable host so that they can develop and grow, eventually causing a problem if not dealt with promptly.

The best way to combat pests and diseases in container and patio planting is to ensure that the plants are healthy and thriving. Regular thorough and gentle care combined with an understanding of the needs of the plants and good hygiene are the basic means to keeping plants in top form. Regular feeding and watering, growing the plants in the right position under the right conditions and tending them regularly will reduce the incidence of pest and disease problems far more effectively than any amount of preventative chemical treatments.

Container culture of plants is, by definition, stressful and will always leave plants vulnerable. Root runs are restricted, there is no ingress of ground water and so plants are vulnerable to drying out, especially in the sun, frost and the wind. But it can be of advantage to plants to be grown in special soil, and in containers raised off ground, as it is easier to keep the plants clean and pest free, and to maintain their special requirements.

One major advantage of growing plants in containers is that if the plants look in poor health, or for some reason need special treatment, the container can be moved to another position, or even be totally removed until the problem is rectified.

Natural controls to plant problems
Nature will generally control any plant pest or disease problem given enough time. If the plants are not basically healthy and thriving, a lot of damage will have been caused before the situation reaches equilibrium. Hence it is very important to keep the plants healthy.

The best natural control for pests and diseases is one of attitude and approach to the garden. Treatment of pests and diseases must be one of encouraging the plant to help itself. A fight against a problem that is fought on behalf of the plant may rid the plant of the problem, for the moment, but does nothing to correct the underlying cause, and leaves the plant weakened and vulnerable to further attack of the same or other pests or disease.

There are often simple situations that occur that make the control of a problem nearly impossible, but once seen and dealt with, enable the visible problem to be remedied easily. For instance, there is no point repeatedly treating a plant for an infestation of greenfly without first dealing with the ants nest in the adjacent paving. The ants will systematically bring in more greenfly to replace those killed off by chemical treatment, as they farm the aphids for their honeydew in a similar manner to a man farming cattle for the production of milk.

Other natural controls consist of the use of predatory insects, some of them introduced into this country purely to control pests. The most commonly used natural control of this sort is the encarsia wasp, introduced and used to control whitefly in greenhouses. Some of these introduced insects only thrive under the controlled conditions within a greenhouse, and are of little use on the patio or for container plants, but considerable research is being done on the subject and new ideas are being continually investigated.

There is generally a treatment for most pest and disease problems based on an organic extract of another plant or naturally occurring substance which can be used instead of a commercially prepared chemical treatment. Organically based treatments are as effective as chemical treatments in dealing with the problem, a lot more gentle on the plant and kinder on the environment. As with all herbal and organic treatments, within the many naturally occurring chemical substances a naturally occurring antidote is included, thus making the organic treatment much safer than conventional treatment.

Pesticides
In the context of house and garden, pesticides are generally considered to be the chemicals used to kill pests. Pesticides fall into several different categories – synthetic and organic, surface acting and systemic. The difference between synthetic and organic chemicals is the source of their active ingredients; organic chemicals come from a natural source, whereas synthetic chemicals are manufactured by man. The difference between surface acting and systemic chemicals is their mode of action; surface acting pesticides kill the insects by direct contact, systemic pesticides are absorbed into the sap of the plant and kill the insects when they drink the sap.

Fungicides
Fungicides are generally considered to be the chemicals used to keep fungal infections under control. Fungal problems are often exacerbated by physical and climatic conditions, and some fungal problems can be alleviated by a change in location or growing conditions. Other fungal infections indicate a condition within a plant, such as coral spot, which usually only attacks dead or dying wood. No amount of fungicide will control coral spot,

and it is best to cut out and burn all affected wood. Leaves, wood and other prunings affected with a fungus should always be burnt and never composted, to ensure that the infection is not knowingly spread to other plants.

Mineral deficiencies

The symptoms of mineral deficiency diseases are often similar to the symptoms of a mild attack of a viral disease, but the cause is a shortage of one or more of the chemical elements essential for plant growth. The symptoms show as somewhat smaller leaves which develop coloured patches in the blades or discolouration in the veins and leaf edges. These effects may also show in the flowers and fruit. Each deficiency has its characteristic pattern from which the problem can be diagnosed.

There are many reasons for the shortage of the essential mineral that is causing the deficiency symptoms, especially in container grown plants. Too much of one nutrient can 'lock up' and give deficiency symptoms of another element. This often happens when reliance is placed upon the use of chemical fertilizers rather than high quality soils and composts. Excess use of chemical fertilizers gives as a consequence a deterioration in soil humus, and so poor growth in the plants. The cure and prevention for most of the deficiency diseases is to give the plants a healthy, well-balanced diet, to increase the resistance to disease and to avoid vitamin and mineral malnutrition.

Excess watering, especially in dry weather can leach many nutrients out of the soil or compost, and container grown plants are particularly vulnerable to this. Ensuring that the plants are growing in the container in good quality, moisture retentive soil, and ensuring that the plants never dry out or are subjected to over-watering will help prevent mineral deficiencies.

Magnesium shortage

Commonest among crops which are greedy for potassium, a good example being tomatoes. It has variable symptoms, often with the lower leaves of the plant turning yellow with the veins remaining green, where the plant has absorbed potassium in preference to magnesium. A shortage of humus will make it less easy for a plant to take up magnesium, especially in dry summers, and so we return to the need of ensuring that the soil is well fed and in good heart.

The quick remedial answer to magnesium deficiency is to water with a solution of Epsom salts (magnesium sulphate) at the rate of 28g (1oz) in 4.551 l (2 gal) of water sprinkled over 1.8 sq m (2 sq yds), or to use this mixture as a foliar spray. For a long term solution, ground dolomite limestone should be dug into the ground at the rate of about 1.1 kg per sq m (2 lb per sq yd). Ground dolomite limestone contains up to 45% magnesium carbonate, and lasts for years, especially with lots of good compost.

Calcium shortage

Can be a problem on sandy soils and acid soils, especially those where pines, heathers, rhododendrons and azaleas grow well. It can also be caused by the sulphates from ammonium sulphate and potassium sulphate in fertilizers combining with the calcium carbonate in the soil, turning it into calcium sulphate, which is less available to plants.

The symptoms of calcium deficiency is brown patches at blossom ends of fruit, the growing points of shoots die back, young leaves fail to expand and in extreme cases the leaves turn purple-brown and die off. The remedy for a calcium deficiency is the application of lime, but also to stop using large quantities of sulphate of ammonia and to use large quantities of good ammonia and well rotted manure instead.

Boron deficiency

Can cause serious symptoms, mostly in vegetables, generally with plants like beets and turnips rotting from the inside. It is usually caused by heavy liming, or by naturally very chalky soils, and is usually overcome by the use of plenty of compost. Borax can be added to the soil, but it is very easy to overdose the ground, so the use of compost is recommended.

Potassium shortage

Can be caused by too much nitrogen or too much phosphorus. Clay soils usually have plenty of potassium, but sandy soils tend to run out fast, as all potassium fertilizers, including wood ashes, are very soluble. Symptoms can include brown spots and scorch marks on leaves and fruit. The best quick remedy is to water with comfrey liquid manure, and the long term answer is more good compost.

Phosphorus shortage
Rare as phosphorus is plentiful in most soils, and there is no other mineral nutrient that locks it out of root reach, but occasionally it can be scarce in an acid soil. A shortage produces stunted leaves and purple tints in older foliage. The remedy is a good dressing of bonemeal in the autumn.

Iron and manganese shortages
Can both occur on soils that are naturally very chalky. The symptoms of both are very similar, with a yellowing of the foliage too early in the season to be due to drought. Where lack of iron is the problem, the youngest leaves lose their colour first. Manganese shortage also causes hollow centres in the seeds of plants.

The best and easiest remedy, rather than try applying a rather rare chemical, is again more compost and less lime. In practical terms, soil improvement with the addition of good compost or well rotted manure is the most effective method. A short term remedy is to water with Epsom salts (see magnesium deficiency for dilution rates), to lock up the excess lime and release some of the missing minerals.

Chlorosis
The yellowing of plant foliage due to the lack of chlorophyll in the plant. The symptoms can also look similar to magnesium deficiency, with distinctive green veins in the yellowing leaves. This is usually due to an iron deficiency, caused by excess lime in the soil or the water, and occurs in acid loving plants growing in neutral or slightly alkaline soil. It can also occur in container grown plants that are watered frequently, where nutrients are gradually leached out of the compost.

The remedy for chlorosis is to water with 'iron sequestrene', which will counteract the effects of the lime in the water and in the soil

and make the iron available to the plants. A foliar feed of comfrey or nettle is also helpful.

Pests and diseases
Every problem, pest infestation and disease has both a chemical treatment and a natural treatment. Choice of treatment is a matter of practicality and personal preference. It may be easier to spray a plant with derris or fenitrothion to rid it of caterpillars, but the chemical may be much more damaging than the original problem and then leave the plant open to a further infestation by aphids, for instance. To pick off the offending caterpillars by hand will take a little longer than a spray of chemical, but will deal with the problem just as effectively. Also, in removing the caterpillars by hand, the plant will benefit from an all over inspection and handling where any other minor problems may come to light and can be dealt with before they become serious enough to be obvious.

However well any plants are cared for, they will always be at risk from pests and diseases. The basic caring for the requirements of the plants will reduce the incidence of any problem, good hygiene and the use of sterile pots and potting mixtures will help, and the regular inspection of plants, especially checking the undersides of the leaves, will detect any infection or infestation at its early stages, before it becomes a problem.

Pests
Container-grown plants are vulnerable to attack by a wide range of bugs, but their feeding habits give clues to their identity, and their subsequent method of control. Some insects, such as caterpillars and weevils, feed by chewing and biting, leaving the leaves ragged and full of holes. Other insects, such as aphids and scale insects, feed by sucking the sap of the plant, leaving it weak and stunted. Other pests leave characteristic identification marks, such as the slime trails left by slugs and snails.

Adelgids are sap sucking aphid-like insects that cause stunted growth in conifers, with small galls on the shoots and stems. Honeydew and sooty moulds generally appear with the galls. Treat with a systemic insecticide or BHC.

Ants feed on the honeydew produced by aphids, and move the aphids around to fresh areas and fresh plants like a farmer will move his cattle around to find the best pasture. This can make the control of an aphid problem very difficult. Ants will also eat the roots of any plants in the vicinity of their ant-hill or nest. Use a proprietary ant treatment. It will take a little while to act, as the ants will take it back into the nest and it will gradually infect the other ants in the colony. A mixture of borax and icing sugar as a bait is also very effective.

Aphids can form vast colonies on the soft sappy growths of new leaves and flower buds, together with the honeydew that they produce and the sooty moulds which grow upon it. Aphids can be green, blue or black, winged or wingless, and are often specific as to which plants they choose to live on. Greenfly and blackfly are the most common, causing puckered deformed and yellowing leaves, distorted buds, shoots, flowers and fruit, and stunting the plant's growth. Some aphids feed on the roots of certain plants, causing them to become stunted and to wilt in the sun. Worst of all, aphids can spread virus diseases. Treat with a systemic insecticide such as malathion or fenitrothion. Mild infestations should be treated with a nettle solution and soft soap, or quassia. Avoid the use of high nitrogen fertilizers, which encourage the production of large amounts of soft sappy growth which is ideal for feeding aphids.

Bark-boring beetles cause stunted growth with dead shoots and branches. The culprits causing the damage are the creamy white grubs, which bore into the bark, leaving holes, channels and galleries, or chewing the shoots and hollowing them out. Cut out and burn the affected parts, and treat if necessary with BHC.

Capsid bugs attack the young leaves and growing points of many plants, causing brown spots to develop and enlarge to holes, distorting and stunting the plant growth. Fruits on affected trees are deformed with sunken areas. The sap-sucking yellowish striped nymphs do the damage before they mature into bright green winged insects. Treat with a fenitrothion, BHC, or nicotine.

Caterpillars are the immature larval stage of different butterflies and moths, and they eat the leaves, buds and shoots of plants, leaving holes and ragged leaves and occasionally totally defoliating a plant. The larvae of other moths, including the cutworms, feed on roots and underground stems, often severing seedling shoots from their roots just below the soil surface. Some tortrix moth caterpillars conceal and protect themselves while feeding with a fine webbing attached to the leaves or shoots. Treat by spraying with fenitrothion, nicotine or derris, but better by regular manual removal and destruction.

Chafers are adult winged beetles, and they feed mainly on flowers. The shiny blue-green rose chafer feeds on rose blooms in summer, whereas the May chafer attacks late flowering apple blossom. The immature chafer grubs also feed on the roots of plants for up to four years before emerging as adults. Treat by removing the beetles off the plants and destroying them, or dust with BHC.

Earwigs, shiny brown fast moving creatures with pincer like tails, feed at night on the buds, petals and leaves of plants. The favourites are clematis, dahlias and chrysanthemums. Treat with BHC, but better to use traps made of upturned flower pots filled with hay or dry grass, suspended high in the plant foliage. The earwigs caught in the traps should be shaken out into a cup of paraffin.

Eelworms are microscopic creatures that invade the leaves, stems and roots of many plants. They can attack at any time of year, especially in wet conditions, as they move along the film of moisture in the sap stream. They block the sap stream, showing up in dark patches and causing stunted, distorted and shrivelled growth. Any infected plants should be burnt immediately the pest is identified, and do not grow the same crop in that position for at least five years.

Flies, carrot fly, onion fly and cabbage root fly are all very small, widespread and very destructive. Their maggots eat into the bulb of the onion, into the carrot and into the root of the cabbage, causing the plant to wilt and giving a reddish tinge to the foliage. The flies are attracted by the smell of the vegetable, so it is essential to dispose of thinnings immediately, and not to damage the plants. The problem can be controlled by growing early crops, as flies are more active later in the season, and to plant onion alternated with carrots, as the smell of one crop is reputed to be distasteful to the flies of the other crop.

Froghoppers, or cuckoo spit are yellowish sucking insects, enveloped in frothy patches on the undersides of leaves and in new shoots. They attack mainly in spring and summer, causing wilt and distorted growth. Hygiene is the best form of control, and all infected plant material should be burnt.

Leaf miners are maggots that mine their way through leaves, leaving wriggly channels within the leaf tissue, generally attacking in late summer. Infected leaves should be removed and burnt, and the plants can be sprayed with a systemic insecticide if necessary.

Magpie moths have conspicuous black and white caterpillars that feed on leaves in spring, leaving plants completely defoliated. The adult moth is black and white with buff and orange markings. Treat by spraying with fenitrothion, BHC or preferably, derris.

Mealy bugs are sap sucking, aphid-like insects with a covering of whitish wax that makes them impervious to spray insecticides. Treat by spraying with BHC, malathion or other systemic insecticide, or preferably, remove the insects manually with a sharp pointed knife and crush them. Sometimes they can be easily removed with white petroleum oil or methylated spirits.

Millipedes are slow moving creatures (centipedes are very fast moving and beneficial in the garden) with worm-like, often coiled bodies. They attack all year round, and eat roots and stems, bulbs and tubers, resulting in stunted growth and wilting in the sun. The most effective method of control is to trap them and kill them with nicotine.

Red spider mites are very small sap sucking insects and a very difficult pest to control. They proliferate in hot dry conditions, particularly in greenhouses. They feed on the undersides of leaves and flowers, enveloping the plants in a fine webbing that takes the brightness out of the flower colours and can cause mottling. Treat with a systemic insecticide, malathion or preferably, derris.

Slugs and snails favour wet conditions, where they eat young plant shoots, leaves and subterranean shoots and roots. They leave a distinctive silvery slime trail on the soil surface. In containers, they love tuberous roots, bulbs and corms, and can do vast amounts of damage overnight. The eggs are laid just below the soil surface and this is one point of control. The best controls for slugs and snails are hedgehogs, and they should be encouraged in the garden at all times. Methaldehyde baits can be used for the slugs and snails, but methaldehyde is poisonous to animals, especially hedgehogs, and will cause paralysis.

Slugs and snails are scavengers, eating the droppings of a large number of creatures as well as the bodies of pests killed with pesticides. These pesticides accumulate in the bodies of the molluscs, and when a hedgehog eats a large quantity of these poisonous slugs, it too accumulates a large amount of these pesticides in its fat. When a hedgehog loses weight during the course of its winter hibernation, these pesticides are released into the blood stream and the creatures are found dead in spring for no apparent reason. This risk of poisoning also applies to other slug and snail eaters like thrushes and blackbirds.

Another effective method of slug and snail control is to trap them, with beer used as the bait. Many traps are needed, and they must be emptied regularly, as there can be up to 60 000 slugs in the garden in a year! Another effective natural method of control is to water a mulched soil surface with a mixture consisting of 1 teaspoon of potassium permanganate and one teaspoon of salt in 9 litres (2 gallons) of water, and to water this mixture over an area of 10 square metres (12 square yards). This will bring the slugs and snails to the surface for the robins, thrushes and starlings to eat, or for the hedgehogs if the watering is done in the evening.

Thrips are tiny, nimble louse like winged insects that attack the petals and leaves of herbaceous plants and leave them streaked and silvered with whitish speckels and distorted. Treat by spraying with a systemic insecticide, BHC or malathion, or preferably, derris.

Wasps are known for their damage to ripe fruit caused by them enlarging existing holes or making fresh cavities. They will also damage flower stems of herbaceous plants by eating through the stem just below the blossoms. Destruction of wasps nests by trained operatives is one method of control, but often the insecticides that are used are exceedingly poisonous, often including cyanide. A safer remedy is to dilute one tablespoon of Quassia in 450 ml (1 pint) of water with a large amount of brown sugar or treacle and paint this mixture on a fence or other wooden surface close to the wasp nest. This will not only catch and kill a few moths, but will be scraped up and taken back to the wasp nest to kill them at home.

Weevils are long snouted small beetles that bite and bore, leaving ragged holes and scolloped edges in the foliage, ribbed bark and chewed off leaf and bud stalks. Larvae or adults can feed on the roots and cause the plants to wilt. Treat with BHC or fenitrothion.

Whitefly attack many plants by sucking the sap, and betray their presence by flying off in quick moving clouds. The nymph stage secretes honeydew onto the hosts' leaves, stems and fruit, which is then followed by sooty moulds, particularly in summer. The plants show signs of weakness and stunting. They are difficult to control effectively, even with malathion. Fumigate greenhouses with BHC smoke, or very strong ammonia.

Winter moth caterpillars have a distinctive looping habit, but their colour depends on the species. They eat the foliage of trees, giving the leaves brownish curling edges, and in severe cases can defoliate the tree and leave the buds holed and bored. The damage generally occurs in late spring. Control is by the use of grease bands on the trees and spraying with tar oil.

Woolly aphids are sap-sucking aphids with a covering like cotton wool, impervious to sprayed surface insecticides. They weaken and disfigure plants, accumulating in the leaf axils and beneath the leaves. Treat with a systemic insecticide, or manually remove the aphids with a pointed knife or using methylated spirit.

Fungal diseases

Humid and overcrowded conditions encourage the spread of fungal diseases by air, water or soil borne spores. Some fungal diseases are specific to a particular plant, like tomato blight; other fungal diseases, like downy mildew, will attack almost any plant, provided the conditions are right.

Black spot is a common fungus disease confined to roses. Infection of the new leaves begins in spring with small circular black spots on the leaves which gradually increase in size and finally result in premature leaf fall and weakened plants. Treat by spraying regularly with benomyl, and by removing all infected leaves from the plant and the ground and burning them.

Botrytis or grey mould attacks leaves, stems, flowers and fruit, gaining entry by insect damage or by injury. The affected tissue turns yellow and if left, will rot and develop a grey furry mould, which releases clouds of dust like spores when disturbed. Botrytis flourishes in cold damp conditions, and is often seen in cool greenhouses in winter. Burn all infected material and treat with benomyl. Good ventilation and a little warmth, combined with impeccable hygiene helps to prevent it.

Canker is a disease of fruit trees, developing a deep oval wound with a gnarled corky edge that exposes the wood below. Cut off all infected wood and burn it. Treat the wounds with Arbrex and spray with Bordeaux mixture.

Coral spot is a fungus that lives on dead and dying wood, leaving its distinctive signature of coral pink spots. There is no effective treatment, and all infected wood should be cut out and burnt. Some species are particularly prone to infection by coral spot, such as *Cercis siliquastrum*, the Judas trees.

Damping off kills small seedlings at ground level, causing them to topple over, wilt, wither and die. It thrives in warm moist conditions, such as those necessary for the germination of seedlings, and an outbreak can wipe out complete pots or boxes of seedlings. Treat with Cheshunt compound when sowing and pricking out.

Leaf curl affects peaches, almonds and nectarines, causing curled and twisted leaves, with red or yellow blisters. Treat by spraying with a copper based fungicide or benomyl.

Mildews attack many kinds of plants whenever the conditions of warmth and moisture prevail, giving white or grey powdery growth on leaves and stems, or a whitish downy covering on leaves, buds, and shoots, disfiguring the foliage and spoiling buds, flowers and fruit. Burn all infected material and spray with benomyl.

Rusts form rusty red-brown pustules on the undersides of the leaves, and release into the air yellow and orange powdery spores to spread the disease. All infected leaves and other parts should be burnt, and the plants should be sprayed with benomyl.

Bacterial diseases
Bacterial complaints are encountered less frequently than fungal diseases, but when they do attack, the effects are often lethal. In container growing, the main bacterial problems are some of the root rots, some kinds of wilt, and canker. These diseases are spread in a similar manner to fungal ailments, and hygiene is especially important in preventing their spread.

Viral diseases
Viral diseases are carried in the sap of the plant, and can be spread from one plant to another by insects, especially sap sucking insects, and by contact. There are no practical cures for viral infections, so prevention is the best policy. Ensure that all purchased plants are of healthy stock, and immediately destroy any plants suspected of viral infections, to prevent any infection spreading.

Virus diseases affect plants in a wide variety of ways. They often cause stunting of growth, or unusual mottling of both the flowers and the leaves, sometimes accompanied by severe distortion. All viral diseases can be carried from one generation to the next in cuttings, and this is how some of the more unusual and bizarre variegated forms of some plants have been developed.

Chemical treatments
This list of chemical treatments contains both conventional and organic treatments. Many of the chemicals listed are obtained as proprietary mixtures, sometimes combined with other chemicals so that a wide range of pests or problems are controlled. The information included is of a general outline nature, and not fully comprehensive, as chemical formulations are continually under review, different and new dangers are discovered, and new 'safe' products become available.

Generally, none of these chemicals are available at a strength to be very dangerous,

but it is essential that all chemicals are locked away when they are not being used. Protective clothing should always be worn when handling and spraying any chemical. Some have a bad or distinctive smell, others will taint fruit and vegetables if picked too soon after spraying, and some will accumulate in the body for serious long term effects that no-one knows much about. Always read the label and follow the instructions.

If in doubt as to whether to use a chemical, or as to which chemical to use, always decide to use the safest approach and do not use a chemical at all. Only use them when there is no other option. The garden is a place for all creatures to live in harmony, and that includes the occasional greenfly, too. It is not necessary to kill every insect seen in the garden, as many of them are beneficial and help to keep the balance with the more destructive insects. Never spray any open flowers with any insecticide, as it will kill the bees, and where possible choose chemicals from a natural source that will break down in the soil or air without producing more harmful substances.

Arbrex
A proprietary paint used for sealing wounds on trees after any sort of surgery. Some people prefer not to seal the wounds but to let them heal naturally, but there is no scientific evidence to show which is more effective.

Benomyl
Usually sold under the trade name of Benlate, is one of the most useful all-round systemic fungicides, to be used according to instructions at the first sign of fungal infection.

BHC
Also known as Gammexane and Lindane, is as valuable toxin for many plant and soil pests. On fruit and vegetables, use 'gamma-BHC', but not within 14 days of eating the crop. BHC should not be used on a fair number of plants, usually listed on the bottle.

Bordeaux mixture
A mixture of copper sulphate and slaked lime, made up in given proportions and used as a fungicide and preventative spray. It was originally used on grape vines in the Bordeaux

area to control mildew. It can be bought as a powder ready to mix up with water for use, but do not mix it in a metal container due to the corrosive action of the copper sulphate. There are now various commercial improvements on Bordeaux mixture, all using copper as the active ingredient.

Cheshunt compound
The copper-based fungicide for use against damping off disease in seedlings. Apply to the soil when sowing or pricking out.

Derris
Contains the alkaloid rotenone and is harmless to all warm blooded animals. It is a good all-round insecticide, but it kills ladybird larvae and eggs, and the larvae of the lacewing fly, both of which are consumers of aphids. It also kills bees and hoverflies. Derris stays toxic for about 48 hours.

Fenitrothion
A poison deadly to caterpillars of all sorts, raspberry beetle and aphids.

Formaldehyde
A powerful and very pungent sterilizer for soil borne fungi like honey fungus, and for cleaning pots, boxes and geenhouses. Always obey instructions for use.

Malathion
A strong contact poison for sucking insects, aphids including woolly aphid, thrips, mealy bug, red spider, leafhoppers, whitefly and many other insect pests. It is a real killer with a nasty smell.

Nicotine
A traditional insecticide, often found in proprietary mixtures and as a greenhouse fumigant. It spares ladybirds, ladybird larvae and hoverfly larvae, and breaks down within 48 hours, so there is no build-up in the soil. It can also be used for caterpillars, and combined with soft soap for a nicotine soap wash.

Pyrethrum
Non-toxic to warm blooded animals, but kills ladybirds, their larvae and other predators. A good insecticide for sucking insects, breaking down within 12 hours, which makes it safe for bees if used at sunset after the bees have gone to bed.

Quassia
Made from chips of wood from the tree *Picrasma quassioides*, and the active ingredients are obtained by boiling the chips in water. Mixed in solution with soft soap, it is a good insecticide for small caterpillars, wasps and aphids. It spares bees, ladybirds, their larvae and eggs, but not hoverfly larvae.

Sulphur
Used for dusting against mildews and other fungi, and is harmless to most tender plants and fruit. It is used as a preventative against fungi, not as a cure.

APPENDIX

SUCCESSFUL PATIO GARDEN PLANS

1. Productive Kitchen Patio Garden

This garden combines the growing of vegetables and fruit with the need to relax and entertain friends, as a vegetable garden can look as good, if not better, than any other type of garden if properly planned.

A broad paved patio allows the use of table and chairs to supplement the permanent seating. To the right of the patio doors, but hidden from immediate view is a small glass house, beyond which, in a sunny place, a variety of herbs are grown. Beyond the seat is a cold frame. Behind the seat is a backdrop of sweet peas and other annual plants, and their fragrance can be enjoyed from the patio.

To separate the patio partially from the central section of the garden is a small self-fertile apple tree, beyond which is the area for cut flowers. A curving path frames the lawn on one side, and on the other side, roses are enclosed by a trellis, beyond which is an area for growing salad and beans etc. A rosemary hedge (*Rosmarinus officinalis* 'Miss Jessup's Upright') screens the formal vegetable garden, the paths of which are of textured concrete. Soft fruit surrounds this part of the garden, and a small self fertile pear tree with an upright habit provides both blossom and fruit. A small weeping tree provides an important focal point around which the whole garden appears to revolve.

Fig. A.1
Productive kitchen patio garden.

Fig. A.1 Productive kitchen patio garden.

242

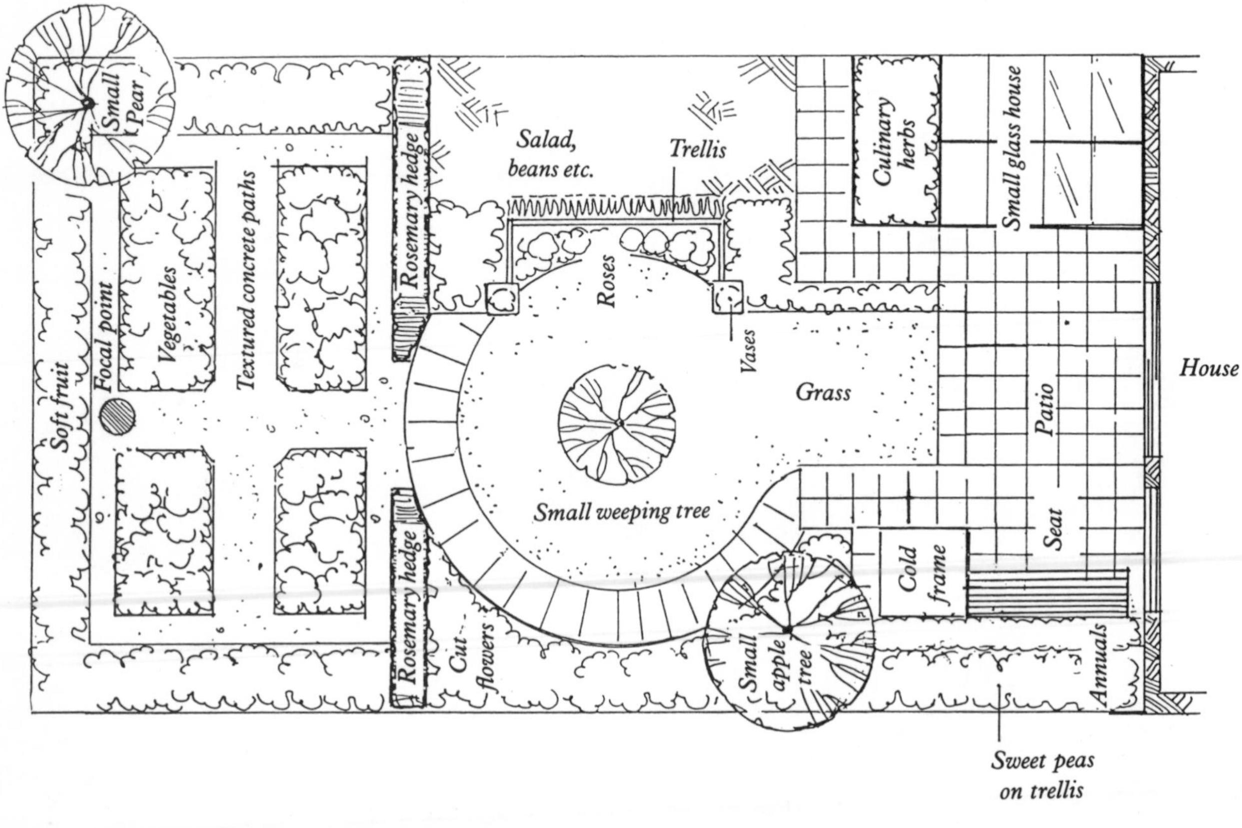

2. Patio Garden for a Disabled Person

Since there are many forms of disability, our garden cannot cater for all of them, but can be adapted. This is a garden for an ambulant person, but can be easily redesigned to accommodate wheelchair access, by making pathways broader, for example. In this instance, the ramp shown would be essential.

The patio next to the house, and all the other paved surfaces, are laid with an even but non-slip paving material. Beds are raised to the extent that they can be also used as seats, but to be comfortable they would need wide tops. The beds themselves are narrow enough to make all plants within reach. Where this is not

possible, permanent evergreen plants should be grown, as they require less maintenance.

The lawn is surrounded by a mowing edge which is at a common level with all the other paved surfaces. The far area is randomly paved, with plants growing in joints in the paving. More garden furniture can be added to supplement the permanent seat as required. Plants in the paving may not always be appropriate and should be omitted if there is any question of loss of safety. The raised beds provide a little formality and can be used for growing herbs, salads, vegetables or cut flowers.

Fig. A.2 Patio garden for disabled person.

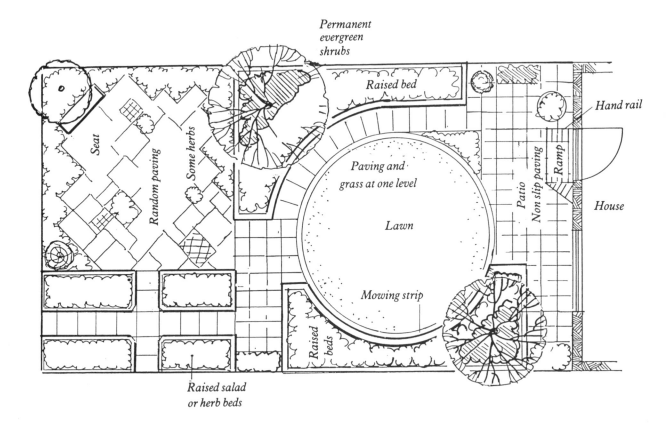

Permanent evergreen shrubs

Raised bed

Hand rail

Seat

Random paving

Some herbs

Paving and grass at one level

Lawn

Patio

Non slip paving

Ramp

House

Mowing strip

Raised beds

Raised salad or herb beds

3. Patio Garden for Children

The majority of areas in this garden are laid to flat non-slip paving, to facilitate safe play and cycling. A playhouse at the farthest end of the garden acts as a focal point, framed by an archway from which a swing is suspended. The seat can be hooked to one side when not in use. The arch can support a climbing plant, demonstrating its dual purpose. Naturally, thorny climbers will be avoided here.

The paddling pool and sand-pit are permanent features, sited in full view of the window for safety. A low seat is positioned to perform its proper function and to act as a play bench. An evergreen shrub, such as bamboo, is planted adjacent to the seat, and provides both a sense of mystery and encloses the pool.

Beyond the arch is the children's garden, where the slightly raised bed is at the right height for children to work in, and not directly in view from the house. The lawn is of hard-wearing grass, always a pleasant surface on which to play and should be included if possible. If conditions are such that grass is not appropriate, granulated pine bark can be used, but it is not an easy surface for children's wheeled toys.

Plants necessarily will need to be robust and quick to recover from any damage.

Fig. A.3 Patio garden for children.

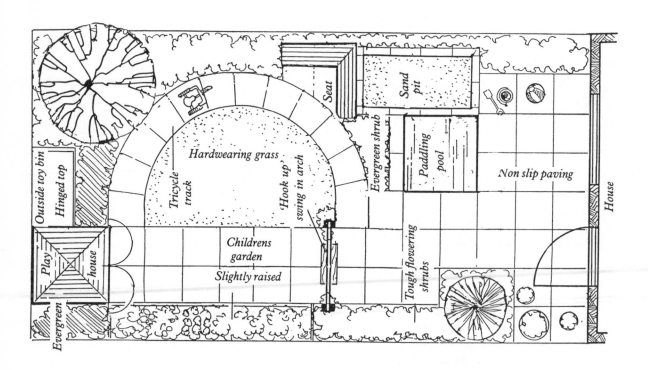

4. The Plantsman's Patio

Where a varied collection of plants is the primary consideration, a good, strong design is essential to ensure that unrelated plants are set in a comfortable yet well defined context, particularly where an area is inherently formal.

The paving shapes are strong and geometric.

Stepping stones of equal size lead to a focal point through planting, also providing access for maintenance. The garden furniture is permanent giving the paved area an obvious purpose, and there are plenty of places for special plants in containers.

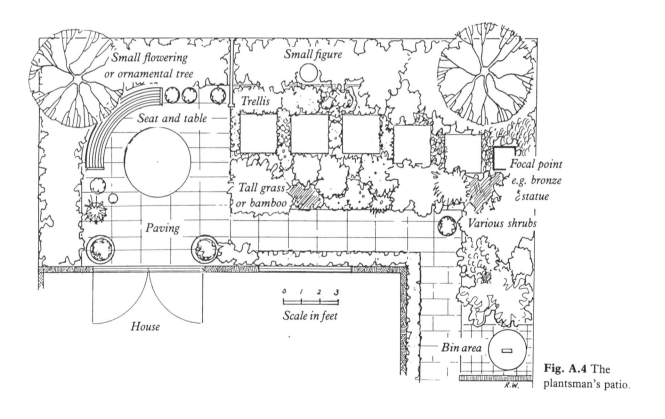

Small flowering or ornamental tree

Small figure

Trellis

Seat and table

Tall grass or bamboo

Focal point e.g. bronze statue

Various shrubs

Paving

House

0 1 2 3
Scale in feet

Bin area

R.W.

Fig. A.4 The plantsman's patio.

5. Patio Within a Larger Garden

This angled garden follows two sides of a house. On the opposite sides it has a 1.8 m (6 ft) high wall, the other side of which is a road.

The main patio for family use and entertaining is close to the garden door and has an evergreen hedge to act as a backdrop and to shelter it from prevailing winds and neighbouring property. A seat, placed as much for aesthetic as for practical reasons, is tucked into two arms of the hedge. At the left is a barbecue, and to the right is a wall-mounted fountain discharging into a low semicircular pool, the top of which may be used for informal seating.

Distributed randomly about the patio are groups of containers with bright seasonal planting.

A broad sweep of lawn curves intriguingly from sight, and a stepping-stone path echoes this. Care has been taken to position some of the stepping stones close to the windows, to give access for cleaning and maintenance.

The area not visible from the main patio accommodates children's play and equipment, often not the most attractive of garden features.

The focal point in the top right hand corner serves both the main patio and the seat within the children's play area.

A balanced planting providing both colour and interest throughout the year sets the scene, with more robust varieties growing adjacent to the children's play area. Ornamental trees detract from the high wall and are an important part of the design, whilst being features in themselves.

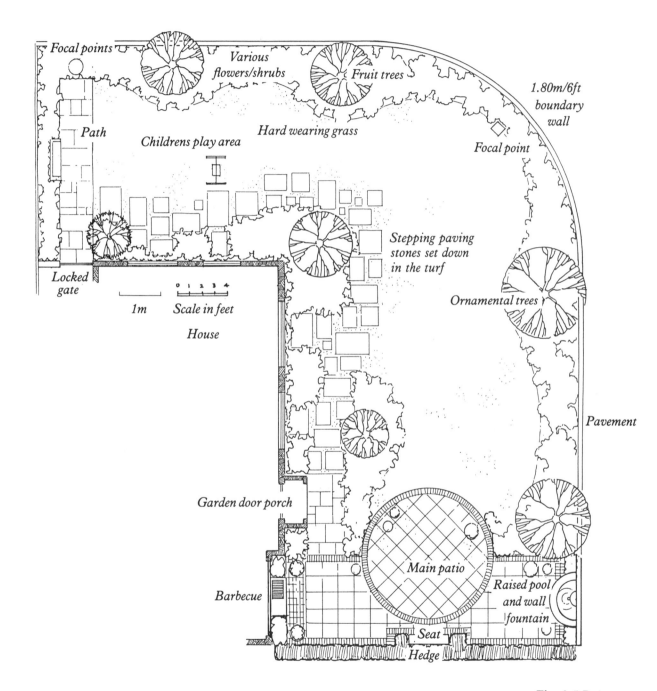

Focal points

Various flowers/shrubs

Fruit trees

1.80m/6ft boundary wall

Path

Childrens play area

Hard wearing grass

Focal point

Stepping paving stones set down in the turf

Locked gate

1m   Scale in feet

0 1 2 3 4

House

Ornamental trees

Pavement

Garden door porch

Barbecue

Main patio

Raised pool and wall fountain

Seat

Hedge

Fig. A.5 Patio within a larger garden.

247

6. Town Patio Garden

This garden has been designed along asymmetrically formal lines and is intended for relaxation and entertaining. Consequently, most of the garden is paved to reduce the need for regular maintenance, with planting confined to peripheral borders and raised beds.

A small pool and fountain is at the heart of the garden and forms the main focal point from all directions. In the far right hand corner of the patio garden is a light pergola with a tree growing up through its centre, and outwards to form a canopy. This creates a secret sitting area, with its own distinctive paved surface. The raised bed makes an excellent foil for the water and fountain immediately adjacent.

There is another focal point, hidden from the house by planting, yet visible from the covered sitting area.

The planting will contain a high proportion of evergreens chosen for interesting foliage and shade tolerance. Any extra colour can be added with plants in containers.

Fig A.6 Town patio garden.

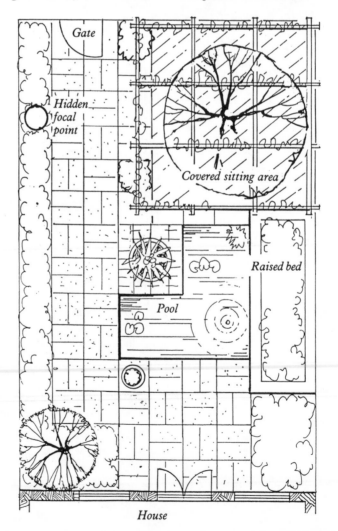

7. Coastal Patio Garden

The coastal patio garden may be for a weekend home, and so there is a need to have low maintenance demands and plenty of space for leisure activities. The main patio is almost entirely covered with a pergola, and depending upon the orientation and the need for shade, could either have more crossbeams, or support a canvas awning.

To the left of the patio doors is a permanent barbecue with sufficient spce at the rear to accommodate 'chef'. The adjacent planting could contain suitable herbs such as *Rosmarinus officinalis* (rosemary). *Salvia officinalis* (sage) and *Origanum vulgare* (marjoram) for use in cooking.

The rest of the planting is in raised containers, to ensure that the plants are growing in a sufficient depth of good quality soil. An automatic watering system is essential if the patio garden is used only for weekends and holidays. A choice would need to be made, therefore, between gravel and grass for the sitting/sunbathing area, as gravel would be self-maintaining, not needing the attention that a lawn would require. Local rocks and pebbles would be appropriate with gravel, forming a natural sculpture and link with the landscape and seascape.

The surround to the garden could be close trellis on a wall, which would be preferable in very windy positions as a toughened glass screen will cause wind turbulence within the garden.

The planting must be salt tolerant, and wind tolerant, the salt wind will tend to cause dehydration.

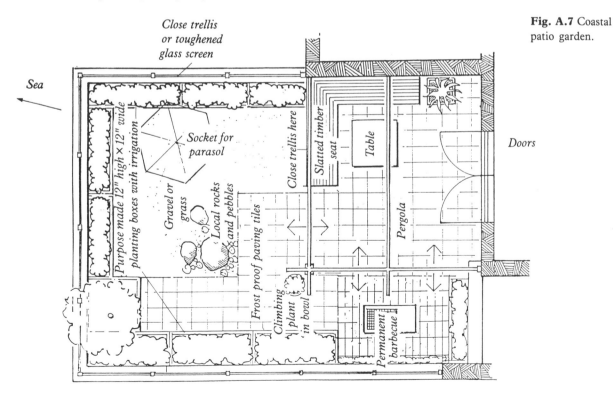

Fig. A.7 Coastal patio garden.

249

8. Wildlife Patio Garden

Even the smallest patio garden can be designed to encourage wildlife. The vast majority of the space has been given to this purpose and has been planted accordingly.

The randomly sized, yet carefully positioned, stepping stones lead towards a seat beneath a rustic pergola. Depending upon the plants and climbers chosen, this retreat could be totally hidden from the house. From here, the small pool is seen across the low marginal planting. Since the pool is formally shaped, with vertical sides, a frog ladder has been positioned to allow frogs and other amphibians to gain access to and from the pool. This works best if the water level is kept high, and then this enables birds, hedgehogs and other animals to drink.

The thirst of bees and other insects, however, will need to be quenched by some wet moss, placed in a flat dish. A bird table is located close to the house, so that the birds can be enjoyed, via the window, all year round.

Fig. A.8 Wildlife patio garden

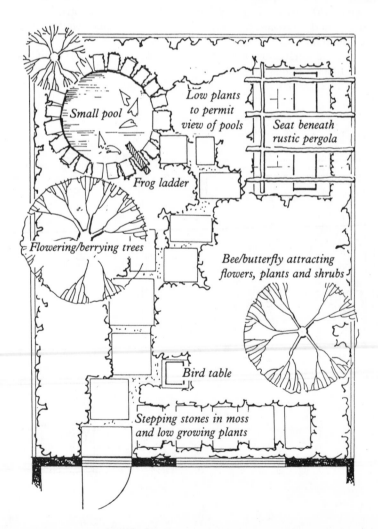

Small pool

Low plants to permit view of pools

Seat beneath rustic pergola

Frog ladder

Flowering/berrying trees

Bee/butterfly attracting flowers, plants and shrubs

Bird table

Stepping stones in moss and low growing plants

9. South-facing Patio Garden

The south-facing patio has a broad area of paving with a linking path to the side gate. This should be ideal for the sun worshippers and should be large enough to accommodate summertime parties. In the hottest weather, a pool and fountain set within the centre of an area of brick paving will bring the cooling sounds of tumbling water. At the four corners of the brick paving are formally clipped evergreen shrubs in matched planters, emphasizing the formality of the square and important in terms of design.

The lawn is approached from two directions, and on the eastern boundary is a permanent seat, which catches the evening sun. Sitting here will permit a view back towards the pool and fountain, which again make an excellent focal point.

Trellis with planting on the north side makes the lawn area more private and at the same time screens the traffic through the side gate. Apart from the south boundary, which will be slightly shaded and may well contain flowers in blue and other pastel shades, to give the impression of distance, other areas will contain sun loving plants in more vibrant colours, appropriate to the bright light. The main patio area is ideal for the grey-leafed aromatic plants, and for brightly coloured annual plants in containers.

Fig. A.9 South-facing patio.

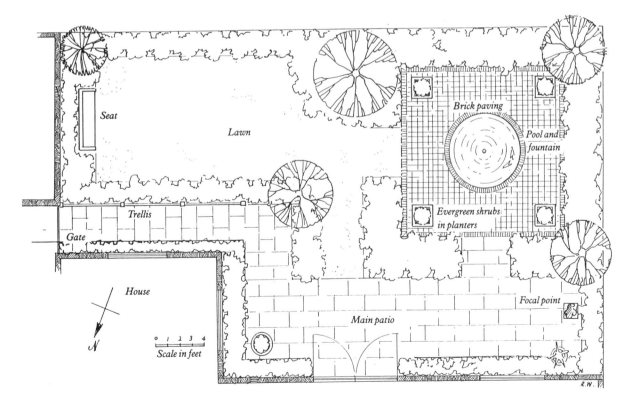

251

10. North-facing Patio Garden

Here in a north-facing patio garden there will be little sun against the house. As many people enjoy the benefits of sunshine, adjacent to the house is not then the best place for the patio. It needs to be move to a sunnier spot.

However, moving the sitting area away from the house may place it in full view of overlooking windows, creating a need for privacy. This can be achieved by screening, but not in such a way as to create another area of shade. An overhead pergola which is not overly planted with climbers will do this, since it allows light to pass through the crisscross arrangements of overhead beams, but when viewed obliquely from neighbouring upper windows can create a total screen. This effect will depend on the relative spacing and depth of the pergola beams in relation to the angle at which it is viewed.

The terminal focal point is partially screened and draws the eye from the shade to the sunlight, effecting a feeling of greater distance. Stepping stones are set into the ground to make moving safe and easy, whilst the birds table, also partially screened, is glimpsed *en route* from the house to the sitting area.

A small shed or store could be easily concealed in the right-hand corner.

The choice of planting is made more interesting because many plants need to be shade tolerant; some will be in total shade close to the house all day. The planting near the sitting area will be chosen to enjoy the sunny position further from the house.

Since a high proportion of shade tolerant shrubs are winter flowering, there will be plenty of interest in the garden in the winter, especially close to the windows.

Trees will need to be selected so that, on maturity, they do not cast too much shade.

Fig. A.10 North-facing patio garden

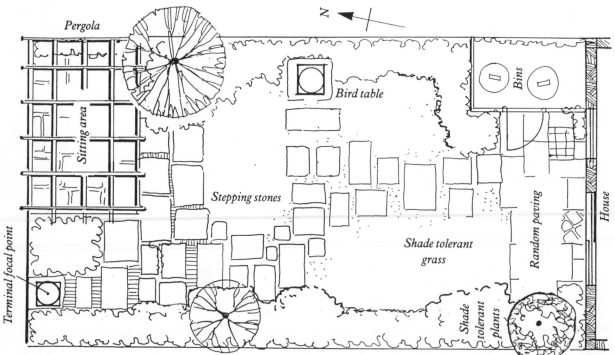

Index

Page numbers in *italic* refer to the illustrations